RSPB

RSPB HANDBOOK OF
SCOTTISH
BIRDS

PETER HOLDEN
and STUART HOUSDEN

Illustrations by
Hilary Burn, Martin Elliott, Alan Harris, Peter Hayman,
Laurel Tucker and Dan Zetterström

First published 2009, reprinted 2012 by Bloomsbury Publishing Plc,
50 Bedford Square, London WC1B 3DP
www.bloomsbury.com

ISBN 978 1 4081 1232 8

A CIP catalogue record for this book is available from the British
Library.

This book is produced using paper that is made from wood grown in
managed, sustainable forests. It is natural, renewable and recyclable.
The logging and manufacturing processes conform to the
environmental regulations of the country of origin.

Commissioning Editor: Nigel Redman
Project Editor: Julie Bailey
Typeset and designed by D & N Publishing,
Baydon, Wiltshire, UK

Printed in China by C & C Offset Printing Co., Ltd.

10 9 8 7 6 5 4 3 2

Previous page: Crested Tits (Laurel Tucker)
Front cover: White-tailed Eagle (Stephen Message)
Inside front cover: Snow Buntings (Laurel Tucker)
Cover spine: Dotterel (Peter Hayman)
Back cover (top to bottom): Scottish Crossbill (Laurel Tucker);
Snow Buntings (Laurel Tucker); Capercaillie (Hilary Burn)

Map on inside front cover by Brian Southern

CONTENTS

ACKNOWLEDGEMENTS

The inspiration for a book like this comes from the birds themselves, and from the magnificent countryside in which they live; however, it is the work of early naturalists, current field workers, scientists and teams of volunteers who have gathered information over the years that provides the basis of all that we currently know about birds in Scotland. It is our privilege to have access to much of that data through books, reports, papers and databases, and it is that information, together with our own observations, that is summarised in this work. One book, more than any other, has been our touchstone: the wonderful *Birds of Scotland*, published by the Scottish Ornithologists' Club in late 2007, is a mine of information for anyone seriously interested in this subject.

However much effort we, as authors, put into the words, it will be the illustrations that will attract many readers. We have been very fortunate to have had access to artwork produced by six of our most notable bird illustrators. Sadly, Laurel Tucker is no longer with us, but her work is very much alive in this volume. Each artist has depicted families or groups where his or her skill and knowledge can show a particular insight and capture not only the plumage detail but also the characteristics of the birds.

The original plans for this book were conceived in the offices of A&C Black with the help of Nigel Redman and Julie Bailey. We are grateful for the help of Tim Cleeves, and to Susi Bailey who has skilfully edited our words. As with other books in this series we benefited from the design team at D & N Publishing, especially Peter Davies and David Price-Goodfellow. The maps are at a scale of detail unusual in field guides and are the work of Marianne Taylor.

A book like this is the result of a team effort, and so we thank everyone who helped in its development and production. The result is impressive and we are confident that with the endorsement by the RSPB, and the promotion of this book in Scotland, we will help win over a new and ever-growing number of enthusiasts for birds, birdwatching and conservation.

Peter Holden and Stuart Housden

Snow Buntings, Plectrophenax nivalis, *male (left) and a fresh, autumn female (right).*

FOREWORD

As a child growing up in Scotland, I was always fascinated by birds. I was fortunate to come from a family that encouraged my interest, but there was little knowledge or expertise to guide me as my skills developed. In those days, the available books were either learned and weighty tomes found in libraries, or delightful pocket books with vignettes of the commoner species. Like many of my generation I gleaned much useful information from the *Observer's Book of Birds*, but the detail about what I saw on my travels around Perth and Edinburgh was often lacking. Nevertheless, the voyage of unending discovery that is birdwatching had been started, and it has stayed with me to this day. I wonder how quickly I would have progressed had I been able to buy a handbook such as this, with its excellent illustrations and detailed text aimed at the birdwatcher in Scotland.

Despite a busy career I have always made time to watch birds: geese flying over a clear Edinburgh sky in October as I travel to work, or a Blackcap singing in a shrub on a visit to a client's rural office. Birds can be found everywhere, being adaptable, sometimes confiding, and still mysterious as they come and go on their migrations – reminding us of what it is to be truly wild and free. Whenever I can, I try to put something back to help bird conservation, knowing that to safeguard birds will help much other wildlife too.

I contribute to projects that monitor breeding and wintering bird populations. I encourage others to watch and enjoy birds, and I volunteer with the RSPB, Scottish Ornithologists' Club (SOC) and British Trust for Ornithologists (BTO). By participating in census and monitoring programmes I help conservation bodies track the fortunes of birds, and ensure that special sites are properly managed and protected. So, birdwatching has its serious side too.

Above all, however, birdwatching is great fun. It encourages enquiry and travel, and the opportunity to share new observations with the thousands of others also addicted to birds in all their great variety. So whether you are just interested in the birds in your garden, or wish to visit some of the remoter and more beautiful parts of Scotland, this handbook will help you discover the birds of our diverse and attractive country. The authors are to be congratulated in distilling so much information into such an attractive and readable format. Like them, I hope this stimulates you to discover more about birds and the challenges facing bird conservation, and to find time to enjoy birds and birdwatching in Scotland.

Ian Darling, FRICS
Chairman of the RSPB Council
Past President of the Scottish
Ornithologists' Club

RSPB SCOTLAND

The RSPB has been active in Scotland since at least 1904, when it campaigned for the better protection of seabirds on St Kilda and guarded nesting Peregrines near Edinburgh. Its current campaigns to protect the marine environment and its work to reduce the illegal killing of raptors are the modern equivalents of these early efforts.

The RSPB now manages over 65,000 ha of Scotland as nature reserves, from Shetland to Dumfries & Galloway. Reserves with facilities for visitors are shown on the map on the inside cover flap. Today, supported by a growing membership of almost 80,000 and with a strong science base underpinning its land management and advocacy, the RSPB is one of Scotland's foremost environmental and conservation charities.

The RSPB manages extensive livestock farms on Islay, has some of the best Caledonian pinewoods on its Abernethy Forest reserve, is restoring blanket peatland in the Flow Country of Caithness and Sutherland, and is enhancing wetlands at the Loch of Strathbeg. Add to these the scenic splendour of the Hoy reserve, including the famous 'Old Man', and the wildlife spectaculars offered by wintering geese at Mersehead and Loch Gruinart, or breeding seabirds at the Mull of Galloway, and it is easy to see why the RSPB's Scottish reserves are recognised as some of the jewels in the crown of conservation. They represent real assets for visitors to Scotland, and help boost rural economies.

RSPB Scotland is a champion for all wildlife, giving a strong voice to nature in a country where development pressures on land remain high and the fortunes of some species, especially the Hen Harrier and Golden Eagle, remain blighted by illegal killing. Much of its advocacy is focused on the Scottish Government and its agencies, seeking to ensure that the interests of wildlife and their habitats are at the heart of policy-making.

To underpin its advocacy, the RSPB researches the problems facing wild birds and their habitats, and proffers workable solutions to decision-makers. This same understanding informs management on its reserves. In Scotland, RSPB research has provided the impetus to improve the fortunes of Corncrakes, proven the effects of illegal killing of Hen Harriers and Red Kites, and demonstrated the economic value of wildlife tourism to island communities such as Mull.

When necessary, the RSPB fights to protect special sites from destruction. Its site safeguard campaign has been successful in preventing the construction of poorly located windfarms and damaging port developments, open-cast mining and the destruction of peatlands.

In Scotland, the RSPB is supported by an increasing membership and has over 250 staff spread across the country. These staff manage reserves, respond to development consultations, lobby the Scottish Parliament, deliver research and survey programmes, and offer innovative environmental education for young people. They are always happy to offer advice on visiting reserves or other matters to ensure our wildlife heritage is appreciated by as many people as possible. Why not support their work by becoming a member?

The principal office of RSPB Scotland is in Edinburgh, with three regional offices covering north Scotland (Inverness), east Scotland (Aberdeen), and south and west Scotland (Glasgow). There are also area offices in Shetland, Orkney, Perth and Dumfries & Galloway.

RSPB Scotland is part of the RSPB, the UK charity that speaks out for birds and other wildlife. Much more information about the organisation and its work in Scotland is available at www.rspb.org.uk/scotland.

Stuart Housden, OBE
Director, RSPB Scotland

BIRDS IN SCOTLAND

A carpet of native Bluebells in old coppice woodland beloved of Redstarts and Wood Warblers.

SCOTLAND

Scotland is an amazingly diverse and interesting place for the birdwatcher. It has a land area of 79,000 sq km, encompassing about 30% of the UK. Yet it has the highest peaks, over 30,000 freshwater lochs and some 11,800 km of coastline. Add to this the 800 vegetated islands, many of which are famed migration points, and you can immediately see why Scotland continues to attract people interested in wildlife, especially birdwatchers.

For a relatively small country, perched on the north-west corner of Europe, Scotland punches above its weight in bird terms. The Scottish list now exceeds 500 species. Of these, 190 are regular breeding species. Another 30 or so are found wintering in Scotland. The remainder are passage migrants, some of which are exceedingly scarce, having been seen less than 20 times – often on remote islands like Fair Isle, Foula, North Ronaldsay or St Kilda. Few British birdwatchers consider their birding education complete until they have spent a week or so visiting one of these islands, which remain at the forefront of migration study and offer the excitement of a personal rare bird find.

In this handbook we cover all the regularly breeding and wintering species, plus the regular passage migrants seen in Scotland. Some scarcer passage and wintering species have also been selected. True vagrants, many of which test the skills of the birdwatcher, are not treated in this volume in order to keep length – and thus costs – to a minimum.

BIRD HABITATS

Scotland is distinctly upland in character. Intensively managed arable farmland is largely confined to those parts of the south and east of the country that are flatter, and whose climate is influenced by the sea. This is also where most of the towns and cities are found. Like all other areas of Britain, the Scottish landscape has been much altered by man's farming activities, and in more recent decades by large-scale afforestation of less agriculturally productive hill areas. In the lowlands of the

Central Belt and along the east coast, industry, roads and the spread of towns and cities has fragmented areas of countryside, and has reduced the extent of inter-tidal habitats, particularly on the Forth and Clyde.

Despite man's influence, there are still significant areas where semi-natural vegetation predominates, and the main use of the ground is largely extensive grazing by sheep and cattle. On these open landscapes may be found breeding Lapwing, Curlew, Snipe and other waders, whilst on the heather moors Red Grouse can occur at high densities. Scotland's uplands support some 420 pairs of Golden Eagles, plus Peregrines, Hen Harrier, Short-eared Owls, Merlin and Kestrels. The moors and mountains are of great landscape and wildlife value.

On the grouse moors, heather is burnt periodically to stimulate fresh growth. This encourages high densities of grouse, which are shot in the autumn. These open, heather-dominated landscapes benefit Golden Plover and other species. Sadly, however, some managers of these sporting estates illegally kill Hen Harriers and other protected raptor species. In spring, the Scottish uplands can be alive with birds. But come the cold, wet, short days of winter and they are deserted even by Meadow Pipits. A few Ravens, the resident eagles and some hardy grouse are all that remain.

Scotland has a very long, indented coastline. It ranges from huge, open expanses of sand and silt flats, such as those on the Solway, to the rocky shores and dramatic cliffs of coastlines exposed to the full force of the waves. Scotland supports nearly half of all the breeding seabirds found in the European Union. The spectacular seabird colonies of Fowlsheugh, Troup Head and St Abb's Head are easily accessible to visitors, but the chance to visit some of the awe-inspiring island colonies should not be missed. St Kilda, Ailsa Craig, Bass Rock, Handa, and stacks and cliffs around Orkney and Shetland are a cacophony of sound, as Gannets, guillemots, Razorbills, Puffins, Shags, Kittiwakes and Fulmars stream

Golden Eagles range widely in the uplands of Scotland.

back and forth. Shetland and Orkney are where most of the Arctic Skuas and Great Skuas (Bonxies) breed. They nest on moors near the coast and other seabird colonies, which they raid for food.

In the autumn and winter, the coastal marshes and inter-tidal flats support tens of thousands of wading birds – Knot, Redshank, Dunlin, Curlew, godwits and Grey Plover. Many pass through on migration, but large numbers remain throughout the winter. Offshore, favoured bays and sea feeding areas support wintering sea duck and large numbers of divers, which come here from their Arctic breeding grounds to find refuge. Where salt marshes and merse occurs, flocks of Twite and Snow Buntings gather in winter, seeking out the seeds of the plants that grow here.

Compared to the rest of the UK, Scotland is quite heavily afforested. About 17% of the country is under plantation and forest. However, only a small fragment of this is native woodland. The majority was planted after the Second World War, and comprises dense stands of Sitka Spruce, larches and other non-native species. In establishing the forests, many raised bogs, dune systems and heather moors rich in birds and other wildlife were lost. Today, some of these areas are being restored, and modern forestry planting designs are an improvement on the dense, dark stands of the past. Plantation forests are not altogether devoid of birds, especially when restructuring as part of the harvesting cycle has occurred. Forestry Commission Scotland (FCS) and other woodland managers have created many access routes, where interesting birdwatching can be had. Species to look for include Siskins and other finches, and in some years crossbills are very visible. Sparrowhawks and buzzards are also common. Black Grouse are found on the edges of clear fells and on some wide heathery rides. In February, Goshawks display on warmer days, over large, mature forest blocks.

A still loch set among Caledonian pine forest.

In the west of the country are found oak, birch and other deciduous woods. The trees here can be festooned with moss and lichens, and support high densities of Willow Warblers, Wood Warblers and Redstarts. Pied Flycatchers are found in Dumfries & Galloway and in some woods in central Scotland.

In the Highlands, particularly Speyside, Deeside and the Beauly catchment, are found the best Caledonian pinewoods. Comprising Scots Pine, birch, Holly, Juniper and other native trees, these woods support some very special birds. In the woods themselves are Capercaillie, now numbering some 1,500–2,000 individuals, while Black Grouse enjoy the woodland edges and Ospreys nest each summer in old pines. The Crested Tit is found in this habitat also, although it is absent from Deeside. The best places to see Caledonian pine forests in all their glory is in Abernethy Forest, run by the RSPB, and in Glen Affric, which is managed by FCS.

In the Argyll islands and Outer Hebrides, a thin strip of fertile coastal land is found. This is farmed by crofters, who traditionally grazed it with cattle and shallow ploughed the drier sandy soils for crops. Dunes and white-sand beaches protected this farmed area from the driving winter gales. These machair habitats are unique to Scotland's western seaboard and a few areas on the west coast of Ireland. They are very special for birds. The machairs of the Outer Hebrides support over 16,000 pairs of nesting wading birds, including Redshank, Dunlin, snipe and Lapwing. They still have Corn Buntings and Twite, and the endangered Corncrake breeds in the wetter meadows and iris beds. The machair is also very important for its flowering plants and rare bumblebees. Good areas to visit include the RSPB's reserves at Balranald on North Uist, and the Argyll islands of Tiree, Coll and Oronsay.

The high mountains of Scotland, and especially the Cairngorms, give a glimpse of Arctic tundra in the British Isles. Here, at 1,000 m or so, the temperatures plunge in winter and wind speeds in excess of 160 kph regularly occur. The vegetation comprises sedges, mosses and arctic-alpine plants, which grow very slowly in the harsh environment. Snow beds may have snow lying until midsummer. It is on these high plateaux that Ptarmigan occur, their cryptic plumage protecting them from Golden Eagles and Foxes. The Mountain or Blue Hare is also widespread. Each spring, Dotterels return from Morocco to nest on these mountains, and a few Snow Buntings nest in the rocky screes. These sensitive

Snowfields on the Cairngorm plateau, haunt of Ptarmigan.

habitats are the nearest thing we have to wilderness in the British Isles and therefore will be very vulnerable to the impact of climate change.

As you push northwards into Sutherland, the landscape becomes more rounded, with the peaks rising from rolling moorland pock-marked with small pools and lochs. Finally you reach the 500,000 ha of the Flow Country, a huge expanse of blanket peatland where Golden Plover, Dunlin and Greenshank breed. On the larger lochs, Black-throated Divers display, and Common Scoters nest on the more sheltered water bodies. The Flow Country is one of the largest expanses of blanket bog in the world and it has some special birds to match. The best time to visit is between mid-May and the end of June. Hunting Hen Harriers, Merlins sitting on old fenceposts, and the trilling display of Dunlins or call of the Greenshank greet the visitor. The RSPB's Forsinard Flows visitor centre can give guidance on the best places to explore in this huge landscape.

MIGRATION

Scotland is at a crossroads on the great travels made by birds, whose migration can be highly visible at times. Large numbers of geese and wild swans arrive in September and October each year from Greenland, Iceland, Spitsbergen and other Arctic breeding areas. They make landfall and then move through the country to their regular wintering areas. These spectacular arrivals – especially on Islay, the Loch of Strathbeg and other sites – is exciting indeed. Greylag and Pink-footed geese from Iceland are quite widespread on farmland. The White-fronted Goose from Greenland is more local, and found in the Argyll islands and the Ken-Dee Marshes in Dumfries & Galloway. The Greenland population of Barnacle Geese winters mainly on Islay, whereas those from Spitsbergen are found on the Solway – and can be seen at Caerlaverock and Mersehead reserves. Autumn also brings large parties of Fieldfares and Redwings to the east coast, joined in some winters by flocks of colourful Waxwings.

Seabirds also migrate, often far out of sight of land, but when the wind conditions are right spectacular movements of shearwaters, petrels, skuas and other species can be observed. The best areas for watching are headlands, where birds are channelled along the coast before continuing onwards. In August and September, Manx and Sooty shearwaters may be joined by Great Shearwaters from the southern oceans. All four species of skua are seen each year, along with rarer species like Sabine's Gull. The extensive network of CalMac and other ferries that run from the mainland to the various islands can also provide excellent sea-watching opportunities!

In spring, birdwatchers are increasingly visiting the Uists and Lewis to look for migrating skuas, particularly Pomarine and Long-tailed skuas seen from the RSPB's Balranald reserve. But careful searching is also turning up many Great Northern Divers in summer plumage, together with small numbers of Yellow-billed Divers in April and May, particularly off Lewis.

In autumn, when easterly winds occur for a few days, many coastal headlands and the Northern Isles are visited by small migrants, including Pied Flycatchers, Wheatears, Redstarts, various warblers, and the occasional Red-backed Shrike, Wryneck or Bluethroat. Favoured mainland sites include St Abb's Head, Barns Ness, Fife Ness, Girdle Ness and Rattray Head. On Orkney and Shetland, migrants can turn up just about anywhere – which is what makes an autumn visit so exciting. Migrant songbirds are attracted to areas of scrub, tangled vegetation, copses and weedy crops. Careful searching may produce something unusual, but a day by the east coast in the autumn watching common species like Whitethroats, Willow Warblers, Chiffchaffs or Redstarts is most enjoyable.

In spring, migration is less obvious, as the birds move north on a broad front through the country. That said, places like the Isle of May or Fife Ness can still reward birdwatchers with an overshooting Golden Oriole or Subalpine Warbler. Birdwatching during migration time is never dull – always expect the unexpected.

The red sandstone cliffs of the RSPB Hoy reserve, with the 'Old man' in the foreground.

NATURE RESERVES AND FACILITIES FOR BIRDWATCHERS

Scotland has numerous excellent nature reserves, many of which have nature trails and hides to assist birdwatchers and other visitors. The RSPB in Scotland has 75 nature reserves, found in all parts of the country. A number of these have visitor centres, and nearly all have trails and good information to help the visitor (see www.rspb.org.uk/reserves).

Scottish Natural Heritage (SNH), the government conservation agency, also manages a number of important National Nature Reserves (NNRs), some owned directly but others run in conjunction with private owners or other conservation bodies (see www.nnr-scotland.org.uk for more details). The Scottish Wildlife Trust (SWT) and the National Trust for Scotland (NTS) also own or manage properties that have facilities for birdwatchers (see www.swt.org.uk and www.nts.org.uk).

Much of the wider countryside and coastal areas of Scotland outside the reserves can offer equally exciting birdwatching. The country has progressive access legislation, offering a right of responsible access to most parts of the countryside. Those accessing private land do, however, have responsibilities and should act accordingly. Basic common sense should be employed, but anyone who is unsure of the outdoor access code should contact Outdoor Access Scotland (www.outdooraccess-scotland.com), which offers detailed guidance for visitors to the countryside.

One of the fundamental rules is that birds or other wildlife should not be

Over 2 million people have watched Ospreys at Loch Garten.

disturbed – either during the breeding season or at winter roosting sites. Waders in particular are stressed during cold periods and will use precious energy if repeatedly bothered. Some scarce species such as Capercaillie are protected by law when displaying (lekking) in the breeding season, and it is illegal to disturb other species listed on Schedule 1 of the Nature Conservation (Scotland) Act 2004. Always put the well-being of birds first, and if they are at or near the nest and are calling out in alarm, please move on quickly. Finally, when visiting private estates, farmland or nature reserves, do take the advice offered, so that you don't accidentally spoil the enjoyment of others (such as anglers or deerstalkers), or put yourself at risk from normal farming or forestry operations.

However, taking responsible action when watching birds and wildlife need not spoil your personal enjoyment. Scotland is a very special country with spectacular and diverse habitats that are rich in birdlife. The secret is to know where and when to go, and what to look for. There is no end to the enjoyment to be had. We hope the following pages will provide a source of information that will help the reader, old or young, resident or visitor to experience the sights and sounds of Scotland and understand a little more about the birdlife that surrounds us, if only we take the time to look.

Dainty Crested Tits occur in old pine forests in the Spey and Beauly catchments.

USING THIS BOOK

This book aims to help as many people as possible develop a greater understanding of the birds that share our towns, our countryside and all the other habitats that make up the rich mosaic of Scotland.

Ours is a reference book for anyone interested in birds. It contains the information a reader is likely to want to know about any bird they are likely to see in Scotland, without having to resort to scientific books or journals, or needing to be familiar with technical details and scientific language.

The contents describe 252 species that regularly occur in Scotland – either as residents or as visitors.

The birds are arranged in the usual scientific order, with related species appearing close together. Each species study begins with the most commonly used name, followed by its scientific name. We have chosen not to use the names that have been recently published by the British Ornithologists' Union and favoured by some other authors because we believe our audience may find these confusing.

IDENTIFICATION

This book is not principally intended to be a field guide. Identification is only a beginning, not an end in itself. The book is intended to be a key to discovering much more about the life of each species and how it is faring in our modern world.

All the most common plumages are described – adult, summer, winter and immature – as are flight actions and other key aids to identification. There are also a few words about the annual cycle of moult as this may influence what a species looks like at a given time and how it behaves.

At the end of Identification the SEE ALSO notes cross-refer to other species that appear similar. These may be closely related, as in the case of Chiffchaff and Willow Warbler, or appear superficially similar as with Red-throated Diver and Cormorant.

HABITS

This describes special characteristics that may aid identification, but also tell the observer more about bird behaviour.

VOICE

The section on sounds is also intended to aid identification. Descriptions of song and calls are highly personal and we advise the reader also to take advantage of the many excellent CDs and other recordings that are on the market and will help to bring our descriptions to life.

HABITAT

It is important to know where a species normally lives. We have looked beyond the breeding habitat and included the places where the bird may be found in other seasons. Readers should note, however, that many species will often be seen away from their usual habitats – this is one of the joys, challenges and frustrations of birdwatching!

FOOD

We have attempted to be quite specific by giving the common name of the most usual food items (for example we have given 'Bullheads, loaches, Minnows, sticklebacks and small Chub' as the food of Kingfisher, rather than the rather bland statement that the bird eats fish).

BREEDING

This summary for each species includes a description of the nest site, the number of eggs laid, the respective roles of male and female, the length of incubation, the time taken for the young to fledge and the age at which they become independent. Readers should note that the times given can sometimes vary by a few days, depending on local environmental conditions. We also state when there is more than one brood in the year; where this number is not given it is implicit that only one brood is reared.

MOVEMENTS AND MIGRATIONS

The movements and migrations of birds are among the natural wonders of the world and we cover this topic for each species. We have also included here the maximum recorded age. It must be emphasised that this is not the 'average' age, but the oldest that is known in Britain or Europe. As this information is based on a small sample of ringed birds, it is likely that many individuals exceed this age.

POPULATION

We have reproduced the latest known estimations of the total number of birds, or breeding pairs. All bird numbers fluctuate from season to season and from year to year; but where we know about long-term trends, either up or down, we have included this information.

CONSERVATION

Following naturally from the current population we include a section on topical conservation issues. Here we summarise some of the influences on bird populations and some measures conservationists are taking to reverse declines.

DISTRIBUTION

The section describes where the species may usually be found in Scotland. We have also tried to put this into a world context.

We are privileged to have been able to select illustrations from the excellent *Handbook of Bird Identification*, as well as commissioning additional material especially for this book. The result is an extensive series of illustrations by some of the best wildlife illustrators, which help to bring both the birds and their characteristics alive on the page. In addition, the specially commissioned maps show the breeding and wintering range of the species in Scotland.

COLOUR-CODED SPECIES

The coloured boxes that head each page follow the UK-agreed system for recognising birds of conservation concern.

indicates the most threatened species in the UK, because either the number of birds is rapidly falling or their ranges are contracting.

indicates a moderate decline or a moderate contraction of the species range.

indicates species that breed widely in Europe. Number often fluctuate from year-to-year but there is currently no discernible rapid or moderate decline, and some may be increasing.

indicates all other species.

KEY TO MAPS

The maps in this book give an approximate indication of the distribution of each species at different seasons of the year.

Green: resident, areas where species may be seen throughout the year and where they breed

Yellow: summer visitor, areas where the species may be seen in summer and usually breed

Blue: winter visitor, areas where species spend the winter, but do not breed

Pink: passage migrant, areas that species visit at times of migration – generally spring and autumn

For distribution at sea, colours are restricted to areas where birds will be visible

to observers and therefore only inshore waters have been mapped.

BIRD TOPOGRAPHY

HOUSE SPARROW

- ear coverts
- nape
- crown
- neck side
- hindneck
- forehead
- mantle
- upper mandible
- scapulars
- bill
- back
- lower mandible
- tertials
- chin
- secondaries
- throat
- rump
- (upper) breast (chest)
- uppertail coverts
- lesser coverts
- tail
- breast side
- median coverts
- (lower) breast
- alula (bastard wing)
- undertail coverts
- greater coverts
- primaries
- primary coverts
- vent
- flank
- claw
- belly
- toe

LITTLE STINT

- brace
- mantle
- upper scapulars
- lower scapulars
- tertials
- lesser coverts
- greater coverts
- median coverts
- tibia
- tarsus
- hind toe

BLACK-HEADED GULL

- terminal band
- secondaries
- trailing edge
- leading edge
- primaries

worn adult male (spring)

Some songbirds change their appearance radically through feather wear rather than moult.

fresh adult male (autumn)

REDSTART

MUTE SWAN *CYGNUS OLOR*

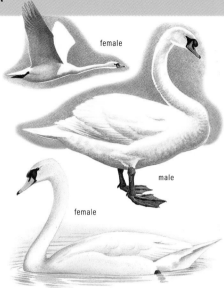

female

male

female

IDENTIFICATION
125–155 cm. One of our largest birds. Has a rounded head with a long, graceful, S-shaped neck and pointed tail. Adult is white with an orange bill that has a black base. Black knob at base of bill is largest on male. Head and neck are sometimes stained rusty orange. Juvenile is brownish grey, becoming whiter by its first autumn. Immatures have a washed-out orange bill. Large black feet sometimes rest on bird's back. When up-ending, the tail is pointed, unlike Whooper and Bewick's. Moults between June and November and becomes flightless for 6–8 weeks. Female moults before male. SEE ALSO: Whooper Swan p17, Bewick's Swan p18.

HABITS
Waddling walk. Takes off from water by running along the surface before becoming airborne. Flies with neck extended and regular, slow wingbeats. Flocks fly in diagonal lines. Aggressive posture has arched wings, neck drawn back and rapid, jerky advance across the water. Courtship takes place in late winter, with syn-chronised head-dipping and necks and breasts pressed together. Normally strictly territorial, but there are a few traditional nesting colonies. Feeds mainly during the day, but continues after dark.

VOICE
Mostly silent, but makes a loud hiss when angry and other snorting sounds. Loud, throbbing 'waou, waou' noise made by wings in flight. Young birds make a high-pitched whistle.

juvenile

HABITAT
Breeds on ponds in parks and on lowland lochs with shallow areas for feeding; also slow-flowing rivers, canals and sheltered coastal waters.

FOOD
Feeds by dipping its head into water and sometimes up-ending. Also picks up grit from river bottoms. Eats aquatic plants and other vegetation. Plant food includes stoneworts, starworts, hornworts, water-crowfoots, various pondweeds, soft grasses and algae. Also eats small animals including insects and snails. Sometimes grazes on short grass.

BREEDING
Pairs first breed at 3 or 4 years. Once paired, divorce is rare. The nest is built of reeds, rushes and other vege-tation near water – on a bank, an island or in a reedbed. The nest may be 4 m wide and built by both sexes, male passing material to female. 5–7 eggs are incu-bated by female and guarded by male. Eggs hatch after 36 days. Young feed themselves. When small, the young may be carried on their parents' backs, which helps to keep them warm and protect them from Pike. Young fly after 120–150 days and usually leave their parents' territory during their first autumn.

MOVEMENTS AND MIGRATIONS
Some stay on their territory all year, while others move short distances and form winter flocks. Juveniles join these winter flocks and non-breeders remain in flocks in summer. Some travel to traditional areas to moult. Oldest bird was over 26 years.

POPULATION
Once prized as a food for banquets, these swans were introduced to many parts of Europe, so that the present population is a mixture of wild and semi-feral flocks. There are over 1,000 pairs breeding in Scotland and a wintering population of over 5,000 birds

CONSERVATION
In Scotland the species has expanded its range in recent years, increasing in the south but slightly declining in the north. Increases may be due to better protection. The problem of lead poisoning of birds on lowland rivers has been largely solved by a ban on the sale of lead fishing weights and the prohibition of lead shot in cartridges used over wetlands. Vandalism, however, is a significant cause of nest failure in some urban areas.

DISTRIBUTION
This swan breeds wild in northern and eastern Europe and also in parts of Asia. It has been introduced to North America, South Africa, Australia and New Zealand. Notable concentrations in Scotland occur on Loch Bee, South Uist, and Loch of Harray, Orkney.

WHOOPER SWAN _CYGNUS CYGNUS_

juvenile

IDENTIFICATION
145–160 cm. Slightly smaller than Mute Swan, with a long bill giving it a 'Roman-nosed' appearance. Neck is usually straight but sometimes forms a graceful curve, and appears long and thin – often with an obvious kink at the base. Adult is white with a black and yellow bill. Yellow on bill extends beyond the nostril and ends in a point. Some have rust-coloured staining on feathers, which is lost during the winter moult. Immature has a grey body that becomes whiter during the winter. Some grey feathers remain until its second winter. Its bill is reddish grey until the black and yellow appear. Larger than Bewick's Swan, with a longer body, longer wings, angular head, longer neck and triangular, not rounded, yellow patch on its bill. When up-ending it has a square-ended tail. Adults moult their flight feathers after breeding and are flightless for several weeks. Female moults when young are small, but male waits until female is almost ready to fly.
SEE ALSO: Mute Swan p16, Bewick's Swan p18.

HABITS
Often feeds by up-ending. In flight, it looks heavier than Bewick's Swan, with a larger head, slower wingbeats, and longer neck and body. It is not colonial when nesting, but forms flocks at other times. Flocks include family units and non-breeders.

VOICE
Loud whooping or trumpeting call.

HABITAT
In winter, visits lowland farmland and lochs. It may also be seen on the sea in sheltered bays. It feeds in shallow water or on farmland during the day, and roosts on open water at night. Some Icelandic feeding areas are rich in iron compounds, which stain the birds' head and neck feathers.

FOOD
Eats the leaves, stems and roots of aquatic vegetation, including pondweeds, stoneworts, Marsh Yellow-cress and horsetails. Also feeds on water snails. On farmland it eats potatoes, grain from stubble fields, grass and winter cereals.

BREEDING
It does not nest until 4–5 years old. Courtship begins in winter and most pairs probably stay together until one dies. The nest is close to water, often on a small island, and is a large mound of reeds and sedges that is built by both sexes. 3–5 eggs are laid as soon as the ice melts and are incubated by the female for 35 days. Both parents tend the young, which feed themselves and are brooded at night. They fly after about 87 days, and remain with their parents for their first autumn and winter and the start of the return migration.

MOVEMENTS AND MIGRATIONS
Migrants from Iceland arrive in Scotland in October and leave before mid-April. Generally, the species winters further north than Bewick's Swans. Scandinavian and Siberian populations winter in eastern Europe and the Black Sea. Oldest ringed bird was 23 years.

POPULATION
The winter population of Scotland's Whooper Swans numbers more than 4,000 birds and there has been no significant change in recent years. Fewer than 30 individuals remain for the summer, of which up to 10 pairs may breed in the Northern and Western Isles.

CONSERVATION
Specially protected. The main threats to the species are from collisions with overhead power lines, disturbance of the few pairs that do nest, and lead poisoning from shotgun cartridges. The estuaries and wetlands visited by birds during their migration and for winter roosts need special protection.

DISTRIBUTION
Breeds on the tundra in Iceland and Scandinavia, and also nests in northern Russia and northern Asia. Winters as far south as the Mediterranean. Most Icelandic birds migrate to Britain and Ireland, while those from Scandinavia winter in Europe and a few arrive in eastern England.

BEWICK'S SWAN *CYGNUS COLUMBIANUS*

IDENTIFICATION
115–117 cm. Smaller than Mute Swan – our smallest swan. Rather goose-like, with a rounded head, smaller bill and shorter and proportionally thicker neck than Whooper Swan. Adult is white with a black and yellow bill. Yellow pattern at base of bill is highly variable, but generally rounder or squarer than the pointed wedge pattern on a Whooper's bill. Neck and underparts may become stained rusty orange. Juvenile is uniformly grey with a flesh-coloured bill that darkens and becomes partly yellow during the first winter. Immatures have some grey feathers on their head and neck until their second winter. When up-ending has a blunt-ended tail.
SEE ALSO: Mute Swan p16, Whooper Swan p17.

HABITS
In flight, neck and body are shorter, and wings beat faster than Whooper Swan. Feeds and roosts in flocks in winter; feeds in water less than 1 m deep, and also on salt marshes and arable fields. Roosts on water, where it can continue to feed after dark. Also grazes in fields at night.

VOICE
Call is a soft, mellow, yelping 'oop, oop', or 'hoo, hoo'.

HABITAT
Breeds on the Russian tundra where there are low, swampy, grassy areas with pools, lakes and rivers. Visits low-lying wet pastures, flooded grasslands, salt marshes, lakes and reservoirs in winter. Sometimes feeds on arable land close to its wetland roosts.

FOOD
Leaves, shoots and roots of pondweeds, milfoil, Floating Sweet Grass, Marsh Foxtail, Marsh Yellow-cress and other aquatics, and rye-grass and clovers. Visits farmland to feed on waste potatoes, carrots and winter wheat.

BREEDING
Does not breed in Britain or Ireland. Nests further north than any other swan and the breeding cycle needs to be completed in 100–110 days before the Arctic weather deteriorates. Pairs stay loyal and 'divorce' is unknown. When one bird dies over half will find a new mate within a year. Young form pairs during their second or third year. Breeding usually starts between 4 and 6 years old. Family groups stay together for the winter and travel back to their breeding grounds as a group. Some young associate with their parents for several years until paired.

MOVEMENTS AND MIGRATIONS
Bewick's Swans leave Siberia in the first half of September and arrive in Britain in mid-October; peak numbers in Scotland occur in November. The Netherlands and Germany are the other main European wintering areas. Some migrants also reach France and other European countries. Most start their return migration before the end of March. The oldest wild bird was 20, but an individual survived for 30 years in captivity.

POPULATION
A rare bird in Scotland, with seldom more than 100 seen most winters – and many of those will move south into England during the winter. The UK population is in modest decline, but Scottish numbers remain stable, with birds regularly seen in Dumfries & Galloway.

CONSERVATION
Specially protected. Many deaths are inflicted directly or indirectly by man: flying into overhead cables, lead poisoning from shotgun cartridges and illegal shooting on migration are all threats. The loss of traditional wetlands has resulted in 90% of the European winter population being concentrated on just 10 sites in England. In Siberia, the growth in oil, gas and mineral exploration also causes some concern for the future of this species.

DISTRIBUTION
Breeds in northern Russia and in North America. Migrants fly to traditional wintering areas. The Russian population reaches western Europe, especially the Netherlands, Britain and Ireland. There are only a small number of sites where the majority of birds congregate.

juvenile

BEAN GOOSE *ANSER FABALIS*

IDENTIFICATION

66–84 cm. Slightly smaller and less bulky than Greylag Goose. This is a tall goose with a long, wedge-shaped bill, a slender, almost swan-like neck, orange legs and a yellow and black bill with a variable pattern. The male is generally a little larger than the female. The adult is brown, with a very dark sooty-brown head and upper neck, uniform brown upperparts with pale barring, and white under the tail. The brown breast has fine, pale barring and there is a white line at the edge of its folded wings. The juvenile is similar to an adult but duller and sometimes paler. Some birds have white feathers around the base of the bill, but not enough to be confused with a White-front. In flight, the upperwing is uniformly dark. It moults all its flight feathers simultaneously and is flightless for about a month before its autumn migration.
SEE ALSO: Pink-footed Goose p20, White-fronted Goose p21, Greylag Goose p22.

HABITS

It swims well but less often than most other geese. The dark brown upperwing and rather long, slender neck are obvious in flight. It is usually sociable, except when nesting, although the flocks tend to be smaller than those of other geese. In autumn, the flocks are first made up of families, and these are then joined by non-breeders. Flocks fly to their roosts at dusk and leave again at dawn. When airborne they generally fly in 'V' formation or in lines.

juvenile

VOICE

Not as noisy as other geese – gives an 'ung-ank' or an 'ow, ow, ow, ow' call.

HABITAT

In Scotland it spends the winter in open country. The winter evening roosts are on undisturbed lochs close to the feeding grounds. The northern breeding grounds are either within dense coniferous forests (Taiga) or birch scrub, or in open areas of low, wet tundra, on small offshore islands or near pools or streams.

FOOD

It feeds by grazing grasses and their seeds, clover, cereals, potatoes and other crops.

BREEDING

This species does not breed in Britain or Ireland. Both parents tend the young, and in autumn families migrate together and then stay together until the following breeding season.

MOVEMENTS AND MIGRATIONS

Family parties from Scandinavia arrive in Scotland during late September and early October and leave again in March. On their breeding grounds some of the forest birds move north to the tundra after they have finished breeding and before migrating for the winter. Sometimes a small number of tundra Bean Geese accompany White-fronted Geese from Russia and arrive in Scotland. Oldest bird was 25 years.

POPULATION

Around 250 are found in Scotland through the winter. Birds of the taiga race are regular on Slamannan plateau, but scarce elsewhere.

CONSERVATION

In winter, protection of the wet grasslands and semi-improved agricultural fields on the Slamannan plateau is essential. The RSPB has established a reserve here at Fannyside Loch for the species. There are now fewer pairs breeding in Sweden and Norway than there were 20 years ago; this may have been caused by increased human disturbance, changes in agriculture and some direct persecution.

DISTRIBUTION

Lowland Scotland and Norfolk are the only places that these birds are regularly seen in Britain in winter. Small numbers are occasionally seen elsewhere, usually in the company of other geese. There are several races of Bean Goose. The western race breeds in northern Scandinavia and north Russia. Other races breed in northern Russia and north Asia. Most of the western race of Bean Goose winter in southern Sweden, Germany and the Netherlands, and a few of these visit Britain in winter.

PINK-FOOTED GOOSE ANSER BRACHYRHYNCHUS

IDENTIFICATION

60–75 cm. Smaller than Greylag Goose. Pinkish grey with a dark head and neck, and a short pink bill with variable dark marks. At a distance it appears compact and daintier than other geese. It has a shorter neck, a darker, rounder head and a greyer body. Legs and feet are pink. Pale edges to back feathers give a barred effect and its underparts are closely barred. Has a white line on body below its wings. In flight, shows a blue-grey forewing that is not as pale as that of Greylag. Juvenile is darker with dull yellowish legs, less distinct barring on back and mottled underparts. Adults moult their flight feathers simultaneously and are flightless for about 25 days before autumn migration. SEE ALSO: Bean Goose p19, White-fronted Goose p21, Greylag Goose p22.

HABITS

A sociable goose except when nesting. Winter flocks contain up to 40,000 birds, which mainly consist of family groups. Flocks move from their night-time roosts to their feeding areas at dawn and return at dusk. Feeding flocks travel up to 30 km, and both roosts and feeding areas are used year after year. It also has 'rest stations' on grasslands or marshland pools. When landing, it frequently side-slips and tumbles as it loses height.

VOICE

Call is higher-pitched and less harsh than other geese – often an incessant and rather musical 'wink, wink'.

HABITAT

Roosts on estuaries, mud flats and freshwater lochs near the coast, and visits nearby farmland to feed. Prefers large fields, especially stubble in autumn, root crops such as potatoes and winter cereals or grassland towards the end of winter.

FOOD

Feeds on vegetable matter, including grain, winter cereals, potatoes and root crops, and also on grass. In summer, it eats leaves and shoots, roots and fruits, especially bistort, horsetails and cotton grass.

BREEDING

Does not breed in Britain or Ireland. The pair bond generally lasts for life. In Iceland it nests in inaccessible river gorges and boggy floodplains, where it is safe from ground predators. In Spitsbergen, which has fewer predators, it nests in flatter habitats. Both parents tend young and families remain together in the first winter, breaking up only at the start of the next nesting season.

MOVEMENTS AND MIGRATIONS

When the young are 10–20 days old, family groups come together to moult and form large, flightless flocks. Some of the moulting flocks travel considerable distances on foot. There is also a massive moult migration of mainly non-breeding birds from Iceland to Greenland in June. Once their new feathers have grown, Greenland birds fly first to Iceland and then the majority move on to Scotland or England. Migrants arrive in Britain in early October and return north in April. Oldest surviving bird was over 38 years.

juvenile

POPULATION

Numbers increased during the 20th century and now almost 150,000 birds overwinter in Scotland – around half of the total British winter population.

CONSERVATION

Protected in the close season. The recent population increase is probably a result of larger fields, accessible food on farmland in winter and better protection in the UK. Although these geese graze farmland, they seldom cause economic damage. The main threat to the species is in its breeding areas in Iceland, where its numbers are affected by hunting and by the establishment of hydro-electricity schemes.

DISTRIBUTION

There are two European populations: one in Spitsbergen and another in Iceland and Greenland. Greenland and Iceland birds winter in Scotland and England. Spitsbergen birds winter in western Europe, especially Denmark and the Netherlands. Notable Scottish concentrations occur at Loch of Strathbeg, Vane Farm RSPB reserve and Montrose Basin.

WHITE-FRONTED GOOSE   *ANSER ALBIFRONS*

IDENTIFICATION
65–78 cm. Smaller than Greylag Goose. Appears larger and longer-necked than Pink-footed Goose, with a deep chest and rather square head. Has a grey-brown head, neck and body, with a white forehead and variable black blotchy bars on underparts. Back is brown and crossed with pale lines. Legs are orange and bill of Eurasian race is pink. Distinctive Greenland race is generally larger and darker, with a longer, heavier orange bill and heavy barring on chest. Juvenile lacks the white forehead and black breast bars. The white forehead is gained during the first winter but it is the second autumn before black bars appear on the belly. Flight feathers are moulted simultaneously and this goose becomes flightless for 25 days after nesting.
SEE ALSO: Bean Goose p19, Pink-footed Goose p20, Greylag Goose p22.

young have hatched, families join together. A few feral birds are free-flying and sometimes nest in Scotland.

MOVEMENTS AND MIGRATIONS
The race that breeds in Greenland almost exclusively winters in Scotland or Ireland. It crosses the North Atlantic via Iceland and arrives in October. The European race that breeds in northern Europe and Russia, and that visits England in winter, is rarely seen in Scotland. Most birds begin their return migration in March or April. Oldest ringed bird was over 18 years.

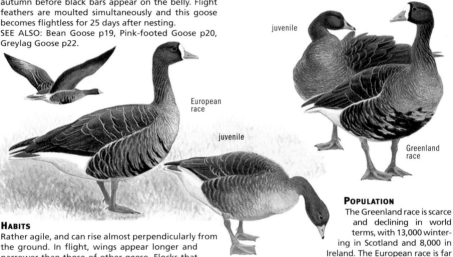

juvenile

European race

juvenile

Greenland race

HABITS
Rather agile, and can rise almost perpendicularly from the ground. In flight, wings appear longer and narrower than those of other geese. Flocks that roost together comprise many family groups. Large flocks cross the sky in lines, 'V's and chevrons, especially at dawn and dusk. These big flocks break up into smaller feeding groups during the day.

VOICE
Cackling calls that are higher-pitched than Greylag and with a laughing sound to them.

HABITAT
Traditionally wintered on peatlands and roosted on estuaries or large lochs at night. Now the species more commonly feeds on wet grassland but still requires proximity to large water bodies for roosting. Breeds on the Arctic tundra, close to lakes, rivers and pools.

FOOD
Vegetarian. Eats leaves, stems, roots and seeds of a variety of plants. In winter, feeds on grain, potatoes, Sugarbeet, horsetails, rhizomes of couch grass and roots of cotton grass. Feeds during the day, and sometimes at night.

BREEDING
Wild birds do not breed in Britain or Ireland. Pairs form after 2 years, but do not normally breed until 3 years old. Once formed, pairs generally stay together for life. Both parents tend young and the family stays together until the adults start breeding the following year, and even then the previous year's young may associate with their family group. On their breeding grounds, after the

POPULATION
The Greenland race is scarce and declining in world terms, with 13,000 wintering in Scotland and 8,000 in Ireland. The European race is far more numerous, but remains rare in Scotland, with passage birds on the east coast.

CONSERVATION
Protected in Scotland. The chief threat has been from hunting in Iceland, although a recent hunting ban there may help this species. A recent decline in the Greenland population is attributed to the expansion of the Canada Goose population and increased hunting. There are also problems with disturbance of White-fronts at feeding and roosting sites, and with the development of windfarms in remote areas.

DISTRIBUTION

There are two races that visit the British Isles. One comes from the west coast of Greenland and mostly winters in Ireland and western Scotland, especially on Islay in the Inner Hebrides and on the Ken-Dee Marshes RSPB reserve in Dumfries & Galloway. The other race comes from northern Russia and winters in western Europe, including southern England, especially around the Severn and Swale estuaries.

GREYLAG GOOSE _ANSER ANSER_

IDENTIFICATION
75–90 cm. Usually smaller than Canada Goose. Grey-brown with a thick neck and large head. Neck has 4 or 5 dark lines down the side, formed by ridges of feathers. Back has a barred appearance and the pale grey breast and belly are slightly mottled with darker marks. Forewing and underwing are noticeably pale. Feathers under the tail are white. The large bill is orange with a white tip and the legs and feet are flesh-pink. Juveniles have darker bills and legs, and less noticeable pale barring on the back. Flight feathers are moulted simultaneously, so birds are flightless for about 4 weeks between May and August. Non-breeding birds moult before breeding pairs.
SEE ALSO: Bean Goose p19, Pink-footed Goose p20, White-fronted Goose p21.

HABITS
Flocks fly in lines or 'V's, but are less organised over short distances. In the air the Greylag Goose looks powerful and flies fast on broad wings. It runs further than other geese when taking off. Swims frequently, and can dive to avoid danger.

VOICE
Loud cackling and honking calls – can sound rather like sheep at a distance.

FOOD
Eats roots, tubers, leaves, stems, flowers and seeds of plants such as grasses, sedges and rushes. Grazes on land or takes floating vegetation such as pondweed and duckweed. On farms it eats spilt grain, grass and root crops.

BREEDING
Breeds near fresh water and some nest close together in colonies. The nest is often under a tree or bush, and comprises a mound of vegetation and sticks lined with grass and feathers. In Scotland, the nest may be amongst heather. Egg-laying starts in April and the female incubates the clutch of 5–7 eggs while the male guards a small territory around the nest. The eggs hatch after about 28 days. Young and adults flock together with other families after a few weeks. Young fly after 50 or 60 days. Families stay together for their first year.

MOVEMENTS AND MIGRATIONS
Icelandic Greylags migrate to Scotland in September and October and return to their breeding grounds by April or May. The oldest known wild bird was 18.

POPULATION
The native Scottish breeding population is thought to be around 20,000 birds after a breeding season, and is increasing in range and numbers. A further 85,000 birds arrive in autumn from Iceland, wintering on Orkney, along the east coast and in inland Perthshire.

CONSERVATION
May be hunted in the wildfowling season. The species has reduced its European range because of drainage of its nest sites. Organised introductions in the 1930s and 1960s in many parts of the UK successfully established new breeding populations. Traditional wintering sites for the Icelandic birds, as well as the natural population, need protection and management. Conflict with agricultural interests may need to be addressed in the future, particularly in Orkney, where numbers of Greylags are increasing.

HABITAT
In Scotland, breeds near freshwater lochs and rivers, often on islands, and visits local farms and meadows to feed. Elsewhere in Europe it nests in marshes, reedbeds and tundra. Winter flocks roost on estuaries, marshes, river islands and lowland lochs. By day it feeds on farmland. Feral birds may be found in parks.

DISTRIBUTION
Most domestic geese are descended from the Greylag. Native wild population in northern Scotland and the Western Isles. Further south there is a growing population that originated from introductions during the 20th century. Migrant Greylags winter in northern England and Scotland. The species was once widespread in Europe, but breeding sites are now scattered in the north and east. These birds winter as far south as the Mediterranean and North Africa.

Canada Goose *BRANTA CANADENSIS*

Identification
56–110 cm. There is a wide variety of sizes of Canada Geese, depending on which race a bird belongs to, although most birds in Britain are among the largest at 90–100 cm. Male is larger and heavier than female. Large brown goose with a black neck and head, a broad white band from back of face joining under chin, pale brown breast and flanks, and white under the tail. Bill and feet are black. Juvenile is similar to adult. Flight feathers are moulted simultaneously and the bird is flightless for 3–4 weeks in June–July. SEE ALSO: Barnacle Goose p24, Brent Goose p25.

Habits
Gregarious outside the breeding season. Swims frequently and up-ends to reach food in deeper water. Also grazes on land. Flies with powerful wingbeats, often in rather ragged flocks, but will form lines of 'V's on longer flights. Roosts in large flocks on water or mud banks. Flocks either walk or fly to these roosts at dusk.

Voice
Deep, resonant, trumpet-like calls.

Habitat
Lives in lowland parks and by shallow lochs, and also around flooded sand and gravel pits and reservoirs. Tolerates lochs that are surrounded by trees, but these geese also need short open grass areas for feeding.

Food
Feeds on roots, tubers, stems, grass, leaves, fruits and seeds. Other plants include winter wheat and other cereals, grain, beans, clover, rushes and pondweeds. Also eats the leaves of Crack Willow and strips leaves from the Common Reed.

Breeding
Often nests in loose colonies in which there are separate territories that are defended, especially by the male (gander), until the young have left the nest. The nest is built on the ground by the female. She gathers twigs, leaves, reeds and grasses, and lines the nest with down feathers from her body. Nests are usually near water and under the shelter of a bush or at the base of a tree – often on islands. The female generally starts laying in late March and incubates the 5–7 eggs while the gander stands by. The eggs hatch after 28–30 days; goslings leave the nest soon after hatching and are tended by both parents, the female brooding them at night while they are small. The young can fly after 40–48 days. Young birds stay with their parents until the following breeding season and breed when 3 years old.

Movements and migrations
In its native homeland of North America different races of Canada Geese vary from being long-distance migrants to being totally sedentary. In Britain, a regular moult migration has gradually developed, with some young birds from England flying to northern Scotland to moult. They leave their breeding areas in late May and return in early September. A very small number of truly wild Canada Geese of the smallest races in North America are very occasionally seen in Scotland as winter migrants, usually with Barnacle or Pink-footed geese. The oldest known wild bird survived 24 years.

Population
There may be 300–800 pairs of Canada Geese breeding in Scotland.

Conservation
May be hunted in the wildfowling season and is protected at other times, although it is often considered a nuisance in some public parks.

DISTRIBUTION

This species was introduced to Britain from North America in the 17th century, becoming a popular addition to large lakes in country estates. It has also been introduced to other parts of northern Europe. A few of the smaller, northerly races occasionally arrive in Britain and Ireland in winter as genuine wild vagrants among flocks of Pink-footed, Barnacle or Greenland White-fronted geese.

BARNACLE GOOSE *BRANTA LEUCOPSIS*

IDENTIFICATION
58–70 cm. Smaller than Canada Goose. Black, white and grey goose with a creamy white face and dusky marks between eye and bill. Back of head, neck and breast are all black. Back is blue-grey crossed with black and white bars. Flanks are pale grey and lower belly is gleaming white. Black legs are proportionally longer than in most other geese. Black bill is small and rather delicate. Pale face of juvenile is more mottled and back is greyer with less distinct bars. Flanks are less clearly barred than on adults. Moults flight feathers simultaneously, becoming flightless for 3–4 weeks before autumn migration. SEE ALSO: Brent Goose p25, Canada Goose p23.

HABITS
Wings appear rather pointed in flight, and the black and white head, neck and breast help to identify it, even at a distance. Usually seen in noisy flocks that contain family groups as well as single birds and pairs without young. Flies in 'V's and lines like other geese.

VOICE
Call is a single bark that is higher-pitched than most other geese. Can resemble yapping of dogs – especially when heard from a distance.

The goslings jump from their nests soon after hatching. Although many perish, the fact that cliff-nesting continues must mean it is far safer than losing eggs or small young to foxes and other predators on flatter, more accessible ground. After breeding the young geese stay with their parents until the following breeding season. Pairs stay together for life.

MOVEMENTS AND MIGRATIONS
Two separate populations from the Arctic start to arrive in Scotland in October and stay until late March, April or even early May. Greenland birds fly first to Iceland before migrating to the Western Isles, particularly Islay. Spitsbergen birds migrate via the Norwegian coast to winter on the Solway Firth, passing over the Scottish east coast en route. The oldest known wild Barnacle Goose survived for 26 years.

POPULATION
80,000 winter in Scotland. Numbers have recovered over the last 50 years, although the increase has recently slowed. There are now also feral birds, which sometimes breed.

CONSERVATION
20% of the world population winters in Scotland. Protected at all times. Where the birds are most numerous there have been conflicts with farmers. The enrichment of pasture has created an ideal habitat and birds are now competing with the needs of livestock. A combination of bird-scaring, the provision of conservation refuges and government payments to farmers have helped to solve this problem in some places.

HABITAT
Visits coastal lowlands and offshore islands in winter, sometimes feeding on salt marshes or bogs, but more often on nearby farmland with clover, grass and stubble, and in fields with some shallow water nearby. In the Arctic it nests on steep, dramatic cliffs, either near the sea or overlooking fjords with rich feeding areas close by.

FOOD
Grazes vegetation, especially leaves, stems and seeds. Also uses bill to pull up roots and crush harder matter. In winter, eats plants such as rushes, grasses, clover, plantains, Thrift, samphire, buttercups and daisies.

BREEDING
On its Arctic breeding grounds some colonies nest on islands, but many are on tall, inaccessible cliffs.

juvenile

DISTRIBUTION
Breeds in Greenland, Spitsbergen and Arctic Russia. Greenland and Spitsbergen birds winter in Ireland and Scotland. The Russian birds winter in Europe. In winter, flocks of Barnacle Geese visit traditional feeding and roosting sites – often on offshore islands. The largest numbers are in Ireland, the Hebrides in western Scotland (especially Islay) and the Solway Firth. Smaller numbers may be seen in eastern Britain.

BRENT GOOSE *BRANTA BERNICLA*

dark-bellied juvenile

dark-bellied

pale-bellied

IDENTIFICATION
56–61 cm. Similar in size to Mallard but more upright and with a longer neck. Plump with rather short black legs and a small black bill. Head, neck and upperparts of the body are dark, apart from a small white neck patch. Underparts are variable, but under the tail is always white. Two races are usually seen in Britain and Ireland: dark-bellied birds from Siberia and Russia, and pale-bellied birds from Greenland and Spitsbergen. Dark-bellied race has breast and belly almost as dark as its back, with some mottling. Pale-bellied race is similar except that the breast and belly are paler grey-brown. Juveniles are similar to their adults but lack the white collar and have pale edges to the folded wing-coverts. Flight feathers are moulted simultaneously and the geese become flightless for about 3 weeks in July and August, before migrating in autumn.
SEE ALSO: Canada Goose p23, Barnacle Goose p24.

HABITS
Swims frequently and rides high in the water. Often up-ends to reach food. In flight, wings look pointed and rather duck-like. Flies in lines that undulate, but less often in 'V's than other geese. Generally in flocks, but birds may spread out across their feeding grounds.

VOICE
Single 'waruk' calls that mix together in a flock to create a dog-like yelping and babbling that is far-carrying. Clamour grows as the flock takes to the air.

HABITAT
Winter feeding grounds are along sea coasts and estuaries where there are mud flats and inter-tidal zones with sufficient plant food. In recent years has often moved on to adjacent farmland to feed. Breeds on the Arctic tundra, often well away from water.

FOOD
Grazes vegetation on land or finds food in water. Traditional food is eel-grass, which grows in some estuaries. Also eats algae, and salt-marsh plants such as glasswort and Sea Aster. Birds that visit agricultural land graze the shoots of winter cereals, grass and Oilseed Rape.

BREEDING
Does not breed in Scotland. With only about 100 Arctic days in which to rear a family, bad weather or the early onset of winter significantly affect breeding success. Families migrate together and remain together until the following breeding season.

MOVEMENTS AND MIGRATIONS
Breeding birds start to arrive at their wintering sites in October. They return in March or April. A few dark-bellied birds from Siberia are seen along the east coast of Scotland. Pale-bellied birds from Spitsbergen winter in northern England and are occasionally seen along Scotland's east coast, while others from eastern Canada pass through the Western Isles on migration to and from Ireland. Small parties are seen on Loch Ryan in most winters. Some survive 28 years or more.

POPULATION
Numbers of these geese have increased in recent years. Up to 5,000 may be seen on passage.

CONSERVATION
Following a shortage of eel-grass in the 1930s, the wintering population dropped sharply. Conservation of wintering sites, restrictions on hunting and the move onto farmland have all helped the species' recovery. Loss of sites to sea-level rise, disturbance by human recreation, conflicts with farmers and a lobby to allow birds to be shot are all issues that need delicate management.

DISTRIBUTION
Breeds further north than any other goose. Dark-bellied race that breeds in Siberia and in northern Russia winters mainly in England and France. Pale-bellied race from Canada and Greenland winters in Ireland. A few winter at Loch Ryan. Other pale-bellied birds breed in small numbers in Spitsbergen and winter in Denmark and on the Northumberland coast.

SHELDUCK *TADORNA TADORNA*

IDENTIFICATION

58–67 cm. Larger than Mallard. Large white duck with a bottle-green head and neck, chestnut breast-band and black 'shoulders'. The broad bill is blood-red and the legs are pink. Male is larger and brighter than female, with a pronounced knob at the base of his bill in spring. The black and white wing, black-tipped tail and a dark streak down centre of the belly show in flight. Juvenile is less well marked, with a grey-brown back and head and whitish face and throat. During moult, the adults look whiter and less well marked. Flight feathers are moulted simultaneously and adults are flightless for 25–31 days between July and October. SEE ALSO: Shoveler p33.

female

male

juvenile

HABITS

Swims high in the water and up-ends to reach submerged food. Also wades, sweeping bill from side to side to sift food out of mud. In flight, looks heavy, with slow wingbeats. Outside the breeding season forms loose flocks.

VOICE

The male is usually silent or makes sweet-sounding whistles. The voice of the female is lower, giving a growling 'ark-ark-ark' call.

HABITAT

Most numerous on sheltered coasts and estuaries where there are sandbars and mud flats. In recent years has adopted a few inland sites. Also visits farmland near the coast. In western Europe favours coastal habitats, but in central Asia lives around salt lakes and marshes, often in steppe and semi-desert many kilometres from the sea.

FOOD

Feeds on invertebrates, including shellfish, crabs, shrimps, worms, sandhoppers and larvae of flies and other insects. The chief food on many estuaries is a tiny snail called *Hydrobia*. Small fish and some plant material are also eaten.

BREEDING

Nests amongst dense vegetation, in a hole (often an old rabbit burrow), or in other crevices or gaps under buildings; also occasionally off the ground in a tree or building. Nests comprise straw, grass and down feathers from the female's breast. 8–10 eggs are laid in April or May. Incubation is by the female and lasts for about 30 days. Young feed themselves within hours of hatching. Female leads her young to a food-rich area where they often mix with other young Shelducks. A few non-breeding adults (aunties) often tend the crèches of young while the parents migrate to their moulting areas. Young fly after 45 days.

MOVEMENTS AND MIGRATIONS

After breeding most Shelducks migrate to traditional moulting areas. Many Scottish birds join thousands that gather in the Heligoland Bight off the German coast. Other moulting areas include some British estuaries, including the Forth. Shelducks return gradually and territories may not be reoccupied until spring. Additional birds from Scandinavia arrive in eastern Scotland in winter. Oldest bird was 24 years.

POPULATION

In summer there are up to 1,750 pairs in Scotland and in winter numbers increase to around 7,000, although the population is declining slightly overall. The Forth, Solway and Montrose Basin hold the main populations.

CONSERVATION

Estuaries and coastal dunes have long been regarded as ripe for development and many Shelduck feeding areas were destroyed during the 20th century. Port and marina developments, new harbours and recreational pressures all threaten the habitat on which the Shelduck depends. Any sea-level rise is also likely to reduce the inter-tidal zone on which Shelducks feed.

juvenile

MANDARIN *AIX GALERICULATA*

IDENTIFICATION
41–49 cm. Smaller than Mallard. Plump duck with a thick neck, large head and small bill. For most of the year male is striking, with a green and purple crest, chestnut-orange ruff, broad pale stripe from eye to nape, white eye-ring, purple breast, orange-brown flanks and dark back. The uniquely shaped innerwing feathers form 'sails' on the back. Bill is red. Female is grey-brown with spotted flanks, a spectacle-like mark around and behind the eye, and a tiny grey bill. In flight, shows dark wings with a white trailing edge and a pale belly. Moults between May and August and is flightless for about a month during that period. Male in 'eclipse' plumage resembles female but with less obvious face marks, a redder bill and glossier plumage.

male eclipse

male

HABITS
Swims with body high in the water, seldom up-ending. Frequently perches on fallen tree trunks and on tree branches overhanging the water. Takes off easily from water or land and flies rapidly, even among trees.

female

VOICE
Usually rather silent. Displaying males have a variety of calls, including a soft whistle. Female has a soft croak, often given in flight.

HABITAT
Breeds around lowland lochs and rivers where there are trees and bushes, and where branches overhang the water. Also common in wildfowl collections and as an 'ornamental duck' in public and private parks.

FOOD
Omnivorous. Feeds on aquatic insects in spring and summer, and mainly vegetarian at other times, eating seeds and nuts, especially acorns in autumn. Also eats snails.

BREEDING
Mandarins may begin breeding in mid-April. The nest is associated with trees, and birds may use natural holes or nestboxes that have been erected for species such as Goldeneye. Natural nest sites may be at ground level or off the ground – up to a height of 10 m and sometimes more. Little nest material is used, but the clutch of 9–12 eggs is laid into a cup of down feathers. The eggs are incubated by the female for about 28 days. Young soon leave the nest and feed themselves. The female continues to care for them and the male sometimes roosts close by. Young fly after 40 days and can breed when 1 year old.

MOVEMENTS AND MIGRATIONS
The Scottish population appears to be sedentary, although individual birds will travel considerable distances and young birds may disperse from their original breeding areas. Northern and western populations of Mandarins in Asia are migratory, whereas the population in Japan is mostly sedentary.

POPULATION
There are probably around 50 pairs of Mandarins nesting in Scotland, although they can be surprisingly easy to overlook during the breeding season.

CONSERVATION
The species was present in Britain before 1745, but the small Scottish population dates back only to the 1960s and is mainly a result of accidental releases from wildfowl collections. In Asia the species appears to be declining, for reasons that are unclear. There are now probably as many Mandarins in Britain as there are in Japan.

male

female

DISTRIBUTION
The species originated in the Far East, where it is native to eastern Siberia, China, Korea and Japan. In the British Isles feral populations have become established in parts of southern England, and smaller populations in parts of Scotland, Wales and Northern Ireland. Elsewhere the species has become established in parts of Europe, especially Germany.

WIGEON *ANAS PENELOPE*

IDENTIFICATION

45–51 cm. Smaller than Mallard. Medium-sized duck with a round head and small bill. Head and neck of male are chestnut, forehead is yellow, breast is pink and body is grey with a white stripe on the wing. Tail is black and pointed. In flight, male shows white wing-patches. Female is a similar shape to the male, but is mottled reddish or grey-brown, with pale pinkish flanks. Both sexes have a dull green speculum and a white belly in flight. Juveniles resemble females. Immature males resemble adult male, but lack white wing-patches. A complete moult occurs between June and September, and birds are flightless for several weeks. The eclipse male is a rich mottled chestnut. SEE ALSO: Pochard p35.

male

HABITS

In flight, neck appears short, wings narrow, and tail longer and more pointed than in many other ducks. Migrating birds often move their necks up and down in a conspicuous way. For most of the year Wigeon are found in large flocks, but when nesting they are generally solitary.

VOICE

Call of male is a far-carrying, musical, 2-syllable whistle, 'wee-ooo'. Call of female is a rather harsh growl.

HABITAT

Breeds near shallow upland lochs, pools and bogs where there is also cover nearby for nesting. In northern Europe, breeds close to the tundra, but will also nest in wooded areas, although not dense forests. Traditional wintering grounds are estuaries and coastal marshes, but in recent years some have moved inland and winter around lowland lochs and reservoirs.

rufous female

grey female

FOOD

Grazes on land or finds food in the water. Sometimes follows other species such as Coots and swans to benefit from their waste food. Eats mainly vegetation, especially stems, leaves and roots of plants such as grasses, buttercups, algae, pondweeds, and especially eel-grass (*Zostera*), which grows on estuaries.

BREEDING

Nesting begins in April or May. The nest is a hollow amongst thick cover, lined with grasses and leaves, and the female adds her own down feathers. The clutch is 8 or 9 eggs. Only the female incubates and the male generally leaves during incubation. The eggs hatch after about 24 days. The young are able to feed themselves straight away, but are brooded by the female while they are small. They fly after 40 days and become fully independent at this time.

MOVEMENTS AND MIGRATIONS

Northerly populations are migratory. In Scotland the largest numbers arrive from Iceland and northern Europe in October. Additional birds may arrive from Europe if the weather there is severe, and some may move south to England. At least one wild Wigeon survived more than 34 years.

POPULATION

Up to 400 breeding pairs in Scotland, mainly in the north; numbers rise to 76,000–96,000 birds in winter.

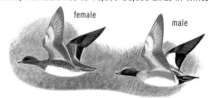

female

male

CONSERVATION

The species is protected during the breeding season and may be hunted in the wildfowling season. Wigeon congregate on salt marshes and coastal wetlands, and drainage and habitat loss have concentrated the birds at a number of important sites, some of which are now reserves. The birds will seek out areas free from disturbance and wildfowling. Increased recreational use of coastal sites and the loss of wet grasslands and salt marshes remain the main threats.

DISTRIBUTION

Wigeon nest in central and northern Scotland and also in northern England. There are individuals that spend the summer further south, but these do not usually breed. Other Wigeon breed in Iceland, Scandinavia and northern Russia. Most of these winter around the ice-free coasts of Europe, especially in Britain and Ireland. Other European Wigeon reach the Mediterranean and the coast of North Africa. Notable gatherings in Scotland are found at Aberlady Bay, the Solway and Cromarty Firth.

GADWALL ANAS STREPERA

male

IDENTIFICATION
46–56 cm. Smaller than Mallard. A rather undistinguished duck with a bold white speculum. Seen at close quarters, male has finely barred or freckled plumage that appears grey at a distance. Rear part of the body and tail are black. White speculum frequently shows clearly as a patch on sides of a swimming bird and is obvious in flight. Bill is grey. Female resembles a slim female Mallard, but with greyer plumage, a whiter belly, white speculum and orange sides to bill. During their summer moult, Gadwalls become flightless for about 4 weeks and it is then that the male resembles the female, but is greyer with plainer upperparts.
SEE ALSO: Mallard p32.

HABITS
Appears buoyant on the water. Wings are rather pointed. Often follows other feeding waterbirds such as Coots and Mute Swans, and forms small, loose flocks in winter. Does not nest in colonies, but several females may sometimes nest within 5 m of each other.

VOICE
Usually rather silent. Male has a deep, rasping croak, often given in flight. Female's call is more like higher-pitched version of Mallard's 'quack'.

HABITAT
Breeds on eutrophic lowland lochs or slow-flowing rivers with vegetation growing in or under the water. In winter it is more widespread, using larger areas of water, including shallow estuaries.

FOOD
Mainly vegetarian, feeding on plant material in water, either on the surface, by up-ending or by following other more wasteful feeders such as Coot or swans. The most common food includes stems, leaves and seeds of pondweeds, sedges, rushes, grasses and stoneworts. Insects, water snails and small amphibians may also be eaten, probably accidentally.

male eclipse

BREEDING
Nests on the ground, often on small islands. The nest is usually among dense vegetation and quite close to water. In some places nests in more open locations close to terns or gulls, which help the Gadwall by chasing away predators. The 9–11 eggs are laid into a hollow lined with grass and the duck's own down. The female alone incubates, and the male usually deserts her during the 24-day incubation period. The young are able to feed themselves after hatching and continue to be brooded by the female while small. They fly after 45 days and become independent of their mother at about the same time.

MOVEMENTS AND MIGRATIONS
Small numbers are found in Scotland in both summer and winter. It is more widespread in winter, with additional migrants from Iceland and northern Europe passing through Scotland on their way south. Oldest bird was 23 years.

POPULATION
150 pairs nest in Scotland and less than 200 birds winter here. The greatest numbers are at Loch Leven and the RSPB's Vane Farm reserve. Generally, numbers are steadily increasing in Scotland.

CONSERVATION
Protected during the breeding season. Wild birds may have colonised some Scottish sites in the early 1900s, but other British populations were artificially introduced in the 1800s. It is important that their wintering areas are left undisturbed. In Russia, where most European birds breed, there has been a recent decline in numbers.

female

male

female

DISTRIBUTION
Most numerous in the south and east of England, but has spread to Scotland as a breeding bird. It is also found in widely scattered locations in central and southern Europe, and in Asia and North America. In winter, it is more widespread and migrants are found around the Mediterranean.

TEAL *ANAS CRECCA*

IDENTIFICATION
34–38 cm. Smaller than Mallard. Small, compact duck with a short neck. Male has a chestnut head, dark green eye-patch extending to back of head, grey body with white lateral stripe, and spotted breast. Also has a yellow patch on side of black tail. Female is like a small, delicate, boldly marked female Mallard, but with a small bill, dark crown and dark green speculum bordered by white stripes that show in flight. Wings are pointed and flight is very rapid. Moults during summer. Eclipse male resembles female, but with darker upperparts and grey bill. Flight feathers are moulted simultaneously and birds are flightless for about 4 weeks. SEE ALSO: Mallard p32, Wigeon p28.

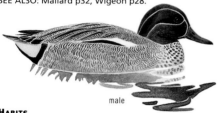

male

HABITS
Frequently in small flocks except when nesting. An agile duck that can rise vertically from the water if disturbed. Teals in flight will twist and turn, and their rapid wingbeats and pointed wings can make them appear more like waders than wildfowl. Often inactive during the day and feeds mainly at night.

female

juvenile

VOICE
Call of the male is a piping, far-carrying whistle, 'prip-prip'. Female's call is a rapid, high-pitched quacking.

HABITAT
Breeds mainly on wet moorland, peatlands and marshes in upland areas. Some birds nest in lowland marshes or near the coast. Breeding sites may be close to woodland. In autumn and winter, birds visit lochs, flooded farmland and coastal areas. In Europe and Asia it ranges from the edge of the Arctic tundra to the fringes of arid deserts.

FOOD
Eats a wide variety of food that it finds in mostly shallow water. Feeds by pecking from the surface, filtering water through its bill, or up-ending. Its chief food is the seeds of rushes, grasses and other plants such as pondweed, dock, birch and buttercup. In summer, animals such as water snails, fly larvae, water beetles and worms are also eaten.

BREEDING
Pairs form during winter before moving to their breeding sites. Nesting begins in mid-April. Teal nest closer to the water's edge than any other duck species, which helps deter predators. A hollow is lined with leaves and grass, plus down from the duck's breast. The female incubates 8–11 eggs and the male often leaves as incubation begins. Young hatch after about 21 days and can feed themselves soon after hatching. They become independent at about 30 days. They are able to breed at 1 year old.

MOVEMENTS AND MIGRATIONS
Most Teal are migratory, with birds from Iceland, northern Europe and Russia reaching Scotland during autumn and leaving again in March. Some birds seen in Scotland in autumn may travel as far as Spain. In Europe many undertake a summer moult-migration after breeding. Oldest ringed bird was over 21 years old.

male   female

POPULATION
2,000–3,500 pairs nest in Scotland. The range and size of this population appears to have declined in recent years. In winter, the average population is around 40,000, with large concentrations at Loch Leven, Mersehead RSPB reserve and Moray Firth.

CONSERVATION
Protected in the breeding season and may be hunted in autumn and winter. Planting commercial forests in the Teal's traditional upland breeding areas may have caused some declines. Safeguarding remaining breeding areas and lowland wintering sites is essential.

DISTRIBUTION

Breeds in scattered locations, especially north and west Scotland and northern England. Found in winter in wetland locations throughout Britain and Ireland, although scarcer in upland and northern areas. Breeding range extends across northern Europe and Asia. Winters in central and southern Europe, and in parts of North Africa and Asia.

GARGANEY ANAS QUERQUEDULA

juvenile

IDENTIFICATION

37–41 cm. Smaller than Mallard but longer than Teal. Slightly oblong head shape, with a flat crown and straight grey bill. Male has broad white stripes over the eyes that curve down and meet at back of neck. Breast is mottled brown, flanks are finely barred with grey, belly is white, and back has black and white drooping feathers. In flight, shows blue-grey forewing. Female is similar to female Teal but paler with a whiter throat, pale patch at base of grey bill, darker eye-stripe that contrasts with pale stripe over eye, diffuse dark line across face and darker crown. In flight, forewing of female is grey. Juvenile is like female but with a stripy head and lacks Teals' pale patch near tail. Moults between May and August, with the male starting first. Flight-feathers are lost simultaneously and adults are flightless for 3–4 weeks. Eclipse male resembles female, but with sides of head heavily streaked.
SEE ALSO: Teal p30.

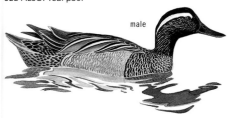

male

HABITS

In flight, the Garganey looks a little heavier and longer-necked than a Teal. Outside the breeding season, it is usually seen in pairs or small groups.

VOICE

Calls of male include a dry rattle and a burping sound used in display. Female has a quiet 'quack' like a Teal.

HABITAT

Breeds in water meadows, flooded grasslands and reedy and marshy pools or ditches with plenty of vegetation cover. It searches out similar habitats outside the breeding season. In Scotland, most birds are seen in the spring on lowland wetland reserves.

female

FOOD

Mostly feeds while swimming, either from the surface or by up-ending. It eats insects and their larvae, including water beetles, flies and midges. It also feeds on water snails, freshwater shrimps, worms and the spawn and young of frogs. Plants are also eaten, especially the stems, leaves or seeds of water weeds, reeds, sedges, grasses, rushes, docks and duckweed.

BREEDING

Pairs form in winter and arrive together on their breeding grounds, where a small territory is established. Nesting begins in April, with the nest consisting of a depression lined with leaves, grasses and down. The female incubates the 8 or 9 eggs for about 22 days. During incubation the male generally leaves the area. The young can feed themselves soon after hatching and fly after 35–40 days.

MOVEMENTS AND MIGRATIONS

The Garganey is our only summer migrant duck. It arrives in Europe in March and returns to Africa between July and October. Western European birds have two autumn migration routes, one through Spain and the other through Italy. In spring, however, most birds return via Italy. One ringed bird survived for 14 years.

POPULATION

About 100 pairs breed in Britain in most years. In Scotland the number of breeding pairs varies between 0 and 10, although the number of birds seen on passage has increased.

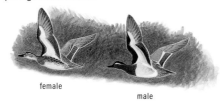

female

male

CONSERVATION

The species is protected in Britain by special penalties at all times. Wetland drainage and poor management of the Garganey's breeding sites is responsible for the decline in Europe. Good management of wetlands in Europe and Asia is therefore essential for the future of this species.

DISTRIBUTION

The Garganey breeds in a few sites in Scotland, and scattered locations in England, but it is much scarcer in Wales and Ireland. Garganeys also breed in France, northern and eastern Europe, Russia, and in central and eastern Asia. Most spend the winter in tropical Africa, although a few winter around the Mediterranean.

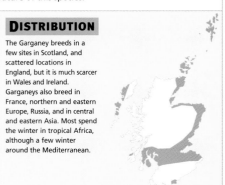

MALLARD ANAS PLATYRHYNCHOS

IDENTIFICATION
50–65 cm. Our most familiar duck. Large and heavy-looking, with a long body and long, broad bill. Speculum is iridescent purple/blue, edged with white. Male has a dark green head, yellow bill, white neck-ring, purple-brown breast, mainly grey body and curly black upper tail feathers. Female is brown with darker mottling, a dark crown, dark eye-stripe, pale breast, orange bill and orange legs. Juveniles resemble females but have more finely streaked flanks. Mallards have been domesticated for centuries and various plumages have evolved: from almost black to pure white. Mallards moult after breeding and are flightless for 4–5 weeks. Males resemble females during moult, but have a blacker crown and yellowish bill.
SEE ALSO: Gadwall p29, Teal p30.

small twigs and lined with down, usually situated among vegetation such as nettles, or sometimes in woodland, in the crown of a tree or in a hedge bottom. The female incubates 11–14 eggs. During incubation, the male generally deserts the female and plays no part in tending the young. Eggs hatch after 27 days. The young are able to swim, dive and feed themselves soon after hatching. They are independent after 50 days. There is usually 1 brood, but the female may re-lay if the clutch is destroyed.

MOVEMENTS AND MIGRATIONS
Mallards in Scotland may be resident or migrant. Many that breed in Iceland and northern Europe arrive in autumn. There is a record of a Mallard surviving for over 29 years.

POPULATION
17,000–43,000 pairs breed in Scotland. Peak winter numbers may reach nearly 100,000 birds. Populations in Europe have declined slightly, resulting in smaller numbers wintering in Scotland than in the past.

male / male eclipse

female

male

HABITS
Usually seen in small flocks. Can rise straight out of the water if disturbed. Mallards are often very tame where they live close to humans, but may be timid in remote locations. Pairs form in autumn and stay together for winter and spring. Some males have two mates, and promiscuity and rape are not uncommon. Ducklings will dive to avoid danger and adults also dive occasionally.

female

juvenile male

VOICE
Calls of the female are varied and include the familiar 'quack', which is often repeated many times in quick succession. The male's call is a quieter, low, rasping 'crrrib'.

HABITAT
Lives on large and small lochs and slow-flowing rivers that are fairly sheltered and have shallow margins for feeding, including park lakes, reservoirs, small pools and coastal marshes. In winter, flocks visit larger water bodies, estuaries and, sometimes, the open sea near the coast. Breeds in a variety of wetlands, from the Arctic tundra to the sub-tropics.

juvenile female

CONSERVATION
Protected during the breeding season; may be hunted at other times. The British population is made up of wild birds and others that have been deliberately released for sport. Hunting pressures and habitat destruction may be a problem in future.

FOOD
Feeds by day or night, on land or in water. Food is picked off the surface, found by submerging the head and neck, or gathered from deeper water by up-ending. Plant food includes the leaves, shoots and seeds of water plants, and cereals. Animal matter includes insects and their larvae, fish and also, rarely, small mammals and birds.

BREEDING
Nesting starts in February if the weather is mild. The nest is a shallow depression ringed with grasses or

DISTRIBUTION
Widespread in Britain and Ireland in summer and winter, wherever there are suitable wetland habitats, although scarce in upland areas. The most widespread duck in the world, breeding in Europe, Asia and North America, and introduced to Australia and New Zealand.

SHOVELER ANAS CLYPEATA

IDENTIFICATION

44–52 cm. Smaller than Mallard, with a heavy-looking body, flatter head and much longer, broader bill. Male has a white neck and breast, dark green head, orange flanks and belly, and white patch before black undertail. Dark back has long black, blue and white feathers. Female is similar to female Mallard, but with white underwings and a dark belly. In flight, both sexes show powder-blue on wings, male's being brighter than female's. Juvenile resembles female, with young males only gradually acquiring adult plumage. Moult takes place between June and September, with males beginning first. A simultaneous moult of flight feathers results in birds being flightless for about 4 weeks. Male in eclipse resembles female, but with darker upperparts and redder underparts.
SEE ALSO: Shelduck p26, Garganey p31, Mallard p32.

BREEDING

Shovelers establish a small territory that they defend vigorously in the early stages of nesting. Nest is on the ground, close to water, in a hollow lined with grasses and down; 9–11 eggs are laid from April onwards. Incubation is by the female for 22 days, the male abandoning his mate. The female tends the ducklings until they become independent after 40–45 days.

MOVEMENTS AND MIGRATIONS

Shovelers are migratory. Most Scottish breeding birds leave by October and fly to England, Ireland and some even as far as Spain. Others from northern Europe and Russia arrive in Scotland; a few will remain all winter but others will continue southwards. Between February and May, breeding birds gradually return to their territories. Oldest ringed bird survived over 20 years.

POPULATION

260–300 pairs breed in Scotland. During the peak autumn migration there may be over 1,000 individuals, with around 800 remaining all winter. Recently the breeding numbers have fluctuated, with increases in some areas and decreases in others.

male

female

male eclipse

CONSERVATION

The Shoveler is protected during the breeding season and may be hunted in the wildfowling season. Its lowland wet grassland habitat has been under pressure from drainage and changes in agricultural practices for many years. The provision of nature reserves like Mersehead on the Solway and Vane Farm on Loch Leven have therefore helped this species.

HABITS

Swims with breast low in the water and huge bill nearly touching the surface. When up-ending, the long wings cross over at the tips, unlike in a Mallard. Sometimes a group swims in a line or a circle, filtering the water disturbed by the bird in front. Shovelers are agile and their pointed wings appear set far back owing to the thin neck and big bill. Usually seen in small groups and, sometimes, bigger flocks outside the breeding season.

male   female

VOICE

Generally rather quiet. Male has a quiet 'took, took' call that is often heard as rival males chase each other. Female makes a soft quacking sound.

HABITAT

Breeds in marshes or lowland wet grassland that is close to shallow open water. In winter, found on inland marshes, small lochs and pools, and sometimes around the fringes of larger water bodies. Small numbers visit coastal marshes.

FOOD

Up-ends and occasionally dives for food, but usually filters surface water through serrations along edges of the bill. Feeds on tiny creatures, including crustaceans, small water snails, insects and their larvae. Also eats seeds and leaves of water plants.

DISTRIBUTION

Breeds in Scotland and other parts of Britain, especially eastern England. More widespread in winter, frequenting any suitable habitat in lowland Britain or Ireland. Breeds in Europe from the Baltic almost to the Mediterranean and eastwards across Asia to Mongolia. Also found in North America. European birds winter as far south as tropical Africa.

PINTAIL   *ANAS ACUTA*

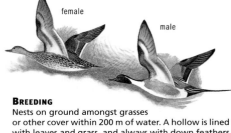
female

male

IDENTIFICATION
51–66 cm. Slightly larger than Mallard. Elegant duck with a long, thin neck, long tail, rounded head, long, delicate grey and black bill, and dark green speculum, edged with white at the rear. Male has a chocolate-brown head with a broad white stripe running down neck. Body is finely barred grey with a black line along side, often covered by the long cream and black drooping back feathers. Tail is black and white, with two greatly elongated black feathers. Female has a shorter tail, looks long-necked and is mottled brown, but is paler and greyer than other female ducks, with a slender grey bill, pale brown head, and neat scalloped brown and buff flanks. Juvenile is similar to female but with a darker back and heavier streaking and spotting. Moults between July and September. In eclipse, males resemble females, but are greyer and more uniformly marked. Both sexes are flightless for about 4 weeks. SEE ALSO: Mallard p32, Shoveler p33.

HABITS
In flight, the Pintail's long neck, small head, curved back, pointed wings and tapering tail distinguish it from other ducks. Seen mainly in small flocks, which sometimes fly high, in a 'V' formation. The sexes form separate flocks in late summer.

VOICE
Generally less noisy than other ducks. Variety of calls similar to Mallard, but quieter. Male has a drawn-out 'greee' and female has a series of deep quacks.

BREEDING
Nests on ground amongst grasses or other cover within 200 m of water. A hollow is lined with leaves and grass, and always with down feathers from the female's breast. The female incubates 7–9 eggs for 22–24 days. During incubation, the male generally leaves female. The young can swim and feed themselves soon after hatching and are able to fly after 40 days.

MOVEMENTS AND MIGRATIONS
Male Pintails leave breeding sites in May or June and many fly to traditional moulting areas. Females also migrate to moulting sites after breeding. By September the southward migration is underway. Pintails from Iceland and northern Europe spend the winter in Scotland. Oldest known bird was over 26 years.

POPULATION
Fewer than 50 pairs breed in Scotland, on Orkney and at a scattering of other sites. The species has always been a rare breeding duck here. In Russia and Finland there have been large declines. Up to 9,000 birds may winter in Scotland, with the largest numbers along the east coast and on the Solway, where around 1,000 can be seen at the Mersehead RSPB reserve.

CONSERVATION
The Pintail is protected during the breeding season and may be hunted at other times. The reason for the recent decline in numbers is unclear, but protection of its breeding sites is essential. In some places American Mink may limit breeding success. Reduced pressure from hunting in Europe and Russia would help its long-term future.

juvenile

female

male eclipse

male

HABITAT
Usually breeds in wetlands with shallow water, close to grassland and open habitats. In winter, Pintails move to sheltered coasts and estuaries, visiting flooded grasslands. Some are also seen on large inland lochs.

FOOD
The Pintail feeds on a variety of plant and animal material taken from the water – often by up-ending and using its long neck to reach into deeper water. Its food plants include pondweeds, docks, sedges and grasses. Animal matter includes water beetles, fly larvae, snails, leeches and, in salt water, shrimps and marine snails.

DISTRIBUTION
Breeds in a scattering of suitable sites in Britain and, rarely, in Ireland. Winters on coastal marshes, large estuaries and large inland wetlands, and moves from site to site. Elsewhere breeds in northern and eastern Europe, Russia and North America. Many Pintails from western Europe reach the African tropics for the winter.

POCHARD *AYTHYA FERINA*

IDENTIFICATION
42–49 cm. Diving duck, smaller than Mallard and with a short neck and round head. Male is pale grey with a rusty-red head and neck, and black breast and tail. Female is yellowish brown with a dark crown and rather blotchy cheeks. Juvenile is like female but grey-brown with pale cheeks and neck. In flight, both sexes show pale grey stripe on wing. Moult takes place June–October, with male beginning first. Flight feathers are moulted simultaneously and birds are flightless for 3–4 weeks. Eclipse male resembles female, but with a more uniform brown head and greyer back.
SEE ALSO: Wigeon p28.

male

male eclipse

FOOD
Usually dives to feed. Dives are often preceded by an obvious jump. Females tend to dive in shallower areas than males. Plant food includes leaves, stems and seeds of a variety of water plants, including stonewort, pondweed, milfoil, sedges and grasses. Also eats water snails, small fish, tadpoles, and insects and their larvae.

BREEDING
Pairs may form into flocks in late winter or at their breeding sites. Nesting begins in April, when the female constructs a shallow cup of reed stems and other material close to water or amongst reeds. Nest is lined with down. Female incubates 8–10 eggs for 25 days. Male generally leaves female during incubation. Young feed themselves soon after hatching and become independent before they can fly at 50 days. Sometimes young from several families group together.

MOVEMENTS AND MIGRATIONS
Little is known about the movements of the small Scottish breeding population. Moulting flocks (mainly drakes) form in late summer. Many additional birds arrive in September and October, with the males moving before the females. Many of the birds that winter in Scotland migrate here from northern Europe and Iceland. Oldest ringed bird survived for 22 years.

female

male

HABITS
Appears to spend a lot of time asleep, as it mostly feeds at night. Usually seen in small groups, or larger flocks outside the breeding season. In many flocks in the UK there are often more males than females. Swims rather low with the tail flat on the water and patters along the surface to take off. In flight, its short wings and heavy body give it a dumpy appearance and its rapid wingbeats make a whistling sound.

VOICE
Usually silent except during courtship, when male makes a soft, wheezing 'wiwwierr'.

POPULATION
Fewer than 50 pairs nest in Scotland and 4,000–6,000 individuals are present in winter. The small breeding population appears to be stable, although a decline in wintering numbers has been observed in recent years.

CONSERVATION
Protected during the breeding season and may be hunted at other times. Breeding birds are susceptible to disturbance and require water bodies that are unpolluted.

female winter

female summer

HABITAT
Breeds on lowland lochs such as Loch Leven and other wetlands where there is plenty of vegetation growing in the water. Winters in similar habitats, but also on larger food-rich lochs and reservoirs. Visits estuaries, but rarely seen on open sea.

DISTRIBUTION
In the British Isles, a few breed in Scotland and more in eastern England, and smaller numbers breed elsewhere, including Ireland. In winter, the species is widespread on lowland waters. It also breeds around the Mediterranean, but the largest populations are in northern and eastern Europe and eastwards across Asia. In Europe, it winters as far south as the Mediterranean and a few reach tropical Africa.

TUFTED DUCK *AYTHYA FULIGULA*

male

female

IDENTIFICATION
40–47 cm. Smaller than Mallard. Diving duck with a short neck, rounded head and relatively large, broad bill with a broad black tip. Male is glossy black with white flanks, a white belly and a drooping crest from back of head. Bill is blue-grey and eyes are golden. Female is brown with darker upperparts, paler, yellowish flanks and a white belly. Some females show a whitish patch at base of bill and pale feathering under tail – but these are not usually as well defined as in similar-looking Ferruginous Duck. In flight, an obvious white stripe runs length of wing. Annual moult takes place between June and October. Males moult first and both sexes are flightless for 3–4 weeks. In eclipse, male resembles a female, but has darker upperparts and loses its crest.
SEE ALSO: Pochard p35, Scaup p37.

HABITS
Looks buoyant on water and frequently dives with a distinct jump. Often forms large flocks outside the breeding season. In parks and places where it lives close to people it sometimes becomes very tame. Winter flocks frequently contain more males than females.

VOICE
Male is generally silent, except for a low whistle during courtship. Female makes a harsh 'karr', especially in flight.

HABITAT
Breeds around shallow inland lochs and slow-flowing rivers. Often lives close to built-up areas. Avoids deep water, unless there are also shallow bays and margins. In winter, gathers on larger water bodies and, occasionally, on the sea.

male eclipse

female (pale base to bill variant)

female (white-vented variant)

FOOD
Sometimes up-ends, but usually dives to collect food from the bottom of a lake or river. Eats freshwater mussels – especially the Zebra Mussel – plus freshwater shrimps, crustaceans, and insects and their larvae, such as caddisfly. Plant foods include pondweed and sedges.

BREEDING
Pairs form in late winter or spring. Nesting begins in May, when the female builds a nest of grasses, rushes and reeds that she lines with down. Solitary nests are not uncommon, but Tufted Ducks often nest colonially, sometimes among gull colonies and generally amongst cover and close to water. The female incubates 8–11 eggs for 25 days and during this time the male may leave the area. The young feed and fend for themselves soon after hatching and can fly after 45 days. The female often leaves them before this time.

MOVEMENTS AND MIGRATIONS
After breeding the birds often disperse from their nesting sites and flocks of moulting birds form, particularly on Loch Leven. Some may move south for the winter, but others arrive from Iceland and northern Europe. Oldest ringed bird was 22 years old.

POPULATION
Approximately 2,500 pairs breed in Scotland. In winter, there may be 11,000 individuals. During the 19th

female   male

and 20th centuries the numbers both breeding and wintering significantly increased.

CONSERVATION
Protected during the breeding season and may be hunted at other times. In Britain as a whole the species is increasing, but in Scotland the expansion of the 20th century seems to have stopped and there may even be a slight decline. Freedom from disturbance, especially from water sports during spring, is important to ensure breeding success. The quality of the water at its breeding sites may be a concern, as is the increase of predators such as Brown Rat and American Mink on some of the breeding islands.

DISTRIBUTION

Widely distributed in lowland Scotland, England and Ireland, but rather more scarce in Wales. In winter it is a little more widespread. Tufted Ducks breed in Iceland, parts of France, northern Europe and across Asia as far east as Japan.

SCAUP *AYTHYA MARILA*

male   female

IDENTIFICATION

42–51 cm. Diving duck with a broad body, round head and large, wide bill with a tiny black 'nail' at tip. Male has a black head and neck with a greenish sheen. Sides of body and belly are white, back is greyish white and tail is black. Female is dark brown with a variable pale patch at base of bill and, in summer, a pale patch on side of head. Juvenile resembles a female, but with a narrower pale patch around bill. In flight, it has a broad white stripe running the length of the wings. It moults between September and November and is flightless for 3–4 weeks. In eclipse the male remains distinctive, but much duller than in breeding plumage. SEE ALSO: Tufted Duck p36.

male

HABITS

Seen in flocks for most of the year. Ratio of males to females in these flocks varies, from a preponderance of males in the north to a majority of females in the south. Some flocks can number hundreds or thousands of birds. Generally swims rather low in the water and dives frequently. Rarely seen on land.

VOICE

Generally silent. Male has a soft, dove-like call during courtship and female has a low growl.

HABITAT

Usually on the sea in winter. Visits sheltered sea lochs and firths but also freshwater pools near the coast. Elsewhere it is a species that breeds on or close to the Arctic tundra, or in open northern forests.

FOOD

Its chief food is shellfish, especially the Blue Mussel, which it obtains by diving. Other shellfish include cockles, periwinkles and the tiny marine snail *Hydrobia*. Insects, crustaceans and plant material are also eaten.

BREEDING

Pairs form while still in their winter flocks or on their breeding grounds. Nests singly or in colonies, sometimes among colonies of gulls or terns. The nest is on the ground near to water and usually well concealed by low vegetation. The female incubates 8–11 eggs for more than 26 days, the male usually leaving her. Young sometimes join with other families and are able to fly after about 40 days. They remain with the female until they can fly, and sometimes for longer.

MOVEMENTS AND MIGRATIONS

Moves to the coast for the winter and most undertake long-distance migrations. Moult generally takes place on breeding grounds and then the birds move south in August. A few males delay their moult until they reach their winter quarters. The largest numbers reach Scotland from Iceland and northern Europe in October, remaining until February or March. A few immatures are sometimes seen in summer, especially in Orkney and the Hebrides. Oldest ringed bird survived 13 years.

POPULATION

No nesting has been proven in Scotland since 1989, despite some birds spending the summer in suitable areas. In winter, 4,000–8,000 individuals are present, comprising the bulk of the UK population.

CONSERVATION

Specially protected at all times. The majority of Europe's Scaup population is concentrated in relatively few areas in winter. This makes it vulnerable to pollution and disturbance by recreation, and there is a need for international cooperation to ensure the most important sites are specially protected. Some of the really large wintering flocks that used to gather on the Forth have now dispersed, as the cleaner coastal waters are less rich in food.

female summer

male 1st-winter

female winter

DISTRIBUTION

A few pairs spend the summer in northern and western Scotland and occasionally a pair will nest. Also breeds in Iceland, Scandinavia and northern Russia. In Scotland, regular winter flocks are seen on Loch Ryan, Solway, Islay and off Methil (Forth).

EIDER SOMATERIA MOLLISSIMA

male

female

male eclipse

male 1st-summer

female

male

Incubating females will sometimes eat plant material, including berries.

BREEDING
Courtship starts in winter, when males are seen throwing their heads back, and breeding begins in late April. Eider nests are often within colonies of Arctic Terns. Nest is in a hollow near the sea, sheltered by rocks or vegetation, but may be in the open. It is lined with down from the female's breast. Female incubates 4–6 eggs for 25–28 days and seldom feeds during this period. Male protects female prior to egg-laying but he generally leaves the female during incubation. Young swim and dive soon after hatching, and broods often join together in crèches that are tended by a few females. Young are independent after 55 days and fly at about 65 days.

MOVEMENTS AND MIGRATIONS
Scottish birds do not generally move far from their breeding grounds and there are several traditional gathering places for moulting birds. In autumn, small numbers of migrants from further north may arrive and some Scottish Eider may move south to England. Oldest known Eider was 35 years.

POPULATION
About 20,000 pairs breed in Scotland (around 75% of the UK population). This species expanded its range during the 19th century and this is continuing. The Scottish winter population is about 65,000 individuals.

CONSERVATION
Chief threat is pollution at sea and in estuaries. Large winter flocks are vulnerable to accidental and deliberate discharges of oil. Control of shipping in sensitive waters and rapid response in the case of accidents will safeguard this and other seabirds. Loss of feeding sites owing to commercial development of estuaries is also a concern, as is predation of breeding colonies by animals such as Foxes.

IDENTIFICATION
50–71 cm. Slightly larger than Mallard. Sea duck with a fat body, short neck, large head and long, wedge-shaped bill. Male is white with a black crown, flanks, belly and tail. Breast is tinged pink and sides of head are lime-green. Female is brown with darker barring and mottling, and a distinctive long forehead. Juvenile resembles female, but young males take 4 years to acquire adult plumage; until then they have varied black and white plumages. In flight, male shows large white patches and female has a dark speculum bordered with thin white bars. Eiders moult from June to August and are flightless for a few weeks in July and August. Male eclipse is blackish with white on wing. SEE ALSO: Shelduck p26, Long-tailed Duck p39.

HABITS
Sociable; often seen in groups in summer and forms much larger flocks in winter. Looks heavy in flight, with a drooping head and neck. Flocks frequently fly in lines low over the water. Dives with a splash, with its wings half-open.

VOICE
Silent for most of the year, but male has a dove-like cooing call, 'ar-oooo', when displaying.

HABITAT
A marine species that lives around rocky coasts. In spring it requires suitable islands or low-lying land close to the sea for nesting. After breeding, birds often move to estuaries and other sheltered coasts rich in food.

FOOD
Eiders dive to search for food on the seabed, especially Blue Mussel and other shellfish. Also eats periwinkles, crabs, starfish, sea urchins and, occasionally, fish.

DISTRIBUTION

In the British Isles it breeds in Scotland, parts of northern England and the north of Ireland. In winter it spreads south as far as the south coast of England, and is most numerous on the east coast. The species is found all round the Arctic Circle, with the nearest populations being in Iceland and Scandinavia. It winters as far south as northern France. Some young birds remain in their wintering sites for their first spring and summer.

LONG-TAILED DUCK *CLANGULA HYEMALIS*

IDENTIFICATION
40–47 cm. Smaller than Mallard, but tail of male may add 13 cm. Small, neat sea duck with a small, round head, steep forehead, all-dark wings in flight and white belly. In winter, male is mainly white with a dark brown 'Y' mark on its back in flight, brown breast-band and a large, dark cheek patch. In summer, it has a streaked brown back, dark head and neck, and pale greyish-white face patch. Adult male has greatly elongated tail feathers. Female in winter shows a white collar, white face with dark lower cheeks and dark crown. She has a warmer brown breast-band. In summer, female has a darker face than in winter. Females have short tails. Juvenile is like female in summer, but with a less contrasting face pattern. Flight feathers are moulted between July and September; during part of this time birds are flightless for a few weeks. Has unique moult, as some back feathers are moulted 4 times a year and some head and neck feathers 3 times.
SEE ALSO: Pintail p34, Eider p38.

female autumn

female summer

HABITS
The Long-tailed Duck swims high in the water and dives easily with a small jump and wings partly open. Usually seen in flocks, except in the breeding season. Sometimes winter flocks are large, comprising several hundred birds. Birds chase each other in small parties and splash-land after a short flight. The species is often seen in very rough water. Flies more readily than many other sea ducks and often travels close to the water, tipping its body from side to side like a Puffin or Little Auk.

VOICE
Compared with other sea ducks, the Long-tailed is quite noisy, with the yodelling calls of the males being made throughout the year and at any time of the day or night. The female makes a low quacking.

male 1st-autumn

HABITAT
Winters on the sea, some distance from the shore, and only occasionally visits inland lochs and reservoirs. Breeds on freshwater pools, lakes and rivers, mainly within the Arctic Circle.

FOOD
Dives to search mainly for crustaceans and molluscs, especially Blue Mussels, cockles, clams and crabs. Also eats Sandhoppers, small fish such as gobies and some plant material.

BREEDING
Long-tailed Ducks display in their winter flocks and some pairs form at this time. The species does not, however, breed in Scotland. In spring, the birds wait along northern coasts of Scandinavia until there is a thaw and they can move to their nesting areas in the tundra. Nesting colonies often spread out over a large area. Females lay 6–8 eggs that are incubated for up to 29 days. Males desert females during incubation. Young birds can fly 35 days after hatching and are soon independent.

male winter

MOVEMENTS AND MIGRATIONS
In parts of its range males travel up to 1,000 km to moult. Elsewhere it moults closer to its breeding areas. After moulting, some move south while others remain in ice-free waters close to their breeding grounds. Oldest known bird was 20 years.

POPULATION
The Scottish population in winter consists of around 15,000 individuals, or 95% of the UK population.

CONSERVATION
These ducks are vulnerable to oil pollution at sea. Routing oil tankers away from sensitive sites and feeding grounds, and limiting the development of wind-farms in such areas, will help this and other species that winter at sea.

female winter

male winter

DISTRIBUTION
Mostly a winter visitor to British and Irish coasts, especially northern and eastern Scotland, Shetland and Orkney. A few non-breeding individuals remain in Scottish waters for the summer. Breeds in northern Europe, Asia and North America, mostly north of the Arctic Circle.

COMMON SCOTER *MELANITTA NIGRA*

IDENTIFICATION
44–54 cm. Deep-bellied sea duck with a pointed tail. Male is all black with a narrow yellow patch on top of the bill. Female is dark brown with a darker crown and pale patch on cheeks and upper neck. Juvenile is similar to adult female. In flight, wings are plain with no obvious marks, although flight feathers look a little paler. Common Scoters moult between July and October, with males beginning first and females following later. Flightless for 3–4 weeks. In eclipse plumage male becomes a little duller with browner underparts.
SEE ALSO: Velvet Scoter p41.

male

HABITS
A few large flocks of moulting birds gather in late summer around the Scottish coast, and flocks may stay into autumn and winter. Some smaller flocks of non-breeding birds remain in summer. Swims buoyantly, often with tail slightly cocked, and dives with a small forward jump. Flocks appear restless, with birds often standing on their tails and exercising their wings. Flies frequently and often forms long, straggling lines low over the water or, sometimes, higher.

VOICE
A limited range of calls can be heard while birds are in flocks, especially during courtship, the most frequent being whistling and piping.

male   female

HABITAT
Seen in inshore waters in winter. Breeds near small moorland lochs, or on islands in larger lochs set in blanket bog. Rare inland outside the breeding season.

FOOD
Chief food is molluscs, especially the Blue Mussel, which it finds by diving. Also eats cockles, clams and other shellfish, crabs, insects, small fish and plant material.

BREEDING
Pairs start to form in the winter flocks. They move to their breeding grounds where male defends female until incubation and then he deserts her. Nest is in a hollow lined with grass, moss and down. The preferred site is close to water, on an island, on the margin of a lake and concealed in vegetation. Female incubates

6–8 eggs for over 30 days. Young can swim and feed themselves soon after hatching and some broods merge together. Young can fly after 45 days.

MOVEMENTS AND MIGRATIONS
A few overwinter in ice-free waters near where they breed. Most others migrate. The first movement is away from the breeding grounds to traditional sites where flocks congregate to moult. There are a number of places around the east and south-west coasts of Scotland where flocks gather, and larger concentrations of northern European birds are found off the coast of Denmark. Some remain in the moulting areas all winter, while other populations migrate further south or west. Oldest known bird was 15 years.

POPULATION
There are under 100 pairs nesting in Scotland, and numbers are declining. In winter, the population may be as high as 30,000 individuals, with most on east coast firths and estuaries.

male 1st-winter

female

CONSERVATION
This species is specially protected at all times. Like other marine species that winter in flocks, there is a real possibility of large numbers being wiped out by an oil spillage unless shipping lanes avoid specially identified sites. Disturbance at winter feeding grounds by boat traffic is a problem, often linked to offshore windfarm maintenance. The species is one of our rarest regular breeders, and the lochs where it nests need protection from development and disturbance.

DISTRIBUTION

Small numbers breed in northern Scotland in the Flow Country and around the Great Glen. Larger numbers winter around British and Irish coasts, especially the north-east coast of Scotland and in Wales. The Common Scoter also breeds in northern Europe and northern Russia. It winters along the west coast of Europe and North Africa.

VELVET SCOTER _MELANITTA FUSCA_

male

IDENTIFICATION
51–58 cm. Similar in size to Mallard. The largest of the three scoters. A sea duck, with a long bill rather like an Eider's, a thick neck and a pointed tail. Males have a small knob at the base of the bill. Both sexes have a white patch on rear of wing that shows well in flight or when wing-flapping, but is often hidden when swimming. Male is velvety black with a small white patch under eye, and red legs that are noticeable when it dives. Female is brown with two pale patches on side of head. The Velvet Scoter moults during the summer, with male beginning before female, and both sexes become flightless for 3–4 weeks. While moulting, male is much duller.
SEE ALSO: Eider p38, Common Scoter p40.

HABITS
The Velvet Scoter may be seen in small groups, and it often associates with flocks of Common Scoters. Birds often cock their tails as they swim. They dive without jumping and with their wings partly opened.

VOICE
Generally rather quiet, but sometimes croaking or growling calls can be heard from flocks in winter.

female
female
(well marked)

HABITAT
In Scotland it is found in winter in coastal waters in the east, either on exposed shores or in more sheltered bays and inlets where there is a supply of food. Very rarely seen on inland waters. In the breeding season it inhabits northern lakes, pools and rivers, often in forest areas and sometimes near the coast.

FOOD
Dives to feed on shellfish, especially Blue Mussels, cockles and Dogwhelks. It also eats crabs, sea urchins, small fish, insect larvae and some plant material.

BREEDING
Although some birds are sometimes seen in summer they have never been proved to breed in Scotland. Courtship takes place in the flocks during the winter. The female tends the young and the male leaves the nest site during incubation. Some females look after young from a number of broods. The young can fly after about 50 days.

MOVEMENTS AND MIGRATIONS
There are some gatherings of moulting birds from further north off the east coast of Scotland between June and August. Larger numbers arrive in September and October, and flocks may be found mainly between the Moray Firth and the outer Forth, particularly the Lothian shore, in winter. The return migration is late, often peaking in Sweden in mid-May. Oldest known bird survived more than 12 years.

POPULATION
It is thought that up to 3,500 individuals winter in Scotland, with the majority in the east.

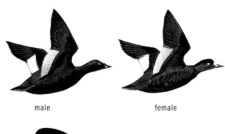
male   female

male 1st-winter

CONSERVATION
Specially protected. Although the European population is currently stable there are concerns for the long-term future of this species. The large concentrations of moulting birds in late July/August and winter make the birds susceptible to oil pollution and development in coastal waters. In addition, there is hunting pressure in Scandinavia and on their breeding grounds. There is a need for the important moulting areas and winter feeding sites to be protected from damaging pollution and the development of coastal windfarms.

DISTRIBUTION

Mainly a winter visitor to the east coast of Scotland and eastern England. Largest numbers concentrate in a few relatively small areas, especially in the Baltic Sea and off the Danish coast. In spring, most return to their breeding grounds in northern Europe or northern Russia. A very small number still breed in Turkey. Also found in North America and in northern Asia. All populations move to coastal areas further south for the winter.

41

GOLDENEYE *BUCEPHALA CLANGULA*

IDENTIFICATION
42–50 cm. Smaller than Mallard. Medium-sized diving duck with a rather large, domed head and small bill. Male appears black and white, with a greenish-black head and circular white patch in front of the yellow eye. Back and tail are black, and breast, underparts and flanks are white. Has white stripes along sides of back. In flight, male shows black wing-tips and large area of white on innerwing. The smaller female is mottled grey, with a chocolate-brown head, square white wing-patch and white collar. Immature female resembles adult but lacks a white collar. Young males develop their dark head during their first winter. Moults between July and September and is flightless for 3–4 weeks. Male moults 3 weeks before female. For a time he resembles female, but has a darker head. SEE ALSO: Goosander p45, Smew p242.

HABITS
Usually in small groups and sometimes forms larger flocks in winter. Adult males may be in a minority in these flocks. Frequently dives. In flight, wingbeats produce a loud, distinctive whistling sound. Courtship displays are frequent in winter as males throw their heads back and show off their white breasts.

In marine habitats it feeds on shrimps, small crabs, Blue Mussels, cockles, periwinkles, small fish and plants.

BREEDING
Pairs start to form in the winter flocks and nesting starts in mid-April. The nest is in a hole in a tree or a special nestbox several metres off the ground. There is little nesting material except for down from the female's breast. At first, the male is territorial, but he deserts the female during incubation. The female incubates 8–11 eggs for 29 days. At a day old the young jump from their nest and the female takes them to a rearing area, often some way from the nest site, where they swim, dive and feed themselves. They are independent at about 50 days and fly after 57 days.

MOVEMENTS AND MIGRATIONS
Males move from their breeding sites while the females are still with their eggs or young. In autumn, additional birds arrive from Scandinavia. Some spend the winter on lowland lochs while others move to the coast. They start to return to their breeding sites in February and March. Oldest known bird was 11 years.

POPULATION
About 150 pairs usually nest. In winter the number of individuals increases to 10,000–12,000.

CONSERVATION
First nested in Scotland in 1970. Since then birds have been attracted to specially designed nestboxes erected on trees close to lochs and rivers. There are limited nest sites in Scottish forests, because of the lack of large, mature trees.

female · male · male 1st-winter · female 1st-winter · male · female

VOICE
Goldeneyes are usually silent unless displaying. A loud 'zeee-ZEEE' and quieter 'rrrrrrrr' usually accompany the displays of the male.

HABITAT
Breeds close to lochs and rivers in forests. Outside the breeding season it visits freshwater lochs (including those in towns), rivers and the sea, especially sheltered bays and estuaries.

FOOD
Feeds on a variety of food, some of which it finds by turning over stones underwater, including freshwater mussels, insect larvae such as stonefly, caddisfly and mayfly, small fish and plant material such as pondweed.

DISTRIBUTION

In Scotland, good numbers are seen on the Moray Firth, Tay, Forth and Clyde, as well as on inland rivers and lochs. Breeds in the Highlands, and a few prospecting birds summer further south. In winter, it visits lochs, large rivers and sheltered coasts. Goldeneyes breed in northern Europe and across Asia and North America, and they generally move south of their breeding areas for the winter.

Ruddy Duck OXYURA JAMAICENSIS

IDENTIFICATION
35–43 cm. Smaller than Mallard. Small, dumpy, thick-necked diving duck with a large, broad bill and stiff tail. Male has a bright blue bill, blackish head and neck, brilliant white cheeks, chestnut body and white under the tail. He also has two small 'tufts' on his crown, held erect during display. From August and through the winter he becomes browner, with black speckles on the white cheeks and a grey bill. Female is dull brown with a blue-grey bill, dark brown cap, and paler cheeks that are crossed with a brown band. Juvenile is like female but paler and with a less obvious cheek-mark. Male starts to moult July–August, and female a month later. Both sexes are flightless for several weeks. During moult, male assumes his winter plumage.

HABITS
Its stiff tail often lies flat on the water or cocked up above its back. Swims buoyantly and dives quickly; sometimes it just sinks below the water without diving. Reluctant to fly, it takes off by running across the water. Remarkable courtship display includes one performance where the male traps air under his dense breast feathers and in a special air sac, then beats this protrusion rapidly with his bill. This has the effect of creating a hollow drumming sound and producing a series of bubbles.

VOICE
Generally silent, but during display there are non-vocal sounds associated with 'breast-beating', as well as various rattles, ticking noises and burps.

HABITAT
Breeds around shallow lowland lochs with abundant fringing water plants, and will occasionally visit coastal waters, especially in North America. In winter it may move to larger water bodies.

FOOD
Feeds during the day on a wide variety of food, including insects and their larvae, water snails, worms and seeds of water plants.

BREEDING
The female builds a platform of reeds, rushes and leaves around vegetation growing in the water. She incubates 6–10 eggs for 25–26 days alone, although the male, and sometimes a second male, remains in the vicinity of the nest and the young family. Occasionally a female 'dumps' a clutch of eggs into the nest of another Ruddy Duck. The young swim and dive soon after hatching. Some females abandon their ducklings after about 3 weeks and rear a second brood. The young fly after 50–55 days.

MOVEMENTS AND MIGRATIONS
In North America the species is migratory. The British population is present all year, although most Scottish birds congregate at a few favoured sites or move south. Recently, a few British breeding birds have started to make long-distance movements into Europe, and are now seen in Spain, Morocco and as far north as Iceland and Norway.

POPULATION
There are thought to be around 50 breeding pairs in Scotland.

CONSERVATION
The Ruddy Duck became established in Britain after escaping from wildfowl collections. The species' subsequent spread to the Continent, and especially to Spain, is a conservation problem. In Spain there is a small and endangered population of White-headed Duck. This is closely related to the Ruddy Duck, and the two species hybridise and produce fertile young. Because the Ruddy Duck is a dominating species, it is feared that it is capable of exterminating White-headed Ducks in western Europe unless its expansion is curbed. Countries across Europe are now carrying out a cull.

DISTRIBUTION
In Britain, breeds mainly in central and southern England, and there are scattered breeding sites in northern England, north Wales, southern Scotland and Northern Ireland. Native Ruddy Ducks breed in both North and South America.

RED-BREASTED MERGANSER *MERGUS SERRATOR*

IDENTIFICATION
52–58 cm. Size of Mallard. Long-bodied diving duck belonging to a group known as sawbills. Smaller and thinner-necked than Goosander, with a wispy crest and long, very thin red bill (thinner than Goosander). Male has a dark green head, white collar, grey and white body and spotted chestnut breast. Female is grey with a reddish-brown head that merges with the pale throat and grey neck. Juvenile resembles a dark female, but with a shorter crest. In flight, male shows white patches on his wings while female has smaller wing-patches. Females have 1 dark bar across the wing-patches, whereas adult males have 2. Mergansers moult between mid-July and September, with male moulting a month earlier than female. During moult both sexes are flightless for a month. In eclipse, male resembles female, but retains much more white on wings.
SEE ALSO: Goosander p45, Great Crested Grebe p58.

HABITS
Swims low in the water and regularly dips its head below the surface when searching for food. Dives frequently. Often seen in small, single-sex groups, but larger flocks form in winter. In flight, looks long-bodied and long-necked.

VOICE
Usually silent, but makes rough croaking or rasping sounds – especially when displaying and nesting.

HABITAT
The Red-breasted Merganser generally breeds near shallow coastal waters but also slow-flowing inland rivers. It favours areas with woods or some other cover. Usually seen on the sea in winter, but occasionally on inland lochs and rivers.

FOOD
Feeds mainly on fish such as young Atlantic Salmon and trout, Perch, Grayling, Herring, Cod, Plaice and sand-eel. It also eats small crabs, shrimps, prawns and aquatic insects. When they first hatch, the ducklings feed mainly on insects.

BREEDING
In winter, makes bowing and stretching courtship displays as pairs begin to form. Nests are on the ground close to water, usually among tree roots or bushes, or in a crevice in a bank or between rocks. Nest is a depression made with some local material and lined with down. Male deserts female during incubation and female alone incubates the 8–10 eggs for 31 days. The young are covered with down and leave the nest soon after hatching. They feed themselves and are cared for by female, but some broods join together. The female frequently leaves before young are fully grown and a single female, or 'auntie', often cares for a crèche of young. They are independent after 60–65 days and then leave the area, often feeding in shallow tidal waters.

MOVEMENTS AND MIGRATIONS
Scottish breeding birds are mainly resident, although some move south in winter. However, Red-breasted Mergansers from Iceland migrate and reach Scotland in autumn. These remain until March, and some immature birds may remain for longer. They may live 21 years or more.

POPULATION
There are 2,000 pairs breeding in Scotland. Wintering birds may total 8,500 individuals. Breeding increased in Scotland between 1885 and 1930. In 1950, birds started to colonise northern England, and in 1953 they reached Wales. The Scottish population now appears to have stabilised and may even be decreasing in some areas owing to culling by game-fishing interests.

CONSERVATION
Its diet of fish has brought the species into conflict with the promoters of sport fishing. Many birds are killed, both legally and illegally, to protect fish stocks. They are also vulnerable to oil pollution and to the siting of windfarms in shallow coastal areas.

male

male 1st-summer

male

female

female

DISTRIBUTION
Breeds in Scotland, especially western and central Scotland and the Highlands and islands; also north-west England, north-west Wales and the west of Ireland. In addition, it breeds in northern Europe, Asia and North America. It is predominantly coastal in winter.

GOOSANDER *MERGUS MERGANSER*

IDENTIFICATION
58–66 cm. Larger than Mallard. Large-headed, long-bodied, thick-necked diving duck with a long, hook-tipped red 'sawbill' that is thicker at the base than that of similar Red-breasted Merganser. Male has a white body, flushed pink in winter, black back and dark green head. Female has a grey body, reddish-brown head (darker than in female Red-breasted Merganser) with a bulbous, drooping crest, an obvious white throat, and a brown neck with a sharp border to the grey breast. Juvenile resembles a dull female. In flight, male looks black and white with black and white wings; female has smaller, squarer white wing-patches. Moult occurs between July and September, and both sexes are flightless for about a month. Male eclipse resembles female, but with larger white wing-patches.
SEE ALSO: Red-breasted Merganser p44, Great Crested Grebe p58.

boxes. Will also nest on the ground, in rock crevices or under buildings. The nest is mainly made with duck down. The female alone incubates the 8–11 eggs for 30–32 days. Young leave the nest after a day or two, those in trees jumping to the ground. Newly hatched ducklings are covered in down and feed themselves. Some ducklings ride on their mother's back. Sometimes several families join together. Juveniles are independent after 65 days, when they leave their nesting area.

MOVEMENTS AND MIGRATIONS
Apart from the annual moult migration to Norway by Scottish males, Goosander live year-round in Britain. Goosanders can live to 14 years or more.

POPULATION
2,000–3,000 pairs breed in Scotland, and around 10,000 individuals winter here. It first nested in Scotland in 1871 and by 1941 had spread to England; it has since continued its southward colonisation.

male

male

female

female

male 1st-summer

HABITS
Swims low in the water. When searching for food repeatedly dips its head under water as it swims and dives frequently. Outside the breeding season it is often seen in small groups, and larger flocks form in winter. In flight, it looks very long-bodied and frequently flies close to the water. Sometimes a pair or group of Goosanders fish cooperatively by swimming in a line as they drive fish forward.

VOICE
Mostly silent. Makes some soft calls during courtship and occasional 'growls' when disturbed.

HABITAT
Breeds on freshwater lochs and large rivers, often close to woods or forests. Outside the breeding season it is mostly seen on large freshwater lochs and rivers, estuaries and sheltered sea inlets.

FOOD
Feeds on a wide range of fish, including young salmonids and Eels. Small mammals and insects are also eaten. When small, Goosander ducklings feed mainly on insects.

BREEDING
Courtship starts in winter, when males can sometimes be seen bowing and stretching. It nests in holes in trees, broken-off tree stumps and also in suitable nest-

CONSERVATION
Its diet of fish and its recent increase has brought the Goosander into conflict with sport-fishing interests. The numbers of licences allowing the killing of Goosanders to protect fish stocks have increased in Scotland, although there is no clear evidence that the species has seriously reduced fish populations.

DISTRIBUTION
Breeds in Scotland, northern England and Wales. In winter, it is found on large inland lochs, reservoirs and some lowland rivers in Britain. Rare in Ireland. The species breeds around the Arctic Circle – in Europe, Asia and North America – and some winter as far south as the Black and Adriatic seas.

RED GROUSE *LAGOPUS LAGOPUS*

IDENTIFICATION
37–42 cm. Larger than Grey Partridge. Plump, with a small head, slightly hook-tipped bill and short black tail. Often appears hunched up, but neck is extended when the bird is alert. Adult has reddish-brown mottled plumage with a white stripe on underwing. Male has a red wattle above its eye and redder plumage than female, although it becomes paler in summer. The legs and feet are covered in off-white feathers. The Red Grouse found in Britain is of the race *scoticus*, a distinct form of Willow Ptarmigan. Moult begins in June with the primary flight feathers. Most of the other feathers are moulted between August and November.
SEE ALSO: Ptarmigan p47, Black Grouse p48.

HABITS
Flight is fast and direct on short, square-ended wings. Alternates between whirring wingbeats and glides on bowed wings. Territorial when nesting, but forms family parties from July, and families may join together in 'packs' in autumn.

VOICE
Crowing call is a loud, gruff 'go-back, back, back'. When disturbed will often make a sharp 'kwok, kok-ok, ok'.

male

female

male

HABITAT
Requires extensive heather moorland away from trees, although areas of upland bog, rough grazing and even some coastal heaths are also inhabited by small numbers. In parts of Europe it lives among Dwarf Willow and other low-growing plants.

FOOD
Feeds mainly on the ground, but also in scrub in winter. Food is mostly vegetable matter, especially young heather shoots. Invertebrates such as crane flies are also often selected. Small young feed on insects, including click beetles, crane flies, sawfly larvae and other small flies, as well as heather and other moorland plants.

BREEDING
Male holds territory and displays by calling, puffing out his feathers, drooping his wings, holding his tail stiffly above his back and moving with a stiff walk. He also rises almost vertically and then, calling, drifts down on deeply curved wings. In late April or May, 6–9 eggs are laid in a hollow that is scraped by female amongst thick heather or soft rush. Female incubates, but male is never far away. Young are active soon after hatching and feed themselves. Flight feathers grow quickly and young are capable of flight at 11–12 days, although they are not fully grown until 30–35 days and remain with their family for 6–8 weeks.

MOVEMENTS AND MIGRATIONS
The Red Grouse is resident in Scotland. Males may travel no further than 1.5 km and females up to 8 km in their lifetime. Snowy weather can force birds from the hills and down to nearby farmland to feed. In Russia, the species is partly migratory. Oldest wild bird survived over 7 years.

POPULATION
There are 100,000–150,000 pairs in Scotland. During the 20th century the population fell as moorland areas became less intensively managed.

CONSERVATION
Protected under the Game Acts, Red Grouse may be shot outside the close season. In some areas populations fluctuate in cycles. This is caused by parasitic worm burdens, and by competition as densities increase, which is then followed by out-migration. Heather moorland, upon which the Red Grouse is highly dependent, has been lost through overgrazing and afforestation. Moorland management is labour-intensive, and the highest densities of Red Grouse are found where gamekeeping occurs.

DISTRIBUTION
In Britain, lives in the uplands of the north and west, with a smaller fragmented population in Ireland. Willow Grouse occurs across northern Europe, Asia and North America.

PTARMIGAN *LAGOPUS MUTA*

female summer

male summer

female autumn

male autumn

IDENTIFICATION
34–36 cm. A little smaller than Red Grouse but similar in shape. Beautifully camouflaged and rather dove-like on the ground. In summer, male is closely barred grey, brown and black, with a white belly and wings. In autumn, the dark parts become grey and, in winter, it becomes totally white except for tail and eye-patch, which remain black year-round. A red wattle above eye is enlarged when breeding. Female has similar plumage to male, but is generally browner in summer and darker in autumn, and lacks a black eye-patch in winter. Juvenile has a grey-brown tail and brown wings. SEE ALSO: Red Grouse p46.

HABITS
More likely to be heard than seen, but often very tame. When disturbed, it is more inclined to crouch and rely on camouflage than to fly. During the breeding season it is usually seen in pairs. Family parties form in summer and it then lives in flocks until March, when territories are established with a song flight. Chooses hollows in snow for roosting at night, even in summer.

VOICE
Call of female is a high-pitched cooing. Male has series of loud and rapid clicks. Call is a harsh croak and rasping noises, and its alarm is a grating sound.

male winter

HABITAT
In Britain it is found only in the Scottish Highlands. Lives in the highest mountains (rarely below 700 m) where there is little vegetation, scattered boulders and bare rock pavements, and where the snow lies longest in summer. Often to be found among the boulders and scree that break up this tundra landscape. Outside Scotland it is associated with Arctic or alpine conditions, and in the far north it lives at lower altitudes, even at sea-level.

FOOD
Eats plant shoots, berries, leaves and seeds, including heather, Bilberry and Crowberry. Uses its feathered feet to dig in the snow to find food. Young eat insects.

male summer

male winter

BREEDING
Breeding starts in late April and May. Both birds make several shallow scrapes before one is lined with a small amount of vegetation. A bush or boulder usually shelters the nest. Female incubates 5–8 eggs for 21 days. Newly hatched young leave the nest quickly and are able to feed themselves. They are tended by both adults and brooded by the female. Flight feathers grow quickly, and young can take to the air in 7 days in exceptional circumstances and are independent after 10–12 weeks.

MOVEMENTS AND MIGRATIONS
Resident and seldom moves far from its breeding sites. Severe winter weather sometimes forces birds down from the highest ground to the edge of forests, but they will also move to higher ridges where the wind blows the snow away.

female winter

POPULATION
There are around 10,000 pairs in Scotland, although an accurate estimate is difficult owing to the inaccessible nature of the habitat. In the last hundred years the Ptarmigan has disappeared from hills in southern Scotland, Orkney and most of the Western Isles, but the numbers breeding in the remaining areas appear mainly stable.

CONSERVATION
Ptarmigan are occasionally hunted in winter, but numbers are more affected by overgrazing by sheep, the increase in crow numbers around tourist attractions and by flying into wires associated with ski development. The potential threat from climate change reducing their habitat is perhaps the most serious long-term threat.

DISTRIBUTION
In Scotland, found only in the highest mountains in the central and eastern Highlands, with outlying populations in Sutherland, Skye and Arran. Found in Arctic regions of Europe, Asia and North America, and also in the Alps and Pyrenees.

BLACK GROUSE *TETRAO TETRIX*

female

male

IDENTIFICATION
40–55 cm. Larger than Red Grouse. Male is glossy black with a red wattle over the eye, white wing-bar and black lyre-shaped tail; white feathers under the tail are used in display. Female is smaller, with grey-brown plumage that has darker freckles and bars, a pale wing-bar and slightly forked tail. Male and female show white under wings in flight. Females show a thin, pale wing-bar on upperwing. Juvenile looks like a small, pale female. Black Grouse moult in late summer, when males become duller for a short time. SEE ALSO: Red Grouse p46, Capercaillie p49.

HABITS
Feeds mainly on the ground. Engages in communal displays at dawn and dusk at traditional sites known as 'leks'; these are used year-round, but especially in autumn and spring. In a lek, males strut and posture to each other, trying to establish dominance, all the time making a far-carrying bubbling song and harsh, scolding sounds. Leks attract females and mating takes place nearby. In winter, gathers in flocks during the day and roosts in groups at night, often in long heather or trees.

VOICE
Mostly silent except around the lek. Male makes a loud, pigeon-like 'cook-roo'. Female makes a loud cackle or 'kok, kok' flight call.

HABITAT
Its home is the uplands, where woodland meets the edges of moors and also hill farms. In some areas it is found in young forestry plantations. Also found around the edges of ancient pine and birch forests. Lives at lower altitudes further north.

FOOD
Mainly vegetarian, feeding on Bilberry, heather shoots, cotton-grass buds, annual meadow plants, birch catkins and buds and Juniper berries. Females eat the flowering tips of cotton grass prior to laying their eggs. Will

also feed on spilt Oat grains and search for seeds in hay fields. In winter, often feeds in trees and shrubs, eating berries, leaves and shoots. Chicks eat insects for the first 2 weeks, especially sawfly larvae and caterpillars.

BREEDING
Breeding begins in April. After displaying and mating, male has nothing to do with the family. Female makes a shallow scrape on the ground that she lines with grasses and mosses. The 6–11 eggs are incubated for 25 days. Newly hatched young are mostly able to feed themselves while being tended by the female. If danger threatens, young can fly from about 10 days, but they are not fully independent for about 3 months.

MOVEMENTS AND MIGRATIONS
In Scotland the species is sedentary. Males may remain within 1 km of where they hatched, although young females may wander 10 km or more. Oldest bird was 12 years.

male
displaying

POPULATION
Around 3,500–5,000 males are estimated to display each spring in Scotland. There has been a huge decline in the range and number of Black Grouse over the last century.

CONSERVATION
The species has declined throughout Europe. The causes of this include ploughing or draining traditional meadows, overgrazing by sheep and deer, blanket afforestation and habitat fragmentation. Wire fences, erected to keep deer out of plantations, have caused numerous casualties, and increasing numbers of crows and Foxes may be adding to the decline. Conservationists are trying to remove or mark fences, and improve forest management and related open-ground habitat.

female

male

DISTRIBUTION

Lives in the uplands of Scotland. Elsewhere in Britain it is found in the Pennines of northern England and in north Wales. There are 7 subspecies, with those found in Scotland being of the *britannicus* race. The species is also found from the Arctic to the Alps and east across Asia.

CAPERCAILLIE *TETRAO UROGALLUS*

IDENTIFICATION
60–87 cm. A huge grouse with broad wings and tail. Male is turkey-like, glossy black with dark brown wings, white marks on belly and under tail, and bold white shoulder-patches. Has a red wattle over eye and a pale bill. The long, broad tail is raised and fanned when bird is displaying to intruders, including humans. Female is smaller, brown, heavily barred black; a reddish patch on the breast and paler underparts distinguishes it from female Black Grouse. Juvenile resembles female.
SEE ALSO: Black Grouse p48.

HABITS
Seen singly and in groups. Despite its size this can be an elusive species, often sitting quietly in pine trees or on the forest floor. Males gather at dawn in spring and 'lek' to attract females. They are aggressive towards rival males and fighting is fairly common. Many females may be attracted to a lek, at which larger alpha males are generally dominant and mate with the most females. Flight is like that of other gamebirds, a succession of rapid flaps followed by a glide on down-curved wings. The long neck is stretched outwards in flight.

VOICE
At the lek the males have an amazing song that is a series of double 'clicks' ending in a loud 'pop'.

HABITAT
Found in the remaining tracts of ancient Caledonian pine forest and a few other established Scottish forests with mature trees, open clearings, an understorey of Blaeberry and naturally regenerating pine. In other parts of Europe the species sometimes lives in deciduous woodland.

FOOD
Mainly vegetarian. Usually feeds on the ground, but also flies into woods to find food, especially in winter. Eats needles, buds and small cones from the Scots Pine, other conifers and Juniper. Also eats berries from plants such as Blaeberry. Chicks feed on a large number of insects when small.

BREEDING
Makes a shallow scrape on the ground, lined with grass and pine needles, usually amongst dense cover and often at the foot of a tree. Mating takes place at the 'lek', usually during late April, and males have nothing further to do with the family. Female incubates 7–11 eggs for 25 days. The young soon leave the nest and are able to feed themselves. They are capable of flight to escape danger from 2–3 weeks, and fully grown at 2–3 months, when they also become independent.

MOVEMENTS AND MIGRATIONS
Not a migrant in Britain, although some young birds may disperse up to 20 km from their breeding sites. Oldest known wild bird lived for more than 10 years.

POPULATION
The population has declined to around 1,000 birds, although that decline may recently have been halted thanks to concerted management by forestry, conservation and landowning interests.

CONSERVATION
Extinct in Britain and Ireland by 1785, the species was reintroduced into Scotland in the 19th century. For a time it was fairly widespread, but since 1970 its range has contracted. It now survives only in well-managed woodlands where there is reduced grazing from deer and a mixture of old and young Scots Pine. The Capercaillie suffers from collisions with deer fences and predation by Foxes and crows. Wet springs have also reduced breeding productivity. Disturbing the birds at leks is illegal; instead, birdwatchers should visit the RSPB's Loch Garten centre in spring.

female

male

male

Hilary Burn

female

DISTRIBUTION
Found near Loch Lomond and parts of Perthshire, although the main population is in Strathspey, Deeside, Moray and Easter Ross. In Europe it breeds in northern and eastern forests and in mountain ranges further south. Also found in Russia.

RED-LEGGED PARTRIDGE   *ALECTORIS RUFA*

IDENTIFICATION
32–34 cm. Slightly larger than Grey Partridge and smaller than Pheasant. This attractive gamebird has plain grey-brown upperparts, boldly striped black, white and chestnut flanks, and a white chin and throat bordered with black, with black spotting spreading like a necklace on the bluish breast. Feet and bill are red. Female is smaller than male. Juvenile lacks the bold head markings of the adult but has more stripes on face and spots on the neck than Grey Partridge. It flies with a whirr of wings followed by a glide on down-curved wings, and the red tail is usually obvious. SEE ALSO: Grey Partridge p51, Quail p52.

HABITS
Often more obvious than the Grey Partridge. More active during the day and tends to walk away or scatter when disturbed. Males will frequently perch on vantage points in their territories, such as straw bales, stone walls or even a barn roof. Like the Grey Partridge, generally seen in groups or 'coveys', some of which can be quite large – up to 40 or more – where the species is common.

VOICE
Can be quite noisy, with the adults giving a loud, chuffing 'chuck-chukka-chuff'.

juvenile

HABITAT
The Red-legged Partridge is found mainly on large, modern, open fields, but releases are now occurring on the edges of hill ground and moorland fringes.

FOOD
It feeds on the seeds, leaves and roots of a wide variety of plants that grow in and around agricultural land, and on larger seeds such as Beech. A few insects are also eaten, especially by chicks.

BREEDING
The male makes several shallow scrapes on the ground. In late April or May, the female chooses one and lays 10–16 eggs. Many pairs produce a second clutch that is incubated simultaneously by the male. Incubation lasts for about 23 days. Young are able to fly from danger after 10 days, but are not fully grown until 50–60 days. If 1 clutch is laid both parents tend the family, and if there are 2 clutches each parent leads their own brood, although eventually families will join together to form coveys. The young stay with their family throughout their first winter.

MOVEMENTS AND MIGRATIONS
The Scottish population is resident. Most individuals seldom move more than a few kilometres from where they hatched or were introduced. Oldest known wild bird survived for more than 6 years.

POPULATION
The population in Scotland depends on the number of birds released each year for recreational game shooting. There are perhaps only 500 pairs in the self-sustaining population, but in autumn many thousands are found owing to releases for game shooting

CONSERVATION
The species was deliberately introduced into southern Britain as a gamebird in 1673 and again in 1770. In Scotland, the early releases were unsuccessful, but from 1963 commercial rearing became more common and most (probably all) of the current population originate from this and subsequent releases. The increase has coincided with a decline in the Grey Partridge population, although there is no evidence that the Red-leg has driven out the Grey. Indeed, where both species are numerous, it is the Grey that is dominant. The Red-legged Partridge is protected under the Game Acts, and may be shot outside the close season.

DISTRIBUTION
Released first in England and then in Scotland. There are also small populations in Wales and Ireland. Its traditional home is southern France, the Iberian Peninsula, northern Italy and some Mediterranean islands.

GREY PARTRIDGE *PERDIX PERDIX*

IDENTIFICATION
29–31 cm. Smaller than Pheasant. Plump, with a small head and short legs. Well camouflaged, with brown- and grey-streaked plumage, chestnut bars on its flanks and a grey breast. Face is orange and it has a dark brown horseshoe mark on belly. Female is smaller, with a less obvious horseshoe mark. In flight, shows a red- dish tail. Juvenile lacks marks of adult and is streaked like a young Pheasant. Moults between June and Octo- ber, with the female beginning when the eggs hatch. A second, partial moult takes place before breeding. SEE ALSO: Red-legged Partridge p50, Quail p52, Pheasant p53.

HABITS
For most of the year 6–15 individuals form flocks called 'coveys'; pairs form in late winter. It is most active at dawn and dusk. When feeding or resting it appears hunched up. If disturbed, it is reluctant to fly and will often crouch and rely on camouflage for protec- tion. In flight, the wingbeats are rapid, followed by a glide on bowed wings, but it seldom flies far.

selves. After about 15 days they can fly to escape dan- ger, but are not fully grown until about 100 days. Juve- niles stay with their parents for their first winter.

MOVEMENTS AND MIGRATIONS
Resident. Birds seldom move more than a few kilo- metres from where they hatched, although severe winter weather may occasionally drive them from their traditional fields for a time. In parts of eastern Europe some are migratory. Oldest known bird sur- vived for over 5 years.

POPULATION
During the last 25 years the UK population has fallen by over 80%, and the species has also declined in Scotland and in other parts of Europe. There are now fewer than 15,000 pairs in Scotland.

CONSERVATION
Protected under the Game Acts, and may be shot outside the close season. It was once widespread in lowland Scotland, and had even been introduced to

male — female — male — juvenile

VOICE
A grating 'kerr-ick' is given during the day and night, especially around dawn and dusk. It makes a 'kip-ip-ip' flight call if disturbed.

HABITAT
A bird of open grassland that has adapted to live on farmland. Prefers open areas of low grass or arable fields, with dense cover for nesting and dry areas for dust-bathing. Most numerous where there is both pasture and cereal fields with thick hedges. Benefits from uncultivated areas, wide (unsprayed) field margins and stubble fields in winter. Mostly found in lowland areas, but also occurs on hill farms.

FOOD
Mainly eats the leaves and seeds of plants such as Knotgrass and Common Chickweed. Also feeds on insects, especially caterpillars and other larvae. The young feed on a range of invertebrates, including aphids, sawflies, ant larvae, weevil and beetles.

BREEDING
The nest is on the ground, under cover of a thick hedge or among dense vegetation. The female makes a shal- low depression lined with grass and leaves. Occasion- ally, 2 females use the same nest. An individual will lay 13–16 (sometimes up to 29) eggs in late April or May. Incubation is by the female and lasts for about 24 days. The young soon leave the nest and mostly feed them-

Orkney and the Argyll islands, but the decline since the mid-20th century has been remarkable. The cause is linked to changes in farm management, including the loss of wide field margins and sheltering hedgerows (needed to give cover for nests), autumn cereal sowing that eliminates winter stubble, insecti- cides that reduce food, and herbicides that control weeds. The increase of ground predators such as Foxes probably exacerbates the problem.

DISTRIBUTION

Breeds in lowland Scotland. Most common in the Lothians, Fife and along the east coast south of Aberdeen. Scarce elsewhere. Also found in England, Ireland and a few parts of Wales; also central and southern Europe and parts of Russia, and has been introduced to North America.

QUAIL *COTURNIX COTURNIX*

male

IDENTIFICATION
16–18 cm. Smaller than Grey Partridge. Tiny gamebird with yellowish-brown streaked upperparts, paler under-parts and a yellow stripe through the dark crown. Male has a plain reddish-brown breast and variable head marks that consist of dark bands round throat and through eye. Female has a spotted breast and less distinctive head marks. Juvenile resembles female. It has a different wing shape from a young Grey Partridge: wings are broader at base but distinctly narrow at tip – like a Snipe. Quails moult between June and September, but they sometimes suspend their moult and migrate with old and worn flight feathers, resuming their moult once they reach their winter quarters.
SEE ALSO: Grey Partridge p51.

female

HABITS
A secretive bird that is reluctant to leave cover and is more easily heard than seen, even where numerous. If disturbed it often drops back into cover after a short, direct flight. On longer flights its action is freer and more like a Starling.

VOICE
'Whip, whip-whip' (said to sound like 'Wet my lips') is the most commonly heard call. It is repeated up to 8 times at a burst. The call may be heard at any time of day or night in spring, but especially around dawn and dusk. Males also make a curious little growling noise – like a cat.

juvenile

HABITAT
Lives in open country, especially grassland, large cereal fields and hay meadows. In Scotland it especially favours spring Barley. On migration it appears in almost any habitat, but on its wintering grounds it lives in grasslands and other low vegetation.

FOOD
Eats the seeds of plants such as poppy, Fat-hen, hemp-nettle and dock, and also insects and their larvae, including beetles, ants and grasshoppers.

male

BREEDING
In Scotland, breeding may begin in May or even later in the summer. Males arrive first and call to attract females. The nest is on the ground in dense cover. The female incubates 8–13 eggs for 17–21 days. The young feed themselves soon after hatching and are cared for by female. Males may mate with more than one female and generally do not stay with their families. The young can flutter off the ground at about 11 days, but are not fully capable of flight until 19 days old. They stay together for 30–50 days before becoming fully independent.

MOVEMENTS AND MIGRATIONS
The Quail is the only member of this family that is a migrant to the British Isles, and winters in Africa or possibly the Mediterranean. Breeding starts early in the year in the south, and birds arriving in Scotland may be males attempting to breed for a second time or young birds. They arrive from May onwards and numbers vary from year to year. Oldest known wild Quail survived for at least 8 years.

POPULATION
In recent years up to 100 calling males have been heard in Scotland, usually in the south-west and on cereal fields in the east.

CONSERVATION
The Quail is specially protected at all times. It is declining over most of Europe owing to agricultural intensification in its breeding areas, hunting during its migration and drought in its wintering grounds.

DISTRIBUTION
Summer migrant to Scotland from winter quarters in Africa or the Mediterranean. Arrives in variable numbers and at unpredictable locations. Generally more are seen south of the border. Also breeds in Europe, from southern Sweden to the Mediterranean coast, and in Asia and Africa.

PHEASANT *PHASIANUS COLCHICUS*

IDENTIFICATION
53–89 cm. This large game bird has a rather long neck, small head and long tail. Male is brilliantly coloured, with an iridescent copper-coloured body marked with dark scallops on the breast and flanks, a metallic green head and neck, a red face and small 'ear tufts'. The very long ginger tail is crossed with dark bars. Interbreeding of different races has produced a variety of plumage colours. Some have an obvious white neck-ring, while others are dark bottle-green. The smaller female is brownish yellow with dark flecks on upperparts and flanks, and a long tail. Juvenile is similar to female, but with a less regular patterned plumage and a shorter tail. Pheasants start their annual moult in June and males appear rather scruffy for about 3 months.
SEE ALSO: Grey Partridge p51.

between March and June, and are incubated by the female. The male has little to do with the young, which hatch after 23–28 days. Chicks are brooded by the female and can feed themselves. By 12 days they can lift off the ground if danger threatens, but they are not fully independent until 70–80 days old.

MOVEMENTS AND MIGRATIONS
Resident in all its breeding areas. Wild Pheasants may live for more than 7 years.

POPULATION
It is difficult to estimate the total Pheasant population owing to the large number released each year for shooting. There may be around 350,000 breeding females in Scotland.

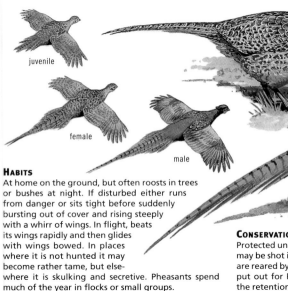

female

juvenile

female

male

male

HABITS
At home on the ground, but often roosts in trees or bushes at night. If disturbed either runs from danger or sits tight before suddenly bursting out of cover and rising steeply with a whirr of wings. In flight, beats its wings rapidly and then glides with wings bowed. In places where it is not hunted it may become rather tame, but elsewhere it is skulking and secretive. Pheasants spend much of the year in flocks or small groups.

VOICE
Its most usual crowing call is a far-carrying, resonant 'kor-ork, -ok- ok' often accompanied by an energetic and noisy flapping of wings. This call is often heard at dusk and in response to sudden loud noises such as gun-shots or thunder.

HABITAT
Found in lowland farmland, woodland edges, copses and shelter belts, and also in more open country.

FOOD
Takes a wide variety of foods, including grain and other seeds such as acorns, plus berries and fruits of Bramble, Hawthorn and many other shrubs. Eats leaves and roots of daisies and other related plants. Insects are eaten in summer, especially ants and beetles.

BREEDING
A cock Pheasant often has a harem of 2 or more females. The usual site for a nest is on the ground amongst vegetation, but some are off the ground on, for example, a straw bale. The 10–14 eggs are laid

CONSERVATION
Protected under the Game Acts. As many as 4.5 million may be shot in Scotland outside the close season. Birds are reared by keepers and released for shooting. Grain put out for Pheasants often benefits wild birds, and the retention of woodland for Pheasant shooting also benefits other species. This species is not a native to western Europe. It was first introduced to England by the Romans, and was then introduced to Scotland in the 16th century.

DISTRIBUTION
Found in suitable habitat throughout most of Scotland except the north-west. Truly wild Pheasants breed in south-east Russia and Asia. They have been introduced to most of Britain and Europe, North America and New Zealand.

RED-THROATED DIVER GAVIA STELLATA

IDENTIFICATION
53–69 cm. Size of Mallard. Has a more rounded head and slimmer neck than other divers, and a rather delicate, up-swept bill. In summer, adult has a grey body, velvety grey head, delicate streaks on hind-neck and a dull red throat patch that appears dark in poor light. In winter, it is grey-brown and white, with fine white spots on its back. Neck is white at the front and sides and dark at the back. The white on the face extends around the dark eye. Immatures look browner and less well marked. Adult plumage is moulted after breeding, when it becomes flightless. Between February and April it moults into breeding plumage.
SEE ALSO: Black-throated Diver p55, Great Northern Diver p56, Cormorant p68.

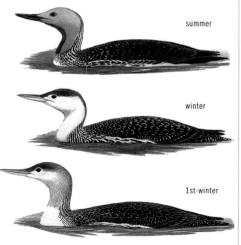

summer

winter

1st-winter

HABITS
Swims low in the water with its bill pointing slightly upwards. Often remains partly submerged when alarmed. Frequently rolls on its side in the water as it preens its white belly. In flight, looks thin-necked and hump-backed, and head and neck move up and down. Wingbeats are rapid, with wings lifted higher above the back than other divers. Flocks, sometimes of 100 or more, gather on the sea in winter. Flies high when commuting between breeding pools and feeding areas. Takes off easily and, when landing, planes down and strikes the water with considerable force. It performs noisy displays in the air during the breeding season.

VOICE
Usually silent. At breeding sites it can be noisy, giving an excited crescendo of calls like a high-pitched, wailing 'ya-roo, ya-roo, ya-roo'.

HABITAT
Breeds around shallow pools and lochans on upland moors and bogs, and also around larger lochs. May fly some distance to the sea to feed and bring back food for young. Almost always found on the sea in winter – especially inshore waters and shallow bays.

FOOD
Feeds mainly on marine fish such as Cod, Herring, sand-eel and sprat. Freshwater fish taken include small Atlantic Salmon, trout and Roach. Some crustaceans and insects are also eaten.

BREEDING
The nest is a heap of moss or aquatic vegetation built close to the water's edge or in water among vegetation. The 1 or 2 eggs are spotted with dark marks and incubated mostly by the female for 26–29 days. The young leave the nest within 24 hours and are fed by their parents. They fly after about 50 days, and they first breed at 2–3 years.

MOVEMENTS AND MIGRATIONS
Breeding birds move to the coast in autumn. Some remain in Scottish waters for the winter but others move south to England and Ireland, and first-year birds may reach the Netherlands or France. Birds that winter in Scotland may be local or have come from Scandinavia, Iceland or even Greenland. Oldest bird was 23 years.

POPULATION
Up to 1,500 pairs breed in Scotland, with almost half of these in Shetland. More than 2,250 winter around the coasts, with concentrations off Aberdeen, the Firth of Forth and the Clyde. There was a decline in the numbers breeding in the 1980s, and this decline may be continuing, albeit more slowly.

CONSERVATION
Specially protected. Floating islands created to help Black-throated Divers in particular have also benefited Red-throats. The species is threatened by winter oil spills, changes in fish populations (especially sand-eels) and the location of windfarms. Disturbance to breeding sites from recreation, birdwatching, fishing and tourism is also a problem.

winter

summer

DISTRIBUTION
In Britain, breeds only in north-west Scotland, especially Orkney and Shetland, with a few in Ireland. It winters all round the coast. Also found in northern Europe, Russia and North America.

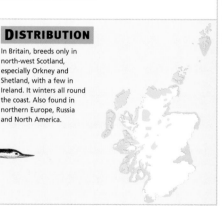

BLACK-THROATED DIVER   *GAVIA ARCTICA*

IDENTIFICATION
58–73 cm. Larger than Mallard. Larger, with thicker neck than Red-throated Diver, and heavier, straighter bill. Head appears rounded, or with a steep forehead. In summer, body is dark with a block of white marks on the back. Head is grey with a black throat, black and white stripes on side of neck and a small single white 'chin-strap' mark. On the water in winter it has contrasting dark and white plumage, prominent white thigh patches and less white on the sides of neck and cheeks than the Red-throated. The dark cap comes down to level of eye and the bill looks pale. First-winter birds are less clearly marked. Breeding plumage is moulted in September or December and flight feathers are moulted in spring.
SEE ALSO: Red-throated Diver p54, Great Northern Diver p56, Cormorant p68.

HABITS
Swims low in the water. Bill is usually held horizontal but may sometimes point slightly upwards, resembling Red-throated. Can look slim and elegant or chunky, depending on the way the neck is held. Like other divers it frequently rolls on its side to preen its belly feathers. In flight, it looks black and white and heavier than Red-throated, with the neck held straighter and the wings more central on the body. It is more solitary than Red-throated, but small flocks form outside the breeding season and groups often gather at fishing sites in the early morning.

VOICE
Mostly silent except on breeding grounds, where it has a loud, drawn-out wail.

HABITAT
Mostly breeds on larger freshwater lochs in the north and west of Scotland that have small islands and plentiful fish supplies. After breeding, it moves to sheltered bays and coastal waters, occasionally visiting inland waters in winter.

FOOD
Dives to chase prey underwater. Feeds mainly on fish, such as Arctic Charr, small Brown Trout, Herrings, Sprats, sand-eels and Minnows, and also on insects and crustaceans.

BREEDING
Pairs usually remain faithful for life. The male builds the nest of moss and water weed with help from the female, in shallow water close to the shore, often on a small island. The female incubates the usual clutch of 2 eggs for 28–30 days with help from the male. Young leave the nest within 24 hours and are fed by their parents. Chicks are often left alone by the parents and are aggressive to each other. They fly after about 60 days.

MOVEMENTS AND MIGRATIONS
Most birds move to the coast after breeding and a few move south to winter off the coasts, south of the border. A few other Black-throated Divers from northern Europe may join the Scottish birds for a time or pass through our waters on their way further south. These divers can live for 27 years.

POPULATION
About 200 pairs breed in Scotland, with 700–800 individuals in Scottish coastal waters in winter. The breeding population appears to be slightly increasing thanks to conservation measures.

CONSERVATION
Specially protected. Breeding birds are affected by changes in water levels, the introduction of Pike and other predatory fish (which compete for food), the development of fish farms and disturbance by recreation at nest sites. Some nesting birds use artificial floating islands specially developed to help them overcome the problem of changing water levels. At sea the species is threatened by pollution, changing fish populations, recreational sports and the unsuitable siting of windfarms.

summer

winter

summer

winter

juvenile

DISTRIBUTION
In Britain, this species breeds only in north-west Scotland. It also breeds on the Arctic tundra in Europe, Russia and North America. Northern populations move south in autumn, with some birds reaching the Mediterranean.

GREAT NORTHERN DIVER *GAVIA IMMER*

IDENTIFICATION
70–90 cm. Substantially larger than Mallard. Large, heavy-looking diver with a dagger-like bill, large head, thick neck and steep forehead. In summer, it is black and white with a chequered back, black head and neck that can appear iridescent green, and a barred white collar. In winter, it is dark grey and white. Dark crown descends below the eye and is broken by a pale eye-ring. Head and neck are generally darker than the back, with a suggestion of a dark half-collar at the base of the neck. Black and white areas are less clear-cut than on Black-throated. First-winter birds have brown backs that are barred with paler feather edges. This diver moults its black and white feathers after breeding and has a full moult in late winter, when it becomes flightless.
SEE ALSO: Red-throated Diver p54, Black-throated Diver p55, Cormorant p68.

HABITS
Swims low in the water and dives smoothly and powerfully. Often searches for food with head partially submerged. If alarmed, will swim with only its head and neck above water. Frequently preens its underparts while rolling on its side. Needs large areas of water to launch into the air.
In flight, it is heavy-looking, with slower, more shallow wingbeats than other divers and large feet that project behind the tail. Usually solitary in winter, but small groups may form, especially in the north. Dives regularly for a minute or more.

VOICE
Makes a variety of eerie howling calls in the breeding areas, but is mostly silent at other times.

HABITAT
In winter, many Great Northerns visit coastal waters and sheltered bays, especially in the north and west. Occasionally, a few arrive on large inland lochs. Usually feeds some distance from shore, but in spring passage birds in summer plumage are found in shallows along the west coast and around the Northern Isles. Its breeding areas (not in the British Isles) are around medium or large lakes.

FOOD
Mainly fish, especially Haddock, Herring and sand-eel. Also eats insects and their larvae, and crustaceans.

BREEDING
Takes place in Iceland, Greenland and Arctic Canada. Usually lays 2 eggs in a nest made of vegetation and built close to the water's edge. The young frequently ride on the parents' backs when they are small.

MOVEMENTS AND MIGRATIONS
Migrants start to arrive on the Scottish coast from Iceland in September and October. More follow later and a few winter as far south as the Mediterranean. Most leave by early May for their breeding grounds, although a few remain in Scottish waters all summer.

POPULATION
Despite frequent summer sightings in the north-west, and suspicion that some have nested, this species is thought to have nested here successfully only once – in 1970, when two adults were seen with two young. In winter, numbers increase up to almost 3,000 in Scotland.

summer

juvenile

winter

CONSERVATION
Specially protected. The main threats are from oil pollution in winter, declining fish stocks, and fishing nets that trap and kill feeding birds. Tight controls and enforcement of measures to reduce oil pollution, both deliberate and accidental, and the sympathetic management of inshore fisheries will help protect this species.

winter

summer

DISTRIBUTION
Most Great Northern Divers seen in Scotland in winter come from Iceland, but some are from Greenland or Arctic Canada. A few non-breeding birds spend the summer around the coast of north-west Scotland and on a few large lochs in Scotland and Ireland. The species breeds in North America, Greenland and Iceland, and on Bear Island off the north coast of Norway.

LITTLE GREBE   *TACHYBAPTUS RUFICOLLIS*

IDENTIFICATION
25–29 cm. Smaller than Moorhen. A small, dumpy bird, with a pale 'powder-puff' below its tail. Head is rounded, and the neck shorter than in other grebes. The small bill has pale patches at its base that become yellow in summer. Breeding plumage is dark brown with a chestnut neck and cheeks. Winter plumage is brown with a darker crown and paler cheeks and neck. Juvenile resembles adult in winter, but has 2 short, dark stripes behind the eye, and first-winter birds are paler and sandier than an adult. In flight, the wings look plain. A complete moult occurs after the breeding season. Flight feathers are moulted simultaneously, resulting in a flightless period of 3–4 weeks.
SEE ALSO: Slavonian Grebe p60, Black-necked Grebe p61.

HABITS
Very secretive and more likely to dive than to fly. Sometimes scuttles across the water. Dives frequently and hunts food underwater. If disturbed it will dive and emerge out of sight among waterside vegetation. If seriously alarmed, remains submerged with only its head above water. Frequently swims with undertail feathers fluffed up. Usually solitary outside the breeding season, but small groups may form in sheltered waters and sometimes roost together. A small territory around the nest is defended fiercely. These territories may be occupied all year, but some only for the breeding season and others only in winter.

summer

The 4–6 eggs are white when laid, but become brown through staining. Both sexes incubate the eggs, which hatch after 20 days. The young are covered with down and soon leave the nest. They may ride on the adults' backs or, more often, return to the nest platform to rest safely. Both parents feed them. They are also given feathers to eat, which might help in the formation of pellets. They become independent at 30–40 days and fly at about 45 days. There are 2–3 broods each year.

MOVEMENTS AND MIGRATIONS
Some northern breeding sites are deserted in winter as birds move to sheltered coasts and larger lochs and reservoirs. Birds from northern Europe migrate south in autumn. Some of these migrants visit Scotland, and while some may join Scottish breeding birds others will continue south into England. Oldest known bird was 13 years.

POPULATION
It is estimated that 1,650 pairs may breed in Scotland. In winter, numbers increase with the arrival of young and migrants from elsewhere and may reach 5,000–6,000 individuals. It appears the Scottish population is stable or slightly increasing.

CONSERVATION
Although the Scottish population is stable, in other parts of Britain unsympathetic management of lake and river banks may be affecting breeding success. In addition, recreational watersports and the introduction of American Mink may be a potential problem.

winter

VOICE
The most common call is a loud trilling, or whinny, that is used during courtship or territorial disputes. This is sometimes given by a pair of birds as a duet.

HABITAT
Found mainly on small lowland lochs and lowland pools with shallow water, both in open country and near woodland. Moves to larger lochs and sheltered coastal waters outside the breeding season.

FOOD
Mainly feeds on insects and their larvae, water snails, and small fish such as Minnows and young Carp.

BREEDING
The male and female together build a floating nest of water weed among plants growing in shallow water, or attach it to branches that are touching the water.

DISTRIBUTION
Found in most parts of Scotland and in most of the rest of Britain. Widespread in Europe, parts of the Middle East, Asia, and central and southern Africa.

juvenile

GREAT CRESTED GREBE *PODICEPS CRISTATUS*

juvenile riding on parent

IDENTIFICATION
46–51 cm. Smaller than Mallard. Has a long white neck and dagger-like bill. In summer, has a chestnut and black frill around the head. Blackish head plumes are raised during courtship. In winter, it is grey and white with a dark back and black crown, and a black line from the bill to the eye. Small young are striped black and white. Juveniles have dark stripes across their faces. A complete moult follows the breeding season. Flight feathers are moulted simultaneously and birds become flightless for 3–4 weeks.
SEE ALSO: Red-throated Diver p54, Red-necked Grebe p59.

HABITS
In flight, the long neck is extended, the feet trail and the large white patches on the front and back of the wings are visible. If disturbed, will usually dive rather than fly. Often swims with the head and neck resting on the back, revealing a very obvious white breast. Dives frequently to hunt food. Elaborate courtship displays involve a pair facing each other and head-shaking. Courting pairs also make synchronised dives, then emerge holding water weed and engage in a short 'weed-dance' as they rise out of the water. Small young regularly ride on their parents' backs to protect them from predators such as Pike. The young of first broods sometimes help to rear small young of second broods.

BREEDING
The nest is built among vegetation or branches growing in the water, or sometimes out in the open, and often comprises a floating heap of water weed and other plants. Both adults build the nest and take turns to incubate the 2–6 eggs. Eggs are covered when the adults leave the nest as a defence against crows and other predators. Incubation takes 28 days and begins with the first egg, so that the young hatch over a period of several days. Both adults feed the young. The diet includes feathers, which may help in the formation of pellets. The brood is split between the parents and the two groups live largely independently. After about 8 weeks the young are able to feed themselves, but the parents may continue to feed them for a further 15–23 weeks. They fly at about 10–11 weeks.

MOVEMENTS AND MIGRATIONS
After breeding, most birds move away from their nesting sites to winter on larger water bodies, and many visit sheltered estuaries and firths in southern and eastern Scotland. It is possible that these wintering flocks are joined by migrants from northern Europe. Oldest known bird lived for over 19 years.

POPULATION
Fewer than 400 pairs breed in Scotland, with possibly as many as 1,500 individuals in winter. Notable gatherings occur in autumn and winter on the Firth of Forth. Numbers increased in the late 20th century and are now thought to be stable.

CONSERVATION
The survival and spread of this once persecuted grebe is partly due to better protection and habitat creation – especially gravel workings and reservoir construction in southern Britain. In Scotland, the main concern is oil spillage in the species' wintering areas and disturbance from recreational activities.

winter

summer

winter

juvenile

VOICE
Occasionally makes a growling 'gorr, gorr', especially during courtship and when nesting.

HABITAT
Breeds on relatively large inland lochs, reservoirs and other water bodies with emergent vegetation, including slow flowing rivers. In winter, many birds move to larger lochs and also to sheltered coastal waters.

FOOD
Feeds mainly on fish, including Roach, Rudd, Minnows and Eels. Also takes aquatic insect larvae and small amphibians.

DISTRIBUTION
Found mainly in southern Scotland. Also occurs in other parts of lowland Britain and Ireland, Europe, the Middle East and Asia. There are other populations in Africa and Australia.

RED-NECKED GREBE *PODICEPS GRISEGENA*

IDENTIFICATION
40–50 cm. Smaller than Mallard. This grebe has a thick neck and a stout, dark bill with a yellow base. It is less elegant than a Great Crested Grebe, with a wedge-shaped, sometimes rounded head, making it look more front-heavy. In summer, it has whitish cheeks and a reddish-brown neck and breast. Its crown is black and its body dark brown. Juveniles have dark marks across their pale faces and paler chestnut on the neck. In winter, it is duller with dusky sides to the face and neck, a white collar and a white breast. The black cap comes down to the level of the eye. Sides of body can look whiter than Great Crested Grebe's body. It moults from its breeding plumage between July and September.
SEE ALSO: Great Crested Grebe p58, Slavonian Grebe p60, Black-necked Grebe p61.

HABITS
It flies strongly with rapid wingbeats. Two white wing-patches show in flight, but a much smaller area of white on the forewing than on Great Crested. When swimming it looks rather buoyant – more like the smaller grebes – and it jump-dives very energetically. Usually seen singly or in pairs. Catches fish underwater. Most dives last less than 30 seconds.

winter

BREEDING
Red-necks sometimes associate with gulls when breeding. The nest site is usually among reeds or other plants growing in the water. The nest is a floating heap of aquatic vegetation built by both male and female. The 4 or 5 eggs are incubated for 20–23 days. The brood is split between the adults and the young fly at about 72 days.

MOVEMENTS AND MIGRATIONS
The Red-necked Grebe leaves its northern breeding sites after nesting and moves to coastal waters or large lochs to moult and spend the winter. Birds from north-east Europe move south or west in late summer and a few reach Scotland, where the species is a regular sight on the Forth.

POPULATION
Between 50 and 100 birds may be present in Scottish waters, and a few are seen in summer in suitable breeding habitats. However, successful nesting has been confirmed only once.

CONSERVATION
Potential nest sites should be kept secret and some birds that were suspected of nesting have been given special protection. In winter, there is some danger from fishing nets and inappropriately located windfarms. Both breeding and wintering sites may be affected by human recreational activity.

summer

winter

VOICE
Mostly silent. A surprisingly loud hooting or wailing song is given in courtship and territorial encounters during the breeding season.

HABITAT
Mainly seen in Scotland in winter along sheltered sea coasts and estuaries like the Firth of Forth. A few summer inland, on lowland lochs and other water bodies where there is emergent vegetation.

FOOD
In winter, it feeds mainly on fish, such as Herrings, gobies and sand-eels, and also shrimps and prawns. In summer, it feeds on insects and their larvae, and on fish such as sticklebacks.

DISTRIBUTION
Mostly seen around the east coast of Britain in winter. Nesting has taken place at a secret location in Scotland. Also found in Europe, parts of Russia and North America, close to the Arctic Circle. Most populations migrate south for the winter.

SLAVONIAN GREBE *PODICEPS AURITUS*

IDENTIFICATION

31–38 cm. Similar size to Moorhen. Has a long neck, stubby bill and flat crown. In summer, has large yellow tufts (horns) on the sides of head, black cheek feathers, chestnut neck and flanks, and dark back. It is black and white in winter, with a flat crown, wedge-shaped head and white cheeks that almost meet at the back of the head. Breast and front of neck are pure white and the well-defined black cap comes down to eye-level, but often with a pale patch between eye and bill. Juvenile is dusky, less well marked and with traces of dark stripes across cheeks. Male moults August–September, while the female probably starts a month later.
SEE ALSO: Little Grebe p57, Great Crested Grebe p58, Red-necked Grebe p59, Black-necked Grebe p61.

summer

winter

juvenile

winter

HABITS

Usually seen singly or in small numbers on the sea in winter, but forms small groups at times of migration. In flight, shows 1 and sometimes 2 white patches on wings. When nesting, has courtship displays that include pairs rearing up and facing each other in a 'penguin-like' position and head-shaking. There is also a 'weed-rush', where the birds dive, surface with water weed, meet face to face, turn and rush side by side for 5–10 m across the water. In summer, snaps insects from the air or off plant leaves, or catches them by skimming the water surface with its bill or by diving. Dives last less than 30 seconds, but it can stay under water for a minute or more.

VOICE

Mostly silent. Has a hard, guttural trill during courtship, and various threat and contact calls while breeding.

HABITAT

Breeds on inland lochs, both at sea-level and at higher elevations, mainly around the Great Glen. These waters usually have emergent vegetation such as sedges and horsetails. In winter, it is found mainly in estuaries and sheltered coastal waters.

FOOD

Eats small fish and invertebrates. In summer, catches insects such as stoneflies, other flies and water beetles, plus Three-spined Sticklebacks, small trout and Eels.

BREEDING

Pairs form in winter or on migration. Nest is built from water weed by both adults, and anchored to water vegetation. Lays 4 or 5 eggs that are incubated by both birds for around 24 days. Young are covered with down and swim soon after hatching, also regularly riding on their parents' backs when small. They are fed by the adults, become independent at 45 days and fly after 55 days.

MOVEMENTS AND MIGRATIONS

Breeding lochs are generally abandoned at the end of summer, when birds congregate to moult, especially on Loch Ashie and Loch Ruthven. Wintering birds visit Orkney, the firths of the east coast and Loch Ryan. These flocks may include birds from Iceland and Scandinavia.

POPULATION

First nested in Scotland in 1909, with breeding numbers increasing to 30–80 pairs and wintering birds numbering up to around 500. The breeding population suffered a decline in the 1990s, then stabilised at around 35 pairs, but it appears to be declining once more.

CONSERVATION

Specially protected. Wave action and flooding is a natural threat. Many breeding sites are kept secret. The best breeding site to see the birds is the RSPB's Loch Ruthven reserve. The wintering populations are internationally important and need safeguarding from changing fish stocks and pollution.

DISTRIBUTION

The most northerly and most coastal of the grebes. Breeds at a few sites in the Scottish Highlands; also in Iceland, Scandinavia, Russia and North America. Found in coastal waters south of its breeding areas in winter.

IDENTIFICATION
28–34 cm. Smaller than Moorhen. Has a small head and a steep forehead, peaked crown and delicate, up-swept bill. Often shows fluffy white feathers under its tail. In summer, has an untidy tuft of yellow feathers behind eye; the rest of head and neck is black. Reddish brown on sides sometimes extends onto neck. In winter, it is black and white with a black cap to below level of eye, dusky cheeks and a pale vertical crescent to rear of cheeks. The breast generally looks very white. A dark band on the nape is thicker than Slavonian's when viewed from behind. Flight is strong with rapid wing-beats and shows a white triangle on rear of wing (Slavonian shows white on front and rear of wing). SEE ALSO: Great Crested Grebe p58, Red-necked Grebe p59, Slavonian Grebe p60.

HABITS
This is the most social of the small grebes, with pairs nesting in colonies and small flocks forming outside the breeding season. It dives to find food and is often reluctant to fly. Dives last around half a minute, but it can stay under water for a minute or more. Displays involve head-shaking, a pair rising out of the water with their breasts pressed together, and then rushing across the water side by side. Nesting birds are secretive.

summer

winter

juvenile

winter

VOICE
A chittering trill and plaintive 'wheeooo, wheeooo' are heard at breeding sites. It is mostly silent at other times.

HABITAT
Breeds on shallow inland lochs fringed with water plants and with plenty of insects and small fish. Will take advantage of newly flooded areas. In winter, it visits larger inland water bodies and sheltered estuaries, and is sometimes seen in shallow coastal waters.

FOOD
Mostly eats insects such as water beetles, dragonfly larvae, caddisflies and mayflies. It also eats small fish and water snails.

BREEDING
It often gains protection by breeding among colonies of Black-headed Gulls. Both sexes work together to build a floating nest of water weed among emergent vegetation. Several nests may be built before one is selected and a clutch of 3 or 4 eggs is laid. Incubation is by both adults for about 21 days. The young are covered in down and soon leave the nest. They frequently ride on their parents' backs when small.

MOVEMENTS AND MIGRATIONS
In August the species starts to leave its breeding areas. Birds from central and northern Europe move south-east or south-west, and a few probably reach Scotland and join local birds for the winter. Return migration starts during March, when small groups may arrive on inland waters. Occasionally there may be a sudden colonisation if conditions are right. Maximum recorded age was 7 years.

POPULATION
Breeding was first recorded in Scotland in 1930 in Lothian, following on from Wales in 1904, Ireland in 1915 and England in 1918. Scottish numbers have remained low, with 8–17 pairs nesting in 2000 and a further drop-off since then. Some key sites have also been abandoned.

CONSERVATION
Specially protected. Disturbance to the species' breeding sites by recreational activity is a problem in some places. However, the lack of suitable nesting lochs with emergent vegetation may be more of an issue, as is predation by mammals such as American Mink. South of the border the small population is thought to be stable.

DISTRIBUTION
The Scottish population is at the edge of the species range. Regular wintering sites include Loch Ryan and the Firth of Forth. The race found in Scotland breeds across the western and central Palearctic.

SOOTY SHEARWATER *PUFFINUS GRISEUS*

IDENTIFICATION
40–51 cm. Smaller than Herring Gull. This is a large, dark shearwater with a dark brown, cigar-shaped body and long, narrow wings. The bill is long and dark and the all-dark plumage is broken by the silvery underwing coverts that appear, from a distance, to form a white stripe. The total moult takes place between May and August while the species is in the North Atlantic.
SEE ALSO: Manx Shearwater p63, Fulmar p66.

HABITS
In flight its wings appear to be set relatively far back on the body and also often look swept back. Usually it flies close to the waves with several strong wingbeats followed by a long glide. Sometimes it will bank steeply before gliding down and resuming its direct line of flight. When swimming it sits quite high in the water, looking quite buoyant. It often associates with feeding whales and it scavenges around fishing vessels.

VOICE
Mostly silent while at sea, but raucous calls and screams have been reported.

HABITAT
It lives on the open ocean and is seldom seen close to land while in the North Atlantic. Breeds on remote islands in the Southern Ocean.

FOOD
It eats fish such as Caplins and sand-eels, also squid, crustaceans and offal from fishing vessels. It scavenges around whales, taking damaged and disoriented fish, and probably also feeds on whale faeces.

BREEDING
Does not breed in Britain or Ireland.

MOVEMENTS AND MIGRATIONS
Migrates north from its island colonies in a clockwise direction. After breeding, during the southern summer, it starts to move northwards through the west Atlantic in April and May. It follows the coast of South and then North America and then gathers in considerable numbers off the coast of New England and Newfoundland. In July many start to cross the North Atlantic and pass through Scottish coastal waters between August and October en route back to their South Atlantic breeding grounds.

POPULATION
Numbers seen from Scottish coasts vary from year to year. Records of thousands passing out to sea is probably not an accurate reflection of true numbers passing close to the coast of Scotland, but of birds that are too far out to be observed from land.

CONSERVATION
Protection of the island nesting colonies from introduced ground predators and habitat destruction, and sustainable fishing are needed to protect this species. Global warming may already be having an impact on its food supplies as its numbers are dropping, especially off the Californian coast.

DISTRIBUTION
Seen regularly in small numbers from Scottish 'sea-watching' headlands, mainly in August and September. Breeds on islands close to Antarctica and spends the northern ummer in the North Atlantic. This shearwater also roams the Southern Ocean and the Pacific.

Manx Shearwater   PUFFINUS PUFFINUS

IDENTIFICATION
31–36 cm. Smaller than Herring Gull. It has long, straight, slim wings and a long, slim bill, with blackish upperparts, white underparts and black cap extending below the eye. The white underwing has a dark border. SEE ALSO: Sooty Shearwater p62.

HABITS
This is the most common shearwater around the coast of Scotland. It flies with a series of rapid, stiff wing-beats followed by a long glide as it banks and turns low over the waves or, in strong winds, rises and falls. Often a number will fly in a line, rising and falling as they ride the air currents – they can look alternately black and white as they change the angle of their bodies. Food is taken from the surface of the water or by plunge-diving and flocks gather where food is plentiful. It is colonial when nesting, and some colonies have hundreds or thousands of pairs close together. It swims 'duck-like', and rafts of hundreds of swimming birds will form on the sea close to colonies as dusk approaches and then only approach land after dark.

VOICE
At sea it is generally silent. At the nest it has a variety of weird calls, including crowing, cooing, howls and screams.

HABITAT
A bird of the open ocean except when nesting. Nests on offshore islands with soft soil.

FOOD
Fish, especially Herrings, Sardines and Sprats. Also feeds on other sea creatures such as squid.

BREEDING
Nests in burrows on flat or sloping land close to the sea. Burrows are excavated in soft soil by both sexes, and old rabbit burrows may also be used. One egg is incubated for about 50 days. The pair takes turns to incubate, with each turn averaging almost 6 days. The young are fed only at night on pre-digested fish. Parents may miss one, two or even three nights owing to bright moonlight, bad weather or difficulty in finding food. Parents desert young at about 60 days old. The chick then leaves the nest-burrow 8–9 days later and heads for the open ocean.

MOVEMENTS AND MIGRATIONS
A long-distance migrant that returns to its breeding areas in late February, March or early April. Migration south begins in July as it heads for its winter quarters off the coast of South America. It is possible that it returns by a different route, by crossing the Atlantic and returning northwards along the coast of Africa. It does not breed until 5 or 6 years old and may live for 50 years.

POPULATION
There may be around 125,000 pairs breeding in Scotland. The largest colony is stable but declines have been noticed at smaller colonies, especially where feral cats or rats have been discovered.

CONSERVATION
The largest threat to this species comes from alien mammals introduced to islands where there are shear-water colonies. Rats are the biggest problem, although Red Deer on Rum also regularly kill fledgling chicks. In addition, supplies of small fish are critical to the birds' survival.

DISTRIBUTION

The Manx Shearwater breeds on St Kilda, Rum and a few other islands off the west coast of Scotland, with small numbers on Shetland. It also breeds in Wales and Ireland, and on a few islands off the Atlantic coast of Europe and Africa. Outside the breeding season it ranges widely in the Atlantic.

63

STORM PETREL *HYDROBATES PELAGICUS*

IDENTIFICATION
14–18 cm. Slightly larger than a sparrow. Sooty-black plumage with a vivid white band above the tail and spreading round the sides. Young birds have a very faint thin bar across the wing. Underwing has a thick white stripe down the middle. Compared with other petrels the wings are rather short. Tail short and square-ended. Juvenile similar to adult. Moult starts while the adults have young and continues into the autumn.
SEE ALSO: Leach's Petrel p65, House Martin p161.

HABITS
The fluttering flight and short glides close to the water is rather 'bat-like'. Feeds with wings raised in 'V'-shape and feet pattering on water surface. May feed in large flocks and sometimes follows ships or keeps company with other feeding seabirds. Swims duck-like, sitting high in the water and normally only approaches land after dark. Sometimes solitary, but often in loose flocks and sometimes in larger numbers.

VOICE
Usually silent except at breeding colonies where it makes a far-carrying, purring 'a-rrrrrrr' call from its burrow.

HABITAT
A bird of the open ocean, except when nesting, and then it approaches land only after dark. Rarely seen close to the coast, except when approaching nests or in late summer when strong winds may drive migrating birds closer to the shore. Breeding sites are on islands with rocky outcrops, boulders, walls or ruined buildings with crevices for nesting.

FOOD
Small fish, such as juvenile Sprats and Herrings, plankton, jellyfish and small crustaceans and squid. It also feeds on offal and other waste from ships at sea.

BREEDING
Nests in crevices between boulders, in stone walls, in Rabbit burrows and will sometimes share a burrow with a Manx Shearwater. One egg is incubated by both adults, which take equal turns lasting about 3 days each. Eggs hatch after about 40 days. Young are brooded continuously for a week and then left as their parents forage for food at sea during the day, returning at night to feed the chick on regurgitated food. The young leave their burrow at about 62 days. They are independent almost at once and quickly disperse into the open ocean. They return to their original colony after 2 or 3 years, but will not breed until at least 4 years old.

MOVEMENTS AND MIGRATIONS
Scottish breeding birds leave coastal waters in September and October. Migrants arrive at the wintering grounds off South Africa from mid-November and leave again in March. Breeding birds are present at breeding colonies from early May. Storm Petrels may live to 31 years or more.

POPULATION
About 25,000 pairs are thought to breed in Scotland, which may comprise 4% of the world population. Because of the difficulty of monitoring this species, its long-term population trend is uncertain.

CONSERVATION
Protection of larger breeding colonies is vital to safeguard this species. The elimination of rats and feral cats from breeding islands is an essential first step. In Scotland, the Storm Petrel breeds mainly in colonies on a small number of offshore islands in the north and west that are close to deep water. One of the best places to see them is on a visit to the Pictish broch on Mousa, Shetland.

DISTRIBUTION

In Britain and Ireland it mainly breeds on the west coast, on islands facing the Atlantic. Feeds on the edge, and beyond the edge, of the Continental Shelf, where the water may be 100 m deep or more. Also breeds in Iceland, the Faroes and Norway, with smaller colonies on islands in the Mediterranean, Atlantic islands such as Madeira and the Canary Islands, and Morocco. Winters in the western Atlantic as far south as South Africa.

LEACH'S PETREL *OCEANODROMA LEUCORHOA*

IDENTIFICATION
19–22 cm. Size of Starling. Plumage brownish black with narrow white, horseshoe-shaped rump. A dark line running through centre of the white rump is often very difficult to see. Tail forked. Wings are longer, narrower and more pointed than a Storm Petrel's and have prominent pale diagonal bar on upper surface. Underwing is dark. Body appears long and more slender owing to longer tail. Moults in its winter quarters during November to February.
SEE ALSO: Storm Petrel p64, House Martin p161, Black Tern p136.

HABITS
Oceanic; normally approaches land only to breed, and then only at night, or when forced into coastal waters by severe weather. Generally seen alone or in small groups. Flight light and buoyant, rather like a tern, as it banks and turns. Wings are angled strongly at the carpal joint and, head on, they look kinked. When feeding it will frequently patter the surface with its feet, as if walking on the water, especially when the wind is strong, but it seldom alights on the water. Leach's Petrels often approach ships at sea after dark.

VOICE
Usually silent at sea. Loud calls at breeding colonies variously described as 'musical', 'crooning', 'churring ' and 'purring' or a crowing 'her-kitti-werke'.

HABITAT
Lives on the open ocean for most of the year. Breeds on remote offshore islands among rocks and boulders, and sometimes in stone walls or ruined buildings. Occasionally after rough weather, it becomes stranded on reservoirs or lakes well away from the sea.

FOOD
It takes food from the water surface by feeding on microscopic sea creatures such as tiny shrimps, crustaceans known as copepods and plankton. It will also follow feeding whales and seals and take offal and other waste material.

BREEDING
Pairs remain faithful from year to year. Nests in huge colonies and approaches land only after dark. Uses its feet to dig nesting tunnels in soft soil, but also nests in crevices in rocks and other holes. Sometimes several will use side tunnels off a single main entrance. The male may build a small nest of grass stems. Both birds take equal turns of several days to incubate the 1 egg. Eggs hatch after about 40 days. Young are brooded by an adult for about 5 days and then left during the day while adults forage far out to sea, returning to feed the chick only after dark. Young desert their burrows at around 65 days and quickly leave their breeding colonies. They reach breeding maturity at about 5 years.

MOVEMENTS AND MIGRATIONS
Birds return to their colonies from late April and leave mainly between September and October, although some remain until November. Autumn gales sometimes force them close to land between mid-August and mid-October, when they are seen from ferries and headlands, usually on the west coast. After breeding, Scottish birds – together with those from Ireland – move out into the Atlantic and most migrate southwards to winter in the tropics. Some may reach South Africa and even enter the Indian Ocean. Maximum recorded age was over 29 years.

POPULATION
This is an extremely difficult species to census. There are thought to be almost 50,000 pairs breeding in Scotland, with the main colony on St Kilda and a handful of other colonies on other remote northern islands.

CONSERVATION
Protecting the few colonies from mammalian predators, especially rats and cats is a priority. The species is specially protected.

DISTRIBUTION

One of the most numerous seabirds, yet one of the most enigmatic. Only a small number of colonies have been found in the British Isles, and the majority of those are in Scotland. These petrels feed far out to sea, usually beyond the edge of the continental shelf of Europe. Other colonies are on both the east and the west coasts on North America and on some North Pacific islands.

FULMAR *FULMARUS GLACIALIS*

IDENTIFICATION
45–50 cm. Smaller than Herring Gull. Appears gull-like but has a thick neck and a strong stubby bill with pronounced nostrils. Body is white with a greyish back and tail and grey wings with a pale patch at base of primaries. The white head has a dark 'smudge' in front of the eye. Those from the Arctic are darker, with duskier bodies and more uniform dark grey upperwings. Adult Fulmars have a complete body moult while at sea between August and October. Primary feathers re-grow rapidly.
SEE ALSO: Herring Gull p124, Kittiwake p131, Gannet p67.

dark morph

HABITS
Flight is distinctive with a series of rapid, shallow wingbeats followed by a glide on stiff, straight wings. Often glides low over the sea with wingtips almost touching the water or riding the air currents along cliff edges, flapping its wings only when losing height. Gathers in flocks on the sea or around a source of food. Pairs perform a noisy greeting ceremony when both adults meet at their nest. Feeds by picking food from the water's surface or sometimes making a clumsy dive.

VOICE
Mostly silent at sea. Pairs cackle to each other on their nests.

HABITAT
A true seabird that is often seen many kilometres from land. Breeds all around the Scottish coast, and occasionally inland, where there are suitable cliffs. Also sometimes nests on old buildings close to the sea.

FOOD
Crustaceans, fish and waste from fishing trawlers. Also eats carrion such as dead birds and seals.

BREEDING
Fulmars keep the same mate for life, unless one dies. Colonies vary from a few nests to several hundred and the same birds will use the same site year after year. A single egg is laid on a narrow ledge with no nest material, or sometimes on soft soil. Incubation takes 52 days. The female incubates first and then disappears for about 7 days before returning to share the incubation with her mate. Both parents feed the young, with one or other adult staying on the nest to protect it for the first 2 weeks. Young fly after 46 days and are immediately independent. For the first few years they live at sea, often hundreds of miles from land.

MOVEMENTS AND MIGRATIONS
After breeding most fly out to sea, but colonies are seldom completely deserted. The young

fledge in September and by November many adults are back on their breeding ledges. By December all the breeding sites are usually occupied. Many juveniles find their way to the coast of Newfoundland. They may return to their breeding colony after 4 or 5 years, but will not breed for 6–10 years. Fulmars may live for 40 years.

POPULATION
Fulmars spread from the remote island of St Kilda in the 19th century. They started breeding on Shetland in 1878 and gradually spread round the coast of Scotland and, later, to England, Wales and Northern Ireland. The current breeding population in Scotland is in the region of half a million pairs.

CONSERVATION
After a long period of expansion it appears the Scottish population has now stabilised, and there is even a suggestion of a slight decrease in some areas, perhaps due to food shortages caused by changes in the fishing industry. Other problems come from predators such as American Mink or rats, and from waste material floating on the sea, which is ingested by the birds. Thousands are also drowned by long-line fishing in the North Atlantic.

DISTRIBUTION
Most numerous in the north and west, but breeds all round British and Irish coasts where there are suitable cliffs. In winter, lives in the North Atlantic. Also breeds in Greenland and North America. There is another race of Fulmar in the North Pacific.

GANNET *MORUS BASSANUS*

IDENTIFICATION
87–100 cm. Larger and longer necked than any gull, with a long body, long pointed wings, pointed tail and dagger-like bill. Adult pure white with black wing-tips and yellowish-orange head in spring that becomes paler in winter. Juvenile grey-brown with white flecks. Immatures have a white belly and various intermediate plumages with increasing amounts of white before growing the adult plumage after 4 years. Gradual moult generally starts after the breeding season and continues into the autumn.
SEE ALSO: Herring Gull p124, Fulmar p66.

HABITS
Flies with powerful wingbeats followed by an effortless glide. When feeding it will fly up, steady itself and then drop, folding the wings and dive, bill first. Often large numbers congregate where food is plentiful. Nests are in huge colonies.

VOICE
Dry, cackling calls from feeding groups. Noisy at colonies with growls, especially when greeting mates at the nest.

HABITAT
Lives on the open ocean, far from land, for most of the year, and most feeding takes place in cold waters over the continental shelves. Colonies are on exposed and often precipitous islands or remote sea cliffs.

FOOD
Fish, chiefly Herring and Mackerel in the breeding season, but also Caplin, Sprat, sand-eel and many other species. An individual will sometimes steal fish from other Gannets and, occasionally, other species.

BREEDING
Nest is a substantial pile of seaweed and other material found floating on the sea and mixed with earth and grass pulled from near the colony. This mixture is stuck together with the bird's own droppings and added to year after year – mostly by the male. The Gannet has no brood patch and parents take it in turns to incubate the single egg under their webbed feet. The egg hatches after 44 days. At first the chick is brooded between the parent's webs and both adults feed it. At about 90 days, after being left to starve for about 10 days, it leaves the nest and enters the sea. Here it swims on the surface for 2 to 3 weeks before starting to fish for itself.

MOVEMENTS AND MIGRATIONS
Present in Scottish waters for most of the year, although maybe scarce or absent in winter. Young leave their colonies in August and September and head south, at first swimming. They may winter off the coast of West Africa, as far south as Senegal. Breeding birds start returning to their colonies in January. Gannets live on average for 16 years, and individuals may live for 37 years or more.

POPULATION
Over 180,000 pairs of Gannets breed in Scotland's 14 colonies, or more than 40% of the world population. Some colonies have a stable population, but others are still expanding.

CONSERVATION
Although the population appears to be stable or slightly increasing it is significant that humans have inflicted most known causes of death. Gannets are caught in fishing nets, snagged by polyethylene cord brought to the nest and killed by oil or other pollution. Toxic chemicals polluting the birds' food has caused breeding failure. The establishment of a sustainable fishing policy in the north-west Atlantic will be critical for the Gannet.

juvenile

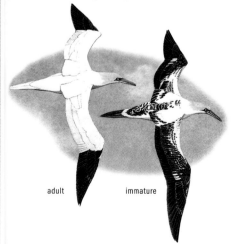

adult   immature

DISTRIBUTION
Most Gannet colonies are in the north and west of the British Isles; Scotland is home to 14 major colonies, including Troup Head, the only mainland colony. It also breeds in northern France, Norway Iceland, the Faroe Islands and on the north-east coast of North America. It is widespread in the North Atlantic for most of the year. Many young move south to African waters and both adults and young feed along the European and North African coasts outside the breeding season.

CORMORANT PHALACROCORAX CARBO

IDENTIFICATION
80–100 cm. Size of a large goose. Large body, long, thick neck, long powerful bill and long sloping forehead and crown. Adult black with white on its face and thighs in spring. Juvenile dark brown, usually with pale, almost white, underparts. Some immatures also have white underparts, while others resemble adults, but without white thighs or faces. Wing and body feathers are moulted between June and December. Head and neck feathers moulted before breeding
SEE ALSO: Shag p69, Red-throated Diver p54, Great Northern Diver p56.

HABITS
Frequently stands with wings extended or swims like a large duck, with bill raised upwards. It dives with a little leap upwards before submerging underwater. Often it is seen singly, but larger numbers gather at roosts and at feeding sites. Nests in colonies – sometimes numbering 100 nests or more. Flies with neck out-stretched, rather like a goose, and sometimes soars over land. Groups may fly in lines or in a 'V' shape. Perches on the ground, on posts, on tree branches and on power lines and pylons.

winter   juvenile

VOICE
Noisy at breeding sites and in roosts. Loud guttural 'agock-agock-agock' call made by adults, but mostly silent at other times.

HABITAT
Traditionally associated in Scotland with rocky coasts, especially sea lochs, estuaries and firths, but also occurs on lowland lochs and rivers away from the sea, particularly in winter. Nests on cliffs, stacks and rocky islets and, rarely in Scotland, in trees.

FOOD
Feeds on fish, especially flatfish such as Plaice and Flounder, but it also catches others such as Butterfish, Cod, Sprats and blennies. On inland waters a wide variety of fish is caught, including trout.

BREEDING
The male builds the nest with some help from the female. Materials include twigs, reed and seaweed. Both adults incubate their 3 or 4 eggs for about 30

days. Young are brooded when small and fed by both parents. They fly after about 50 days but continue to return to the nest to be fed for a further 40–50 days before becoming fully independent. They first breed when 3 years old.

MOVEMENTS AND MIGRATIONS
Present throughout the year, although birds disperse from breeding colonies after nesting. Most remain in Scotland, but some travel to northern England and Ireland, and at least one bird is known to have reached northern France. Maximum age is over 23 years.

POPULATION
There are estimated to be over 3,500 nests in Scotland. Overall, the numbers appear stable, although there have been local changes, including a marked recent decline in the north-west.

summer

juvenile

CONSERVATION
The chief threat to the Cormorant comes from human persecution. Conflict – both real and perceived – with angling interests continues, and Cormorants can now be legally shot under licence. Such laws are hard to monitor and it is likely that many more are killed illegally. Depletion of coastal fish stocks and marine pollution are also a threat.

winter

DISTRIBUTION
Found around the coast of Scotland and sometimes on inland lochs and rivers. Also breeds in England, Wales and Ireland, with more birds breeding inland in recent years. Outside the British Isles, the race found in Scotland also breeds across Scandinavia and Europe; different races breed in Russia, China, India, parts of Africa, New Zealand and Australia, as well as Iceland and, in small numbers, North America.

SHAG *PHALACROCORAX ARISTOTELIS*

summer

winter

juvenile

IDENTIFICATION
65–80 cm. Larger than Mallard. Smaller and slimmer than Cormorant with smaller head and thinner bill. Head shape different from Cormorant, with steeper forehead and peak to the crown above the eyes. Breeding adult is oily greenish black with yellow at base of the black bill and curly crest on the front of the head. At close range it has a scaly-looking back and a purplish sheen. Non-breeding adults are browner with a pale throat and lack the crest. Juveniles are brown, and lack the whitish underparts of a juvenile Cormorant. Immatures are also brown with less blotchy underparts than Cormorant and with pale edges to the wing feathers, creating a scaly pale panel. Complex moult whereby flight feathers are moulted gradually from July to November then delayed until February when moult resumes until all have been replaced and the process begins again.
SEE ALSO: Cormorant p68, Red-throated Diver p54.

HABITS
Frequently stands with wings partly out-stretched. Usually makes a distinctive forward jump before diving and these dives may last for 40 seconds. Often flies close to water surface. Wings are shorter and tips more rounded than Cormorant's, and flight is more rapid, with wings raised higher above the back.

VOICE
Mostly silent. At nest it makes a series of grunts and clicks.

winter

HABITAT
More at home on rough seas than Cormorant. Found in inshore waters close to rocky coasts and islands. Rare on fresh water.

FOOD
Mostly feeds on fish, especially sand-eels, Herring, Cod and many other fish found in inshore waters. Feeds singly or in flocks where there is an abundance of fish.

BREEDING
Nests in colonies. May keep the same mate from year to year, but some change mates and some males may be bigamous. A small territory is defended around nest built on cliff ledges, either just above high water mark, or much higher above the sea. The male selects a site for the nest that is built by both sexes from seaweed, vegetation and material found floating on the sea. A clutch of usually 3 eggs is incubated by both birds for about 30 days. The chicks are fed by both parents on regurgitated food. The young fly after 48 days, but continue to be fed by their parents for several more weeks before becoming independent. The young breed after 3–4 years.

MOVEMENTS AND MIGRATIONS
Present throughout the year. Outside the breeding season seldom moves far from breeding areas, although there appears to be a southern movement by some individuals. After severe storms there may be 'wrecks' that result in Shags being seen at a variety of wetland sites, sometimes far from the sea. Maximum age is over 30 years.

POPULATION
Scotland is home to 30% of the world population. Up to 30,000 pairs breed here, and the winter population may number as many as 60,000–80,000 individuals. The population appears to be largely stable, albeit with some local increases.

CONSERVATION
Like all fish-eating seabirds its future depends on a sustainable supply of fish and appropriate fishing quotas in British waters. Sea temperature changes and the loss of sand-eels presents the biggest, current threat. The species also suffers from oil discharged into the sea. Legislation preventing pollution and stricter controls over shipping routes will help. Predators such as rats, feral cats and American Mink can decimate colonies.

winter

juvenile

DISTRIBUTION

Commonly seen around the coast of Scotland in both summer and winter. Also breeds along the rocky coasts of northern and south-west England, Wales and Ireland. Elsewhere, it is found around the Atlantic coast of Scandinavia, Iceland, the Faroe Islands, France, Spain, Portugal and North Africa, with different races present in parts of the Mediterranean.

GREY HERON *ARDEA CINEREA*

IDENTIFICATION
90–98 cm. Very large, with a long neck, long legs and a dagger-like bill. Adult grey, black and white. Head white with white centre to the black crown that ends in a long, black wispy crest. Whitish neck has rows of black marks. Back is blue-grey and the large flight feathers are dull black. Adult's bill changes from yellow to partly reddish in breeding season. Juvenile appears sleeker and greyer than adult and lacks the long plumes. Adults start to moult after the breeding season and complete this by November.
SEE ALSO: Night Heron p244, Bittern p244.

HABITS
Usually solitary, but also seen in groups. Often stands 'hunched up' with head resting between shoulders. When hunting the neck is elongated. In flight, head is drawn back, neck bulges and legs and feet extend well

juvenile

beyond tail. When hunting, walks with great stealth and stands motionless for long periods with neck curved ready to strike. Sometimes wades in deep water. Crown feathers raised in display.

VOICE
Usually silent, apart from loud 'frank' or 'kaark' call, often given in flight. At nesting colony there is a variety of croaking calls.

HABITAT
Usually seen on the ground, near shallow edges of lakes, slow-flowing rivers, marshes or estuaries, but also stands in fields away from water or perches in trees. Generally it nests in tall trees, but sometimes on the ground in reedbeds or on a cliff ledge.

FOOD
Feeds mainly on fish. From fresh waters the species include Roach, Perch, sticklebacks and also Goldfish from garden ponds. In coastal areas catches Eels, Flounders, wrasse and crabs. Small mammals, birds, amphibians and insect larvae are also eaten occasionally.

BREEDING
Breeds in colonies (called heronries) although single nests are not uncommon. The large nest of sticks is usually at the top of a deciduous or coniferous tree, 25–40 m off the ground and generally in the same tree as several other nests. In the north of Scotland some Grey Herons nest in low shrubs, cliff ledges and even on the ground amongst vegetation. Nests built by both adults; male bringing the material and female undertaking construction. 3 or 4 eggs are incubated by both sexes and hatch after 25–27 days. Young brooded for about 18 days and for the next week or so an adult remains at the nest. At around 20–30 days the young

leave and start to clamber around the branches. They eventually fly when about 50 days old, but may continue to return to their nests for a further 10–20 days. Soon after fledging the young disperse from their colonies.

MOVEMENTS AND MIGRATIONS
In winter, Grey Herons spread out from their heronries, although only a few leave Scotland and move south of the border, with a small proportion reaching the Continent. In autumn, Scottish birds are joined by migrants from Scandinavia. Elsewhere they are long-distance migrants, and some from Europe cross the Sahara. Oldest known bird survived more than 35 years.

POPULATION
There are thought to be around 10,000–15,000 pairs nesting in Scotland. This population appears stable or even modestly increasing in recent years.

CONSERVATION
In the past, the Grey Heron population has been adversely affected by persecution, severe winter weather and persistent use of pesticides. Legal protection, mild winters and cleaner water courses have stabilised numbers, which are even probably increasing in some areas.

DISTRIBUTION
Found throughout Scotland and the rest of Britain and Ireland, except in mountainous areas. Most numerous close to lochs, rivers and burns, and frequently feeds along sheltered shores. Also breeds in central and northern Europe with a few scattered locations farther south. Some northern European birds winter around the Mediterranean. Also found in Africa and Asia.

HONEY BUZZARD *PERNIS APIVORUS*

IDENTIFICATION
52–60 cm. A little longer than Buzzard. Birds vary from pale to dark. Male has grey head, grey-brown upperparts and variable underparts. Head slender and pigeon-like. Has longer tail than Buzzard with dark band at tip and two or three bands near base. Along hind edge of wing has dark band that is 'S' shaped, curving into the body. Paler birds show dark patch on bend of wing. Female is darker, browner and more obviously barred on body. Juvenile is also variable, with darker brown plumage, often a white forehead, almost black tips to wings and dark secondary feathers. Tail is crossed by several indistinct bars. Juveniles with pale heads often have a dark eye-patch. Adults start their moult whilst breeding but finish it in Africa. Juveniles start a protracted moult in their second year.
SEE ALSO: Buzzard p73, Goshawk p76.

male

juvenile

female

BREEDING
Nesting begins in late May. Both sexes build nest on a branch of a large tree and often use the old nest of a large species such as a crow as a foundation. Nest is made of twigs and branches with some live, green material. Both birds share the incubation of the 2 eggs, which hatch after 30–35 days. At first, young are mainly brooded by female. Male provides most of the food for female and chicks for about 18 days, after which both parents share the hunting. The young fly at about 42 days, but are not independent until 75–100 days.

MOVEMENTS AND MIGRATIONS
Breeding birds arrive in Europe in May and leave again in mid-August and September. Large numbers converge at major sea-crossings such as Falsterbo at the southern tip of Sweden, Gibraltar, Messina in southern Italy and Istanbul in Turkey. Maximum recorded age was 29 years.

POPULATION
Between 15 and 20 pairs breed in Scotland, but this a difficult species to pin down and the number of pairs appears to fluctuate from year to year.

CONSERVATION
Specially protected. Scottish breeding birds are usually at secret locations to protect them from collectors. Numbers have increased in recent years, perhaps as a result of occupation of maturing upland conifer forests. Increases in wasp grubs owing to climate change may have contributed to the increase.

male

male
(pale)

HABITS
Different flight profile from Buzzard; wings held either flat or drooped slightly downwards, deep and lazy wing-beats; wings held straight and flat and tail fanned when soaring. When displaying or advertising its territory, male will carry out an undulating sky-dance where the wings are raised high above body. Spends more time feeding on ground than other birds of prey. Shy and usually seen singly except when large flocks are concentrated at narrow sea-crossings on migration.

VOICE
Generally silent, but make a piping 'pi – aa' in the breeding season.

HABITAT
Breeds in mature mixed or pine woodlands in lowland Scotland, and also on wooded hillsides in higher hills. It favours woodland with open rides and open countryside nearby.

FOOD
Uniquely adapted to feeding on the larvae of insects, especially wasps and bees that it digs up with its rather blunt claws and from which it is protected by the scaly head feathers. Also eats lizards, frogs, some mammals and birds.

DISTRIBUTION
A summer migrant to Scotland and a few other parts of Britain. In autumn, Scandinavian birds are sometimes seen along the east coast. Breeds in most of Europe and Russia, and winters in tropical and southern Africa.

RED KITE *MILVUS MILVUS*

juvenile

IDENTIFICATION
60–66 cm. Larger than Buzzard. Elegant and graceful bird of prey with long wings and long forked tail. Has a reddish-brown body with dark streaks, an orange-red tail and a pale streaked head. In flight, underwing is distinctive with black, fingered tips to wings, dark mark at bend in wings and pale patches. Female is larger than male. Juvenile has less distinct streaking on the body, pale brown undertail coverts (reddish in adults) and a thin white line along upperwing. Red Kites moult between May and the autumn, and at this time they may have some flight feathers that are noticeably shorter than others.
SEE ALSO: Buzzard p73, Marsh Harrier p74.

HABITS
Soars with an easy, buoyant flight, constantly changing the angle of its tail to steer, while hardly moving its wings. Often the long wings look angled, but are generally flat when gliding. Often seen singly or in pairs but larger gatherings occur at food supplies and communal roosts outside the nesting season.

VOICE
The call is a shrill, mewing 'peeee-ooow'.

juvenile

BREEDING
Nesting begins in March. The nest of large twigs is usually in the fork of a tree and may be 'decorated' with rags and plastic bags. Sometimes an old nest, such as a Buzzard's, is used. Nest may be used in successive years. Female incubates 2 eggs, with male taking short shifts. Young hatch after 31 days. They leave the nest after 45 days and sit in nearby trees, but it may be another 25 days before they fly properly, and their parents feed them for a further 15 days.

MOVEMENTS AND MIGRATIONS
Northern and eastern European populations are migratory, while those in Britain and southern Europe are largely sedentary. However, juvenile Scottish birds tend to disperse from their nesting areas and many move south of the border. Oldest bird was 25 years.

POPULATION
Approximately 120 pairs now nest in Scotland and the winter population may be as high as 350 individuals. The population is slowly growing. This species is vulnerable to human persecution from poison baits. Occasional migrants from Europe also visit eastern Scotland and the Northern Isles.

CONSERVATION
Specially protected at all times. Red Kites were once common throughout Britain, but persecution drove them to near extinction, with only a tiny population remaining in central Wales at the beginning of the 20th century. Legal protection helped a slow recovery, and from 1989 the species was reintroduced to Scotland, first to the Black Isle, then to the Stirling area and Dumfries & Galloway, and finally to Aberdeenshire. The current population is descended from these birds; although numbers are increasing slowly, the species' expansion into new areas is limited by illegal killing.

HABITAT
Breeds in mature but open woodlands, often nesting in Scots Pine or oak. It hunts over farmland, moorland and open areas, and may scavenge farmyards and roadside verges. Communal roosts form in some woodlands in winter. Elsewhere in Europe it frequents fringes of marshlands and rubbish dumps.

FOOD
Mainly eats carrion, including dead sheep. Also catches live prey by diving from the air or dropping from a post and catching its prey feet-first. Hunts invertebrates, including earthworms, mammals such as rats, mice, voles and small rabbits, a variety of birds including young crows, pigeons and, in southern Europe, reptiles.

DISTRIBUTION
Reintroduced to Scotland. Also breeds in Wales, England and Europe, from southern Sweden to the Mediterranean coast and east to the Ukraine. It is a little more widespread in southern Europe in winter.

BUZZARD *BUTEO BUTEO*

IDENTIFICATION
51–57 cm. Large thickset bird of prey with wide rounded head, short neck, broad rounded wings with 'fingered' ends and a rather short, broad tail. Female larger than male. Colour is very variable, but never has the dark bands in the wings or tail of Honey Buzzard. Common plumage medium-brown with a pale crescent on breast, browner wing linings and paler flight feathers. Upperwing is darker, more uniform brown. Buzzards hold their wings in a shallow 'V' when soaring and gliding. Juveniles are usually dark and streaky. Moult takes place between March and November. Female starts to lose flight feathers during incubation. Moulting Buzzards show obvious gaps in their wings.
SEE ALSO: Honey Buzzard p71, Golden Eagle p79.

juveniles

HABITS
Buzzards soar and glide with head hardly extending in front of the wings. Will hang in the air almost motionless looking for prey, and will also hover, with slower wingbeats than Kestrel. Also spends a lot of time perched in trees, on posts or on poles from where it can easily swoop down on prey. Hunts for worms on the ground. Usually seen singly or in pairs, although migrating birds may gather in larger numbers.

juvenile

VOICE
Call a mewing 'peee-uu', which may be heard at any time of year.

HABITAT
Resident in a wide variety of habitats: forest, woodlands, moorland, agricultural land and upland glens. Recently it has become more numerous in lowland areas, even quite close to cities such as Glasgow and Edinburgh.

FOOD
Small mammals, especially voles and Rabbits, birds such as young pigeons and crows, and also insects, reptiles, earthworms and carrion.

BREEDING
Nest made of sticks and lined with Bracken, moss and other softer materials. Often the same nest is added to year after year. Breeding begins in April or May. Both adults incubate the clutch of 2 or 3 eggs, but the female has the longest shifts, while the male provides most of the food. Eggs hatch after about 34 days. Incubation starts with the first egg, thus hatching is spread over about a week. As the young are of slightly different ages the smallest may not survive. Young fly at about 50 days and remain dependent on their parents for a further 40 days or more.

MOVEMENTS AND MIGRATIONS
Scottish birds are largely sedentary. Young will move away from their nest sites but generally do not travel far. On Shetland the species is seen only in spring and autumn, and these are assumed to be local movements of Scottish birds, although some from the Continent may occasionally reach Scotland in the autumn. Many Buzzards in eastern Europe and Russia are long-distance migrants, with many wintering in Africa. Maximum recorded age was 28 years.

POPULATION
There are thought to be 15,000–20,000 pairs nesting in Scotland, and the population has increased markedly in recent years.

CONSERVATION
Buzzards were once widespread in Scotland, but for much of the 19th and 20th centuries they were persecuted. It is only during the last 20 years, as changing attitudes to birds of prey have encouraged their spread, that they have started to repopulate old haunts and become more widespread again. Illegal poisoning is, however, still a problem in some places.

DISTRIBUTION
Widespread in all but the most mountainous areas in Scotland. Buzzards traditionally bred in northern and western Britain, although there has been a recolonisation of the eastern and central lowlands of the country. Outside the region they breed from the Arctic Circle south to the Mediterranean and across Asia. Some eastern races winter in Africa.

Marsh Harrier *CIRCUS AERUGINOSUS*

IDENTIFICATION
48–56 cm. Size of Buzzard but less bulky. Largest European harrier, with long, rather broad wings and long tail. Has slim body and long legs. Male has pale head streaked finely with dark brown, tri-coloured wings – brown with large grey patches and black wing-tips – and grey tail. Larger female is chocolate-brown with straw-coloured head and similar coloured leading edges to the wings. Juvenile resembles female but often lacks pale marks on wings and sometimes lacks pale head. Moult takes place between April and October. Flight feathers moulted gradually with female beginning before male. SEE ALSO: Red Kite p72, Hen Harrier p75, Buzzard p73.

HABITS
Whether hunting over a reedbed, or soaring and gliding at a greater height, wings are usually 'V'-shaped. Heavier-looking than other harriers. Before breeding, a pair will undertake aerial displays including a sky-dance comprising deep undulations, with male making mock attacks on female. Aerial food passes take place as male drops prey to the female that she catches in mid-air.

VOICE
Mostly silent, but during courtship displays the adults have wailing 'kweooo' call.

male

female

3rd-year

juvenile

male

female

HABITAT
Traditional breeding sites are in large reedbeds, but in recent years it has colonised smaller reedbeds and arable fields, especially winter-sown Wheat and Oilseed Rape close to feeding areas. Some migrants visit tropical marshes and swamps in winter, but on migration it may be seen in dryer places.

FOOD
Feeds mainly on animals that live in or near marshes and other wetlands. Drops onto its prey from the air. Chief food is small birds, ducklings, gamebird chicks and mammals, especially Rabbits.

BREEDING
Nesting begins in April. Female builds a nest from grass, reeds and small sticks, on the ground among thick marshy vegetation or in a crop, while male constructs one or more 'false nests' or platforms nearby. Eggs are laid at 2–3 day intervals. Female incubates clutch of 4 or 5 eggs and male brings her food. Incubation starts with the first egg, and as each egg takes 31–38 days to hatch the brood comprises unevenly aged young. Male continues to provide food and female feeds young until they have grown and scattered into surrounding vegetation. Young fly at about 35–40 days and female stays with them for a further 15–25 days.

MOVEMENTS AND MIGRATIONS
Northern and eastern populations migrate, while southern populations tend to be more sedentary. In Scotland, most birds are seen between April and September, the majority as passage migrants. Young birds disperse after fledging, and it is known that at least two from Scotland have reached West Africa. Maximum recorded age was 20 years.

POPULATION
The British population has been growing in recent years and the first successful nesting in Scotland took place in 1990. There are now 3–8 females producing young each year. Further growth in this population can now be anticipated.

CONSERVATION
Specially protected at all times. Drainage of wetlands and persecution reduced the number and range of this species in the past and it was down to one pair in England in 1971. Since then the protection of wetland sites has helped a recovery and also the birds started adopting arable fields as nest sites. With the co-operation of farmers, these nests have been generally safe and many young have fledged successfully.

DISTRIBUTION

In the British Isles most breed in eastern England, with small populations in suitable reedbed and sedge-bed habitats in northern England and Scotland. A growing number are now wintering in England. The species also breeds in Europe, from the Baltic south to Portugal and east into Russia and Asia. Many of the migrants from northern Europe winter in Africa.

HEN HARRIER CIRCUS CYANEUS

IDENTIFICATION
44–52 cm. Smaller than Buzzard. It has a long tail and long wings with 'fingered' tips. Male has silver-grey upperparts, white underparts, white rump, black wingtips and slight blackish trailing edge to wings that sometimes shows in flight, especially on underwing. Larger female is dark brown with buff marks on wing, grey-brown tail with darker bands and obvious white rump. Disc of stiffer feathers gives an 'owl-like' appearance to face. Underparts are paler and breast is heavily streaked. Juvenile is similar to female but with wing linings and breast more bright ginger brown. Moult takes place between April and October. Female starts first and gaps can sometimes be seen in the wing.
SEE ALSO: Marsh Harrier p74, Buzzard p73.

HABITS
Seen singly during the day but often gathers in communal winter roosts. Buoyant flight when hunting low over ground, with wings forming a shallow 'V' when gliding. In spring, male has a spectacular switchback sky-dance. He also makes food passes to the female by calling to her and either passing food in the air or dropping it for her to catch.

VOICE
Silent except when nesting when it makes rapid 'yikkering' call during sky-dance display and various other scolding calls.

HABITAT
In Scotland, the Hen Harrier breeds on upland heather moors, young conifer plantations and extensive sheep walks. In winter, it visits lowland farms, bogs and coastal marshes, and can be found at communal roosts, usually in reedbeds or fens.

FOOD
Feeds on small birds, such as Meadow Pipits, also voles and mice. Larger prey, such as Rabbits, hares, young waders and gamebirds, may also be taken.

BREEDING
Nesting begins in April. Nests are usually spaced out, but where a male is mated to more than one female, several nests may be in relatively close proximity. Nest is a pile of local vegetation, generally heather, that is built among low, dense vegetation. Female incubates 4 or 5 eggs for about 34 days. Eggs are laid at 1–3 day intervals and there is a noticeable age difference between the young. For the first 10–15 days the female tends the chicks and the male provides food. Later the female helps with hunting. Young fly at 37–42 days and they remain with female for several more weeks.

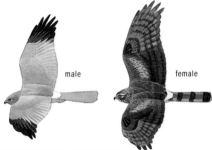

male   female

MOVEMENTS AND MIGRATIONS
It is a migrant in the north and east of Europe. In Scotland it moves from high ground after nesting, and juveniles move further than adults. Many juvenile males cross the border and winter in England or Ireland, with some reaching France, Spain or Portugal. Females and adults tend not to travel as far, and the majority remain in Scotland. Oldest bird was over 17 years.

POPULATION
There are around 600 pairs in Scotland. The population is increasing in the north and west, but is decreasing in the east and in the Southern Uplands owing to illegal killing, particularly on driven grouse moors.

CONSERVATION
Specially protected at all times. As a result of persecution in the 19th century almost exterminated from Britain, but remained in Orkney and some other remote Scottish sites, and Ireland. Has since made a gradual comeback, but still faces illegal persecution on land where there is game shooting. In most European countries Hen Harrier populations are declining owing to habitat loss.

juvenile

female

DISTRIBUTION
Present all year. Breeds in upland areas of Scotland, parts of northern England, Isle of Man, North Wales and Ireland. In winter, it is more widespread. It also breeds from Scandinavia south to Portugal and across much of Asia. There is another race of Hen Harrier in North America.

GOSHAWK ACCIPITER GENTILIS

IDENTIFICATION
48–62 cm. Female almost the size of Buzzard; male is smaller. Looks like huge Sparrowhawk, having round-ed wings, but tail is relatively shorter and rounded at edges, not cut square across tip. Male is grey-brown above with dark patch behind eye giving hooded appearance. Close to, yellow eyes and white 'eyebrow' create fierce expression. Under-parts pale and closely barred, and tail also barred. Female is browner than male. Juvenile has a buff, streaked breast. Moults between April and September, with female starting first.
SEE ALSO: Sparrowhawk p77, Buzzard p73, Hen Harrier p75.

juvenile

juvenile female

HABITS
In flight, appears deep-chested and powerful, with proportionally short wings. Except when nesting, it is generally solitary. An elusive species, but can be seen soaring over its nest site in early spring. When soaring, the wings are held flat with three or four feathers visi-ble at the wing-tip. Secondary flight feathers are long and bulge, giving an 'S' curve to the rear wing. It can point its wing-tips and look remarkably Peregrine-like. Displaying birds have a sky-dance that involves spreading the white undertail feathers, flapping very slowly on straight wings and, eventually, rising and falling dramatically. Female does the majority of sky-dancing. When hunting, it is remarkably agile and weaves through stands of trees.

male

VOICE
Most calls are heard close to the nest or when displaying. The most frequent is 'gek-gek-gek', which is also given when birds are alarmed.

HABITAT
Lives and nests in large mature woods and forests. Inhabits both coniferous and deciduous woodland, but also hunts in open countryside.

FOOD
The Goshawk will use cover to surprise its prey. It makes a rapid chase over a short distance and grasps its quarry in its talons. Will also stoop like a Peregrine to gain speed before attacking. It feeds on birds such as Jays, Woodpigeons, crows, Pheasants, Starlings and thrushes. It also kills mammals such as Rabbits.

BREEDING
Nesting begins in March or April. A nest of twigs and branches, lined with bark and pine needles, is built in the fork of a large tree, although nests from previous years are often re-used. Female incubates the 3 or 4 eggs for 35–38 days and broods the young for their first 8–10 days. She will fiercely attack any potential pred-ators – including humans and male Goshawks. Young stay in the nest for about 35 days before moving onto nearby branches for a further 10 days, by which time they are able to fly.

MOVEMENTS AND MIGRATIONS
Most Scottish Goshawks do not move far from their breeding sites. Young birds disperse in all directions in late summer, with females tending to move further than males. Some northern populations move south for the winter, and it is possible a few from

Scandinavia occasionally reach Scotland. Oldest ringed bird was 18 years.

POPULATION
It is estimated there may be 130 pairs in Scotland.

CONSERVATION
Specially protected at all times. As a result of persecution and reduction of forests the Goshawk became extinct as a breeding species in Britain at the end of the 1800s. The current breeding population originates from birds that escaped from captivity. The colonisation has been ham-pered by the theft of eggs and young and by illegal per-secution, but the establishment of coniferous forests and their subsequent management by the Forestry Commission has helped this species enormously.

DISTRIBUTION

In Scotland the species is widely but thinly distributed. Greatest numbers are in the east and the south, where it is associated with large stands of mature conifer forest that lie close to open ground used for hunting. It is also found south of the border in England and Wales. It breeds across Europe and Russia, and there are other races, includ-ing one in North America.

SPARROWHAWK *ACCIPITER NISUS*

IDENTIFICATION
28–38 cm. Male is smaller than a Kestrel. Sparrowhawks are small, fast-flying birds of prey with long, square-ended tails and broad, rounded wings. Male has a slate-grey back and reddish, barred underparts that can appear orange at a distance. Grey tail crossed with 4–5 dark bars. Female much larger (25% bigger), heavier-looking with brown upperparts and paler barred underparts, white stripe over the eye and fierce expression. Juvenile has reddish-brown upperparts and ragged bars on breast. Moult is between May and October, but may be suspended while young are being fed.
SEE ALSO: Goshawk p76, Kestrel p80.

HABITS
Secretive and usually solitary. Sometimes seen displaying over its nest site as it soars on broad, outstretched wings. When displaying in spring, birds often flap their wings slowly and deliberately as they undulate across the sky. They also close their tail feathers and stick out their pale undertail coverts. These soaring displays may culminate in a spectacular dive with closed wings. In level flight it alternates rapid, flappy wingbeats with a long glide. Takes its prey by surprise, by watching, waiting and attacking swiftly – grasping prey with its foot. Often uses the same flight-path when hunting and, sometimes, dashes along a hedgerow, silently slipping over the top, to startle a flock of small birds on the other side.

female

male

juvenile
male

VOICE
Silent for most of the year. When nesting, most common call is a shrill 'ke-ke-ke-ke'.

HABITAT
Breeds in conifer, deciduous or mixed woodlands, but tends to prefer conifer. Sometimes occupies small woodlands and overgrown gardens in urban areas. Hunts along woodland edges, in open countryside and in coastal areas where prey is available.

FOOD
Mainly birds. Male specialises in taking smaller species such as Chaffinch, Yellowhammer and Great Tit. Female takes larger species such as Blackbird and Starling. Birds up to the size of Woodpigeon may be caught and killed.

BREEDING
New nests of twigs and sticks are built each year in a fork of a deciduous tree or near the trunk of a conifer. Egg-laying begins in late April or May and incubation of the 4 or 5 eggs is carried out by female for 32–36 days.

During incubation male supplies female with food. As young grow female also helps supply them with food. At about 28 days they leave the nest and sit in nearby branches until they fly a few days later. They depend on their parents for a further 20 days until they can hunt and feed themselves.

MOVEMENTS AND MIGRATIONS
In the British Isles it is largely resident. In northern and eastern Europe the species is a migrant, with many moving south in winter. Some, especially from Norway and Denmark, cross the North Sea and are seen in the Northern Isles and eastern Scotland in both spring and autumn. Oldest bird was 20 years.

POPULATION
There are thought to be 8,000–12,000 pairs breeding in Scotland. After a sharp decline in the 20th century there was a dramatic increase, but numbers have recently tended to decline again, especially in intensively farmed arable areas.

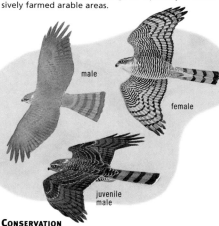

male

female

juvenile
male

CONSERVATION
Once common, the Sparrowhawk was first persecuted by gamekeepers and then suffered from agricultural pesticides. Following the phasing out of such pesticides by the 1980s numbers increased, and the planting of shelter belts and upland areas with conifers provided new nesting habitat. Declines in small bird populations now limit its numbers, although individuals that have moved into urban areas may be faring rather better.

DISTRIBUTION

Throughout Britain and Ireland, except in the most mountainous areas or on the most intensive farmland. Also breeds in Europe, from the Mediterranean to the far north of Scandinavia, and also in Asia.

WHITE-TAILED EAGLE   *HALIAEETUS ALBICILLA*

juvenile

IDENTIFICATION
70–90 cm. Heavier and more bulky than Golden Eagle. Wings are broad, rectangular-looking (like planks!) with obvious 'fingered' tips. Tail short and wedge-shaped. Neck long and strong, with large head and huge powerful bill that is usually obvious, even in flight. Adults are dark with pale heads and white tails. Males are smaller, lighter and with smaller bills than females. Young birds lack pale head and the white tail. Juvenile is dark with streaked underparts and darker head and tail. Second-year birds have paler bellies and third-year birds are darker. It has four or five body moults before reaching adult plumage. Only a proportion of the flight feathers are moulted each year. Moults more or less continuously, though it may pause in winter if food is in short supply.
SEE ALSO: Golden Eagle p79, Osprey p83.

HABITS
Flight is Heron-like, with shallow flaps and glides at low levels; at higher levels it soars with wings held flat. It is usually seen singly or in pairs and spends a lot of time perched, standing on the ground, or even standing in shallow water. In late winter and early spring pairs may be seen in display: 'sky-dancing', with gentle undulations, rolling and sometimes touching talons in flight.

juvenile

3rd/4th-cal-year

VOICE
It makes dog-like yapping, high-pitched woodpecker-like 'kew, kew, kew, kew' and a quieter 'ko-ko ko'. Most calls are made near the nest or during courtship.

HABITAT
A bird of rocky coasts, estuaries, marshes and lochs near the sea. Since its reintroduction it has nested on cliffs and in mature woodlands. After nesting, young may be found away from breeding areas, and even on farmland.

FOOD
Hunts singly or in pairs and often robs other birds of their prey. Will grab food from the surface of the water and sometimes dives in. Eats Cod, Herring, trout and Eels. Also kills other birds, especially gulls, ducks and auks, and takes Rabbits, hares and other mammals. Carrion is commonly eaten. These eagles will take advantage of food supplies from abattoirs and discarded fish from fishing boats.

BREEDING
A pair selects one of several traditional nest sites within a home range. Nests are built from large sticks and driftwood, and lined with grass, seaweed and sometimes wool. Some nests are used for many years and reach a huge size as material is added year after year. 1–3 (usually 2) eggs are laid in late March or April and most incubation is by female. Young hatch after 40 days and are fed by both parents. They fly after 70 days. Once independent, the immatures roam widely and may join other youngsters at good feeding areas.

MOVEMENTS AND MIGRATIONS
Resident in Scotland, but young birds may roam widely and be seen almost anywhere in the UK. A small number of birds from Scandinavia may visit Scotland in winter. Oldest known bird survived 28 years.

POPULATION
There were massive declines in European White-tailed Eagle populations during the 19th and 20th centuries, and the species was driven to extinction in 1916. However, there have also been some local recoveries. A reintroduction programme on the west coast of Scotland has been successful, and the population now numbers around 40 pairs and is slowly increasing.

CONSERVATION
Specially protected. In Scotland, most sites are kept secret for fear of attracting egg collectors or disturbance by birdwatchers. Poison baits have accidentally or deliberately killed some of these birds. In Europe a build up of organochlorine chemicals in the bird's diet has affected breeding success.

DISTRIBUTION
Mull, Skye and parts of the north-west Highlands provide the best chance of seeing the species in Scotland. The species also breeds in northern Europe and Asia. In Europe the largest population is in Norway.

IDENTIFICATION

75–88 cm. Much larger than Buzzard, with powerful bill. Adult uniform dark brown with golden yellow feathers on back of head. Sexes look similar, but female is larger. In flight, wings are long and broad, and trailing edges bulge out. Tail looks longer than that of a Buzzard and head protrudes prominently in front of the wings. Juvenile is darker with white base to the tail, black terminal band and white wing patches. Immature shows whitish tail with dark band and varying amounts of white at base of flight feathers. Golden Eagles moult slowly and some feathers are retained for 2 years. Outer flight feathers are replaced more frequently than inner flight feathers. It takes 7 years to attain full adult plumage SEE ALSO: Buzzard p73, White-tailed Eagle p78.

HABITS

Usually seen singly or in pairs. The huge 2 m wingspan is almost twice that of the Buzzard. On take-off, when carrying prey and in display, flight is slow and laboured with deep wingbeats. Mostly it soars and glides effortlessly using air currents. At these times wings form a shallow 'V' and 'fingered' wing-tips are obvious. Displaying birds circle high up – almost touching – and will fold wings and plunge dramatically before repeating this in a series of loops.

VOICE

Generally silent, but sometimes makes a 'yelping' call.

HABITAT

In Scotland lives in wild, open countryside, high moorlands, rugged mountains and remote islands. Outside Scotland it breeds in mountain ranges, except those covered with dense forests, and also in flatter habitats where there are trees for nesting.

FOOD

Includes birds such as grouse, crows, seabirds and wildfowl, and also mammals varying in size from voles to young Otters and Foxes. Deer and sheep are also eaten, though generally as carrion.

juvenile

BREEDING

Nest, or eyrie, is built of sticks and small branches on a cliff ledge or in a mature tree. Old nests are re-used and new material added each year. Clutch of 1–3 eggs is laid in late March or early April. Incubation mostly by female and generally starts with the first egg leading to a noticeable size difference between chicks. The eggs hatch after 43–45 days. While two chicks frequently hatch, it is not uncommon for the older and larger to kill the younger. Both adults provide food and the young fly from about 65 days, but they depend on their parents for a further 90 days or more.

MOVEMENTS AND MIGRATIONS

Young eagles leaving their nest sites range more widely than adults and there is a tendency for most to head east. Adult Golden Eagles in Scotland seldom move far from their territories, but other more northerly populations leave their breeding grounds in autumn and return the following spring. The oldest ringed Golden Eagle survived for over 32 years.

POPULATION

There are 440 territories in Scotland. High densities are found on Mull, Skye and the Western Isles where deer and sheep carrion can be abundant.

CONSERVATION

Specially protected. Historically it was more widespread, breeding in England, Wales and Ireland. The decline was caused largely by persecution. Current problems include lack of food due to overgrazing by sheep and deer, and afforestation of its upland hunting grounds. Birds in the west generally produce fewer young. It also suffers from attacks by egg thieves and poisoning and illegal killing. Windfarms pose a new risk.

DISTRIBUTION

In Britain the Golden Eagle breeds mainly in the Scottish Highlands and Islands. In Europe it breeds from Scandinavia to the Pyrenees and other races are found in southern Europe, North Africa, Asia and North America.

KESTREL *FALCO TINNUNCULUS*

male

female

IDENTIFICATION
32–35 cm. Small bird of prey with short neck, long wings and long tail. Frequently hovers when hunting. Male has spotted, reddish-brown back, grey head and tail and buff underparts with dark spots. It has a black band at the end of its tail. Female slightly larger and browner with variable pattern of black bars on upperparts and pale breast with dark streaks. Juvenile resembles female, but more boldly streaked below and with broader dark bars on back. Moult lasts almost all year. Main flight feathers are lost gradually between May and September. Feathers are moulted in a sequence, but the most noticeable gaps appear in August and September.
SEE ALSO: Sparrowhawk p77, Hobby p245, Merlin p81.

HABITS
Usually seen singly. Hunts during daylight and also during and after dusk. When hunting it will either hover effortlessly, with tail fanned and wings beating rapidly, or hang motionless, supported by the wind. Also hunts from a prominent perch such as a telegraph pole, or sometimes chases small birds. When soaring, wings appear more rounded at the tips and tail is fanned.

female soaring

male

male hovering

VOICE
Usually silent. Most common call is a shrill 'kee-kee-kee' that is most usually heard near the nest.

HABITAT
Found in a variety of habitats, especially moorland, upland pastures, sea cliffs and farmland. In some places it has moved into towns and cities. Frequently hunts over rough grass in young conifer plantations and beside roads and railways.

FOOD
Mainly small mammals, especially Short-tailed Voles. Other mammals include shrews, mice and occasionally larger prey such as Moles and Rabbits. Larks, pipits and Starlings are commonly caught and larger birds such as Blackbirds and Collared Doves are also hunted. Kestrels regularly eat beetles, other insects and worms.

BREEDING
Does not build a nest, but scrapes a depression for its eggs. Uses cliff-ledges or buildings, holes in trees and disused nests of large birds. Breeding begins in February with aerial, territorial displays. Female incubates 4 or 5 eggs, the male sometimes taking a turn. Young hatch after 28–29 days. For the first 10–14 days they are brooded by the female and then both parents feed them. The young fly after 32–37 days, but rely on their parents for a further month.

MOVEMENTS AND MIGRATIONS
Once independent, young Kestrels move away from their nest site. Northern-bred birds tend to travel furthest, with many reaching southern England, Ireland or France. Adults of northerly and upland populations, where there is winter snow, are more likely to migrate south in autumn, and some from Scandinavia reach Scotland between August and October. Oldest known Kestrel lived for 16 years.

POPULATION
Around 7,500 pairs nest in Scotland. The population appeared largely stable for most of the 20th century, with fluctuations due to the changing density of vole populations. However, since about 1994 the Kestrel population has fallen, possibly by as much as 30%.

CONSERVATION
The decline of the Kestrel has been linked to similar declines of other species that depend on agricultural land. Although the causes are not fully understood, the more intensive management of grassland, with fewer areas supporting voles, more widespread use of insecticides and the loss of wide field margins mean that small mammal populations have reduced. Schemes aimed at restoring permanent meadows, providing beetle banks and restoring field margins may be helping.

DISTRIBUTION

Found throughout most of Britain and Ireland although scarce in north-west Scotland and in higher mountains. Also found in most of Europe, Africa and Asia.

MERLIN *FALCO COLUMBARIUS*

IDENTIFICATION
25–30 cm. Smaller than Kestrel. Our smallest falcon, with short, broad-based, pointed wings and shorter tail than Kestrel. When perched, wing-tips reach about three-quarters along the tail length. Male has blue-grey back, rusty breast with dark streaks and very dark primary flight feathers. Cheeks and nape are rufous. Female larger and browner with pale buff breast streaked heavily with brown and barred tail. Juvenile resembles dark female and has white flecks on nape. Moults between June and September. Female moults earlier than male. SEE ALSO: Kestrel p80.

provides the food. At about 18 days the young leave the ground nests and crouch in the surrounding heather. They can fly after about 32 days and depend on their parents for food for a further month.

MOVEMENTS AND MIGRATIONS
Many Scottish Merlins move away from their breeding areas in autumn, visiting lowland and coastal areas. Icelandic and Scandinavian birds are seen in the autumn, particularly in the Northern Isles. Some Scottish birds move to England or Ireland and a few reach the Continent. Oldest Merlin lived for 12 years.

male

female

male

female

HABITS
Usually a solitary species although occasionally two birds will hunt in unison. Small and compact-looking predator, male not much bigger than a Mistle Thrush, but with direct and dashing flight. Rapid wingbeats are followed by short glides – often low to ground. Chases small birds with agile twists and turns. Regularly perches on posts, walls and boulders. Occasionally has been seen to surprise its prey by approaching on foot.

VOICE
Usually silent, but near a nest the shrill 'kek-kek-kek-kek' call may be heard when the bird is excited or is chasing off intruders such as crows.

HABITAT
Breeds mainly on ground on heather moorland in uplands and in some coastal areas. Increasingly nests in the fringes of maturing conifer plantations. In winter, moves to lowland areas, particularly coastal salt marshes and farmland. In Canada has recently colonised several cities where it breeds in the old nests of crows.

FOOD
Mainly small birds such as Meadow Pipit, Skylark, Chaffinch and Wheatear. Also takes larger birds such as Mistle Thrush. Other food includes voles, bats, moths and beetles.

BREEDING
Traditionally Merlins in Britain nested on the ground among heather, but in recent years increasing numbers of tree nests have been found, usually in old crow nests on the edge of conifer plantations. The clutch of 3–5 eggs is incubated by male and female for 28–32 days. At first the female tends young and the male

POPULATION
There are around 800 pairs nesting in Scotland. The population is mostly stable, or increasing in some areas. Most birds nest in mature heather on open hillsides.

CONSERVATION
The Merlin is specially protected at all times. There has been a historical decline in its population. The population is now stable or increasing due to reduced persecution and fewer environmental pollutants used in agriculture. However, many of its former breeding sites are now planted with commercial forests and much heather moorland is lost. Quality of moorland is affected by overgrazing. Some pairs have adapted to artificial nests in trees.

DISTRIBUTION
The Merlin breeds in the uplands in the north and west of Britain, and also parts of Ireland. In winter it has a wider distribution and regularly visits lowland farms and coastal marshes. The species also breeds in northern Europe, Asia and North America. It winters in central and southern Europe, and in North Africa.

PEREGRINE *FALCO PEREGRINUS*

IDENTIFICATION
36–48 cm. Large and powerful falcon with long, broad-based, pointed wings and relatively short tail. Adult has blue-grey upperparts and dark blue wings and head. The crown is blackish and it has a conspicuous black moustache contrasting with white face, giving it a hooded look. Pale breast finely spotted and underwing barred. Female is noticeably larger. Juvenile has dark brown upperparts with pale tips to feathers, streaks on underparts and broad buff tip to tail. Moult takes place between April and November, but may be suspended while adults are feeding young.
SEE ALSO: Hobby p245.

juvenile

HABITS
Away from nest it is usually solitary. Swift and agile in flight with fast wingbeats and long glides. Chases prey and attacks it from below or will spot prey a long way off, rise very high and fly fast towards it, dropping (stooping) with wings folded to increase momentum. Soars with wing-tips slightly splayed.

VOICE
Usually silent, but may be noisy at nest. If female is disturbed she produces a grating, 'scraa, scraa, scraa', often building to a crescendo. Male's call is higher.

HABITAT
A bird of open country. Nests on crags or other rock faces, sea-cliffs, offshore islands, quarries and, increasingly, on buildings in towns. Hunts over marshes, estuaries and agricultural land outside the breeding season.

FOOD
Feeds mainly on birds captured in flight, either by out-flying them, or stooping on them. Feral Pigeon, Wood-pigeon, Lapwing, Black-headed Gull, Blackbird and Starling are among the prey, but mammals, such as Rabbits, are occasionally taken and carrion is eaten during extreme weather conditions. Coastal nesters will take seabirds.

BREEDING
Some nest sites have been used for hundreds of years. They are usually on ledges of cliffs, although old crow's nests in trees may be used. Pairs return in February and perform breathtaking aerobatics as they plunge, dive, roll and stoop. Male supplies female with food, sometimes dropping prey that she catches in flight. The 3 or 4 eggs are laid in March or April. Incubation is mostly by female and lasts 28–33 days. At first young are tended by female while male provides food, as they grow both adults hunt. Young fly after 39 days and gradually become independent.

MOVEMENTS AND MIGRATIONS
Most Peregrines move away from their nesting sites after the young fledge, but many do not travel far and very few leave Scotland. Those that leave may reach England, Ireland and Wales. Some from northern England winter in Scotland and others arrive from Scandinavia. Peregrines from northern Europe may be long-distance migrants, with some reaching Africa for the winter. The oldest wild Peregrine survived for 17 years.

POPULATION
Following a decline in the Peregrine population in the 20th century, there has been a welcome recovery and around 600 pairs now breed in Scotland. However, from a peak in the 1990s there appears to have been another decline in some localities, particularly in the northern highlands.

CONSERVATION
Historically, the Peregrine was prized for falconry, but has also been persecuted by gamekeepers and landowners and became a target for egg thieves. It was killed during World War II to protect homing pigeons and suffered disastrously from the effects of agricultural insecticides. Control of chemicals and legal protection have helped it partly to recover, but the species remains at risk across much of Europe. There also remains the threat of continuing illegal persecution on some sporting estates.

juvenile

DISTRIBUTION
The Peregrine's stronghold in Britain is the uplands of the north and west, especially the Scottish uplands and rocky sea coasts. Recently the English south coast has been re-occupied in places. Peregrines now breed on buildings in some towns and cities. In winter it visits many lowland areas although still most frequent in the west. Elsewhere, other races are found in rocky or coastal areas in Europe, Africa, Asia, America and Australia.

OSPREY *PANDION HALIAETUS*

IDENTIFICATION
55–58 cm. Slightly longer bodied than Buzzard but has much longer wings – looking almost gull-like at times. Light brown breast-band, clean white underparts and wing linings and a dark patch at bend of wings. Tail is short, dark above and barred below. Adult has uniform brown upperparts and a white head with a thick black stripe through and behind its yellow eye. Juveniles have buff tip to their brown feathers giving a scaly appearance. Annual moult begins in June, but is 'suspended' for annual migration and then continued in Africa.
SEE ALSO: Buzzard p73.

HABITS
Generally seen singly except at nest. Often perches near feeding areas, favouring dead branches or a post in the water. In flight, long wings often appear kinked at the joint. When hunting for fish it half folds up the wings and hurtles into the water, stretching its legs out in front to grasp the prey. It can also grab fish quickly from the water's surface. It carries its prey head first to limit air resistance.

juvenile

VOICE
Usually silent but near the nest a shrill 'pieu-pieu-pieu'.

HABITAT
Lives near inland lochs, large rivers, coastal lagoons and estuaries. In Britain associated with places that have both lakes for feeding and mature trees for nesting. In winter, in Africa also inhabits coastal regions.

FOOD
Although a few small mammals, reptiles and amphibians are taken the vast majority of food is fish. Among the fish it catches are Perch, Pike, trout and Salmon.

BREEDING
Male generally returns to the nest site first. When female returns he performs an aerial switch-backing display. In Britain the nest of sticks is usually built in a tree, but in other parts of its range it will nest on cliffs and man-made structures such as pylons. The 2 or 3 eggs are laid in April. Female mostly incubates the eggs, with male taking occasional turns. Incubation begins with the first egg. Young hatch after about 37 days and are fed by both adults. They fly at about 50 days, but depend on their parents for a further month or two before beginning their migration.

MOVEMENTS AND MIGRATIONS
They leave their breeding grounds in mid-August and head south on a broad front. They will stop at good feeding areas and reach their African winter quarters in late September. Adults return the following March, young may remain in Africa or follow more slowly. The oldest known Osprey was 26 years old.

POPULATION
Almost 200 pairs are currently nesting (or attempting to nest) in Scotland, a remarkable increase in the last 50 years. The species' numbers and range continue to expand.

CONSERVATION
Specially protected. Once relatively common, it was exterminated in Britain by 1916. It returned and, despite robbery by egg-thieves, it eventually re-established itself on Speyside, thanks to round-the-clock protection by the RSPB. Secret sites, helpful landowners, artificial nests and hard work by volunteers and professional conservationists all contributed to the re-colonisation.

DISTRIBUTION
Migrating Ospreys stop and feed at suitable habitats almost anywhere, especially at reservoirs and large lochs. They breed in central and northern Scotland, with a few pairs in Dumfries & Galloway, and some now also breed in England and Wales. The species nests from Scandinavia south to the Mediterranean, across Asia, in Australia and in North and Central America. European birds winter in tropical Africa.

WATER RAIL *RALLUS AQUATICUS*

IDENTIFICATION
23–28 cm. Smaller than Moorhen. Upperparts streaky brown, underparts blue-grey, grey and white barring on the flanks and white under the tail. Bill is long and red. Long legs and toes trail in flight. Juvenile has a browner face with a pale stripe over the eye, paler, more mottled underparts with no blue-grey, a pale throat and dark bill. After nesting, adults undergo their annual moult. Flight feathers are lost simultaneously and they are flightless for about 3 weeks.
SEE ALSO: Moorhen p86, Spotted Crake p85.

HABITS
Usually shy and skulking, and more often heard than seen, but sometimes in winter, or where it becomes used to people, it can be surprisingly confiding. Usually solitary outside the breeding season and defends a winter territory. Its slim body allows it to slip through dense waterside vegetation. Walks cautiously, flicking its tail when alarmed and will run, head-down, for cover. Frequently swims over short distances. Flight appears weak and fluttering on rather long wings.

juvenile

VOICE
Makes a variety of grunts and squeals during the day and night, especially when nesting. Most obvious call is a drawn out, squealing shriek rather like a piglet.

HABITAT
Breeds in dense reedbeds and marshes with thick, low cover and some open muddy areas. Also found alongside rivers, around the edges of lochs and ponds and, in winter, in ditches and other wet places. Usually associated with fresh water, but will visit brackish lagoons and salt marshes.

FOOD
Feeds in the water and on land. Catches small fish, freshwater shrimps, frogs, small snails, insects and their larvae. Eats berries and other fruit, and shoots

downy young

and roots of plants such as Watercress. Will catch and eat small birds and it also eats carrion.

BREEDING
Nest is on ground amongst dense vegetation close to water. The 6–11 eggs are laid between March and June. Incubation is for 19–22 days by both parents, although the female takes the largest share. Young are brooded in the nest for a few days and fed by both parents. Once out of the nest they soon feed themselves. They fly at 20–30 days and become independent after about 55 days. A second brood is normal, with breeding often continuing into August.

MOVEMENTS AND MIGRATIONS
Its secretive nature makes this a difficult species to study. Mostly resident, although upland breeders move to lowlands for the winter. Some Scottish birds may move south of the border and migrants from Scandinavia arrive in autumn, either to join the Scottish wintering population or to pass through and winter further south in England or Ireland. Oldest ringed bird lived for over 8 years.

POPULATION
A very difficult species to census. It is estimated that there may be 1,250–1,400 pairs breeding in Scotland and up to 3,000 present in winter. The Scottish population appears stable, although the species is declining elsewhere in its range.

CONSERVATION
Once common, but drainage of marshes and fens and loss of vegetation along waterways has reduced its numbers. It is adversely affected by severe winters that freeze shallow water, and dry summers may also present problems. Conversely, changing water levels during wet summers destroy active nests. Recent initiatives by the RSPB and other conservation organisations to protect and enlarge reedbeds should assist this species.

DISTRIBUTION

Thinly distributed in Scotland, mostly in the south and east. More common in Ireland and lowland England and Wales, and especially in East Anglia. Breeds in Europe, from Scandinavia south to the Mediterranean and east into Russia. Also found in Asia and North Africa.

SPOTTED CRAKE PORZANA PORZANA

IDENTIFICATION
22–24 cm. Similar size to a Starling. This small marsh bird has a green-brown back with dark streaks and white flecks and spots, and blue-grey on the face and throat. The olive-brown breast is covered in pearl-like white spots. The flanks are barred black and white, it has orange feathers under the tail, fine lines at the tips of the folded wings and the leading edge of the outer flight feather is white. The bill is dull yellow with a red spot at the base. The female resembles the male, but is slightly smaller. The juvenile has a pale stripe over the eye, lacks any blue-grey, has no black between eye and bill and has a pale throat and browner breast. Adults moult completely after breeding, and lose all flight feathers. Juveniles start by moulting the head and body, but can suspend this moult while they migrate.
SEE ALSO: Moorhen p86, Water Rail p84.

HABITS
This secretive species skulks in dense vegetation, but some birds can be confiding, especially juveniles in autumn. It is most active at dawn and dusk. If surprised in the open it will run for cover or spring up and fly with dangling legs and fluttering flight before dropping into cover. Usually seen singly. It walks with legs bent, body close to the ground and tail flicking nervously. It swims with an action rather like a Moorhen.

days they leave the nest and feed themselves. They fly after 25 days. There may be two broods in a year.

MOVEMENTS AND MIGRATIONS
Spotted Crakes are summer migrants to Scotland. Most arrive in April or May and leave between mid-July and November. At times of migration, especially in late summer, migrants from Scandinavia may arrive in the Northern Isles and around the Scottish coast. Oldest known bird was 7 years.

POPULATION
There are generally thought to be up to 15 calling males in appropriate breeding habitat in Scotland each year, but a detailed survey in 1999 found 33 birds, more than half of the British total. Always rare and difficult to census as it calls at night, the species declined in late 18th and early 19th centuries, but may now be increasing again.

CONSERVATION
The Spotted Crake is specially protected. Most of the marshes that it breeds on are nature reserves and the plans by the RSPB and other conservation bodies to re-create large fens may help this species in future.

male

female

juvenile

male

VOICE
Usually silent during the day, but adults call at dusk and throughout the night. The call is a rapid 'whit, whit', repeated at approximately 1-second intervals and likened to a whip cutting through the air.

HABITAT
Breeds in large freshwater marshes and other wetlands with shallow water and dense vegetation. On migration and in winter it visits similar habitats where it may be found feeding along muddy wetland margins.

FOOD
Among the wide variety of small prey items are insects such as caddisflies, beetles (including water beetles) and moth larvae. It also eats small water snails, fish and worms. Plant material such as seeds, shoots and roots of rushes and rice are also eaten.

BREEDING
The nest is on the ground near water. Both adults incubate the 10–12 eggs for 18–19 days. Young remain in the nest until all the eggs have hatched. After a few

DISTRIBUTION
This species is widely distributed in Britain, with most Scottish breeding attempts being in the north and in the Hebrides. Others breed in southern and eastern England. In autumn, migrants may be widely scattered. It breeds from northern Europe to the Mediterranean and also in parts of Africa and Asia. Migrants from Europe winter in central and eastern Africa.

MOORHEN GALLINULA CHLOROPUS

IDENTIFICATION
32–35 cm. Smaller than Coot. From a distance appears black with a ragged white line along its body, but the back is olive-brown and the head and underparts are blue-grey. Bill is red with a yellow tip and it has a red 'shield' on its forehead. Long legs and toes are yellowish green. Under its tail it has white feathers divided by a black line. Juvenile is dark brown with a pale throat and chin and a less obvious line along its body. The body feathers are moulted between May and November. Flight feathers are lost simultaneously and birds are flightless for a short time between June and August. SEE ALSO: Coot p87, Water Rail p85, Corncrake p88.

HABITS
Constantly flicks its tail as it walks or swims, revealing white undertail feathers. When taking off it runs across the water, trailing its legs as it takes to the air. Once airborne, the legs protrude beyond the tail. It uses its long toes to clamber around in vegetation and it often roosts in trees and bushes. Swims with a distinctive pumping motion and sometimes dives to escape danger. Seen singly or in family groups in summer, but larger groups sometimes form in winter.

VOICE
Wide range of calls, the most familiar being a loud, abrupt 'kurr-uk' that seems to echo across the water. It makes other harsh, croaking calls.

HABITAT
Typically breeds around freshwater lochs, slow-flowing rivers and streams, and in ditches and small ponds. Also found in town parks, farmland and, sometimes, on coastal marshes and other water bodies.

FOOD
Eats both plant and animal material, feeding on land and in water. Plant food includes duckweed, pondweed, seeds from sedges, docks and buttercup and also berries from Blackberry, rose and Elder. Animal food includes worms, snails, spiders, insects, small fish and eggs of other birds.

BREEDING
Breeds between March and August. Both parents build the nest among aquatic plants in or near water. It consists of dead reeds and other vegetation. Occasionally it nests in bushes. Both birds incubate the 5–7 eggs for about 21 days. It is not uncommon for two, sometimes three or four, females to lay in one nest. Young are fed by the parents and also by young of earlier broods. By 25 days they can feed themselves, but continue to be fed by their parents until they fly at about 45 days. They become independent between 52 and 99 days. There may be two or three broods.

MOVEMENTS AND MIGRATIONS
There is some movement away from upland nesting sites in autumn, presumably to lowlands, but most Scottish birds do not travel far from their breeding areas. Moorhens from northern and eastern Europe mostly migrate south-west in autumn; some of these birds reach Scotland between October and November, leaving again in April. Oldest bird survived 18 years.

1st-winter

juvenile

POPULATION
The breeding population has been estimated at 10,000–25,000. In Britain as a whole it is increasing, but there are some indications of a slight decline in parts of Scotland.

CONSERVATION
Threats come from the methods of managing waterways that often remove bankside vegetation. Maintenance of channels and banks needs to be on a rotation, where some vegetated areas are left uncut, to allow Moorhens and other wildlife feeding and nesting sites. Feral Mink may also be a threat to local populations.

DISTRIBUTION
In Scotland the species is found mainly in lowlands of the south and east, and is scarce elsewhere. It is common in the rest of Britain and Ireland. Moorhens are widely distributed throughout the world, being found across Europe and North Africa and east to Japan. Subspecies are present in North and South America.

COOT *FULICA ATRA*

IDENTIFICATION
36–38 cm. Larger than Moorhen. Dumpy water bird, swims strongly with nodding head motion. Adult is slate-black with a white bill and forehead. In flight, shows a pale bar along the trailing edge of the inner wings. Legs are grey with long toes that are partly webbed. In flight, feet project well beyond the tail. Juvenile is grey-brown with pale face and throat. Adults begin to moult in May. The flight feathers are moulted simultaneously and birds are flightless for a short time between June and September. Juveniles start to moult their body feathers after fledging and finish by late October.
SEE ALSO: Moorhen p86.

young on the nest for the first 3–4 days and male feeds them. The parents divide the brood between them and continue to feed the young for about 30 days. The young fly at about 55 days.

MOVEMENTS AND MIGRATIONS
Present in both summer and winter. After breeding, flocks form at a few favoured places, where the birds undergo their annual moult. After moulting they disperse to wintering waters, such as Loch Leven, and are joined by migrants from elsewhere in Scotland and others from northern Europe. A few Scottish Coots move further south and may visit England or Ireland. Oldest bird survived for over 20 years.

juvenile

1st-winter

HABITS
Frequently seen in flocks and often accompanies ducks, swans and other waterbirds, picking up discarded food or food disturbed by other birds. It can be noisy and quarrelsome and engages in territorial fights during the breeding season. It makes a long, pattering run across the water as it takes off. Spends most of its day on water and dives frequently when feeding. Also grazes on short grass where it walks rather awkwardly, and runs with wings flapping.

VOICE
The most usual call is a loud single note, 'kowk', that may be heard during the day and at night.

HABITAT
Frequents large, food-rich stretches of water such as lochs, lakes in parks and slow-flowing rivers. It will sometimes visit estuaries or shallow coastal waters in winter, especially in cold weather.

FOOD
Eats both plant and animal material. Plants include algae, pondweeds, duckweed, Bull Rush, hornwort and young grasses. Animals include freshwater mussels, water snails, larvae of flies, moths and beetles.

BREEDING
Most nests are built among reeds and other aquatic vegetation and close to other Coot's nests. Some nests are out in the open with little surrounding cover. Sometimes two broods are reared in a single summer. The large nest is made of plant leaves and stems and lined with smaller material. Nesting begins at the end of April. Incubation of the 5–7 eggs is by both parents and lasts for 21–24 days. Female broods newly hatched

POPULATION
There may by 1,500–2,500 pairs nesting in Scotland. Unlike in other parts of Britain, Scottish numbers may be slightly declining. Also, it appears that fewer Coots from Europe are now visiting Scotland in winter.

CONSERVATION
The overall British population has been helped in the south by the creation of many new artificial water bodies such as gravel pits and reservoirs, and numbers here have consequently increased, but this trend is not apparent in Scotland.

DISTRIBUTION
Common in the lowlands of the south and east of Scotland, but may also be encountered in autumn and winter on lochs with emergent vegetation in many areas of the country, including the Northern Isles. Breeds throughout Europe as far north as Finland. Also found in Asia and parts of North Africa, with another race present in Australia.

CORNCRAKE *CREX CREX*

IDENTIFICATION

27–30 cm. Smaller than Moorhen, and rather chicken-like, with a short, pointed bill and thick neck. Mainly yellow-brown with dark streaks on its upperparts, reddish-brown underparts, with pale barring on its flanks and grey face and breast. The rusty-red wing feathers show at rest and in flight. Wings are quite rounded at the tips, but in full flight look longer and sleeker. Adults moult in July and August. Flight feathers are lost simultaneously and it becomes flightless for a short time.
SEE ALSO: Quail p52, Grey Partridge p51, Spotted Crake p85.

HABITS

Generally solitary except when nesting. Very secretive and more likely to be heard than seen. On the ground walks with high steps and runs swiftly. Able to thread its way through dense vegetation. Usual flight is fluttering, with legs dangling, but over longer distances the flight is more direct and the legs are drawn up under the body.

VOICE

The distinctive song, 'crex-crex', is mostly heard at dusk and during the night. It has been likened to drawing a comb across a matchbox and is the origin of the Corncrake's scientific name.

HABITAT

Found in low vegetation such as grasslands, nettle and iris beds, and especially meadows and pastures that are mown or grazed in late summer. It will also frequent stands of irises and Meadowsweet in dry ditches on the margins of wetlands. In Europe and Russia, it nests in grasslands on river plains. In Africa it follows the winter rains, inhabiting grassland and savannah close to rivers and marshes.

FOOD

Feeds on insects, including beetles, flies, grasshoppers and ants. It also eats spiders, snails and worms as well as seeds, leaves and stems of plants.

BREEDING

The nest is a shallow cup lined with leaves and built on the ground among dense vegetation, sometimes with longer stems pulled over the top to make a loose canopy. Lays 8–12 eggs, which are incubated by the female for 16–19 days. Young are fed by female for the first few days after hatching until they feed themselves. They can fly after about 34 days. There may be two broods.

MOVEMENTS AND MIGRATIONS

A summer visitor to Europe arriving in mid-April and leaving again in August or September. Capable of sustained long-distance flights, over the Sahara Desert.

POPULATION

Over 1,200 calling males are present in Scotland. This follows more than a century of decline, with the population reaching a low of 480 pairs in the early 1990s. Numbers are gradually increasing again.

juvenile

CONSERVATION

Specially protected. The Corncrake was once common in much of Britain and Ireland, but numbers started to decline when hay fields were first mown mechanically. Cutting of silage and grass earlier in the year destroyed nests, adults and young. Suitable habitats were also lost to drainage and agricultural intensification. Towards the end of the 20th century the species was virtually extinct in England and Wales, and declines were also noted throughout Europe. However, it hung on in parts of Ireland and, especially, the Hebrides. More recently, conservationists have been working with farmers and crofters to ensure overgrown field corners are available in spring, and that fields are mown after 1 August and from the centre outwards, allowing young birds to escape unharmed.

DISTRIBUTION

Birds can be heard and occasionally seen from late April onwards – Tiree, Coll and Balranald RSPB reserve on North Uist are good locations. In Britain breeds mainly in the north-west of Scotland, especially in the Hebrides. The species is also found patchily across Europe, from the Pyrenees to the Arctic and east into Asia. Winters in south-east Africa.

OYSTERCATCHER *HAEMATOPUS OSTRALEGUS*

summer

summer

winter

summer

juvenile

IDENTIFICATION
40–45 cm. Large, stocky, black and white wader, with long, orange-red bill and reddish-pink legs. Head, breast and back are black and underparts white. In flight, has wide, white wing-bar, black tail and white rump that extends as a 'V' between wings. In winter, many have wide, white chinstrap. Juvenile has brown fringes to feathers on its back and grey legs. Adults moult in July, after breeding. Flight feathers are moulted symmetrically and never more than two at a time. Juveniles have partial moult between August and December.
SEE ALSO: Avocet p246.

HABITS
Noisy and excitable, both in winter flocks and on breeding territory. Piping displays are important when establishing a territory, and sometimes 5–30 will come together in 'piping parties' as they run side-by-side calling loudly. Also in spring it has an advertising display flight and flies with shallow wingbeats, calling above its territory. Outside breeding season gathers in flocks. Sometimes thousands roost together at high tide, when forced off feeding grounds.

VOICE
Usual call is a loud, shrill, piping 'kleep, kleep'.

HABITAT
Breeds on pebbly beaches, on shingle banks of large rivers, in pastures and meadows and, in a few cases, on grassy moors. It is also sometimes found nesting on flat roofs and even car parks! In winter found mainly around the coast, especially on estuaries.

FOOD
In coastal areas chief food is shellfish such as mussels and cockles. Inland the main food is worms. Also eats crabs and lugworms.

BREEDING
Nests on ground, in the open or among low vegetation. Occasionally a nest is off the ground on a tree-stump or the flat roof of a building. There are usually 2 or 3 eggs. Incubation is by both sexes and lasts 24–27 days. Unusually for waders, the young don't feed themselves, but depend on their parents until they fly after 43 days and may not be fully independent until 26 weeks old.

MOVEMENTS AND MIGRATIONS
Oystercatchers that breed inland move to the coast for winter. Northerly populations migrate south, and most Scottish birds move to England, Wales or Ireland, with a few travelling as far as Spain. Others from Scandinavia and Iceland take their place, with the largest numbers arriving during July and August. One German bird survived over 43 years.

POPULATION
Widespread. Around 100,000 pairs breed in Scotland, 71% of the UK breeding population. Recent declines noted on farmland, particularly in the south and east.

CONSERVATION
Those nesting on the coast, or visiting to feed and roost, face increasing disturbance from human recreational activities, which may either cause nests to fail or disturb birds at high tide roosts, at times when they need to conserve energy, especially in the depths of winter and during migration. The largest impact on breeding numbers comes from changes in agricultural practices, particularly the rolling of fields and a switch to winter cereal crops.

DISTRIBUTION
Found around the Scottish coast and also inland, especially on lowland farmland and by rivers. Common around the coasts of Britain and Ireland. In winter it ongregates in large numbers on estuaries, especially the Solway, Forth, Clyde and Moray Firth. Also breeds in Iceland, northern Europe, Scandinavia and Russia. Others breed further east, in Siberia and parts of Asia. Some European birds reach West Africa in winter.

LITTLE RINGED PLOVER *CHARADRIUS DUBIUS*

IDENTIFICATION
14–15 cm. Small wader with round head, short dark bill and rather short slender flesh-coloured legs. Adult has brown back and crown, white collar and black breast-band. A slimmer wader than Ringed Plover and has a distinct yellow eye-ring, white forehead bordered above with black and a thin white stripe above the black band. In flight, wings are plain with no wing-bar unlike Ringed Plover. Juvenile has an incomplete brown breast-band and lacks black markings of adult and pale stripe over its eye. Adults moult between July and November, some starting before their migration and completing it on the winter grounds. Juveniles start to moult body feathers and some tail and wing feathers in autumn.
SEE ALSO: Ringed Plover p91.

HABITS
Not generally seen in flocks or groups except sometimes in Europe during migration. Feeding action more rapid than that of Ringed Plover. Often noisy and very aggressive towards rivals at start of breeding season, but can be very secretive once it has eggs or young. When displaying a stiff-winged 'butterfly-like' flight at a low level over its territory.

VOICE
Most usual call heard from breeding birds is a loud 'pee-u' that is often given in flight. It also makes a rapidly repeated 'pip-pip-pip' and a repeated 'gree-a' call during its song flight.

They fly at 25–27 days, but remain dependent on their parents for a further 8–25 days.

MOVEMENTS AND MIGRATIONS
A summer visitor that spends the winter in Africa. In England it arrives quite early, from mid-March onwards, but the peak arrival time in Scotland is early to mid-May, and most are seen in the south or east of the country. Return migration starts in July, when small numbers are seen at sites like Musselburgh lagoons near Edinburgh. Oldest bird was over 13 years.

POPULATION
Still a rare breeding bird in Scotland, with around 10 pairs. Numbers seen each year have increased following the comparatively recent colonisation and its gradual spread northwards.

CONSERVATION
First colonised England in 1938. The Little Ringed Plover has been gradually spreading north and west, finding suitable man-made habitats in which to rear its young. Working with quarry managers to secure safe nesting areas is the main priority.

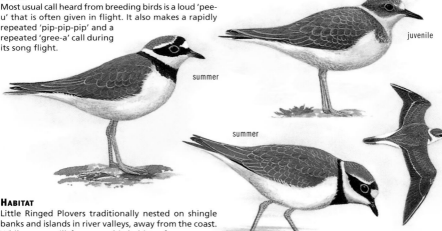

juvenile

summer

summer

HABITAT
Little Ringed Plovers traditionally nested on shingle banks and islands in river valleys, away from the coast. While some still frequent this habitat, far more use man-made sites such as gravel quarries. Many of these sites are transitional, with breeding birds moving on after a few years. In winter in Africa, migrants are found on muddy or sandy shores, flooded ground and short grassy areas near fresh water.

FOOD
Feeds chiefly on insects, spiders and other small creatures found in or close to shallow water. Includes beetles, flies, larvae of mayflies and dragonflies, freshwater shrimps, worms, small water snails, and also some seeds.

BREEDING
Nest is on bare ground or among low vegetation. The simple scrape is one of several made by male and chosen by female. Both birds share the incubation of, usually, 4 eggs. Young hatch after 24 days and feed themselves, although they continue to be brooded by their parents while small and during wet and cold weather.

DISTRIBUTION
In Britain it is most numerous in England, with only a small Scottish population in the south-eastern lowlands. Elsewhere it breeds from the Arctic Circle to North Africa and east to Japan. European birds winter in central Africa.

RINGED PLOVER *CHARADRIUS HIATICULA*

IDENTIFICATION

18–20 cm. Similar to Little Ringed Plover but larger and bigger chested. Adults in summer have white foreheads with black band above, black mask through the eyes, white collar and complete black breast-band. Upperparts are brown, underparts white. Bill is orange with black tip and legs are orange. In flight, there is an obvious white wing-bar and tail has a brown centre and white sides. Juvenile lacks bold black and white head pattern, has a smaller, browner breast-band (often broken in the middle) and back and crown have a scaly appearance. Bill and legs are dark. Adults moult between July and November, and some of the flight feathers may be moulted before migration. Juveniles start moulting their tails, body and some wing feathers between August and January.
SEE ALSO: Little Ringed Plover p90.

HABITS

Feeding actions are typical of plovers: a short run before suddenly pausing and quickly tilting the whole body forward as it picks prey from the ground. When suspicious it will bob its head. May be seen singly, but also forms small flocks and will associate with other small waders. Flight rapid, generally low; in spring it has a 'butterfly-like' flight display on stiff wings.

FOOD

Feeds on a variety of small insects, worms, crustaceans and other creatures, including shrimps, marine snails, beetles, spiders and small fish.

BREEDING

Nesting begins in April. Male prepares nest-scrape in the open or sometimes sheltered by short vegetation. The 3 or 4 beautifully camouflaged eggs are incubated by both sexes for 23–25 days. Young are covered in down and can feed themselves. They fly after about 24 days and soon become independent. Occasionally a few pairs have second broods.

MOVEMENTS AND MIGRATIONS

Ringed Plovers may be found around the coast of Scotland year-round, but this conceals significant seasonal movements. After breeding, Scottish birds move to their winter areas on the coast; a few may move south, but most remain in Scotland. However, large numbers of other Ringed Plovers from Scandinavia, Iceland and even Greenland move through Scotland along the east and west coasts in spring and autumn. The oldest Ringed Plover survived for over 19 years.

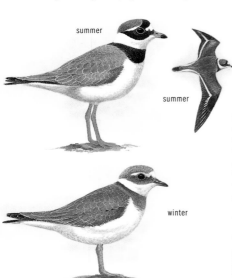

summer

summer

juvenile

winter

POPULATION

Over 5,000 pairs of Ringed Plovers breed in Scotland, comprising 60% of the UK population. Numbers are declining on the Western Isles.

CONSERVATION

Threats come from disturbance to nest sites by tourists, dog-walkers and recreational activities, and also from a rise in sea-level. The introduction, by humans, of Hedgehogs to the Outer Hebrides significantly reduced breeding success. Action is being taken by the RSPB and Scottish Natural Heritage to address this.

VOICE

Call a distinctive low whistle, 'toolip'. Song during its display flight is yodelling 't'lew, t'lew, t'lew'.

HABITAT

A bird of shingle and sandy beaches; also of dunes and grasslands close to the sea, and of the machair grasslands of the Western Isles. Smaller numbers nest inland around lochs and rivers, and occasionally on man-made habitats such as gravel quarries. Outside of the British Isles many breed on the Arctic tundra. Those that reach Africa in winter may feed on beaches, on mud close to rivers or on areas of short grass.

DISTRIBUTION

Breeds around the coast of Scotland wherever quiet sandy or shingle beaches are found. Also breeds on English, Welsh and Irish coasts, although it is scarce in south-west England. Winters around the coasts of the British Isles and as far south as South Africa. Outside the region it breeds from northern France north to Scandinavia, and also in northern Asia, Iceland, Greenland and Canada, especially on the Arctic tundra.

GOLDEN PLOVER *PLUVIALIS APRICARIA*

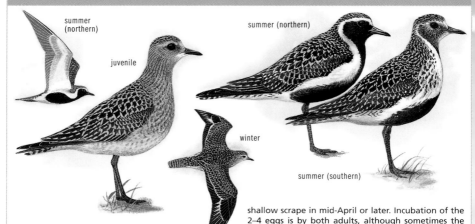

summer (northern)

juvenile

summer (northern)

winter

summer (southern)

IDENTIFICATION

26–29 cm. Medium-sized, upright wader with small rounded head, plump body, medium-long legs and short bill. In summer, brown and gold spangled back is separated from black face, neck and belly by white line which gets wider towards belly. Males are generally blacker below than females. Northern populations are even blacker on face and belly, but similar birds are found at some British breeding sites. In winter, yellow is duller, breast lined with buff and belly white. In flight, has a white line in the centre and underwing is white. Adults start to moult while nesting and complete this in autumn. Breeding plumage is acquired between March and May.
SEE ALSO: Grey Plover p93, Dotterel p94.

HABITS

Typical plover that runs, stops and tilts forward to pick food. Often feeds at night. Flight usually rapid, but has butterfly-like display flight. Flocks throughout the year and, in autumn and winter, thousands gather at traditional sites, often with Lapwings. Some individuals on their breeding grounds are accompanied by a Dunlin that benefits from the early warning of danger given by alarm-calling Golden Plover.

VOICE

Most usual call is lonely-sounding 'pu-we'. Song-flight has a longer, far-carrying 'per-we-oo-, per-wee-oo'.

HABITAT

Breeds amongst short vegetation on upland moors, peatlands and blanket bogs, and will sometimes visit nearby pastures to feed. In northern Europe it also breeds on Arctic tundra. In winter, it gathers at traditional inland and coastal sites – often lowland grassland or arable fields – and sometimes roosts on ploughed land or estuarine mudflats.

FOOD

Eats a variety of small creatures, especially beetles and earthworms. Also caterpillars of moths, larvae of crane-flies (leatherjackets), ants, earwigs, spiders, snails and plant material including berries, leaves and seeds.

BREEDING

Females sometimes take a second mate, even leaving the first male with eggs and moving to a new territory and a new partner. Both male and female prepare a shallow scrape in mid-April or later. Incubation of the 2–4 eggs is by both adults, although sometimes the male spends most time on the nest. Young hatch after 28–31 days and are cared for by both parents. They fly after 25–33 days and soon become fully independent.

MOVEMENTS AND MIGRATIONS

Most Golden Plovers that nest in Scotland remain here for the winter. They move from high ground to lower pastures and estuaries, and a few may fly south, some even reaching Spain and Portugal. In winter, Scottish birds are joined by many migrants from the north, especially Iceland, which arrive mainly in September and October. In severe weather birds may be forced to move on to new wintering areas further south. Oldest recorded bird was 12 years.

POPULATION

There are 15,000 breeding pairs in Scotland, or 80% of the British population. However, numbers are declining, particularly in the south of its range.

CONSERVATION

Protected in the close season. Decline may be a result of a combination of factors. Planting upland forests destroys moorland, and these waders seldom nest within 400 m of plantations, which further reduces the area available to them. In addition, predators such as Foxes and crows, attracted by the forests, have increased. Much moorland has been drained and many peatlands lost. Drainage and ploughing up of old pastures reduce food supplies both in summer and in winter.

DISTRIBUTION

It breeds in the uplands of Scotland, northern England, Dartmoor, Wales and the west of Ireland. In winter, it avoids land over about 200 m. It also breeds in the Faroes, in Iceland, across northern Europe and into Siberia. In winter, some northern birds reach the Mediterranean and North Africa.

GREY PLOVER *PLUVIALIS SQUATAROLA*

winter   winter

summer

IDENTIFICATION
27–30 cm. Medium-large wader that appears larger and stouter than Golden Plover and with larger head and heavier bill. Legs are dark grey. In spring, has silver and black spotted upperparts, black face, neck and belly and broad white line running from forehead and down the sides of breast. In winter, loses the black feathers and has a more uniform grey-brown back than Golden Plover. Juvenile has neatly spotted yellow-brown upperparts that are retained through first winter. In all plumages shows a white wing-bar in flight, white rump and has an obvious black patch under the wing, where the wing joins the body. Moult takes place between July and December. Birds starting in July may suspend their moult during their migration and continue on their wintering grounds.
SEE ALSO: Golden Plover p92.

HABITS
Feeding birds tend to be solitary and defend their own area of shore. Flocks sometimes form when feeding birds are driven off their feeding grounds by a high tide, but generally it is seen in smaller numbers than Golden Plovers. Feeding action similar to other plovers and also feeds at night.

VOICE
Most usual call is a lonely-sounding and far-carrying 'plu-oo-wee', often given in flight.

HABITAT
Breeds in the high Arctic on tundra and has not nested in Scotland. Here it is mainly found around the coast, especially on estuaries and muddy or sandy beaches. Sometimes roosting flocks are forced onto adjacent farmland during high tides, where the birds may mix with Golden Plovers.

FOOD
Feeds on cockles, other small shellfish, marine snails, lugworms, ragworms and bristle worms.

BREEDING
Does not breed in Scotland. In its northern breeding areas it nests on the ground in a scrape made by both adults. The female usually leaves the male with the young when the chicks are about 12 days old and begins her migration ahead of the male. The young take 35–45 days to fledge.

MOVEMENTS AND MIGRATIONS
This is an impressive migrant. Adults leave their Siberian breeding grounds and many pass through Scotland in August and September on a southerly journey to West Africa, while others remain around the coast of Scotland for the whole winter. Favoured haunts here include the Montrose Basin, the Solway and the Firth of Forth. Non-breeders and failed breeders move first, then females; after that come the males that have been rearing young and, finally, the juveniles. Migrating birds are capable of non-stop flights of 6,500 km and return to their breeding grounds in May. Oldest bird was 23 years.

POPULATION
Up to 2,800 winter around the Scottish coast, but at peak migration times numbers may reach 5,000–10,000. Following a period of population increase numbers are falling again for reasons that are far from clear.

CONSERVATION
The main threat to Grey Plovers is the loss of habitat along their staging grounds on both the European and North American coasts.

summer

winter

juvenile

DISTRIBUTION
Found on the Scottish coast in most months of the year, with the largest numbers in spring and autumn. Many overwinter and a few non-breeders remain all summer. This species breeds in Arctic Russia, Siberia and North America. It winters on the coast of Europe, Africa, southern Asia and North and South America.

DOTTEREL CHARADRIUS MORINELLUS

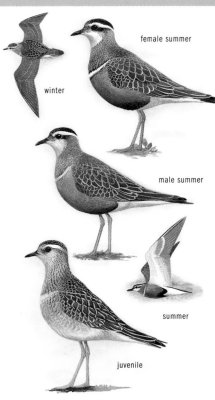

female summer

winter

male summer

summer

juvenile

IDENTIFICATION
20–22 cm. Medium-sized wader with, unusually, female more colourful and more clearly marked than male. Adult has pale face, dark crown and broad white stripes above eyes that meet at back of head. Upperparts grey-brown and belly black. Chestnut underparts are separated from grey breast by distinctive white band. Throat is white. In autumn and winter less colourful, with scaly-looking brown upperparts, and less obvious eye-stripe and breast-band. In flight, apart from a white streak on the leading flight feather, the wings are plain. Juvenile is like a small Golden Plover, with well marked upper-parts, an indistinct breast-band, a finely striped buff breast, dark crown and long creamy stripe over eye. SEE ALSO: Golden Plover p92.

HABITS
Dotterels can be very confiding and ignore humans on their breeding grounds. Nesting occurs on short vegetation, usually above 1,000 m. This is one of the few species where the male does almost all the incubating. The female is more colourful than the male and has a butterfly-like display flight. Most females abandon their partners after egg-laying and move to other hills in search of new males. Some leave Scotland altogether, nesting again, with other males, in Norway.

VOICE
Not generally a noisy species, but if disturbed it makes a 'wet-e-wee' call. Migrants make contact calls which carry a long way, 'pilk, pilk, pilk' or a soft 'kwip'.

HABITAT
Breeds in the Arctic tundra and on mountains. In Scotland inhabits high, wide plateaux on largely barren mountaintops, with scattered areas of moss, short grass, sedges, bilberry, heather and lichens below the snow line. In Austria and Russia breeds at over 2,000 m but in northern Europe it may be only 100 m above sea level. On migration, visits low-lying arable farmland, hills and areas of short grass such as golf courses. In Holland has bred on arable sites reclaimed from the sea.

FOOD
Eats spiders, worms, beetles, weevils, sawflies and craneflies, including their larvae (leatherjackets).

BREEDING
Nesting begins in mid-May. Both sexes make a shallow scrape lined with moss, lichens or leaves on bare ground or amongst short vegetation. Male incubates the 2 or 3 eggs for 24–28 days. Female may share the incubation of a second or subsequent clutch. Young are covered in down and feed themselves. They are tended mainly by the male. They fly after 25–30 days and quickly become independent.

MOVEMENTS AND MIGRATIONS
Small flocks (known as 'trips') break their flight from North Africa and spend a few days at traditional sites, such as the Pentland Hills (Lothian) – some sites have been used for hundreds of years. After egg-laying many females fly on to other northern breeding grounds. Few are seen on their return, and most make non-stop flights back to their winter quarters, where they move around to take advantage of available food supplies. Oldest bird was 10 years.

POPULATION
In good years some 630 males breed in Scotland. The population varies widely from year to year. Found on high mountains in central and northern Scotland, with occasional breeding elsewhere.

CONSERVATION
Specially protected. Scotland now holds all the UK breeding population. Numbers fluctuate from year to year, and some breeding sites are under pressure from disturbance from hillwalkers, birdwatchers and ski development. This is a species that may come under increasing threat from loss of habitat due to climate change.

DISTRIBUTION

Stronghold in Britain is the Scottish Highlands, but it is also found on a few hills farther south. In Europe strongholds are in Scandinavia and northern Russia. Breeds across northern Asia and in a few mountain ranges farther south. Scottish Dotterels winter in Morocco, European birds mostly winter in Spain or North Africa.

LAPWING VANELLUS VANELLUS

male summer

female winter

IDENTIFICATION
28–31 cm. Medium-large wader with broad, rounded, black and white wings. Back dark green, breast black, underparts and face white, and undertail orange-brown. Adults have long upsweeping black crest on back of head, the male's being the longest. Males also have whiter faces and blacker breasts. In winter, neat buff edges to back feathers give scaly pattern. Juvenile has shorter crest, more scaly back and face is less well marked. Adults moult between June and October and then moult head and some body feathers in February to May. Adult's wings look narrower when moulting.

HABITS
Forms large flocks in autumn and winter that are highly mobile. Flight appears lazy with relaxed wingbeats, and flocks flicker black and white. In courtship, tumbles in aerobatic display during which the stiff flight feathers make a humming sound. Has the 'walk, stop and tilt' feeding action typical of plovers.

VOICE
Call, from which it gets its alternative name of Peewit, is a rather wheezy, drawn-out 'pee-wit'. The song that accompanies its display is 'pee-wit, wit, wit-eeze wit'.

HABITAT
Breeds mainly on farmland, especially amongst crops cultivated in spring where there is bare soil and short grass. Also on pastures, wet grassland, fens, bogs, marshes and occasionally industrial sites where there is bare ground and damp areas for chicks to feed.

summer

summer

FOOD
Eats a variety of invertebrates living on or in the ground, including earthworms, leatherjackets, beetles, flies, moth caterpillars and ants. Also spiders, small frogs, snails, and some plant material.

BREEDING
Nesting begins in March. Male makes several scrapes on bare ground from which female chooses one. Scrape is lined with some grasses or leaves. Incubation of the 4 eggs takes around 28 days and is mostly by female. Young are covered with down. They feed themselves soon after hatching and are cared for by both adults. They fly after 35–40 days and become independent soon afterwards.

MOVEMENTS AND MIGRATIONS
Lapwings are seen in Scotland throughout the year. Some do not move far from their nesting areas. However, many fly south, some to Ireland and others to France, Spain or Portugal. Winter flocks tend to be nomadic, and will move to avoid severe weather and prolonged periods of frost or snow. From May to August, migrant Lapwings arrive from Scandinavia and eastern Europe and join our local birds, when large flocks are seen on farmland near firths and estuaries. Oldest ringed bird survived 21 years.

POPULATION
There may be 100,000 pairs nesting in Scotland, forming a significant proportion of the UK population. Breeding numbers are declining, particularly in the lowlands.

CONSERVATION
The recent decline has been linked to agricultural changes, especially the move from spring to autumn sowing of cereals, which has resulted in the crops being too tall to suit breeding Lapwings in spring. There has also been a reduction in mixed farming and a loss of unimproved damp grasslands, both of which have reduced the feeding areas for chicks.

juvenile

DISTRIBUTION

Widespread. The highest concentrations are in the Hebrides and Northern Isles, and on grazed moorland and in fields. Declining on lowland farmland. Large flocks occur on ploughed fields and by the coast in winter. Common across Britain and Ireland. Breeds from Arctic Scandinavia south to the Mediterranean, and also in parts of Asia and northern Russia. Winters in western Europe and some reach North Africa.

SANDERLING *CALIDRIS ALBA*

IDENTIFICATION
20–21 cm. Small, plump, energetic wader, slightly larger than Dunlin, with short straight black bill and medium-long black legs. For most of year has pale grey upperparts; underparts and most of head are white and there is a black mark at shoulder of folded wing. Breeding plumage reddish brown above with mottled back, rather like Knot. Juvenile grey, sometimes with buff head and breast and scaly-looking back. In flight it has a prominent white wing-bar and white on either side of a dark rump. Adults have partial moult between March and May, and then start moulting completely between July and November.
SEE ALSO: Knot p100, Dunlin p101.

HABITS
Runs with head hunched in. An extremely active and restless wader that often runs like a 'clockwork toy', following retreating waves in its search for food. It feeds in scattered groups and sometimes forms small flocks. Larger flocks form at high-tide roosts and when migrating.

also left. Body weight increases up to 60% to provide energy to fly non-stop for up to 5,000 km. Breeding birds return to their territories in May or June, but some non-breeding birds remain on Scottish beaches in summer. Oldest ringed bird survived for 17 years.

POPULATION
Up to 5,500 winter around the coast of Scotland, but this number may rise to as many as 50,000 during autumn passage, which commences in late July.

CONSERVATION
Like other waders, Sanderlings need to feed undisturbed to obtain enough food to sustain their long flights and survive the winter. Disturbing feeding birds in winter should therefore be avoided. Developments and hard engineering works on the coastline remain a threat. Climate change may cause a problem through sea-level rise and changes to its Arctic breeding sites.

summer

summer

summer

winter

winter

VOICE
Call given in flight or when flushed is a liquid 'twick, twick'.

HABITAT
In Scotland usually a coastal species, especially liking sandy shores and estuaries. Infrequently on migration it may visit the edges of large lochs and reservoirs away from the coast. It breeds on the high Arctic tundra near freshwater lakes where there are usually some low-growing Arctic plants such as saxifrage.

juvenile

FOOD
Takes food from the surface or probes in mud. Eats small crabs, shrimps, shellfish, sandhoppers and marine worms that live in mud and sand or are washed in by the tide. On its Arctic breeding grounds eats insects and some plant material, including buds, seeds and shoots.

BREEDING
Does not breed in the British Isles. On breeding grounds female makes nest scrape. Once a clutch of 4 eggs is complete some females make a second nest and produce a second clutch that they incubate themselves while leaving the male to incubate the first clutch and look after the first family. Incubation takes 23–27 days and the young fly after about 17 days and quickly become independent. It may have one or two broods.

MOVEMENTS AND MIGRATIONS
Long-distance migrant. Adults leave their breeding grounds by mid-August and by September young have

DISTRIBUTION

Found on sandy beaches throughout Scotland on passage. Its main wintering areas are the Hebrides and east coast beaches, including Aberlady Bay. Also found on much of the coast of Ireland, Wales and England, except in the south-west. Breeds in the high Arctic, on land closest to the North Pole, in Siberia, Spitsbergen, Greenland and North America. Reaches the far south of the major land masses of South America, South Africa and Australia, as well as India and South-east Asia.

LITTLE STINT   *CALIDRIS MINUTA*

IDENTIFICATION
12–14 cm. Tiny wader that is smaller than House Sparrow and much smaller than Dunlin. Has short straight bill and rather short black legs. Adult in spring has reddish head and upper breast, finely streaked dark brown back with some delicate mottling and the suggestion of a yellow backward-facing 'V' along its back. The bright spring plumage becomes worn and duller during summer. After moult adult becomes plainer and greyer with a paler face. Juvenile, which is commonly seen in Britain and Ireland, is brown like adult in late summer, but has prominent white 'V' on its back and white stripe below this. Has a pale stripe over the eye that splits to form a second, shorter stripe. In flight, has a white wing-bar, dark centre to its rump and grey outer tail-feathers. Adults moult completely between August and March, and have a partial moult in spring.
SEE ALSO: Dunlin p101, Sanderling p96.

MOVEMENTS AND MIGRATIONS
Long-distance migrant. Leaves Arctic breeding ground in August, moves on a broad front across land masses and gathers at suitable wetland feeding places. Starts moult around the Mediterranean and then flies on to Africa. It is possible that juveniles travel further than adults. As so few are seen in Britain in spring it is possible that the birds use a different route for their return migration and arrive back in the Arctic in May or June. Oldest ringed bird was 12 years.

POPULATION
Numbers in Scotland vary considerably from year to year, with 5–30 in spring and up to 1,500 in late summer and autumn.

CONSERVATION
There are no specific conservation measures for this wide-ranging species although carefully managed and protected wetlands help the survival of this and other waders migrating through western Europe after the breeding season.

summer

juvenile

summer (worn)

juvenile

HABITS
Feeds very rapidly with a shuffling movement, pecking quickly at the surface of the mud and hardly ever, apparently, looking up. In some places feeding flocks form on migration. In Scotland in spring it is usually only ever seen in ones and twos, often with other small waders such as Ringed Plover. Larger numbers are seen in autumn.

VOICE
When disturbed it will give a 'chit' or 'tit' call that is repeated about three times.

HABITAT
In Scotland, it visits areas of shallow water around the edges of lochs and estuaries, and brackish pools near the coast. It also sometimes visits inland freshwater pools. Its Arctic breeding grounds are on coastal tundra or large islands.

FOOD
Feeds by picking food from the surface or from water, but rarely probes in mud. Eats insects, especially flies and beetles, small worms, tiny shellfish, shrimps and plant material including seeds.

BREEDING
Does not breed in Scotland. In the Arctic it nests on the ground, making a shallow nest cup lined with leaves and grass. Lays 4 eggs in late June. Some females lay one clutch of eggs and leave their care to the male while she incubates a second clutch. Breeding is quick with incubation taking only about 20 days. Young fly at about 17 days old. Single-brooded, but can have two clutches and parents look after a brood each.

DISTRIBUTION
Passes through Scotland on its way to and from its high Arctic breeding grounds, with a variable number of juveniles occurring in late August and September, mainly along the coast. It is seen regularly on the Ythan, Montrose Basin and the Musselburgh lagoons. It breeds in northern Norway and across Arctic Siberia, and winters in Africa, India, the Arabian Peninsula and even as far afield as Australia.

CURLEW SANDPIPER *CALIDRIS FERRUGINEA*

summer

IDENTIFICATION

18–19 cm. Similar in size to Dunlin, but with a longer neck, longer black legs and a longer, finer and slightly more down-curved bill. In all plumages the white rump is distinctive, although this shows best in flight. In spring, it resembles a small Knot with brick-red underparts and mottled back, although underparts of the female appear scaly. In autumn and winter, it is dusky-grey above and white below, similar to a Dunlin in winter, but cleaner, whiter, with a long white stripe over its eye and fine grey streaking on its breast. The juvenile is paler and cleaner-looking than a Dunlin, with a stripe over the eye and the breast and belly are unspotted, often with a pink flush. In flight it shows a thin white wing-bar as well as the white rump. Adults begin the moult of their small body feathers on their breeding grounds in July. Their moult is suspended while migrating and completed on their wintering grounds when the larger flight feathers are also moulted. It has a further partial moult into breeding plumage between January and March, and this is sometimes suspended and completed after migration.
SEE ALSO: Dunlin p101, Knot p100.

HABITS

Can resemble a Dunlin, but more often wades in water when feeding. It will often associate with other feeding waders, especially Dunlin, and is seen singly or in small groups.

juvenile

VOICE

The most common flight call is a rippling, dry 'chirrup'.

HABITAT

On migration Curlew Sandpipers are found in similar places to Dunlins, including salt marshes, brackish pools and the fringes of freshwater lochs and pools, often near the coast. It breeds in the coastal lowlands of the high Arctic where there are bogs and pools.

FOOD

Probes in mud or wades in water to find prey such as flies, beetles, shrimps, a small marine snail called *Hydrobia* and worms.

BREEDING

Does not breed in Scotland. It nests on the ground in the Arctic on south-facing slopes that are free of snow. Both parents share the incubation of the eggs. The chicks fledge quickly, but adults migrate ahead of the young, and the males leave 21–35 days before the females.

MOVEMENTS AND MIGRATIONS

Many of the Curlew Sandpipers that cross Europe from their Arctic breeding grounds fly down the west coast of the Continent and on to West Africa. Some of these birds arrive in Scotland, especially along the east coast. Other migrants use more easterly routes. Numbers in Scotland vary from year to year depending on the success of the breeding season, with adults (especially males) migrating first, and then, between August and October, juveniles. Relatively few are seen on the spring migrations northwards. Oldest known bird survived 19 years.

POPULATION

Exceptionally, up to 1,900 may be present in Scotland in autumn, but birds are usually seen in small groups of up to six at sites like the Musselburgh lagoons, Ythan and Loch of Strathbeg RSPB reserve. In spring, there are usually less than 25 in total.

CONSERVATION

Long-distance migrants require safe, food-rich places to 'refuel' after their long migratory flights. Many wetland sites have been drained for agriculture or are disturbed by recreational pursuits. Many of the best sites for these birds are now specially protected sites such as nature reserves.

winter

winter

DISTRIBUTION

In Scotland most are seen on the coasts bordering the North Sea, although they do appear farther west, including regular sightings in Ireland. These birds breed in Arctic Siberia and winter from Africa, around the Indian Ocean, to Australia and New Zealand.

Purple Sandpiper *CALIDRIS MARITIMA*

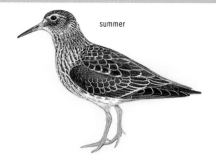

summer

IDENTIFICATION
20–22 cm. Medium-sized wader that is larger, stockier and darker than Dunlin. Bill is slightly down-curved and short legs are bright orange or yellow. In spring, head, back and sides of breast are dark purplish brown with white streaks around head and neck, and back scaly with white and rusty marks. In winter, it is darker with more uniform upperparts and yellowish base to bill. It has dark streaks along its flanks. Female is larger with slightly longer bill. Juvenile is greyer with pale edges to feathers on its back and some chestnut on the crown. In flight, all show a dark tail with white sides and pale, narrow wing-bar. Adults moult completely between July and September, while they are still close to their breeding grounds, and have a partial moult in spring.
SEE ALSO: Dunlin p101,
Turnstone p118.

juvenile

HABITS
In flight, the appearance is of a very dark, rather small wader. Small groups fly swiftly, low over the sea, and often land with a flutter on rocks close to the water where they actively search for food among the rocks and seaweed and avoid the breaking waves by jumping, fluttering and sometimes swimming. Frequently associates with Turnstones. Can be quite tame.

VOICE
Although usually silent, flocks sometimes make a Swallow-like twittering 'wee-wit' as they take off.

HABITAT
Outside the breeding season this is a coastal species that feeds on rocky beaches and islets, around piers and groynes, and also stony beaches or on mussel-beds at low tide. Breeds on tundra and, in Scotland, on Arctic-Alpine heath where there are sedges, mosses and lichens interspersed with rocks, scree and gravel.

FOOD
Picks up food left stranded by the tide or pecks amongst mussels or seaweed. In winter, eats small winkles, mussels, dog-whelks, shrimps, small crabs, insects and other tiny creatures washed up by the tide or living among the seaweed. In summer, feeds on insects and spiders and plant material such as seeds.

BREEDING
Nesting starts in June or July. Male makes several scrapes on the ground and female chooses one in which she lays 3 or 4 eggs. Male mostly incubates. Female helps, but sometimes leaves before the eggs hatch. Incubation takes 21–22 days. Young feed themselves and are tended by the male for 3–4 weeks.

MOVEMENTS AND MIGRATIONS
Those that nest in the high Arctic are long-distance migrants. Some from Canada probably winter in Scot-

land and therefore 'leapfrog' others that nest in southern Greenland and Iceland, which may remain on the coasts of those countries for the whole winter. Females leave their breeding grounds first, followed by the males and the juveniles. Many Norwegian birds spend the winter in Scotland. Migrants start to arrive in July and leave for their breeding grounds in April or May. Oldest bird was 19 years.

POPULATION
1–5 pairs have nested in Scotland since 1978. This is the only breeding population in the British Isles. In winter there may be 16,000 birds around Scottish coasts, or more than 90% of the UK total.

CONSERVATION
Specially protected. First discovered nesting in Scotland in 1978. Breeding areas are secret to protect it from egg thieves and disturbance. There is no other conservation measure as the habitat it requires is widespread in northern Scotland.

winter

winter

DISTRIBUTION

A winter visitor to rocky coasts of Scotland, with the largest numbers in Orkney, Shetland and the Outer Hebrides. Elsewhere it is found wherever there are exposed rocky shorelines. There is a small Scottish breeding population on high mountain plateaux. Outside the region it breeds from Canada, Greenland and Iceland to Scandinavia and Siberia. It winters as far south as northern Spain.

KNOT *CALIDRIS CANUTUS*

summer

summer (worn)

winter

winter

juvenile

IDENTIFICATION

23–25 cm. Medium-sized stocky wader, larger than Dunlin, with relatively short grey-green legs and short straight bill. Breeding plumage brick-red with mottled orange, black and grey back. For the rest of the year, when it is most numerous in Britain and Ireland, it is grey with grey marks on breast and flanks, short pale stripe over eye and white belly. In flight, shows pale rump and dull white wing-bar. Juvenile a little browner than non-breeding adult; back and wings grey with each feather neatly edged black and off-white giving a scaly look. There is an obvious pale stripe over its eye. Adults moult completely between July and November, the flight feathers are moulted over a long period of 90–100 days. SEE ALSO: Dunlin p101, Sanderling p96.

HABITS

In Scotland Knots are generally seen in large flocks, sometimes several thousand or more. They fly in close formation and perform breathtaking aerial manoeuvres over their feeding grounds as they twist and turn in unison, looking alternately grey and white. At high tide they roost in tight packs close to the water's edge, on salt marshes, rocky islands, on a shingle bank or a nearby field. When feeding, they spread out to search, head down, for food.

VOICE

Most frequent call is a low-pitched 'knut' and a higher pitched 'quick-ick', the latter call is usually given when it takes flight.

HABITAT

In western Europe this is a bird of the seashore, especially estuaries and mudflats, and some feed on rocky coasts. It is rare inland, although single birds, often juveniles, will appear on the fringes of large lochs. Its breeding grounds are on peninsulas, islands and barren plateaux in the Arctic.

FOOD

It probes in the mud for a small shellfish called the Baltic Tellin, and also for small cockles, mussels and a snail called *Hydrobia ulvae*. In summer in the Arctic it feeds on a wide range of flies, beetles, worms and plant material including seeds, shoots, buds, leaves and flower heads.

BREEDING

The Knot does not breed in the British Isles. It needs to breed fast during the short Arctic summer. It lays 3 or 4 eggs. Incubation is by both parents and takes only 21–22 days. The young fly after 18–20 days and are quickly independent. The female leaves the family before the young can fly.

MOVEMENTS AND MIGRATIONS

Long-distance migrant. Most have left their breeding grounds by August. The females depart first, followed by the males and then the young. All make long flights to traditional sites, usually estuaries, to moult and feed before the next leg of their journey. Those that visit Scottish estuaries will have nested in Arctic Canada or in Greenland, and usually rest in Iceland or Norway before flying on to Scotland. Some will overwinter, while others travel on to England, the European coast and even West Africa. Oldest bird was 27 years.

POPULATION

Up to 25,000 winter in Scotland and the numbers appear to be largely stable.

CONSERVATION

A large proportion of the Knots depend on a few European estuaries to feed and moult. They are, therefore, vulnerable to any changes to these sites, such as barrages, sea-level rise and human disturbance.

DISTRIBUTION

In Scotland, Knots are found on most major firths and other river estuaries. The species is also numerous on estuaries south of the border. Large flocks occur on the Forth, Cromarty Firth and inner Solway. It breeds in Alaska, Canada, Greenland and northern Siberia. Different populations winter in South America, Australia and New Zealand, all returning to the Arctic to breed.

DUNLIN *CALIDRIS ALPINA*

IDENTIFICATION
16–20 cm. Smallest common wader, with medium length black legs and gently down-curved black bill. Adult in summer has reddish-brown back, white underparts with black patch on belly. In winter, has grey-brown back, grey breast and white underparts. In flight, has white wing-bar and white sides to dark rump. Juvenile in autumn has dark spotting on lower breast and flanks and neat buff edges to back feathers. Different races moult at different times. Adults moult between July and September, and have a partial moult into summer plumage between March and June.
SEE ALSO: Sanderling p96, Curlew Sandpiper p98, Little Stint p97.

summer

winter

HABITS
Gathers in flocks outside breeding season. Some flocks number thousands of birds at important feeding sites where they fly in compact formation, showing alternately white and grey as they bank and turn. When feeding they spread out, but at high tides they form tight roosts on the shore or on nearby fields. Feeds intently, hunched up with head down. On breeding grounds may associate with a Golden Plover, which helps to give warning of danger. Breeding male has an aerial display over his territory. Climbing steeply, he hovers against the wind and then switchbacks, alternately fluttering and gliding until drifting down and settling with wings held above his back in a 'V'. A far-carrying trilling call is given during this display.

VOICE
Usual flight call is rough 'treep'. Display song on breeding grounds is a piping trill.

HABITAT
Breeds on wet upland moors but also in salt marshes and among pools in the wet grassland (machair) in the Western Isles. At other times visits estuaries and mudflats, coastal pools and shallow water inland.

FOOD
Food is taken from the surface, by probing mud or wading in water. Eats insects such as beetles and fly larvae; also molluscs, microscopic crustacea and worms.

BREEDING
Nests on ground, on a tussock or under low vegetation. The 4 eggs are laid in May and usually incubated by male during the day and female at night. Some females lay a second clutch and leave male to incubate the first. Young hatch after 22 days and run about and feed themselves. They fly and become independent at about 20 days, but may be abandoned by the female before this. After nesting, adults and young quickly move to the coast.

MOVEMENTS AND MIGRATIONS
The Dunlin is both a winter visitor and a breeding species in Scotland. Three subspecies are involved. Breeding birds are of the southern subspecies and gather around the coast before and after the breeding season, but move south, out of Scotland, for the winter. A northern subspecies that breeds in Scandinavia and Russia, and another from Greenland, arrive in Scotland after the breeding season. Some pass through and fly on south, but many remain in Scotland for the winter. Oldest bird was 28 years.

POPULATION
8,000–10,000 pairs breed in Scotland. There may be 37,000–50,000 birds present in winter. There have been serious declines in the number of breeding birds in recent years, and Scotland holds about 85% of the British and Irish population.

CONSERVATION
The decline in the breeding population is due to increased forestry and changing agricultural practices in the uplands. The species depends on the conservation of wet upland moors and the machair in the Western Isles for nesting. Conservation of estuaries is essential for wintering populations and also for passage migrants. Recreational activities on the coast can disturb roosts, especially in winter.

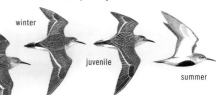

winter

juvenile

summer

summer

juvenile

DISTRIBUTION
Breeds in wet upland peatland areas and northern coastal sites in Scotland, and in upland areas in other parts of the British Isles. Other subspecies visit in winter. There are nine subspecies worldwide, which breed in northern Europe, North America and northern Asia. The subspecies breeding in Scotland winter as far south as West Africa, while other populations winter in India and South-east Asia.

JACK SNIPE *LYMNOCRYPTES MINIMUS*

IDENTIFICATION
17–19 cm. Smaller and more compact than Snipe, and with a much shorter bill. It also has a more metallic green and purple back, an all-dark crown with bold buff stripes above the eye and down the centre of the crown. The dark back has four bright straw-coloured stripes running down it. It moults between July and October, before it migrates, and has a second, partial moult starting in January.
SEE ALSO: Snipe p103.

HABITS
A very secretive wader that is most active at dawn and dusk and is more likely to crouch and freeze than fly if disturbed during the day. When it does fly it often takes-off from very close to an observer, lacks the ziz-zag flight of the Snipe and generally lands again close by. When feeding or resting it has a characteristic bobbing movement so that the body looks as if it is on a spring as it bounces slowly up and down. It does not form flocks, although several birds will sometimes feed close together.

Lowlands. Many remain for the whole winter, but some fly on southwards. In severe weather, Jack Snipe may move again to ice-free feeding grounds. Oldest ringed bird was 12 years.

POPULATION
10,000–15,000 pass through Scotland on migration, with up to 5,000 remaining for the winter. There are reports of local increases and decreases, and long-term trends are not clear. In Europe and Russia, numbers are generally declining.

CONSERVATION
The conservation of existing large wetlands and the proper management of those identified as being of special importance is a priority for wintering Jack Snipe and other waders. Many smaller wetlands remain vulnerable to drainage, development and loss to encroaching trees and scrub. The breeding grounds especially need to be protected from drainage or other damaging activities. Hunting is also a threat, as it is possible that owing to confusion with the Common Snipe as many as 30% of wintering birds are shot for sport.

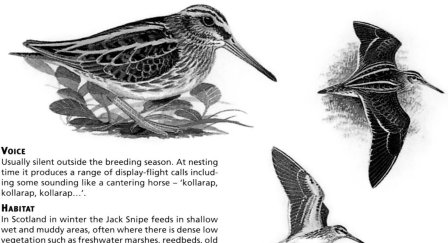

VOICE
Usually silent outside the breeding season. At nesting time it produces a range of display-flight calls including some sounding like a cantering horse – 'kollarap, kollarap, kollarap…'.

HABITAT
In Scotland in winter the Jack Snipe feeds in shallow wet and muddy areas, often where there is dense low vegetation such as freshwater marshes, reedbeds, old fens, flooded grassland and the banks of rivers and streams. In summer, it breeds in wet, open areas within taiga and birch forests of the sub-Arctic.

FOOD
Feeds on adults and larvae of a variety of insects such as beetles and flies, and also small snails, worms and some plant material, especially seeds.

BREEDING
Never known to breed in Scotland, although there are isolated records of birds in suitable habitats in summer. Nests on the ground, with eggs laid in a cup-shaped nest, often on a small ridge close to water. The 4 eggs are incubated by the female for up to 24 days, and there may be two broods.

MOVEMENTS AND MIGRATIONS
The autumn migration begins with birds arriving in the Northern Isles from September onwards. These birds come from the Continent and winter in suitable habitats throughout Scotland, especially in the Central

DISTRIBUTION

It winters in scattered locations in southern and western Scotland and generally avoids upland areas in winter. Migrants may turn up on coastal islands and headlands. It is occasionally recorded in Britain in summer. It breeds in northern Scandinavia and Russia and winters in western Europe and North Africa. The European breeding population winters from west Europe to the Mediterranean and east to south-east Europe.

SNIPE *GALLINAGO GALLINAGO*

IDENTIFICATION
25–27 cm. Medium-sized stocky wader with extremely long straight bill and rather short legs. Back is dark brown and delicately barred and streaked with paler brown and four straw-coloured stripes. These are less obvious than Jack Snipe's. Crown is blackish with a thin buff line down centre, and it has a long buff stripe over eye and across cheeks. Breast is buff with darker arrow marks; belly is white. In flight, has a white trailing edge to pointed wings and a rather short tail. Adults moult between June and October, but there is no obvious change in appearance.
SEE ALSO: Jack Snipe p102, Woodcock p104.

HABITS
Secretive. If disturbed, flies with a zig-zag flight, but often crouches and relies on its cryptic camouflage for protection. Does not form large flocks like other waders, but groups will feed close together and fly in loose flocks called 'wisps'. In spring, it has an undulating display flight over its breeding territory, and on the downward path it makes a whirring sound (called drumming) with its stiff outer-tail feathers.

juvenile

VOICE
In addition to drumming, it has quick, 'chip-er, chip-er' alarm call in spring, used in flight and when perched. It also makes a loud rasping 'scaap' when disturbed.

HABITAT
Breeds on moorland bogs and wet pastures in upland areas and in marshes in low-lying places. In winter, it is more widespread and feeds in almost any lowland marshy place, both around the coast and inland.

FOOD
Probes into wet ground to find food and sometimes feeds in shallow water. Eats worms, insects such as beetles, flies and ants. Also takes larvae and adults of crane-flies, caddisflies and damselflies.

BREEDING
Nesting begins in April, but some breed as late as July. Male builds a nest on ground, usually concealed by vegetation. Incubation of the 4 eggs is by the female and lasts 18–20 days. Young are fed by their parents. Once out of the nest the brood is split between the pair, with the male usually taking charge of the oldest chicks. Young fly after 19–20 days and become independent at about the same time.

MOVEMENTS AND MIGRATIONS
Two subspecies nest in Scotland. Those nesting on the mainland are more likely to be resident, although they will move from upland to lowland areas and some will leave Scotland and travel to England, Ireland and sometimes France. Those in the Orkneys and Shetland are from a northern subspecies and are more mobile after breeding. At times of migration, birds from Iceland and the Faeroe Islands pass through mainland Scotland, with large numbers seen in the Outer Hebrides and Orkney; some of these may remain for the winter while others will fly as far as Spain. Further short movements may be triggered by the onset of freezing conditions. Oldest ringed bird was 16 years.

POPULATION
Between 40,000 and 50,000 pairs nest in Scotland, comprising more than 60% of the UK population. It appears the population is declining in some lowland areas, but this seems to be offset by increases in the uplands.

CONSERVATION
This species can be legally hunted. Its breeding habitat in the lowlands has been reduced over centuries as wet grassland, marshes and bogs have been drained and rivers deepened. Changes in agriculture, such as improved field drainage and the ploughing of traditional grasslands, have further reduced feeding and breeding areas. In parts of Britain and Ireland the population has declined dramatically, but, as yet, the numbers breeding in Scotland remain fairly stable.

DISTRIBUTION
Widespread in Scotland in both summer and winter. There are three subspecies: one breeds in most of the British Isles and in central and northern Europe; another breeds on the Orkneys, Shetland, St Kilda, the Faeroe Islands and Iceland; and a third breeds in North America. The latter may be elevated to species status as Wilson's Snipe.

WOODCOCK *SCOLOPAX RUSTICOLA*

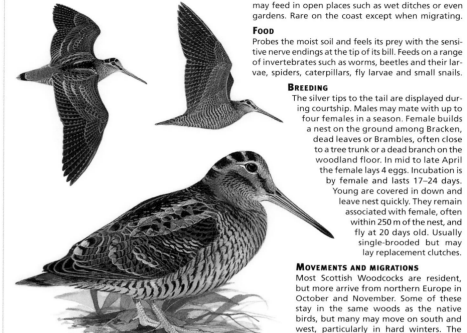

may feed in open places such as wet ditches or even gardens. Rare on the coast except when migrating.

FOOD
Probes the moist soil and feels its prey with the sensitive nerve endings at the tip of its bill. Feeds on a range of invertebrates such as worms, beetles and their larvae, spiders, caterpillars, fly larvae and small snails.

BREEDING
The silver tips to the tail are displayed during courtship. Males may mate with up to four females in a season. Female builds a nest on the ground among Bracken, dead leaves or Brambles, often close to a tree trunk or a dead branch on the woodland floor. In mid to late April the female lays 4 eggs. Incubation is by female and lasts 17–24 days. Young are covered in down and leave nest quickly. They remain associated with female, often within 250 m of the nest, and fly at 20 days old. Usually single-brooded but may lay replacement clutches.

MOVEMENTS AND MIGRATIONS
Most Scottish Woodcocks are resident, but more arrive from northern Europe in October and November. Some of these stay in the same woods as the native birds, but many may move on south and west, particularly in hard winters. The return migration is in March and April. Oldest wild bird was 15 years.

POPULATION
There are between 25,000 and 55,000 breeding pairs in Scotland, with large numbers arriving in late autumn and winter. Some local declines in breeding numbers have been observed, particularly in north-east Scotland and Dumfries & Galloway.

CONSERVATION
Protected during the close season, but may be hunted at other times. Over-hunting, especially in Europe, may be contributing to the species' decline. Has benefited from the planting of conifer plantations since World War II, but as those plantations mature they become less suitable for Woodcock and this may partly account for their recent decline in Britain.

IDENTIFICATION
33–35 cm. Larger than Snipe. Large bulky wader with short legs, very long straight, tapering bill and large eyes. Reddish-brown upperparts have delicate mottling and underparts are buff with dark barring. Broad blackish crown is crossed with several paler brown lines, not striped like Snipe. Tail has a silver tip that is most obvious from below. In flight, wings appear broad-based and rounded, and lack any prominent marks. Adults moult between June and November and also have a second moult before the nesting season begins again. SEE ALSO: Snipe p103, Jack Snipe p102.

HABITS
The beautifully camouflaged plumage, nocturnal habits and secretive behaviour make this species difficult to observe. It is generally solitary and most active at dawn and dusk. In spring, males have an aerial display as they fly over the best breeding habitats with slow, flickering wingbeats, and calling – this is known as 'roding'. The most dominant males rode longest and mate with most females. At other times it flies strongly or, if disturbed, zig-zags between trees with agility before dropping into cover. When probing for food, it has a rocking action.

VOICE
When roding it has two to four frog-like croaks, followed by a thin but far-carrying, 'tsiwick', 'tsiwick'.

HABITAT
Nests in deciduous or mixed woodland, young conifer plantations and sometimes on heather moors. Remains in woodland in the winter, although in cold weather

DISTRIBUTION

Widespread. Found in all suitable woodland habitats in Scotland and also in most other parts of the British Isles. Breeds from northern Scandinavia south to the Azores and east across Asia to Japan. In winter it may reach the Mediterranean area.

RUFF PHILOMACHUS PUGNAX

male summer

male summer

IDENTIFICATION

Male 26–30 cm, female 20–24 cm. Male size of Redshank; female considerably smaller. Long-necked wader with a small head, a rather short, slightly droopy bill and medium-long legs that are reddish, orange or yellow-green. Male in spring is unmistakable, with an exotic ruff and ear-tufts. The 'ruff' can be black, white or orange, but the marks and colours vary. Females in spring are also variable, some appearing very dark. At other times both are grey-brown, with male sometimes retaining white patch on the neck and pale face. Juvenile is buff with dark feathers on upperparts bordered bright buff and giving a scaly-look. In flight, shows narrow white wing-bar and oval patches on either side of tail. After breeding, birds moult completely, often over a long period. Juveniles moult their body feathers and some wing feathers between August and December.
SEE ALSO: Redshank p114.

HABITS

May look 'hunch-backed' but when alert stands very erect. Feeds singly or in small groups. Picks delicately for food at surface of mud. In flight, looks lazy, with relaxed wingbeats and quite long wings. On breeding grounds in spring it has a ritualised display known as lekking. Males dance and display as females choose a mate.

VOICE

Generally very silent, even when lekking, but it can make a low 'tu-wit' especially when disturbed.

HABITAT

The main breeding habitat is lowland wet meadows that are grazed in summer and flooded in winter. At other times visits muddy fringes of pools and lakes, and brackish coastal lagoons. Avoids large open estuaries usually.

regularly on wet grasslands and coastal flashes on the Northern Isles, east coast, Solway and Hebrides. Scotland is at the edge of the main migration route. Passage birds that do arrive here mostly winter further south. Oldest bird was 13 years.

POPULATION

In some years one or two may display and stay to nest, usually on coastal marshlands. Fewer than 20 stay in Scotland all winter. The numbers of birds on passage increased in Scotland during the 20th century.

CONSERVATION

Specially protected. Ruff were first proved to breed in Sutherland in 1980. The main danger to the small breeding population appears to be natural predators, although egg-collectors are also a threat. Beyond the region hunting is a serious issue, as 84% of ringed birds recovered outside Britain are killed by man.

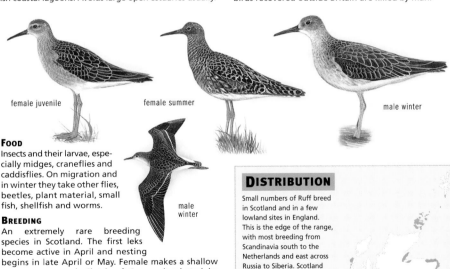

female juvenile

female summer

male winter

male winter

FOOD

Insects and their larvae, especially midges, craneflies and caddisflies. On migration and in winter they take other flies, beetles, plant material, small fish, shellfish and worms.

BREEDING

An extremely rare breeding species in Scotland. The first leks become active in April and nesting begins in late April or May. Female makes a shallow scrape on ground. Clutch of 4 eggs incubated by female alone for 20–23 days. Newly hatched young are covered in down. They are fed by female for first few days and fledge after 25 days.

MOVEMENTS AND MIGRATIONS

Mainly an autumn migrant, seen in August and September, with smaller numbers in spring occurring

DISTRIBUTION

Small numbers of Ruff breed in Scotland and in a few lowland sites in England. This is the edge of the range, with most breeding from Scandinavia south to the Netherlands and east across Russia to Siberia. Scotland has the most northerly wintering birds, with a few more in England; most, however, occur further south, reaching as far as South Africa.

BLACK-TAILED GODWIT LIMOSA LIMOSA

male summer

female summer

winter

winter

IDENTIFICATION
40–44 cm. Smaller than Curlew. Large wader with long straight bill, long black legs and long neck. In flight, has broad white wing-bar and white tail terminating in broad black band. In spring, head, neck and breast are chestnut-red, belly white with dark bars and back mottled grey-brown. After breeding it becomes pale grey-brown above and paler below. There is always a noticeable amount of leg showing above the bend in the leg, unlike Bar-tailed Godwit. Juvenile similar to winter adult, but with warm reddish tinge to neck and breast and coarsely spotted back. Adults moult from their bright spring plumage between June and October.
SEE ALSO: Bar-tailed Godwit p107.

HABITS
A graceful wader that often feeds in deep water. On breeding grounds will sometimes perch on posts or trees. Usually in small groups and sometimes forms larger flocks of several hundred in winter. In spring, performs aerial displays over its territory in which it rises and tumbles several times in rapid succession.

VOICE
Most common call is loud clear 'weeka-weeka-weeka'.

HABITAT
Mainly found around muddy estuaries and coastal pools in winter. The small population that breeds in the Northern Isles are of the Icelandic subspecies that nests on Arctic tundra and fens. The southern subspecies that breeds south of the border nests on wet grasslands and winters further south, usually on wet fields and meadows in North Africa.

FOOD
In spring and summer feeds on insects, especially the adults and larvae of beetles and flies. Also feeds on worms and small snails.

BREEDING
Nesting begins in early April. Male makes several scrapes on the ground and female chooses one or helps to construct another nest. Nest is well hidden in a tussock. Incubation of the 4 eggs lasts for 22–24 days and is by both sexes. Young feed themselves. They are cared for by both adults and are brooded during the day while small. They fly after 25–30 days and become independent at about the same time.

MOVEMENTS AND MIGRATIONS
Birds seen in Scotland are usually the Icelandic subspecies. They breed in Iceland, the Faeroes and other islands (including small numbers annually in Shetland and Orkney), and some overwinter in Scotland, mainly in the south-east. Many more pass through in autumn to winter in England, France and Spain. There is a passage of birds returning to Iceland during April and May, particularly on the west coast, but numbers vary. It is possible that some fly from southern England and France directly to Iceland, stopping in Scotland only if the weather is unfavourable. Oldest bird was 23 years.

POPULATION
5–11 pairs breed in Scotland. The winter population is around 500 birds, with many more present at times of migration in spring and autumn.

CONSERVATION
The species was rare in Scotland in the 19th century but became an increasingly common passage migrant in the 20th century. It first nested in Caithness in 1946, and there then followed colonisation of Shetland and Orkney. The numbers wintering have also increased. These trends match an increase in the number breeding in Iceland and may be linked to climate change. However, the southerly race that breeds in small numbers in England appears to be declining.

DISTRIBUTION
There are three subspecies worldwide: Icelandic birds, which also breed in Scotland; a second subspecies that breeds in England and across most of northern Europe to Russia; and a third in Asia. All move south for the winter, with the Icelandic birds reaching western Europe, the European breeding birds moving south to Africa, and the Asian birds reaching Australia.

male summer

female summer

winter

winter

Identification
37–39 cm. Larger than Redshank and smaller than Curlew. This large wader has a long, tapering, slightly upturned bill and long legs. Unlike the Black-tailed Godwit, often little leg shows above bend in the leg and it lacks the white wing-bar. Its back is more Curlew-like, with a pale 'V' between wings, white rump and brown barred tail. Short pale stripe above the eye, but this is less obvious than on Black-tailed Godwit. In spring male has brick-red face, neck and underparts and mottled grey-brown back. Female is larger than male with a longer bill and is less colourful in spring. After moult, adult loses bright colours, but has boldly streaked back. Juveniles resemble non-breeding adults with scattered streaks on their buff breasts. Adults moult from the breeding plumage between August and November. Juveniles have a partial moult between September and January. SEE ALSO: Black-tailed Godwit p106.

Habits
Has shorter legs and is more robust than the Black-tailed Godwit, and often wades in deep water. It flies with its neck withdrawn making it appear smaller and more compact. Some form flocks outside the breeding season and may perform spectacular aerial manoeuvres.

Voice
Flight note in flocks is a low, nasal 'kirruc, kirruc'.

Habitat
In Scotland this is a coastal species, spending most of its time feeding in the inter-tidal zone or in a high-tide roost close to the coast. It favours sandy or muddy shores, estuaries and sheltered bays, but many are also found on rocky shores. Breeds mainly in the sub-Arctic on peat mosses, swamps and low tundra near the coast.

Food
Feeds mainly on shellfish, lugworms, ragworms and other worms found in coastal sand; also shrimps and small marine snails. On breeding grounds chief food is insects, especially beetles, flies and moth caterpillars, and also snails, crustaceans, worms and occasionally seeds and berries.

Breeding
Does not breed in Scotland. The nest is situated on the ground, and 4 eggs are usually laid. Incubation lasts 21–22 days, and is thought to be by both sexes, although male may take major share. Young feed themselves and become independent at about the time that they learn to fly.

Movements and migrations
The Bar-tailed Godwit is a migrant that leaves its Arctic breeding grounds after nesting and migrates through Europe between July and October. Some adults stop and moult on Scottish firths and estuaries before flying on south, while others remain for the whole winter. Some juveniles stay to feed before continuing on their journey to winter in Africa. Most birds leave in March and April, although a small number of non-breeders may remain for the whole summer. Oldest bird was 32 years.

Population
There are estimated to be 10,000–14,000 birds present in winter. This population grew during the 20th century but may have fallen again in the last few years. Large numbers winter in the Firth of Forth, Montrose Basin, Orkney and the inner Solway.

Conservation
Long-distance migrants depend heavily on relatively few coastal wetlands during migration and for their winter quarters. While many of these sites are protected, others are under threat from development. In addition, the birds are vulnerable to disturbance when resting and feeding, and are under increasing pressure from human interference, often caused by leisure activities. Outside the UK hunting is also a problem.

DISTRIBUTION
In winter, found around Scottish coasts, especially in the east. A few non-breeding birds remain for the summer. Breeds from northern Scandinavia to Siberia, and winters around the North Sea and along the Atlantic coast of Europe and North Africa. Another race breeds in eastern Siberia and western Alaska, and winters as far south as Australia and New Zealand.

WHIMBREL *NUMENIUS PHAEOPUS*

IDENTIFICATION
40–42 cm. Large wader, but smaller than Curlew by about a third, with slightly shorter legs and shorter, straighter bill that curves nearer the tip. It has a dark-centred back, each feather neatly edged buff, with barred flight feathers and finely lined underparts. Unlike Curlew its crown has two broad dark bands separated by a narrow pale stripe. Face pattern is also different from Curlew's with a more obvious buff stripe over the eye, a dark line through the eye and paler cheeks and throat. Flight is lighter than Curlew's and it has a noticeably darker chest, but like Curlew it also has a white rump that extends up between the wings in a 'V' shape. Adults moult their body feathers after nesting, but delay the moult of their flight feathers until they reach their wintering areas.
SEE ALSO: Curlew p109.

HABITS
Often picks food from the surface as well as probing like the larger Curlew. It is usually seen in small groups, often flying in 'V' formation. Larger congregations form at migration stopping places to feed and rest.

VOICE
The commonly heard call is a rippling whistle 'pe,pe,pe, pe,pe,pe,pe'. Sometimes known as the 'Seven Whistler' on account of the usual number of notes. On its breeding grounds it has a bubbling call, rather like a Curlew.

cared for by both adults. They can fly after 35 days and quickly become independent.

MOVEMENTS AND MIGRATIONS
Whimbrels start to leave their northern breeding grounds in June and move rapidly through western Europe. The main post-breeding migration through Scotland is via the Northern Isles and then along both coasts. Migrants will also cross large tracts of land along river valleys, where their distinctive calls attract attention. Some Whimbrels migrate as far south as southern Africa. The return migration through Scotland occurs in April and May, with the largest numbers on the east coast. Oldest bird was 16 years.

POPULATION
The population peaked at around 500 breeding pairs in Scotland, most of them on Shetland, but it is now declining. Scotland holds the whole of the breeding population of the British Isles.

CONSERVATION
The Whimbrel is specially protected at all times. Following an increase in the 1980s–90s, the population has been falling in recent years, even in Shetland. Climate change bringing colder, wetter springs may have caused Icelandic or Scandinavian Whimbrels to stop over and breed. Many birds are found breeding near small colonies of Arctic Skua and benefit from the skuas chasing away predators such as gulls.

juvenile

HABITAT
Breeds on northern heathland, grassland and bogs. Outside the breeding season it visits coasts, favouring inter-tidal zones in particular, but also rocky shores. It will sometimes roost on farmland near the sea at high tide.

FOOD
On the coast it eats periwinkles, Dogwhelks, crabs, sandhoppers and shrimps. Inland it feeds on small snails, slugs, worms, spiders and insects such as beetles and flies.

BREEDING
The Whimbrel nests on the ground, in the open, among short vegetation. The nest is probably built mainly by the female and is a shallow scrape lined with plant material. Incubation of the 4 eggs is by both sexes and lasts about 27 days. The young feed themselves and are

DISTRIBUTION
In Britain and Ireland the Whimbrel breeds only in the north of Scotland, mostly in Shetland. It visits areas farther south during its spring and autumn migrations. The four races of Whimbrels breed in Alaska and Canada, Iceland and western Russia, eastern Siberia and south-east of the Ural Mountains. The North American race has an all dark rump – it has been seen in Scotland. European breeding birds winter mainly in west Africa but some winter as far south as South Africa.

CURLEW NUMENIUS ARQUATA

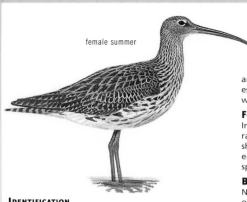

female summer

IDENTIFICATION
50–60 cm. Our largest breeding wader with very long, deeply down-curved bill and long legs. It is grey-brown with long fine dark lines down neck and breast, arrow-shaped barring on flanks and brown barred back. Head is rather plain, lacking the bold stripes on the crown of Whimbrel. In flight, outer flight feathers are darker than the rest of the wing and white rump extends up the back in a shallow 'V'. Female has a longer bill than male. Adults moult completely between June and November.
SEE ALSO: Whimbrel p108, Bar-tailed Godwit p107.

HABITS
Forms flocks outside breeding season – especially near coast. Feeding birds spread out, but congregate at high tide, and often roost on nearby fields. Feeding birds frequently wade in deep water and sometimes swim over short distances. It is a shy bird. Its flight is fast and rather gull-like. On its breeding grounds it sometimes perches on trees and bushes. Male marks its territory with an undulating display flight with shimmering wings and a parachute glide.

VOICE
Common call is a distinctive 'cour-lee' from which it gets its common name. In spring, song flight is accompanied with lonely-sounding, bubbling trill.

HABITAT
Breeds in the uplands on boggy, grassy and heather moorland, hill pastures, hay meadows and also, rarely, on coastal marshes. Some nest on agricultural land in lowland areas. In Europe and Russia nests in river valleys and steppe. In winter, found mainly around coasts, especially estuaries. There are some traditional inland wetland wintering sites.

FOOD
In winter, it probes into soft mud for crabs, lugworms, ragworms, small shellfish, cockles, marine snails and shrimps, and in pastures for earthworms. In summer, it eats insects, especially the larvae of beetles and flies, spiders and worms.

BREEDING
Nests on the ground. Male makes several scrapes and one is selected and lined by female. Site usually in the open on a mound or tussock, but sometimes protected by vegetation. The 2–5 eggs are laid in April or May and incubated for 27–29 days by both adults. Young are covered with down and feed themselves. They are cared for by both parents at first, but female often leaves before they fly at 32–38 days.

MOVEMENTS AND MIGRATIONS
Curlews start to leave their breeding grounds in June. The first to leave are the unsuccessful females, followed by the males and lastly the juveniles. Early movements may be from the hills to nearby coasts, but many Scottish birds will fly on to winter in Ireland. Many breeding birds from Scandinavia start to arrive on Scottish coasts in late summer and will stay for the winter. Oldest known bird reached 31 years.

POPULATION
Around 58,000 pairs breed in Scotland, a population of European significance, and about 85,000 are present in winter. The breeding population appears to be declining in some areas owing to agricultural intensification, habitat fragmentation and, possibly, predation.

CONSERVATION
Curlews have declined in Europe. In Scotland there may have been a similar reduction in numbers. Intensive farming practices, draining of wet pastures and planting of forests have all reduced the available habitat.

male summer

DISTRIBUTION
Breeds in the uplands of England, Scotland and Wales and is widespread in Ireland. Common on Orkney, Shetland and the Hebrides. Major wintering concentrations are found on Orkney, the Firth of Forth, the Clyde and the Solway. Also winters around the coast and a few visit inland sites. Breeds in central and northern Europe and Russia and winters around European and African coasts as far south as South Africa.

GREEN SANDPIPER _TRINGA OCHROPUS_

summer

winter

winter

juvenile

IDENTIFICATION
21–24 cm. Smaller than a Redshank. This wader is shorter legged than Wood Sandpiper and has dumpier looking body, making it less elegant. Has straight bill, longer than Wood Sandpiper's. Back and head are dark green-brown. Has a prominent dark streaked breast contrasting abruptly with white underparts. It has white above and in front of its eye but, unlike Wood Sandpiper, this does not extend behind the eye. In summer, has fine white speckling on its dark back. In flight, the upperwing and underwing are dark which contrasts with the white rump – giving a House Martin-like appearance. Juvenile is neatly speckled and spotted with off-white marks on the back and wings. Adults moult from late July and may not complete it until November or December. Some individuals suspend their moult during their migration.
SEE ALSO: Wood Sandpiper p111, Common Sandpiper p112.

HABITS
Rather shy, nervous and secretive wader that frequently bobs when on the ground, wagging its rear end. When disturbed will take off rapidly with a zig-zag flight that resembles Snipe. Can be seen singly or in small groups.

VOICE
When disturbed it frequently makes a distinctive 'tweet, weet, weet' call in flight – the last two notes being higher pitched.

HABITAT
Breeds in wet woodland and open forests. Outside the breeding season it visits marshes and muddy fringes of lochs, rivers and small pools, sometimes near the coast, but also inland. Some birds will overwinter at similar sites, mainly in lowland areas.

FOOD
In winter, feeds on insects and their larvae, including mayflies, stoneflies, caddisflies and other flies and beetles. Also takes freshwater shrimps, worms, small snails and small fish.

BREEDING
Pairs occasionally breed in Scotland. Unusually for a wader it nests in trees – in the old nests of other species including Woodpigeon and thrushes. Both adults incubate the 3 or 4 eggs. Incubation lasts for 20–23 days and is by both adults, but mainly female. Both parents tend the young at first, but female may leave before they fly at about 28 days.

MOVEMENTS AND MIGRATIONS
Migration begins in June with females moving south before the males and juveniles. Migration takes place across a broad front and many not only cross Europe, but also cross North Africa, including the Sahara Desert. They start to return from March and are back on the breeding grounds by mid-May. Oldest ringed bird was over 11 years.

POPULATION
In some years up to five pairs may breed in Scotland. Fewer than 20 overwinter here, but numbers may increase to over 200 at times of migration, with most seen in autumn.

CONSERVATION
This is such a secretive bird on its breeding grounds that organised protection is almost impossible, and probably unnecessary. It is important that the mixed age forests and wet woodlands in the Scottish highlands are conserved for this and other specialised breeding birds.

DISTRIBUTION

Widespread while on migration, and a small population overwinters in Scotland, often on small lochs or inland marshes. Breeds from the Arctic Circle south to Denmark and also east across Russia to Siberia and China. Apart from the British Isles, small numbers winter elsewhere in western Europe, but most occur in central Africa. Other populations reach South-east Asia and Australasia.

WOOD SANDPIPER *TRINGA GLAREOLA*

IDENTIFICATION

19–21 cm. Smaller than Redshank with straight bill and conspicuous long creamy white stripe from the bill, over the eye to back of neck. Adults have a chequered-looking, brown and white back. Slender neck and fine bill give it an elegant look. Legs are yellowish. In flight, has no wing-bars and lacks the black and white appearance of Green Sandpiper. Has square white rump, barred tail, pale greyish-brown underwing and feet that project beyond the tail. In autumn and winter, back is more uniform grey-brown. Juvenile resembles adult in summer but with dense, buff-coloured spots on back and mottled breast. Adult's moult begins on the breeding grounds in July and is usually suspended and completed on migration or on wintering grounds. Has a second partial moult between January and May into breeding plumage. Juveniles have partial moult between August and January.
SEE ALSO: Green Sandpiper p 110, Redshank p114.

winter

HABITS

Similar to Green Sandpiper, but less shy and can be noisy when migrating. Bobs its body when curious. Agile in flight and climbs steeply. Has an undulating display flight high over its breeding grounds in spring. Often seen singly, but small groups of three or four can be found.

VOICE

Most common call is a rather dry 'chiff-iff-iff', usually given in flight.

HABITAT

Breeds around marshes and swamps in lightly wooded country, often on the fringes of large forests or in flooded birch woods close to large lochs. Outside the breeding season it visits the edges of lochs, flooded grasslands or brackish pools near the coast, but it is essentially a freshwater wader.

FOOD

Feeds on beetles, flies and the larvae of dragonflies, caddisflies, mayflies and moths. Also takes worms, spiders, shellfish and small fish.

BREEDING

Nest is usually on the ground among dense vegetation, but sometimes in a tree – in an old nest of another bird such as a thrush. It lays 4 eggs. Incubation lasts 22–23 days and is by both sexes. Young feed themselves and fly at about 30 days. Both adults care for them at first, but female generally leaves a few days after hatching.

MOVEMENTS AND MIGRATIONS

Adults arrive on their breeding grounds from late April. Post-breeding passage through Scotland is between July and September. Some of these birds may be local, but they are joined by others from northern Europe. They fly on to traditional staging posts close to the Mediterranean, especially the Camargue, where many congregate before their flight into Africa, usually over-flying both the Mediterranean and Sahara Desert. Oldest ringed bird was 11 years.

POPULATION

18–21 pairs nest in Scotland. This small population appears to have been growing slowly in recent years. In most years, the species is a scarce autumn passage migrant, with 40–90 birds occurring in the Northern Isles and along the east coast. Smaller numbers are seen in spring.

CONSERVATION

The Wood Sandpiper is specially protected. It nested in England in the 19th century, but it was not until 1959 that it was proved to have nested again in Scotland. Since then it has bred at up to nine sites. Forestry developments have damaged some sites, but there has been a small increase in the number of pairs in recent years. This species is on the edge of its world range in Scotland, but the re-wetting of some traditional marshes may help this wader in future.

summer

juvenile

DISTRIBUTION

A few pairs breed in the Scottish Highlands. On migration visits many freshwater and brackish habitats in Britain and Ireland. Breeds from Scandinavia eastwards across Russia and Siberia to the Pacific Ocean. Winters in West, central and southern Africa, India and South-east Asia.

COMMON SANDPIPER *ACTITIS HYPOLEUCOS*

IDENTIFICATION

19–21 cm. Much smaller than Redshank, this medium-sized wader has a horizontal posture and constantly wags its rear end up and down. Grey-brown above with neat division between a grey-brown breast and pure white underparts. White from underparts extends up towards neck. Rather small head, short neck, short greenish legs, medium-length straight bill and quite a long tail – extending beyond its folded wings. Adults in summer have short blackish marks across back feathers. Wings have a white bar and rump has white sides and a dark centre. Juvenile has paler buff tips to the wing feathers giving a pattern of scaly bands across the back. Adults begin their moult in August and September and continue until March.

SEE ALSO: Green Sandpiper p110, Wood Sandpiper p111.

summer

HABITS

Flight very distinctive, usually close to the water, on stiff, bowed wings that never seem to rise above the level of the bird's body and alternate between a flickering flight and a glide. Has a rather crouching feeding action and habitually bobs, especially when feeding, after landing or when curious. Usually seen singly outside the breeding season but flocks of a thousand or more sometimes gather on their African wintering grounds. Both adults and young will occasionally dive to escape danger.

winter

VOICE

Call is a shrill 'tee wee wee', usually given in flight as an alarm call. Song is a twittering version of the flight call.

HABITAT

Breeds close to the shores of lochs and fast-flowing burns and rivers, mostly in upland areas. On migration it visits other water bodies – usually containing fresh water, but also brackish pools and sheltered bays and estuaries at the coast, where a few individuals may spend the winter.

FOOD

Usually picks food from the surface rather than probing into sand or mud. Feeds on insects, especially flies and their larvae, beetles, earwigs and grasshoppers. Also eats spiders, worms, freshwater shrimps and small fish.

BREEDING

Nests on ground, usually concealed in vegetation and often close to water. Both sexes make suitable scrapes for the nest and female selects and lines one of them. Both adults share incubation of the 3–5 eggs for about 21 days. Young are covered with down and tended by their parents until they fly at about 27 days.

MOVEMENTS AND MIGRATIONS

Breeding birds leave their nest sites by late July. Juveniles move south more slowly than adults, but most will have left Scotland by late September. It is thought they winter in West Africa. In spring, migrants pass through Scotland in April and May, and while many are local breeding birds, others are heading for Scandinavian breeding grounds. Oldest ringed bird survived 14 years.

POPULATION

Around 20,000 pairs breed in Scotland, with fewer than five being seen in most winters.

CONSERVATION

Once more common in the British Isles, the species has retreated from many southern and lowland areas. Scotland now holds 80% of the British and Irish population. Reasons for the decline may be poor water quality due to the acidification of water courses or run-off from agricultural operations, and recreational disturbance alongside rivers and burns.

juvenile

DISTRIBUTION

Widespread in Scotland, especially in upland areas in summer. Also found in upland areas of England, Wales and Ireland. Widespread in lowland areas while migrating. Breeds from Arctic Europe south to Spain and east to Japan. A few winter in western Europe, including the British Isles, but most fly south to central and southern Africa. Other populations from Asia fly as far as Australia.

GREENSHANK *TRINGA NEBULARIA*

IDENTIFICATION

30–33 cm. Medium-large wader with long slightly upturned bill and long greenish legs. Taller and greyer than Redshank. Grey above and white below, with head, neck and sides of breast pale grey. In flight, wings are uniform grey; long white 'V' up the back and pale tail are conspicuous. In spring, back is darker with irregular black spots and streaks and dark 'arrow-head' marks on neck and breast. Juveniles have darker backs with every feather on the upperparts thinly edged with buff. Adults start to moult in June and July, although some suspend this moult during migration. Partial moult between January and May to acquire breeding plumage. Juveniles have a partial moult between August and March.
SEE ALSO: Redshank p114, Spotted Redshank p115, Green Sandpiper p110.

between 25 and 31 days and male often accompanies them on migration.

MOVEMENTS AND MIGRATIONS

Breeding birds leave nesting areas between June and August, with females and non-breeders departing first and males and juveniles following. They stop at the coast and on some inland waters before continuing south to winter in south-west Ireland, around the Mediterranean or in North Africa. Some birds over-winter in Scotland, but these may include individuals from Scandinavia. Oldest known bird was 24 years.

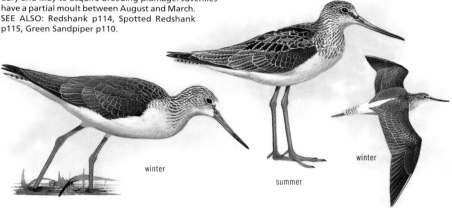

winter

summer

winter

HABITS

When feeding, probes into wet mud, pecks delicately from the surface or sweeps bill from side-to-side. Generally seen singly, but may travel in small flocks. Flight rapid and it sometimes twists erratically. On breeding territories may perch on a post or small tree. Male proclaims territory with a song flight of deep undulations, sometimes reaching a great height, before 'tumbling' back to the ground.

VOICE

Loud, ringing 'tew, tew, tew' call is often given in flight. Also has a rich 'ru-tu, ru-tu, ru-tu' song in spring.

HABITAT

In most of its breeding range inhabits open forest or partially tree-grown areas in the sub-Arctic. In Scotland found on lower moors that may be either dry or boggy, but are usually near small pools or peat bogs. Outside the breeding season it visits the margins of lochs and rivers, and also estuaries and coastal marshes.

FOOD

In summer it feeds on beetles, worms, snails, dragonfly nymphs and small fish. It also eats amphibians such as newts and some plant material. At the coast it eats shrimps, crabs, ragworms and small fish.

BREEDING

Nesting begins in late April. The male makes several nest-scrapes on the ground, in the open, from which the female chooses one. There are usually 4 eggs. Incubation is by both adults and lasts 25–27 days. Young are covered with down and feed themselves. At first both adults tend the chicks, but often the female leaves and begins her migration ahead of the family. Young fly

POPULATION

The Scottish population has been estimated at 720–1,480 pairs, which comprises the entire population of the British Isles. There appears to be an increase in the numbers overwintering, with 50–90 in recent years.

CONSERVATION

Planting of forests on the flow country of Caithness and Sutherland, the drying out of traditional marsh sites and disturbance by leisure activities have all contributed to rob the Greenshank of some its former breeding sites. Climatic changes may also be driving birds farther north. Current restoration of flow country by RSPB may help to restore some breeding sites.

DISTRIBUTION

In Britain it breeds only in the north of Scotland. It occurs widely both inland and on the coast during migration, and some overwinter particularly around Irish coasts. It breeds across northern Europe, north Russia and northern Asia and winters south to South Africa and Australasia.

REDSHANK *TRINGA TOTANUS*

winter

summer

juvenile

IDENTIFICATION

27–29 cm. Medium-sized wader with an orange-red base to its medium-length bill and longish red legs. In spring, adult has a dark brown back with irregular dark markings, heavily lined breast and streaked flanks. In winter, becomes grey-brown with a more uniform appearance, plain grey-brown breast and mottled flanks. Juvenile brown like the summer adult but has neat buff edges to all back and wing feathers and legs are more orange-red. In flight, has very obvious white rear edges to wings and white 'V' up the back. Breeding plumage moulted between June and November; partial moult into breeding plumage between January and May. SEE ALSO: Spotted Redshank p115, Ruff p105.

winter

HABITS

Walks and runs when feeding and also wades and swims. May be seen singly, but not uncommonly forms flocks. Flight sometimes appears a little erratic and it often glides. In spring, has a noisy display as it undulates over territory, calling loudly and gliding to the ground where it pauses with wings raised, displaying the white feathers under its wings. When nesting, frequently perches on posts or on low trees and bushes.

VOICE

Noisy and nervous wader that alerts other birds to approaching danger with ringing 'tew, tew' call. In spring, has a yodelling 'tu-udle, tu-udle' that accompanies its display flight.

HABITAT

Breeds in wet areas, either inland on freshwater marshes, wet grassland and rough pastures, or at the coast on salt marshes. After breeding it moves to the coast, especially sheltered estuaries, salt marshes or where there are brackish pools, although it will also forage on rocky coasts.

FOOD

In coastal areas feeds on shrimps, small fish, shellfish such as cockles, marine snails, small crabs, ragworms and other marine worms. Inland, feeds on earthworms, cranefly larvae, beetles, flies and spiders.

BREEDING

Most eggs are laid in May in a nest made by female in a scrape within rushes or other vegetation. There are usually 4 eggs. Incubation is by both sexes and lasts for 24 days. Young are self-feeding and at first both parents care for the family, but often female leaves before the young fly at 25–35 days.

MOVEMENTS AND MIGRATIONS

From late June numbers on the coast increase as breeding birds move to favoured feeding areas. Some Scottish birds may remain on Scottish estuaries and firths, but many migrate south-west to winter in western Britain, Ireland or south-west Europe. In autumn more Redshanks arrive from Iceland, and while some pass through Scotland and fly on south, many more remain and join the local birds for the whole winter. Oldest bird was 26 years.

POPULATION

11,700–17,500 pairs nest in Scotland, comprising 40% of the British breeding population. Up to 50,000 birds may be present in winter, with large numbers on the Forth, Ythan, Clyde and Solway, and many also on Orkney.

CONSERVATION

Changing agricultural practices, especially increased agricultural drainage, deprive Redshanks of their breeding habitat. Overgrazing of coastal marshes may also be a problem. Future threats may come from climate change and the less predictable weather that is anticipated to accompany this: the species suffers badly in periods of prolonged frost. Rising sea-levels may also cause coastal marshes to be inundated more frequently by summer floods. Breeding numbers have declined in the Western Isles owing to predation by introduced Hedgehogs.

DISTRIBUTION

The greatest concentrations of breeding Redshanks occur in parts of Scotland and north-west England. Others are on the coastal marshes of eastern and southern England. It winters on coasts where there is suitable feeding habitat, from Britain south to the Mediterranean and also in Africa, India and Indonesia. Breeds in Iceland, and from Scandinavia to Spain and east into Asia.

SPOTTED REDSHANK *TRINGA ERYTHROPUS*

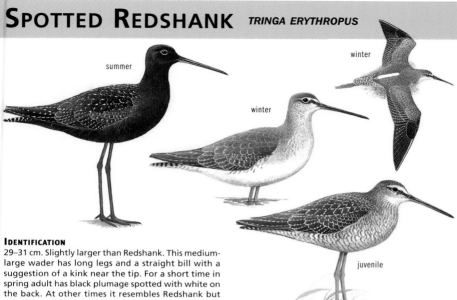

summer

winter

winter

juvenile

IDENTIFICATION
29–31 cm. Slightly larger than Redshank. This medium-large wader has long legs and a straight bill with a suggestion of a kink near the tip. For a short time in spring adult has black plumage spotted with white on the back. At other times it resembles Redshank but with longer bill and longer legs. The back is pale grey with some spotting and the pale head has a black line through the eye with white above. Underparts are white. The legs are red and the lower part of the bill is red at the base. It flight, it has a white lozenge-shape on its back and no wing-bar. Juvenile brown above with dusky belly and barring on flanks. Immature in first summer may become darker with heavily barred underparts. Adults moult completely between July and October. In spring, the body plumage is moulted between March and May. Juveniles have a partial moult between August and February.
SEE ALSO: Redshank p114, Ruff p105.

HABITS
An elegant wader. In flight, it often looks long and slim with legs trailing, but it sometimes tucks its legs under its body giving it a more snipe-like appearance. An energetic feeder that frequently wades in deep water, submerging its whole head in its search for food. Often solitary or in small groups.

VOICE
Usual flight call is a loud and distinctive 'chu-it'.

HABITAT
Breeds on bogs and marshes between the most northerly forests, the taiga, and the Arctic tundra. In Scotland it visits coastal marshes, brackish lagoons and sheltered estuaries, where it especially favours creeks and channels. It will also feed around shallow pools away from the coast.

FOOD
Searches in mud or in water and sometimes chases after prey. Eats adults and larvae of water beetles and flies. Also takes moth caterpillars, shrimps, shellfish, worms and small fish.

BREEDING
Does not breed in the British Isles. It makes a shallow scrape and lines it with leaves and stems. The eggs, usually 4, are incubated mostly by male. Female may leave the breeding site before the eggs hatch or when the chicks are very young. Male looks after young.

MOVEMENTS AND MIGRATIONS
Females leave their breeding grounds from mid-June, before the males and juveniles. Numbers seen in Scotland peak in August and September, when juveniles arrive from Scandinavia. Tiny numbers remain for the winter, but most fly on to winter in southern Britain, southern Europe or Africa. Return migration peaks in April and May, so that females may be present on the breeding grounds for only 4–5 weeks. Oldest bird was 8 years.

POPULATION
Up to 130 are seen during autumn migration, when it occurs most regularly on the east coast and Solway. Usually fewer than 15 are present in spring, and fewer than 10 overwinter.

CONSERVATION
Western Europe sees relatively few of the large number of Spotted Redshanks that move to and from the Arctic each year. The conservation of the estuaries and lowland freshwater wetlands they use to stopover and feed at is as important as the management of the brackish lagoons found near the coast, which are usually specially protected sites and nature reserves.

DISTRIBUTION

Breeds in northern Scandinavia and east across northern Russia and Siberia. Winters in small numbers in Britain and Holland, around the coast of western Europe, around the Mediterranean and in West Africa. Most of the population however winter in a very wide range of countries from West Africa eastwards across India and South-east Asia to Vietnam. Much of the migration takes place overland on a broad front. In Britain and Ireland it is widely distributed on migration but wintering birds are mainly found in the south.

RED-NECKED PHALAROPE *PHALAROPUS LOBATUS*

IDENTIFICATION
18–19 cm. Delicate Dunlin-sized wader that is more likely to be seen swimming than wading. Small head, slender neck and fine straight bill. In spring, female has grey head and upperparts, white throat and underparts, an orange patch on the sides of neck and buff lines on its dark back. Male duller with more buff streaking on upperparts. Juvenile has dark crown and obvious buff lines on back and shows a pale oval near the shoulder. First-winter birds start to show grey lines along the back but retain the neat dark flight feathers, edged buff. In flight, shows white wing-bar on dark wings.
SEE ALSO: Grey Phalarope p117, Sanderling p96.

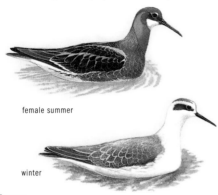

female summer

winter

HABITS
A remarkably tame wader when seen in small groups on its breeding grounds in the Northern or Western Isles. Individuals may also be seen on migration. In winter, it gathers in large flocks on the open sea. It swims buoyantly with neck held straight as it spins and turns on the water, or bobs its head like a Moorhen when swimming.

VOICE
Most common call is a sharp 'twit', or 'whit' given in flight or on the water.

HABITAT
In Scotland it nests mainly on Shetland, with smaller numbers on the Outer Hebrides. The nest is usually near marshy, freshwater pools within a few kilometres of the sea, where there is open water and emergent vegetation. On migration it may visit any body of fresh water, especially brackish pools near the coast. It also swims on the sea and winters on the open ocean.

FOOD
Feeds while swimming, wading or walking. Chief food is insects, especially flies and their larvae. Also eats springtails, beetles, butterflies, moths, spiders and small worms.

BREEDING
Nests on the ground, close to water, usually in a grassy tussock with grass pulled over the top of the nest. Both sexes make nest-scrapes and female selects one in which to lay her 4 eggs. Eggs are laid in late May or early June. Incubation is by male and lasts 17–21 days. Young quickly move to emergent vegetation where they feed themselves and remain well hidden. They are cared for by male until independent at about 14 days and are able to fly at about 20 days. Once fledged, young leave their breeding site within about 5 days.

MOVEMENTS AND MIGRATIONS
Starts to leave its northern breeding grounds from the end of June. Females leave first followed by males in July and juveniles in August. Migration is still little understood, but northern European birds tend to migrate south-east across Europe and gather in large concentrations on the Arabian Sea by late October. There they remain in their winter quarters until the following April and arrive back on their breeding grounds during May. Oldest bird was 9 years.

POPULATION
Less than 50 pairs breed in Scotland. There has been a decline in both range and numbers since the 19th century. Numbers have more recently fluctuated, but have declined on Shetland since 2004. The best place to view breeding birds is the RSPB's reserve on Fetlar.

CONSERVATION
Specially protected. It has been a target for egg collectors and suffered from the drainage of suitable pools. The current breeding sites require protection and careful management to ensure a succession of pools for feeding and nesting. It is important that grazing animals are restricted in the breeding areas in spring, but are allowed to graze down rank vegetation later on. Climate changes may be affecting Scottish breeders too.

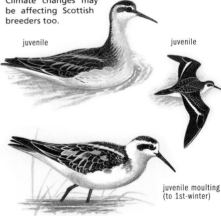

juvenile

juvenile

juvenile moulting
(to 1st-winter)

DISTRIBUTION
The few Scottish sites are the only places where the species breeds in the British Isles. It also nests in northern Scandinavia, Iceland, northern Russia and North America. It winters in the Indian and Pacific oceans, and may sometimes be seen on the coast of western Europe, including Britain, on migration, especially after nesting.

GREY PHALAROPE *PHALAROPUS FULICARIUS*

female summer

IDENTIFICATION

20–22 cm. Dunlin-sized wader that is larger and chunkier than Red-necked Phalarope with shorter thicker bill and longer broader wings. Adults in breeding plumage are rare in Britain and Ireland. Most of the year it is pale grey above and white below, with a dark mark behind eye and an almost plain grey back. In breeding plumage has dark brown back streaked brightly with buff, white face patch, yellow bill with dark tip, and varying amount of red on underparts. Male duller than female in summer. Most common plumages in Britain and Ireland are juvenile and first winter – these birds are brown above with all back feathers neatly edged buff, with varying amounts of grey moulting through. Juvenile has thin buff stripes on dark back and pale buff wash to breast. Adults moult between July and November. Partial moult back into breeding plumage during March–May. Juveniles moult their body plumage and some wing feathers in autumn.

SEE ALSO: Red-necked Phalarope p116, Knot p100, Sanderling p96.

juvenile

HABITS

Very tame wader, commonly swimming and spinning as it feeds. Frequently 'bobs' its head like a Moorhen. The pale non-breeding plumage and buoyant swimming action is reminiscent of a small gull. Will also feed on land near water. Generally seen singly, but larger groups may be seen on migration.

VOICE

Common call is a low 'wit'. Also a 'zhit' call given when a bird is disturbed.

HABITAT

Migrants may visit coastal waters or pools near the coast. Sometimes seen further inland, especially following storms. Breeds near the coast in the Arctic, close to brackish lagoons, pools, boggy meadows and on marshy tundra. After breeding it lives on the open ocean.

FOOD

Feeds on land, or while swimming. Eats mainly invertebrates and some plant material. Food includes flies and their larvae, beetles, bugs, springtails, shrimps, worms and spiders. In winter, feeds on marine plankton.

juvenile

juvenile moulting
(to 1st-winter)

BREEDING

Does not breed in the British Isles. This is a sociable species with birds nesting close together in some places. It nests on the ground, near water. A pair makes a scrape and the female selects one that is then lined by the male. Male incubates the 4 eggs for 18–20 days while female goes off to mate with another male if an excess of males is present. Young feed themselves and are cared for by the male alone until they fly at about 16–18 days.

MOVEMENTS AND MIGRATIONS

An oceanic wader, migrating across the sea and wintering well away from land. Those seen on or near land outside the breeding season are off course, usually owing to bad weather encountered while migrating. There is a staggered departure from the breeding grounds, with non-breeders leaving in June, females in July and then males with, or followed by, young. 'Storm-wrecked' birds mostly occur in September and October, although there are sometimes sightings in winter. Spring sightings are very rare.

POPULATION

10–50 are seen on or near the Scottish coast during times of migration. The number of observations is slowly increasing, particularly on west coast headlands, possibly because more birdwatchers are observing passage seabirds.

CONSERVATION

Too few occur in Scotland for any special protection to be necessary, but birds like Grey Phalaropes that winter in discrete areas of the oceans need plankton-rich seas to feed on and they are potentially at risk from pollution.

DISTRIBUTION

Small numbers visit mainly northern or western Scotland in autumn. Also seen in other parts of the British Isles, especially Cornwall. Breeds in Iceland, Spitsbergen, Siberia, Greenland and North America. Winters out to sea, in the Atlantic Ocean, off the coasts of Africa, South America and the southern USA.

TURNSTONE *ARENARIA INTERPRES*

summer

IDENTIFICATION
22–24 cm. Chunky-looking wader that is smaller than Redshank with large head, short bill and short orange legs. In spring, adult has black and white head, black breast and bright orange and brown mottled pattern on back. In winter, all the upperparts, including the head, become mottled grey-brown. Underparts are white. In flight, looks black and white with white wing-bars, white back and shoulder stripes and black and white tail. Adults start to moult between July and November; partial moult back into breeding plumage between March and May.
SEE ALSO: Oystercatcher p89, Redshank p114, Ringed Plover p91.

HABITS
Generally seen in small groups that can be rather tame. When feeding busily searches shoreline, dodging waves, and often flicking aside seaweed and small pebbles to reach food. Seldom still, running over rocks, but frequently perches on posts and other objects in water. Often flies close to water and can also swim.

VOICE
Usual call in flight is a rather metallic, twittering 'kit-it-it'. It also has rippling song on breeding grounds that ends in rattling 'quitta, quitta, quitta'.

HABITAT
May visit almost all types of coast, especially where rocks are covered with seaweed, but also feeds on softer sandy and muddy shores, often close to mussel beds. Breeds on small islands and near the sea on bare ground. Also breeds on Arctic tundra in dwarf willows or on barren, rocky ground.

FOOD
Feeds on mussels, barnacles, sandhoppers, periwinkles, crabs and insects. An opportunist feeder: a wide variety of food has been recorded, from household scraps to a human corpse washed up on a beach.

BREEDING
Does not normally breed in Britain or Ireland. Birds arrive back on their breeding grounds already in pairs. Nests are a scrape on bare ground or among low-growing vegetation. The clutch of usually 4 eggs is incubated by both sexes for about 23 days. Female leaves before the young become independent at 19–21 days.

MOVEMENTS AND MIGRATIONS
Turnstones that are seen in Scotland breed in northern Europe, Greenland and north-east Canada. Migrants mainly start arriving in July. It is thought that most of the European birds that pass along the east coast of Scotland in July and August go on to winter in Africa, while those from Greenland and Canada arrive to moult and stay for the winter in Scotland or elsewhere in western Europe. Wintering birds gradually leave between February and May, although some non-breeders may remain for the whole summer. Those that return to Greenland and Canada may break their

winter

journey in Iceland, but some probably fly direct to Greenland and then overfly the ice cap. Oldest ringed bird was 20 years.

POPULATION
There is just one possible breeding record, in Scotland in 1976. About 35,000 Turnstones winter in Scotland and more pass through on migration. Wintering numbers appear to be declining in the south of Scotland

CONSERVATION
There are no special conservation measures to protect this species. Changes in distribution of shellfish and other food because of cleaning up of sewage outfalls may affect numbers. Should a small regular breeding population establish itself, then these sites may need special protection.

summer   winter

DISTRIBUTION

Seen around the coasts of Britain and Ireland at all seasons and nested at least once in Scotland. Breeds right round the Arctic Circle, from northern Canada, Greenland, Spitsbergen, Scandinavia, northern Russia, Siberia and Alaska. Winters as far south as Chile, South Africa and Australia, with some birds from North America wintering in western Europe.

IDENTIFICATION

48–53 cm (35–41 cm excluding tail streamers). Small slim skua the size of Black-headed Gull with long wings. The adult resembles a small pale Arctic Skua with slimmer wings and very long delicate tail streamers. It is usually very dusky below with only the upper breast pale. Lacks white on the underside of the wings, and has only one or two pale feather shafts on its upperwing. Upperparts are grey with contrasting dark hind edge to the wing and dark flight feathers. There is only one adult phase – pale. Juveniles are very grey-looking birds. They are barred below and have all feathers of their upperparts tipped pale greyish white. Folded primaries are solid dark, unlike Arctic Skua. In flight, blunt projecting central tail feathers are only just visible. Some juveniles are very dark chocolate-brown but still have barring under the tail and pale edges to their back feathers. Some pale juveniles have almost white heads.
SEE ALSO: Arctic Skua p120, Pomarine Skua p121.

HABITS

An elegant seabird that has buoyant, graceful, almost tern-like flight. It chases terns and Kittiwakes but also, on migration, swims a lot and picks for food on the sea's surface.

juvenile (dark)

juvenile (intermediate)

juvenile (very pale)

summer

summer

juvenile (intermediate)

VOICE

Generally silent when not nesting.

HABITAT

A marine species that sometimes passes through Scottish inshore waters on migration. It breeds in the far north on Arctic tundra and on fells above the tree-line, and it winters at sea. In Scotland second-year and adult Long-tailed Skuas are sometimes present at colonies of Arctic Skuas in summer.

FOOD

Often obtains food by chasing other species. On its breeding grounds its main food is small mammals, especially lemmings and some voles. It also eats eggs of other birds, insects, worms and berries. At sea it feeds on small fish, offal and carrion.

BREEDING

The Long-tailed Skua has been known to nest in Scotland only once, in 1980. Nests are usually on the ground and in loose colonies. Both adults take turns to incubate the 2 eggs for about 24 days and the young fly at about 25 days.

MOVEMENTS AND MIGRATIONS

Post-breeding migration begins in July, with birds passing along Scottish coasts from August to mid-October. Most of these migrants are seen in the North Sea, but others are out in the Atlantic and pass to the north or west of Scotland. They are thought to winter off the West African coast, and others have been seen off Argentinian and Brazilian coasts between September and May. Birds returning north are seen mainly off the Hebrides during mid-May, particularly when winds bring them close inshore. The RSPB's Balranald reserve is a noted locality for observing them on spring migration.

POPULATION

Apart from the single breeding record and few birds present in summer, most sightings are of migrating birds. Numbers passing through Scottish waters are generally small, but occasional influxes have been recorded, so that in any one year there may be between 100 and 1,500 sightings.

CONSERVATION

There are currently no specific conservation measures for this seabird, although it would help to know more about its winter quarters. Like other seabirds this skua would be threatened by unsustainable fishing methods in its winter quarters and in time its northern breeding grounds could be influenced by changes to the climate.

DISTRIBUTION

This species nests in northern Scandinavia, Arctic Russia, Siberia across to Asia, the north of North America and parts of Greenland, with the largest numbers in Russia, Alaska and Canada. It spends the winter in the Pacific, Atlantic and Indian oceans.

ARCTIC SKUA STERCORARIUS PARASITICUS

IDENTIFICATION
41–46 cm. Much smaller than Herring Gull. Resembles dark gull but with long pointed central tail feathers and long pointed and rather narrow wings with white flashes. There are dark and pale colour morphs, but many adults are intermediate. Dark morph is uniform dark brown below. Intermediate birds are warmer, more golden brown below, with paler yellow-brown on side of face and neck. Pale morph has a dark cap, white neck, cheeks and underparts and, sometimes, a pale grey-brown breast-band. Juveniles have buff edges to all feathers on their upperparts and central tail feathers have small points. Intermediate juveniles are warm, gingery brown. No juveniles are cold, grey-brown like Long-tailed juveniles and at rest they show pale marks on dark folded primaries, unlike the other two species. Adults moult completely after breeding. SEE ALSO: Pomarine Skua p121, Long-tailed Skua p119, Great Skua p122.

HABITS
Flight is fast and falcon-like when chasing other seabirds. Twists and turns and harasses them until they either drop their catch or disgorge their food. On its breeding territory it is very aggressive, attacking

MOVEMENTS AND MIGRATIONS
Breeding birds return to Scotland in April and May. There is also a strong passage of light-phase birds in May, most of which move quickly along the west coast as they head for their Arctic breeding grounds. Return migration begins in late June with non-breeders leaving their colonies, and continues until October, mainly along the east coast. A few birds remain in Scotland all winter. Oldest ringed bird survived 31 years.

POPULATION
The species expanded from its stronghold on the Northern Isles during the 20th century, and there are now around 2,000 pairs breeding, with colonies scattered across the Western Isles and north coast as well as Orkney and Shetland.

CONSERVATION
The success of this species is linked to the health of the local seabird population (particularly that of Arctic Terns), which in turn depends on fish stocks. The decline in sand-eels through overfishing or climate change has been disastrous for many seabirds, in particular the terns and kittiwakes from which Arctic Skuas steal fish. The spread of the Great Skua may also have had impact on the smaller Arctic Skua.

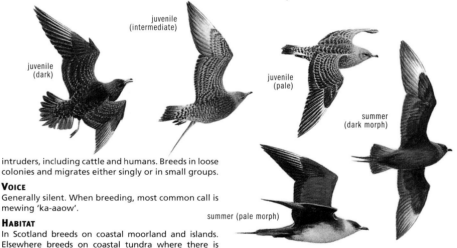

juvenile (intermediate)

juvenile (dark)

juvenile (pale)

summer (dark morph)

summer (pale morph)

intruders, including cattle and humans. Breeds in loose colonies and migrates either singly or in small groups.

VOICE
Generally silent. When breeding, most common call is mewing 'ka-aaow'.

HABITAT
In Scotland breeds on coastal moorland and islands. Elsewhere breeds on coastal tundra where there is moss, grass or other vegetation. There are usually freshwater pools nearby where the birds bathe. Outside the breeding season spends most of the time at sea.

FOOD
Eats mainly fish, especially sand-eels and Sprats, that it obtains by harassing other seabirds. Also a scavenger on dead mammals and birds. Will take eggs from nests, kill and eat young birds and small mammals such as voles. Also feeds on insects and berries.

BREEDING
In Scotland first eggs are laid in May in a nest on the ground in the open. There are almost always 2 eggs and both sexes incubate for 25–28 days. Incubation starts with the first egg, which hatches ahead of the second. Young are cared for and fed by both parents. Young fly after 25–30 days and are independent after 2–5 weeks. They do not breed until at least 3 years old.

DISTRIBUTION
In Britain this species is at the southern limit of its range. Breeds in northern Scotland, especially Shetland. Also breeds in Iceland and around the northern coast of Scandinavia, Greenland, North America and Siberia. European population mainly winters off the coast of South Africa.

POMARINE SKUA *STERCORARIUS POMARINUS*

IDENTIFICATION
46–51 cm. Approaching the size of Herring Gull. Larger and heavier than Arctic and Long-tailed Skuas, with a deeper chest, bulkier body, and a longer, heavier gull-like bill that is pale with a dark tip. Adults have long spoon-shaped central tail streamers, although these are sometimes damaged. Two colour morphs: the rarer (less than 10%) all-dark morph with smaller wing flashes, and paler birds with dark caps, variable white underparts, sometimes a dark breast-band and often with barred flanks. The wings are long, broad at the base and with a pale crescent shape on the underwing. Juvenile is pale or dark grey-brown and closely barred, with strong barring under the tail and pale legs. Juveniles at rest show virtually all dark flight feathers, Arctic Skuas show conspicuous pale tips. The underwing of the juvenile Pomarine has two pale crescents, the Arctic has only one. Adults start to moult in August but do not complete this moult until well away from Britain and Ireland. Juveniles also moult in wintering areas.
SEE ALSO: Arctic Skua p120, Great Skua p122, Long-tailed Skua p119.

summer pale morph

summer dark morph

1st-summer pale morph

summer female pale morph

juvenile intermediate

HABITS
A large aggressive skua that sometimes attacks other birds to rob them of their prey. When hunting it occasionally forces victims into the sea to drown them. Normal flight is steady with measured downbeats and very brief glides and sometimes resembles a large gull. On migration it can be seen in groups of 7–20 at a time, and more rarely 70 or more.

VOICE
Generally silent outside its breeding grounds.

HABITAT
This is a seabird that breeds on the Arctic tundra and lives for the rest of the year in offshore waters, coming closer to land mainly as a result of rough weather.

FOOD
Outside the breeding season it feeds mainly on fish that it catches itself by diving or by robbing other species. It also kills and eats other birds and takes carrion when available. On its breeding grounds it feeds mainly on lemmings and the young of other birds.

BREEDING
The Pomarine Skua does not breed in Scotland. It nests on the ground in the Arctic tundra and usually lays 2 eggs in late June. Incubation is by both adults and lasts about 28 days. Both parents tend the chicks until the young fly at about 32 days.

MOVEMENTS AND MIGRATIONS
Twice a year this skua passes close to the Scottish coast. In April and May, it is mainly seen from the Outer Hebrides. The return movement from its Arctic breeding grounds is between late July and early November, when the birds are more likely to be seen off the Northern Isles and east coast. They then travel to winter in the Atlantic off the coast of Africa. A greater number of juveniles are seen in years when lemmings are abundant on the species' breeding grounds.

POPULATION
Numbers vary widely from year to year, but it is thought that up to 4,500 pass through in spring and up to 2,000 in autumn.

CONSERVATION
As the species does not breed or winter in Britain or Ireland there are no special protection measures for it. In future it might be affected by declining fish stocks, which would reduce its food supply while it passes through British and Irish waters.

DISTRIBUTION
The species breeds in the far north of North America, Asia and Europe. It normally passes well to the west of Scotland and Ireland when migrating and it winters off the coast of West Africa. North American breeders winter off South American coasts and Siberian breeders winter in the Arabian Sea. It is widely distributed across the Atlantic during peak migration times.

GREAT SKUA OR BONXIE *CATHARACTA SKUA*

juvenile

juvenile (dark)

IDENTIFICATION
53–58 cm. This, our largest skua, is the size of a Herring Gull, but more bulky and heavier-looking with broader, slightly rounded wings and heavy bill. Has a proportionally shorter tail than other skuas and no streamers. Plumage usually blackish-brown with straw-coloured streaks and very obvious white flashes in the wings, above and below. Adult in summer may be paler and more yellow-brown, especially on the head and back. Juvenile tends to be uniformly darker, but there is some variation and a few may be noticeably paler. Adults moult their body feathers between June and September, but flight feathers are moulted only gradually between August and January while in its winter quarters.
SEE ALSO: Juvenile Herring Gull p124, Pomarine Skua p121, Arctic Skua p120.

HABITS
In flight, resembles a large gull, but more compact with strong downbeats and a big belly. Accelerates with powerful wingbeats and is surprisingly agile when pursuing other species. Very aggressive and chases large seabirds such as Gannets. On breeding grounds it fiercely attacks intruders, including domestic animals and humans.

VOICE
Usually silent away from breeding grounds. Main calls are a loud 'gek-gek' during attacks on intruders and a rolling 'hah-hah-hah'.

HABITAT
Breeds on rocky islands and moorland near the coast and spends the winter at sea.

FOOD
Specialises in robbing other species of their prey, usually of fish, but also hunts by taking food from the surface of the sea. Main food is sand-eels, Haddock and Whiting. Also eats carrion and offal discharged from fishing boats. Kills other birds such as Puffins and even species as large as a Brent Goose.

BREEDING
Within a colony the Great Skua defends its territory. Nest is a hollow on the ground into which the 2 eggs are laid. Incubation is mainly by female and lasts 26–32 days. Young leave the nest soon after hatching and remain separately within their territory. Female guards young while male obtains most of the food, which he regurgitates for his family. Young fly after about 44 days and are dependent on their parents for up to 20 days. Young can breed when 4 or 5 years old, but more often they are 7 years or older before nesting for the first time.

MOVEMENTS AND MIGRATIONS
Birds arrive back on their breeding territories in April. They disperse again from July, after breeding, and most travel down the east coast of Scotland in August and September. Much of their migration is out of sight of land, unless they are driven close to shore by strong winds. They continue south through the English Channel, and most go on to winter off the coast of West Africa. Those breeding in Iceland may migrate towards North America. Oldest known bird lived for 32 years.

POPULATION
The Scottish population is estimated at 9,650 pairs, comprising a significant proportion of the world population. Most occur on the Northern Isles, but smaller colonies are found on some Hebridean islands.

CONSERVATION
This was a rare breeding bird until the 20th century. At first it was welcomed, but as numbers increased it came into conflict with farming interests as it was alleged to prevent pregnant ewes from feeding on new spring grass. Changes in fishing practices affected sand-eel numbers, and that in turn reduced Great Skua breeding success. Also concentrations of pollutants have been found in Great Skuas, but the long-term effect is unclear. Scotland is important for this breeding bird, holding some 60% of the world population.

DISTRIBUTION
In Britain nests mainly in Shetland and Orkney. May nest in Iceland and other populations breed in the Faroes, northern Norway, Spitsbergen and northern Russia. Seen around British and Irish coasts in autumn and spends the winter in the east Atlantic between the Bay of Biscay and Senegal.

LITTLE GULL   *LARUS MINUTUS*

1st-winter

1st-winter

winter

summer

summer

winter

IDENTIFICATION
25–27 cm. This delicate bird is the smallest gull, noticeably smaller than Black-headed Gull, with small dark bill and red legs. Adult in spring has black (not brown) hood, grey back, blunt-ended pale grey upperwings that have a thin white edge from tip to rear. Underwings are very dark, like charcoal. In winter, black hood is replaced by a black spot behind the eye and dark shading on back of head. Juvenile is blackish-brown and white with a dark crown and an obvious dark 'W' wing pattern across upperwings in flight. First-winter birds have grey backs, a bold dark 'W' wing-pattern, a black tail-band and dusky marks on the head. First-summer birds resemble first-winter birds but have a smudgy dark hood and are in rather worn plumage. Second-winter birds retain some dark marks on their wing-tips. Adults gain their full black hood from February.
SEE ALSO: Black-headed Gull p130, Mediterranean Gull p246.

HABITS
Quick wingbeats and rather erratic, buoyant zigzag flight is reminiscent of a tern. Frequently feeds in flight by dipping down and picking prey delicately from the water.

VOICE
Not normally very vocal but has a 'kek, kek, kek' call.

HABITAT
Visits Scottish coasts and brackish pools near the sea in autumn and winter. It occasionally visits inland lochs and other large water bodies while migrating. Breeds in freshwater marshes, beside rivers and lakes, and sometimes at coastal sites where there is lush vegetation.

FOOD
Much of its food is insects such as dragonflies, mayflies, midges and their larvae, water bugs such as water boatmen, ants and beetles. It also eats spiders, worms and fish.

BREEDING
Breeding has been suspected in Scotland on two occasions, in 1988 and 1991. Nests on the ground in colonies from May to early June. Nest is on tussock of grasses or rushes in a marsh. Both adults incubate the 2 or 3 eggs, starting with the first egg, with the result that the young hatch at different times. Incubation is for 23–25 days. Young wander from the nest when a few days old, but continue to be fed by both parents. They fly at 21–24 days.

MOVEMENTS AND MIGRATIONS
Movements are complex. After breeding birds disperse to coastal waters and sheltered bays to moult and then move out to sea. Many winter in the Irish Sea and a few on the Scottish east coast. Most go south to cross the English Channel, reaching as far south as the western Mediterranean and African coast. A wave of birds appears in Scotland in May and June, mainly in the east, and a second wave in October/November, particularly in the Firth of Forth. Some of these movements can involve hundreds of birds. Oldest bird survived over 20 years.

POPULATION
The spring passage may involve up to 400 birds, while as many as 3,000 may be seen on autumn passage.

CONSERVATION
The species is specially protected. In its major breeding colonies in Russia it appears to be declining owing to drainage of wetlands, natural and man-made flooding during the breeding season and also activities such as fishing, which disturb breeding colonies.

DISTRIBUTION

May be seen at any time, especially along the east coast and around the Forth and Tay. There are three distinct breeding populations – in eastern Siberia, western Siberia and Russia west to the Baltic Sea – plus smaller numbers in eastern North America and a few other scattered colonies, including a number of breeding attempts in the British Isles. The Russia/Europe population winters mainly around the coast of Europe and in the Nile Delta. Other populations winter off the coast of China and even India.

HERRING GULL   *LARUS ARGENTATUS*

IDENTIFICATION
55–67 cm. Large gull, between Lesser and Great Black-backed in size, but with grey back and wings. Fierce-looking, with powerful, slightly hooked yellow bill with a red spot near the tip. Legs and feet are flesh-coloured. Wings are broad giving rather heavy appearance in flight and the wing-tips are black with white spots. In winter, head and neck are heavily streaked with grey. Juvenile is mottled brown and very similar to juvenile Lesser Black-backed Gull. It is not until its second winter that the adult grey colour of the upperparts becomes obvious. Adult moult starts early, often in mid-May, while nesting. Gradual moult and re-growth of flight feathers takes 3–6 months. There is a second partial moult between January and March.
SEE ALSO: Lesser Black-backed Gull p126, Common Gull p125, Kittiwake p131.

juvenile   winter

of vegetation is built by both sexes on the ground, on a cliff ledge or even on a roof of a building. Clutch of 2–4 (usually 3) eggs is incubated for 28–30 days by both adults. Young are well camouflaged and covered with down. They leave nest after 2–3 days but remain within the territory. They fly at 35–40 days old and quickly become independent.

MOVEMENTS AND MIGRATIONS
After breeding there is a general movement southwards, with many remaining in Scotland, others migrating south of the border and a few reaching mainland Europe. Between October and March the Scottish population increases owing to the arrival of other Herring Gulls from Scandinavia and Russia. Some of these migrate on to southern Britain, but many remain in Scotland for the winter. Oldest bird was 34 years.

POPULATION
About 72,000 pairs nest in Scotland, with numbers rising to over 100,000 in winter. Following a rapid increase in the 20th century, the species has now declined markedly as a breeding species in some areas.

CONSERVATION
Increased during the 20th century as it benefited from new food supplies on rubbish tips and around fishing boats and from safe roosts on reservoirs. Recently it has declined in some coastal areas, while urban nesting has increased. Some have suffered from botulism – a disease caught from bacteria found on refuse tips and in shallow pools in warm weather.

summer

winter

HABITS
Individuals may feed singly, but are seldom far from others. Nests in noisy colonies and joins large communal roosts. At the coast follows fishing boats to scavenge for discarded fish. Feeds in ploughed fields and forms large feeding groups at refuse tips. Adaptable, dropping shellfish onto rocks to break their shells, or hunting like a bird of prey in search of small mammals.

VOICE
Variety of loud, wailing and laughing cries, short barks, and a familiar 'kyow, kyow, kyow'.

HABITAT
Found around most coasts and offshore fishing grounds. Largest numbers nest near the sea, on cliffs, dunes, grassy areas and offshore islands, but some breed away from the coast, increasingly on rooftops in towns. It is widespread outside the breeding season, but still most numerous near the coast. It visits town parks, rubbish tips and fishing ports, and roosts on sheltered coastal waters and large lochs.

1st-winter

FOOD
Has a wide range of food, from offal and carrion to seeds and fruits. Sometimes robs other birds of their food, eats the young and eggs of other birds, catches small mammals, scavenges on rubbish tips, catches flying ants and plunges into the water for fish.

BREEDING
Pairs defend a small territory inside a colony. Nesting begins in April and a nest comprising a large mound

DISTRIBUTION
Found almost all round the Scottish coast and the rest of Britain. Can be seen anywhere except in mountainous country in winter. Also breeds in Iceland and parts of western Europe. Winters as far south as Spain.

COMMON GULL *LARUS CANUS*

IDENTIFICATION
40–42 cm. Smaller, but superficially similar to Herring Gull, with blue-grey back and black wing-tips with white spots. Legs and bill are greenish yellow and dark eyes give the bird a gentle appearance. Wings are less pointed than Black-headed's, with no white on leading edge. In winter, has dusky marks on head and neck. Juvenile has mottled brown back and dusky marks on head and underparts. First-winter bird is also mottled on head and underparts, but has a grey back and a thick tail-band. Adults moult between June and October and there is a second partial moult between February and April.
SEE ALSO: Herring Gull p124, Kittiwake p131.

summer

1st-summer

summer

1st-winter

juvenile

2nd-winter

winter

HABITS
Breeds among colonies of other gulls or terns, but sometimes has its own colonies. Sociable outside the breeding season, often feeding and roosting with other gulls.

VOICE
Call is higher pitched than other gulls, an almost mewing 'keee-ya'.

HABITAT
Breeding colonies may be near the coast or miles inland in marshes, on islands in lochs, on moorland and sometimes on the roofs of buildings. Outside the breeding season may be found inland on farmland, around lochs, urban playing fields and reservoirs. Also winters at the coast where many may roost on estuaries.

FOOD
Takes live prey and carrion and sometimes robs other species. In summer, feeds on worms, cranefly larvae and other flies, moths, beetles, eggs, berries, small mammals, young birds and fish. In winter, feeds on invertebrates, fish, crustaceans and also scavenges rubbish tips.

BREEDING
Breeds in colonies, often on fens or near fresh water, and sometimes gains protection by nesting close to other gull species or terns. Egg-laying begins in late April or May in a nest on the ground, in low vegetation or sometimes on cliff-tops or roofs. Nest is made of vegetation or seaweed and is built by both sexes. Both adults incubate the 2–4 eggs for 22–28 days. Young are fed by both parents and leave nest within 3–5 days. They stay in the vicinity of the nest until they can fly at about 35 days and become independent soon afterwards.

MOVEMENTS AND MIGRATIONS
Most breeding birds move south after nesting. Many remain in Scotland, but others head on to southern Britain or Ireland, and a few may reach mainland Europe. From July and August birds from Iceland and Scandinavia arrive; some of these pass through Scotland to winter further south, while others will stay and join the local birds. Return migration takes place in March and April, with both Scottish breeders and those from further north making their way back to their breeding grounds; adults leave first, followed by juveniles. Oldest bird was 33 years.

POPULATION
Over 48,000 pairs nest in Scotland, comprising 67% of the British population. Numbers increase to around 80,000 in winter, but at peak migration times it has been estimated that there be as many as 200,000 birds in Scotland.

CONSERVATION
As the majority of Common Gulls are inland breeders they are likely to be adversely affected by drainage of marshes, agricultural changes and even forestry where it replaces wet moorland. Following earlier increase, some large colonies have recently declined.

DISTRIBUTION
Common Gulls breed widely in Scotland and also in the west of Ireland. There are breeding colonies in the north of England and a few coastal locations farther south and east. The species breeds in northern Europe, Russia, northern Asia and North America. European birds mainly winter in western Europe and around the Black Sea.

LESSER BLACK-BACKED GULL *LARUS FUSCUS*

IDENTIFICATION
52–67 cm. Generally a little smaller and slimmer than Herring Gull with slightly longer yellow (not pink) legs and darker slate-grey back. In winter, heads and necks become streaked with grey. Juvenile is uniformly streaked grey-brown with scaly pattern on back and uniformly barred wings. It is hard to distinguish it from a juvenile Herring Gull, but it has more uniform flight feathers with no pale 'window' like Herring Gull. By the second winter the adult colouring of the back starts to appear. Those breeding in southern Scandinavia have blackish backs, but not quite as black as their wing-tips. Another race occurs further east and has an even more intensely black back. Dark-backed races are separated from the Great Black-backed by smaller size, slimmer bill and smaller head. Annual moult for adults begins between May and August and is not complete on some birds until November. Partial pre-breeding moult between January and April.
SEE ALSO: Great Black-backed Gull p127, Herring Gull p124.

HABITS
The wings are longer and narrower than those of a Herring Gull, giving the species a long-winged appearance in flight. Breeds in colonies, often with other gulls, and is also sociable at other times of year, usually joining large evening roosts with other gulls. It migrates singly or in small groups.

VOICE
A rather gruff 'kaw' and rough laughing cries, 'ga ga gag'.

HABITAT
It breeds around the coast on sand dunes and shingle islands and also inland on upland moors. Also occurs in towns, and sometimes nests on buildings. Outside the breeding season it ranges widely, both inland and near the coast, although in coastal areas it mainly visits inshore waters.

FOOD
It eats a wide range of food, including small mammals, especially voles, and also birds, including Puffins and terns. It eats eggs, fish, insects, shrimps, shellfish, worms and plant material, including seaweed and berries. It eats carrion and scavenges on rubbish tips.

summer

2nd-summer

winter *scandinavian*

winter

BREEDING
Nesting begins in late April or early May. The nest is usually on the ground, sometimes in the open, but often near long vegetation where chicks can hide. Both sexes build the large nest from seaweed, grasses and other local materials. The 2–4 eggs (usually 3) are incubated by both birds for 24–27 days. The young hatch over a period of 1–6 days and leave the nest a few days later but do not generally wander far. They are fed by both parents, and fly after 30–40 days.

MOVEMENTS AND MIGRATIONS
Mainly a summer migrant to Scotland, with most leaving in the autumn to spend the winter further south in Britain, Europe or even Africa. Some remain over winter, especially around the Clyde. In autumn there is a large passage of birds from further north moving south through Scotland, and a return migration takes place in spring. Oldest bird was 34 years.

POPULATION
As many as 25,000 pairs may nest in Scotland, with notable colonies on islands in the Firth of Forth. A growing number now overwinters in the British Isles, 200–600 of them in Scotland.

CONSERVATION
The population in Scotland increased during the 20th century and may still be increasing overall, but there are signs of decline in some areas – especially Shetland, which may be linked to changes in the fishing industry, and at some inland colonies on moorland.

juvenile

winter

1st-winter

DISTRIBUTION
The species breeds in northern and western Europe and northern Russia. It winters as far south as the Mediterranean and North Africa. There are several distinct races. The pale-backed race that breeds in Britain and Ireland also nests in Iceland, France and north-west Spain. A darker-backed race breeds in Scandinavia and western Russia and many of these spend the winter in Britain. Another dark-backed race from Russia only rarely reaches Britain in winter.

GREAT BLACK-BACKED GULL *LARUS MARINUS*

IDENTIFICATION
64–78 cm. Our largest gull. Has larger head, heavier bill, thicker neck, and proportionally thicker wings and legs than Lesser Black-backed Gull. Appears heavy and powerful both on the ground and in flight. Back and wings are black and legs are flesh-coloured. In winter, head and neck are lightly streaked with grey. Juvenile has typical brown plumage of young gulls. Its bill is black, the head and breast are paler than the rest of the underparts and it has a bold chequered pattern on its back. Immatures have paler heads than Lesser Black-backed, but the size and shape of a bird is usually a better identification feature until its third year when it starts to acquire its black back. It takes 5 years to reach adult plumage. Adults start their moult between June and August and do not finish until September or even November.
SEE ALSO: Lesser Black-backed Gull p126.

summer

winter

2nd-summer

1st-winter

1st-summer

HABITS
In flight, looks heavy and ponderous. Frequently seen singly or in pairs, although small groups congregate outside breeding season. Often aggressive towards other species and will attack and rob them of their food.

VOICE
Call is rather gruff bark, 'uk, uk, uk'.

HABITAT
Breeds mostly around rocky coasts and islands, but sometimes on freshwater lochs or moorland. Also visits sandy coasts and estuaries, and joins concentrations of gulls at roosts and feeding sites such as rubbish tips.

1st-winter

summer

FOOD
Hunts in a variety of ways and takes a wide range of food. Kills and eats young seabirds such as Puffins and Kittiwakes, robs others of their food, will catch fish or feeds on carrion, either in the water or washed up on the shore. It sometimes drops shellfish to break their shells and has been observed scavenging road kills. It will kill and eat mammals, such as rabbits.

BREEDING
Nests are built singly or in colonies on rocky outcrops and islands, or sometimes on moorland or even on buildings. Nest is a mound of seaweed built by both sexes. There are usually 2 or 3 eggs, incubated by both parents. The young hatch after 27 days and soon wander from the nest, but they seldom go far. They fly after 49–56 days and become independent soon afterwards.

MOVEMENTS AND MIGRATIONS
Most breeding birds remain in Scotland, although some move south to England and Ireland. Others, mainly from Norway, visit Scotland in winter. There is a tendency for young birds to move further afield – some northwards but most south, with a few reaching mainland Europe. Oldest known bird was 27 years.

POPULATION
About 15,000 pairs nest in Scotland, with the largest colonies found in Orkney. The population is largely stable.

CONSERVATION
This large gull has, historically, been persecuted and its main breeding areas are now restricted to the west coast and to the Northern Isles. During the 20th century the species' range extended southwards along the coast, although this expansion now seems to have largely stopped and the population stabilised.

DISTRIBUTION
Breeds mainly on the western coasts of Britain and Ireland. Outside the breeding season it can be found all round our coasts and at some inland sites as well. The species breeds in north-west Europe, Iceland, Greenland and North America. In winter in Europe it ranges as far south as the Bay of Biscay.

ICELAND GULL *LARUS GLAUCOIDES*

IDENTIFICATION

52–60 cm. Smaller, less bulky and with longer wings than a Herring Gull. This is the smaller of the two species known as 'white-winged gulls' that visit Britain and Ireland. Adults have very pale wings and white wing-tips. Its head is rounder than a Glaucous Gull's, it has a smaller, less vicious-looking bill, a thin red ring round the eye and a more gentle facial expression. The long wing-tips project well beyond the tail when the bird is perched. In winter its head and neck is streaked grey-brown. The female is smaller than the male. The first-winter birds are buff, finely mottled and barred darker brown with pale, white or greyish-buff flight feathers. Extreme tips of folded primaries often subtly edged grey buff. The bills of first-winter birds have more extensive black tips than Glaucous Gull's. The pattern of moult is probably similar to that of the Glaucous Gull.

SEE ALSO: Glaucous Gull p129, Herring Gull p124.

HABITS

In Scotland this species is generally seen singly and can be rather tame. Its flight is light and graceful as it hovers, turns and glides more freely than other large gulls. It is also more agile when feeding, and will take food from the ground, when flying or when swimming. Sometimes it will plunge-dive in shallow water to reach its prey.

VOICE

The call is similar to that of a Herring Gull but more shrill.

HABITAT

This gull is seen mostly on the coast where it visits harbours and nearby rubbish tips. It does occur inland, often roosting at reservoirs where it mixes with roosting flocks of other gulls.

FOOD

It feeds mainly on fish, either alive or as carrion. On its breeding grounds it will take eggs and young birds. Outside the breeding season it frequently scavenges on rubbish tips and around harbours.

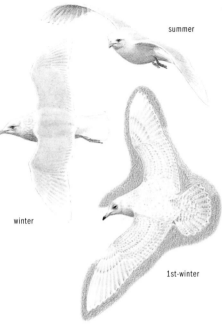

summer

winter

1st-winter

BREEDING

It does not breed in Scotland. Its breeding grounds are on rocky Arctic coasts, mostly on tall cliffs where it may nest among Kittiwakes. In places where the Glaucous Gull also nests, the Iceland nests lower down the cliff and is separated by space from the larger, more aggressive species.

MOVEMENTS AND MIGRATIONS

Breeding birds leave their breeding sites in August and return the following April or May. Some move south down the north-east coast of North America while others cross to Iceland with a small number travelling further to western Europe.

POPULATION

In a normal year there may be 50–100 birds in Scotland during the winter. In some years there are larger influxes, when numbers may rise to 250 or more. The largest numbers are seen in Orkney, Shetland and around fishing ports on the west coast.

CONSERVATION

The few Iceland Gulls that reach our shores benefit from human activity, whether it is the by-products of the fishing industry or domestic rubbish. It can suffer from pollution at sea: 16 Iceland Gulls were killed after the oil tanker *Braer* ran aground off Shetland in 1993.

1st-winter

DISTRIBUTION

In winter, an individual Iceland Gull may be seen almost anywhere around the coast of Scotland, especially in the west. It also visits a few inland sites. Despite its name, the species does not breed in Iceland but in Greenland and Arctic Canada. It winters as far south as New York in the USA and in Britain and Scandinavia in western Europe.

IDENTIFICATION

62–68 cm. Larger than a Herring Gull and approaching the size of Great Black-backed Gull. This is the largest 'white-winged gull'. It is bulky and powerful-looking, with a long, massive bill and rather flat forehead and crown that creates an aggressive appearance. The back of the adult is pale grey and the tips of the wings are white. In winter, its head and neck are heavily streaked with grey-brown. In flight, the long bill, long protruding head and neck and long broad wings give an impression of large size and great strength. The mottled plumage of the first-winter birds is fawn and the wing-tips are pale. The tail lacks any obvious dark marks. Its long powerful bill has a dark tip – less extensive than the dark tip of a juvenile Iceland Gull's bill. Moult lasts from the end of April until November, although some populations moult more quickly than others.

SEE ALSO: Iceland Gull p128, Herring Gull p124.

HABITS

This is a social species and sometimes forms large flocks in the north of its range, but around Scottish coasts is seen singly or in small numbers. It frequently swims, but lacks the 'tapered-end' of the Iceland Gull owing to points of the wings being proportionally shorter. It is an aggressive bird and will rob other species, notably Eiders, of food.

VOICE

Generally silent in winter. Its call sounds similar to that of the Herring Gull.

HABITAT

This gull is chiefly found on our sea coasts, both in inshore waters and further out to sea around fishing boats. It may occasionally be seen inland, feeding at rubbish tips and roosting on lochs and other water bodies. In the breeding season it nests on Arctic coasts where there are rocks and cliffs, and on inland crags.

FOOD

It eats a wide range of foods, especially animal material. It is a predator, a scavenger and a pirate. It eats eggs, young birds, fish, shellfish, insects and carrion. It also appears to associate with marine mammals including walrus, seals and whales and probably feeds on their faeces.

winter

1st-summer

BREEDING

Both adults build a nest of seaweed on rocks or grass or sometimes on snow. The usual clutch is of 3 eggs, which are incubated by both sexes and hatch after 27 days. The young are cared for by both parents and fly after 45 days.

MOVEMENTS AND MIGRATIONS

Birds seen in Scotland may have come from Arctic islands in the Barents Sea, from northern Iceland or even from Greenland. Most are juveniles, which wander further than adults, and the largest numbers are seen in Shetland and the Outer Hebrides. They are mainly seen between October and April, but a few non-breeders may stay for the summer; one individual on Shetland paired with a Herring Gull for several years.

POPULATION

There are probably 50–100 sightings in most years, although during occasional influxes larger numbers are seen.

CONSERVATION

This species is not currently at risk. The few that reach Scotland benefit from our fishing industry and domestic rubbish tips.

1st-winter

winter

1st-winter

DISTRIBUTION

This gull is occasionally seen around the coasts of the British Isles in winter, especially in Shetland. Some birds are seen in spring and summer too. It also visits a few inland lakes and reservoirs. It breeds in the Arctic, including Iceland, northern Russia, northern Asia, Greenland and North America.

BLACK-HEADED GULL *LARUS RIDIBUNDUS*

IDENTIFICATION
34–37 cm. This is the smallest of the abundant gulls of Britain and Ireland. It has slim, pointed wings with obvious white stripes along the front edge. In late winter and spring it has a dark chocolate-brown hood that in autumn and winter is reduced to a dark spot behind the eye. In spring the bill and legs are wax-red, but are duller at other times. The juvenile has ginger-brown blotches on its head, back and sides of its breast. First-winter birds have head markings of an adult in winter, a brown bar across the wings and a narrow black tail-band. First-summer birds start to get dark hoods but keep the brown across the wings and the tail-band. Adult moult begins during June or July and is completed by September or October. The partial moult into breeding plumage is between January and April.
SEE ALSO: Little Gull p123, Mediterranean Gull p246, Sabine's Gull p247.

HABITS
Often the brown head may appear black (hence its name). Quick wingbeats and buoyant flight may resemble a tern and it is agile enough to catch insects in the air. It will sometimes paddle the ground with its feet to attract worms and it often attempts to rob birds such as Great Crested Grebes or Lapwings of their food.

VOICE
The commonly heard call is a rather harsh' 'kree-aaa'.

HABITAT
This gull breeds both inland and near the sea. Breeding sites varying from coastal marshes and sand dunes to freshwater marshes, lochs, flooded gravel pits, reservoirs and moorland pools. It forages for food on areas of short grass, farmland and rubbish tips as well as on beaches.

FOOD
It eats a wide variety of food, including worms, insects such as beetles, mayflies and stoneflies and swarming ants, spiders, slugs, small crabs, small fish and carrion.

BREEDING
Breeding begins in April when birds display at their generally large colonies. The male may select a site and start building the nest, which is then completed by both male and female working together. The nest is a pile of vegetation on the ground, sometimes in water and rarely off the ground in trees, bushes or on buildings. Incubation of the 2 or 3 eggs is by both sexes and lasts for 23–26 days. The young are covered with down and leave the nest after about 10 days. They remain near the nest until they fly at about 35 days, and become independent soon afterwards.

MOVEMENTS AND MIGRATIONS
Breeding birds leave their colonies during July, many remaining in Scotland, while others migrate south to England, Wales and Ireland. From July, other populations from Iceland and Norway also start to move, and many of these will arrive in Scotland. Some will remain for the winter, joining flocks of local birds. Breeding birds return to their colonies in March and April. Oldest bird was 30 years.

POPULATION
More than 43,000 pairs nest in Scotland. In winter the population increases to over 150,000 birds. The breeding population is mostly stable, although there appears to be a reduction in smaller colonies that is largely compensated for by the growth of some larger ones.

CONSERVATION
At present there are no conservation measures necessary for such a successful species.

summer

winter

1st-winter

1st-summer

summer

winter

juvenile

DISTRIBUTION

The largest breeding colonies in the British Isles are in Scotland, with others in north-west England, north-west Ireland and Wales. After breeding, these birds may be seen almost anywhere, especially inland. This species breeds in Iceland, many parts of Europe, especially the north and east, in Russia and in Asia. European birds winter in western Europe, the Mediterranean and around the coast of North Africa.

KITTIWAKE   *RISSA TRIDACTYLA*

1st-summer

summer

IDENTIFICATION
38–40 cm. A little larger than Black-headed Gull. This is a neat, gentle-looking, medium-sized gull with a small yellow bill and dark eye. It resembles a Common Gull, but has a slightly forked tail, short black legs and distinctive triangular black wing-tips with no white spots. The grey back is slightly darker than the grey of the upperwings. In winter, crown and back of head are pale grey. Juvenile has a bold black 'W' pattern on its wings, black half-collar, grey back, black tail-band and small grey mark behind eye. Juveniles lose their black collars during their first winter. Adults have a complete moult between May and October and a partial moult into breeding plumage beginning in January.
SEE ALSO: Common Gull p125, Sabine's Gull p247.

HABITS
Breeds in large, noisy colonies, mainly on cliffs, but may be seen singly or in small groups outside the breeding season. Sometimes large numbers gather where food is plentiful. Approaches boats and picks up food from the surface of the sea. Also plunge-dives to find food. The buoyant flight with stiff wingbeats sometimes resembles a tern. Breeding birds visit freshwater pools near their colonies to collect mud for nests and to bathe.

VOICE
Around its breeding cliffs it shouts its 'kitti-waaark' call from which it gets its name. At other times it is rather silent.

summer

juvenile

HABITAT
In spring and summer, mostly seen around rocky coasts where nests on tall, precipitous sea cliffs and, sometimes, on buildings close to the sea. At other times lives out at sea, often beyond the continental shelf. A truly marine gull, unusual inland, except occasionally after gales.

FOOD
Feeds on fish such as Caplins, Herrings, Sprats and sand-eels, and other marine creatures, including shrimps, planktonic sea creatures, worms, insects and carrion.

BREEDING
Eggs laid in May in a nest of compacted mud, grass and seaweed, built by both sexes on a precipitous cliff ledge. Occasionally nests are on the ledges of buildings close to the sea. Both parents share the incubation of 1–3 eggs (usually 2) which hatch after 25–32 days. The chicks are brooded while small and fed by both adults. Pairs that lay 3 eggs are usually unable to find sufficient food to keep all 3 chicks alive. Young fly after 33–54 days and quickly become independent.

MOVEMENTS AND MIGRATIONS
After breeding, in July and August, birds disperse from their colonies. Some remain around the British Isles, but many juveniles reach the North American coast, and immatures may remain in the western Atlantic for several years before returning to their natal colonies to breed. Adults fly out to sea and tend to move southwest, but some will cross the Atlantic for the winter, returning to their colonies from February onwards. Oldest ringed bird survived for 28 years.

POPULATION
Over 280,000 pairs nest in Scotland, which is 68% of the British population. After a period of expansion the population is now falling again owing to poor breeding success.

CONSERVATION
Following persecution in the 19th century, the species increased during the 20th century. However, recent years have seen a decline in some of the breeding colonies, especially in Shetland and along the east coast. This has been linked to a shortage of food, possibly caused by climate change and exacerbated by overfishing.

DISTRIBUTION

Breeds around the coast of Britain, with the largest colonies being in northern and eastern Scotland. It can be seen at Fowlsheugh, St Abb's Head and some other accessible mainland sites. Most abundant in northern Scotland and along North Sea coasts. It also breeds in North America, Asia and northern Europe, with a few colonies on the Atlantic coast of Spain and Portugal. In winter, it is widespread in the North Atlantic.

LITTLE TERN *STERNA ALBIFRONS*

summer

summer

IDENTIFICATION
22–24 cm. Our smallest tern. A third smaller than Common Tern and its wings and tail are proportionally shorter. Tail is deeply forked, but lacks any tail-streamers and head and bill are noticeably large. Bill is yellow with a small black tip and legs are yellow or orange. It is a white bird with pale grey back and wings, a black cap and a forehead that is always white. By late summer the white forehead becomes larger, the bill darker and the legs paler. Juvenile is noticeably smaller with a dark bill, a pale buff, streaked crown, a dark patch through the eye to the back of the head and a sandy-grey back with darker marks. Adults start to moult when the birds are still feeding young in June–August and then moult is suspended until migration is completed. There is a further moult in winter to acquire breeding plumage.
SEE ALSO: Common Tern p134, Arctic Tern p135.

HABITS
Wingbeats are very fast. It frequently hovers before diving into water. It does not normally form very large communal flocks like the larger terns, but it does breed in colonies of, on average, 30 pairs.

winter

VOICE
The most frequent call is a loud, shrill 'kik-kik'.

HABITAT
In Scotland almost exclusively a marine species, nesting on shingle or sandy beaches. In Europe spreads up suitable rivers and breeds around inland lakes. Outside the breeding season it mainly feeds in inshore waters.

FOOD
Feeds on mainly small fish, especially sand-eels. Also takes shrimps and insect larvae.

BREEDING
Nesting begins in May. Both adults make a nest scrape in the shingle or sand that is often unlined. There are 2 or 3 eggs, which are incubated by both adults for 18–22 days. Young are covered in down and mobile soon after hatching. After a few days they leave the nest and hide among the shingle or nearby vegetation. The location of colonies may change from year to year.

MOVEMENTS AND MIGRATIONS
European breeding birds leave their colonies during July and August and soon start their southward migration along the coasts of Europe and Africa. Some of the European birds that breed inland migrate across land and along rivers, but it does not appear to cross the Sahara like some of the larger terns. The oldest ringed bird was over 21 years old.

juvenile

POPULATION
Over 300 pairs breed in Scotland in most years. The population appears to be more stable than elsewhere in Britain, where numbers have fallen by 25% in recent years.

CONSERVATION
On open beaches Little Terns are vulnerable to predators such as Foxes, Stoats and Hedgehogs, and also crows and even Kestrels. Natural disasters like spring tides and wind-blown sand can wipe out whole colonies, and human disturbance – especially from dog-walkers and vehicles – is an increasingly serious threat.

DISTRIBUTION
In Britain and Ireland there are colonies almost all round the coasts. The main colonies in Scotland are in Argyll and on the Outer Hebrides. Little Terns also breed from the Baltic to the Mediterranean and there are other races in Africa and Asia. European birds winter along the coast of West Africa with some reaching South Africa.

SANDWICH TERN   *STERNA SANDVICENSIS*

IDENTIFICATION
36–41 cm. Slightly larger but slimmer than Black-headed Gull. The largest of the terns that breed in Britain and Ireland. Heavy-looking with yellow tip to its long black bill, and short black legs. It is a very white tern, with its back and long, pointed wings light grey and a short, forked tail that lacks tail-streamers. Forewings show grey wedges. Black cap is perfect only at start of breeding season, and soon shows white speckling above the eyes. By late summer whole forehead is white. In spring, feathers at back of the crown are longer and form a ragged crest. Juvenile has brownish-black spotting on crown and forehead, sandy back with dark tips to feathers, and all-black bill. Moult may start during incubation and the loss of flight feathers may be suspended during migration and resumed in winter quarters. Breeding plumage acquired between February and April.
SEE ALSO: Common Tern p134, Little Tern p132.

HABITS
Often flies higher than other terns and can look very 'angular' and less buoyant. Also looks short-tailed and will often fly with head and bill pointing down. Seldom hovers, but frequently dives with quite a large 'splash' and usually stays under for longer than other terns. Colonies are fickle and will often move location for no apparent reason. Large roosts sometimes form on beaches and sandbars.

VOICE
Noisy, the most common call being a loud grating 'keer-ick'.

HABITAT
Breeds exclusively in coastal locations, using shingle, sandy and sometimes rocky beaches and also islands close to the shore. Outside breeding season inhabits inshore waters and is only occasionally seen inland.

FOOD
Feeds mainly on fish that are found near the surface of the sea, such as sand-eels, Sprats and Whiting.

BREEDING
Breeding begins at the end of April. It nests in large colonies and the nest is a simple scrape on the ground made by both adults, with little or no special lining. The 1 or 2 eggs are incubated by both adults for 21–29 days. Some young stay in the nest, others form crèches, while yet others are mobile and roam around the colony. Both adults feed the young even after they fly at 28–30 days. Juveniles remain dependent on their parents for 3 months or so.

MOVEMENTS AND MIGRATIONS
After nesting, birds soon disperse. Within days juveniles may be many kilometres from their colonies. Large numbers build up in the Firth of Forth during August and early September. At first they may travel north or south, but gradually all head south, and by October most have left Scottish waters. They move mainly along the coasts of Europe and Africa, and first-year birds will remain in Africa for their first summer. Adults generally winter further north than immatures. Return migration begins in February and these are one of the earliest summer migrants to reach Europe. Individuals are often seen near their breeding colonies in March or April. Oldest ringed bird was 30 years old.

POPULATION
About 1,000 pairs nest in Scotland. The numbers fluctuate from year to year, but the trend is towards fewer colonies than in the past.

CONSERVATION
The decline has been attributed to mammalian predators such and American Mink and Fox, but fish stocks and sea-level rise are also potential problems. Colonies on beaches also suffer from human disturbance and several have been abandoned.

summer

winter

summer

winter

juvenile

DISTRIBUTION
There are colonies of Sandwich Terns scattered around the coasts of Britain and Ireland. It breeds in Europe, Russia and North America. European birds winter along the African coast as far as South Africa and extend into the Indian Ocean as far north as Natal, although individuals have wintered as far north as the Firth of Forth in Scotland.

Common Tern   *STERNA HIRUNDO*

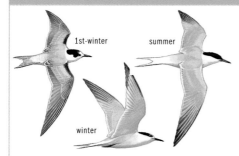

1st-winter   summer

winter

Identification
31–35 cm. Smaller than Black-headed Gull. Back and wings are silver-grey and underparts pale grey. Bill is orange-red with a dark tip and the short legs are red. Longest flight feathers of the upperwing become progressively dark during the summer giving the appearance of a blackish 'wedge'. Tips of flight feathers on the underwing are dusky and there is a translucent patch that appears semi-transparent against a bright sky. Juvenile is grey, white and black with a ginger back, a pale forehead and flesh-pink or yellowish bill with a dark tip that becomes darker during the summer. Moults while in British and Irish waters. Inner flight feathers are lost from July, and in late summer adult birds with missing flight feathers are often obvious.
SEE ALSO: Arctic Tern p135.

Habits
Flight is more direct and powerful than that of the other smaller terns. When fishing, flies with bill pointing down and often rises gently before hovering and diving head-first. A social species, breeding in colonies and often seen in flocks. In spring, may be seen carrying fish crossways in its bill. This may be to feed the young or for the female as part of courtship.

Voice
Most common call is a loud, rasping 'keee-yaah'.

Habitat
In Scotland, most Common Terns nest on or near the coast, whereas in other parts of Britain many nest well away from the sea. They breed on shingle and sandy beaches or on offshore islands. One large colony is found in Leith docks! A few pairs may nest on gravel banks along major rivers. Small numbers are also seen inland during their migration.

Food
Feeds mainly on fish, chiefly small Herrings, Sprats and sand-eels. In fresh water catches Roach, Perch and Minnows.

juvenile

1st-winter

Also takes shrimps and insects – especially cockchafers and water-beetle larvae.

Breeding
Breeding begins in May. Both adults construct a scrape in the sand. Sometimes pebbles and vegetation are added to the rim of the nest before and during incubation. Incubation of the 2 or 3 well-camouflaged eggs is by both sexes and lasts 21–22 days. Young leave the nest after 3–4 days and hide in nearby vegetation or in hollows in the sand while waiting to be fed. They fly at 22–28 days and are 2 or 3 months old before they are fully independent.

Movements and migrations
After nesting some birds soon leave, a few heading north before flying south, while others remain in inshore waters, especially the Forth, until October. These are joined by birds on passage from Europe, especially Norway and Germany. Some fly on to Spain and Portugal, but most winter off the coast of West Africa. Birds from northern populations often travel furthest and winter south of the Equator. Breeding birds return in March and April. Oldest ringed bird was 33 years old.

winter

summer

Population
4,800 pairs nest in Scotland. There has been a decline in recent years, especially in Shetland, were the population has fallen by 90%.

Conservation
The recent fall in numbers in Shetland and Orkney are linked with declines in other seabird populations and are due to local food shortages. These shortages may be explained by overfishing and also climate change. Elsewhere, the birds suffer from human disturbance and from predators such as American Mink and Foxes. Habitat destruction due to afforestation has also been responsible for the loss of at least one large colony.

DISTRIBUTION
Breeds around the coast of Scotland, with a few colonies inland. Also breeds in other parts of the British Isles. The species nests from the Arctic Circle south to North Africa and winters mainly off the coast of West Africa. There are other populations in North America and Asia.

summer

IDENTIFICATION

33–35 cm. Smaller, lighter and more delicate than Common Tern with narrower wings, shorter neck and longer tail-streamers. Upperparts pale grey and rump white. Underparts smoky grey, a shade darker than Common Tern's and contrast more with its white cheeks. Bill and short legs deep red. Upperwing more uniformly grey, becoming paler towards tip and with dark trailing bar, not a 'wedge' on the longest flight feathers. From below against the light the primary and secondary flight feathers appear translucent. Juvenile is grey and white from a distance, but seen close up its back is heavily marked with dark crescents. Has white forehead and black bill with red base. Adults moult in their winter quarters and return in spring with neat new flight feathers.
SEE ALSO: Common Tern p134.

Young stay in the nest for a few days before leaving to shelter nearby. They fly at 21–24 days but remain with their parents for a further month or two.

HABITS

Flight lighter and more bouncy than that of Common Tern. When fishing, appears hesitant as it hovers, dips down and hovers again before plunging into the water. Breeds in large colonies, and groups fish close together. Also flocks during migrations. On breeding grounds it is very aggressive toward intruders, including humans.

1st-winter

MOVEMENTS AND MIGRATIONS

It leaves Scotland between July and early October and migrates along the coasts of western Europe and Africa, eventually reaching the Southern Ocean and the coast of Antarctica, where it may travel along the edge of the pack ice. Most arrive back in Scotland in April or early May. Oldest survived 30 years.

POPULATION

The Scottish breeding population comprises over 47,000 pairs, or more than 80% of the population of the British Isles. The size of colonies fluctuates from year to year, but in general there has been a steady decline in the past decade.

CONSERVATION

Food shortages have resulted in some northern colonies failing to produce any young in some years. Overfishing of sand-eels and other small fish is one cause, but long-term climate change and related changes in the distribution of fish is another more difficult problem to overcome. Several large colonies in Shetland are now much reduced. Predators such as rats, cats, American Mink, Hedgehogs and Stoats have also significantly reduced the success of some colonies.

VOICE

Call a slightly higher-pitched version of Common Tern's call, a harsh, scolding 'kee-aar'.

HABITAT

Breeds in similar habitat to the Common Tern, mostly on the coast or on offshore islands, but also along large rivers where there are shingle islands and stone beaches. Some colonies are on heath and rough pasture, and most nests are in or close to vegetation. Outside the breeding season it becomes a seabird, and sometimes perching on floating objects, including icebergs.

juvenile

FOOD

Feeds mainly on fish including sand-eels, Sprats, Herrings, Caplins and sticklebacks. It also takes insects, crustaceans and even worms from flooded fields.

BREEDING

Nesting begins in May. Nest is a shallow scrape made by both parents. Incubation of the 1 or 2 eggs is shared by both parents until the chicks hatch after 20–24 days.

summer

1st-winter

winter

DISTRIBUTION

Most of the population of the British Isles nests in Scotland, with a few in northern England and more in Ireland. Mainly an Arctic species that also breeds in northern Europe, North America, northern Russia and Asia. Winters at the other end of the world, in the Southern Ocean off the pack-ice of Antarctica, and some British birds reach Australia.

BLACK TERN *CHLIDONIAS NIGER*

IDENTIFICATION
22–24 cm. Smaller than Common Tern with shorter, broader wings, less deeply forked tail and black bill. In spring, has an almost black head and body, slate-grey back, wings and tail, and white under its tail. Underside of wing is almost white. Female is slightly paler than male. After breeding, head and body become white with black marks behind eye and on back of head, and with a prominent dark smudge on shoulder and white collar. Juvenile resembles adult in winter but with brown feathers creating a mottled effect on its back. Adult moult starts in May or June and the dark plumage quickly becomes blotchy, and dark grey feathers are replaced by white ones by September.
SEE ALSO: Common Tern p134, Little Gull p123.

HABITS
Typical flight is rather lazy and it banks from side to side. Often travels singly, but flocks may gather, especially on migration. Has a characteristic feeding action as it dips down to the water and delicately takes food from the surface. Hovers less frequently than other terns, preferring to fly up and down on regular beats, dipping down to feed from time to time. Regularly perches on rocks and posts in the water.

FOOD
Its food is mainly insects and their larvae in summer and fish in winter. Insects include water beetles, flies, dragonflies and grasshoppers. Fish include sticklebacks, Bleak and Roach. It also eats frogs and tadpoles.

BREEDING
Does not breed in Scotland, and has only rarely attempted to breed in England and Ireland. It nests on floating vegetation, in shallow water or among marsh plants. The nest is a mound of water weed that is added to by both birds. The 2–4 eggs are incubated for 21–22 days by both birds taking turns. Young stay in the nest and are brooded by a parent for the first few days, but they soon move into nearby vegetation. They fly at 19–25 days and are quickly independent.

MOVEMENTS AND MIGRATIONS
Autumn migration begins in June with non-breeding birds moving first, followed by adults and then juveniles. Most are seen in Scotland between August and October. At peak times huge numbers gather on some European and African estuaries. Common along the African coast from September, and birds remain there until their return the following March. A few birds pass through Scotland in May, sometimes travelling

winter

summer

juvenile

VOICE
Usually silent, with only very occasionally calling a sharp 'kik, kik'.

HABITAT
In Scotland, the Black Tern is seen on migration along the coast and in estuaries and pools near the sea, and sometimes visits inland lochs, reservoirs or large rivers. It breeds in marshes, fens and lagoons in eastern and central Europe.

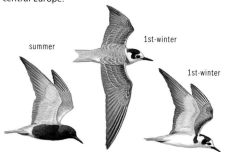

summer

1st-winter

1st-winter

overland, but most return to their breeding grounds by a more easterly route. Oldest ringed bird was 17 years old.

POPULATION
Small numbers, usually less than 50, are seen in spring. Up to 200 may be seen on their return migration, with most in August and September, with occasional influxes, usually on the east coast, of over 1,000 or more.

CONSERVATION
While this remains a non-breeding species no particular conservation measures are required. However, it has attempted to breed in the British Isles on a few occasions, and if this were to happen in Scotland special protection might be required to ensure its success.

DISTRIBUTION
In Scotland mostly seen in the southwest and east in spring, and predominantly the east in autumn. Breeds from Denmark to Spain and east to Russia and Asia. Another race breeds in North America. European birds winter along the coast of West Africa.

BLACK GUILLEMOT OR TYSTIE CEPPHUS GRYLLE

IDENTIFICATION

30–32 cm. Pigeon-sized. Smaller than Guillemot with long neck and bright red legs. Breeding plumage is sooty black with an oval white wing-patch. In autumn and winter, becomes off-white with dark, scaly marks, darker back and dark flight feathers. The oval wing-patch is still obvious in winter. Juvenile is like adult in winter but more heavily barred. In July, after nesting, adults begin to moult and small groups form on the sea. Between August and October they become flightless as flight feathers are regrowing. Between January and March there is a second, partial moult into breeding plumage. SEE ALSO: Guillemot p138, Razorbill p139, Puffin p141, Little Auk p140.

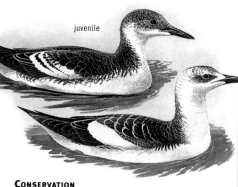

summer

HABITS

Stands upright on land. Flight is usually low, but when searching for good feeding areas it may rise to 100 m or more. When swimming or flying in winter it resembles a duck or grebe from a distance, but the rapidly whirring wings, white oval patch and direct flight are characteristic. Commonly seen swimming and diving close to shore. Usually in ones or twos and although nesting birds do come together to form colonies, these are not large colonies like those of Guillemots. Sometimes Black Guillemots work together: they swim in straight lines or semicircles as they close in on a shoal of fish.

juvenile

VOICE

summer

Mostly silent, but makes a weak, high-pitched whistle 'peeeeeh' at breeding sites.

HABITAT

Found around rocky coasts where there are loose boulders and other potential nest sites. A marine species that is generally seen closer to the shore than other auks.

FOOD

Feeds on fish such as sand-eels, blennies, butterfish, small Cod and sole. Also catches small crabs, shrimps and other animals.

1st-winter

BREEDING

On April mornings groups gather to display, first on the sea and then on land, their red mouths contrasting with their striking plumage. They nest in holes and crevices under boulders and in caves. Sometimes they use man-made structures such as holes in harbour walls and even in the barrel of an old cannon! 1 or 2 eggs are laid in May. Incubation is by both male and female and the eggs hatch after about 30 days. Young leave their nests and swim on the sea before they can fly. They are independent on leaving the colony, but may not breed for 4 years.

MOVEMENTS AND MIGRATIONS

Birds from farther north may move south to avoid winter ice, and young may wander farther than adults. In Scotland, few travel more than 50 km from where they hatched and no breeding colony is totally deserted in winter. Oldest known bird was 22 years old.

POPULATION

Over 18,000 pairs nest in Scotland, comprising 95% of the UK population. There have been significant population changes in some areas, but overall numbers have remained relatively stable.

CONSERVATION

Threats at sea come from oil pollution, but Black Guillemots are less vulnerable than some other members of this family in that their colonies are small and widely dispersed and so numbers affected by single incidents tend to be small. The availability of suitable food is also critical and in recent years, when sand-eel stocks have fallen, the number of young also declined. They are vulnerable to predation by rats; the removal of these predators from Ailsa Craig has encouraged an increase in numbers on the island.

DISTRIBUTION

In the British Isles, Scotland has the largest population, followed by Ireland and the Isle of Man, with only small numbers in northern England and Wales. Found all round Arctic Circle and winters as far north as possible (right up to the edge of the ice). Winters at sea, but usually close to its breeding colonies. Extremely rare inland.

GUILLEMOT URIA AALGE

1st-winter

winter

IDENTIFICATION
38–41 cm. Larger than Jackdaw with short wings, long, dark, tapering bill and a longer neck than other members of this family. Swims well. Head, neck and back are chocolate-brown, and breast and belly are white. Some northern birds have white 'spectacle-like' marks on their faces. The brown plumage of northern birds is darker, almost black. In winter, neck and side of face, behind the eye, become white. Juvenile is smaller, pale headed, with a shorter bill. Moult begins while the adults are feeding young. The flight feathers are lost simultaneously in July and August and the birds are flightless for about 7 weeks. Breeding plumage is gained between January and March.
SEE ALSO: Black Guillemot p137, Razorbill p139, Puffin p141.

HABITS
Stands upright on cliffs or swims like a duck in the sea and dives to find food. Breeds in large colonies and lives in loose flocks outside breeding season. Sometime sits, rather than stands, on its cliff ledges. In flight, wings beat rapidly, appearing blurred at a distance.

summer

winter

summer

the sea. It is 8–10 weeks before the juvenile can fly and it continues to be fed by the adult for up to 12 weeks.

MOVEMENTS AND MIGRATIONS
After breeding, many Guillemots do not travel far, and some move north following food supplies. Juveniles stay with the males for the first autumn and part of the winter before forming separate flocks of adults and immatures. Many Scottish birds stay in Scottish coastal waters, some cross the North Sea and winter off the coast of Norway, and others move south and reach the coast of Spain, with juveniles travelling further than adults. Guillemots from southern Britain, Ireland, Norway and the Faeroes may also winter in Scottish waters. Oldest known bird was 38 years.

POPULATION
It is estimated that about 800,000 pairs nest in Scotland, or 75% of the British and Irish population. Numbers increased during the latter part of the 20th century, but this increase has slowed and some colonies, especially in the Northern Isles, are declining.

CONSERVATION
Guillemots have been killed for sport and food in the past. Recent dangers have included: fine fishing nets that ensnare and drown these birds, oiling incidents and depleted fish stocks due to overfishing and climate change.

VOICE
Usual call is a growling 'arrrr'.

HABITAT
Lives most of year on the open sea, coming to land only to breed. Nest sites are on narrow cliff ledges or the exposed flat tops of tall stacks and offshore islands.

FOOD
Feeds chiefly on fish especially Cod, Herring, Whiting, sand-eels and Sprats. Also eats some crustaceans such as crabs.

BREEDING
Males and females usually winter separately and come together at the nest site, with males generally arriving first. They make no nest, but lay a single pear-shaped egg on bare rock, and both sexes share the incubation. Young is covered in down when it hatches after 28–37 days. It is fed by both parents and usually leaves its cliff within 3 weeks of hatching. At this time it is not fully grown and is unable to fly properly. Male attends chick when it leaves the colony and continues to feed it on

DISTRIBUTION
Breeds on inaccessible sea cliffs around the Scottish coast. Large colonies can be seen at Troup Head, Fowlsheugh, Sumburgh Head and Handa Island. It also breeds on suitable cliffs in England, Wales and Ireland. Most winter in loose flocks around our coasts or go farther south, with many from western colonies reaching the Bay of Biscay and a few travelling as far south as Portugal. Breeds in western Europe, with small colonies as far south as Portugal, and also in Greenland and North America. Other races live in Bering Sea and North Pacific.

RAZORBILL ALCA TORDA

IDENTIFICATION
37–39 cm. Slightly smaller than a Guillemot with a proportionally thicker neck, larger head and bill, smaller wings and longer tail. In flight, looks blacker than a Guillemot with snub-nose effect, not a pointed bill. The black bill is laterally flattened, deep and blunt, with thin white line near the tip. The underparts are white. In winter, the head becomes mostly off-white with a dark crown and hind-neck. The juvenile is smaller and browner than the adult, and has a dark head. Moult begins in July and flight feathers are lost simultaneously between August and October and, for a few weeks, the birds become flightless.
SEE ALSO: Guillemot p138, Puffin p141.

HABITS
It breeds on cliffs, but nesting birds are more difficult to see and its colonies less dense than those of the Guillemot. It may form flocks in winter, but again these tend to be smaller than flocks of Guillemots. It swims and dives, and was once recorded at 140 m below sea surface. When feeding young, the Razorbill will carry 2–3 fish at a time.

VOICE
The call is growling 'caarrrrr' and the juvenile has a plaintive whistle.

HABITAT
A seabird that comes to shore only to breed, and for the rest of the year it lives mostly at sea, but remaining within the continental shelf of Europe. Its nest sites are on rocky cliffs and among boulder scree close to the sea.

FOOD
It feeds chiefly on fish, especially sand-eels, Sprats and small Herrings, and a few marine crustaceans.

BREEDING
Most eggs are laid during May. A single egg is generally laid in a crevice in the rock, either high on inaccessible cliffs or among scattered boulders. Occasionally an open ledge may be used. Incubation is by both sexes and lasts for about 36 days. The young Razorbill is cared for by both parents and leaves the cliff at about 18 days old by jumping or scrambling into the sea. At this stage it is about two-thirds fully grown. At sea, the male cares for the chick.

summer

CONSERVATION
This species shares the fate of the Guillemot. Its future is linked to the health of the marine environment. Fishing nets, climate change, pollution at sea and declining fish stocks all threaten Razorbills.

summer

winter

1st-winter

winter

MOVEMENTS AND MIGRATIONS
In July Razorbills leave their colonies and disperse out to sea. The male and juvenile start by travelling together and both are flightless until September. The juveniles may travel further from their colonies than adults, which return to the breeding cliffs as early as March. Some young birds from around the Irish Sea reach the Mediterranean during their first winter. Young birds will not return to their colonies until they are 2–3 years old. The oldest known ringed bird survived for more than 36 years.

POPULATION
Over 93,000 pairs nest in Scotland. Numbers increased in the 20th century, but there have been several very poor breeding years recently, especially in the Northern Isles, and populations may have started to fall in those places.

DISTRIBUTION
The largest colonies are in the north of Scotland on Handa, the Outer Hebrides and Fowlsheugh. The species breeds in north-west Europe, Iceland, Greenland and the north-east coast of North America. It winters in the North Atlantic, mostly scattered over the continental shelf of Europe and is rather scarce in inshore waters.

LITTLE AUK *ALLE ALLE*

IDENTIFICATION
17–19 cm. Our smallest auk is only the size of a Starling. It is a dumpy bird with a black stubby bill, short neck and tail and a small head. Its upperparts are black with some fine white lines on its back, a white bar on closed wings and the underparts are white. In its winter plumage its neck and lower face become white while it retains a blackish crown that extends lower than the eye. In flight, it has a dark underwing and it rocks from side to side with fast whirring wingbeats low over the sea. The juvenile has the same pattern as a summer adult, but paler. Moult has been little studied, but adults moult their body feathers between May and September and flight and tail feathers are moulted between September and October.

SEE ALSO: Guillemot p138, Razorbill p139, Puffin p141.

summer

winter

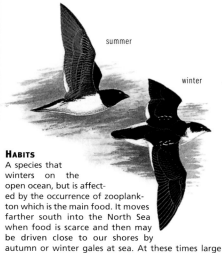

summer

winter

HABITS
A species that winters on the open ocean, but is affected by the occurrence of zooplankton which is the main food. It moves farther south into the North Sea when food is scarce and then may be driven close to our shores by autumn or winter gales at sea. At these times large numbers sometimes appear in inshore waters and occasionally individuals are blown inland. It takes to the air without running across the surface of the water. In flight, it can appear rather like a small wader at times. On its Arctic breeding grounds it nests in vast colonies.

VOICE
It is usually silent away from its breeding grounds. At colonies it makes noisy chattering calls.

HABITAT
The breeding sites are in the Arctic, on islands or the massive sea cliffs of Spitsbergen and Greenland where it nests amongst the boulder scree. Outside the breeding season this species lives out at sea.

FOOD
It feeds on plankton most of which is the larval stage of crustaceans and also other tiny marine creatures. It also eats fish and some shellfish.

BREEDING
Not until the snow has thawed from the breeding colonies do these birds start to nest. Eggs are laid in late June or July in a rock crevice or in spaces under boulders. Both adults incubate the single egg in turns. At first the chick is brooded under the wing of an adult. It leaves after about 17 days and for a time it stays with one of its parents.

MOVEMENTS AND MIGRATIONS
Adults and juveniles leave their colonies in August and slowly move south to their wintering areas. Some remain as close to their colonies as the winter ice-flows allow. Others spread across the North Atlantic with some entering the North Sea.

POPULATION
Relatively small numbers are seen, except when adverse conditions drive these birds close to shore. One estimate has a million birds wintering in the North Sea, and numbers each year seen from the Scottish coast may vary from 100 to 35,000. Most commonly seen off the Northern Isles and east coast headlands in October to December.

CONSERVATION
Its remote Arctic habitat is largely free from development, but like other seabirds its future could be affected by fishing policies that alter the fish populations of the North Atlantic. Climate change affects sea temperatures and thus food supplies. Hunting and trapping of seabirds in Greenland is also a problem.

DISTRIBUTION
Scotland is at the southern limit of the species' normal wintering range. Some birds enter the North Sea in autumn and are regularly seen from sea-watching points on the east coast in late October and early November during north-easterly gales. The species breeds in Greenland, parts of Iceland, Spitsbergen and east to Arctic Russia.

PUFFIN FRATERCULA ARCTICA

summer

IDENTIFICATION
26–29 cm. Smaller than town pigeon. Upright on land, with a black back, white underparts, pale grey face patches that almost meet on the back of the head, huge laterally flattened, colourful bill and colourful skin around the eye giving it a clown-like appearance. Male has a larger bill than female. Legs and feet are bright orange. In winter, the cheeks become dusky and the bill smaller and less colourful. In flight, underwing is grey. Juvenile resembles an adult in winter, but is smaller with a smaller bill and a sooty black patch in front of eye. Adults begin to moult in August and September. Flight feathers are lost simultaneously during the winter and birds are flightless for a time. The colourful bill plates are shed after breeding and regrown in spring. SEE ALSO: Guillemot p138, Razorbill p139, Little Auk p140.

HABITS
In flight wings are flapped rapidly unless landing on the cliff-top or caught in the up-draught. It swims and dives, and uses its wings to propel itself underwater. There are many ritualised displays including males flicking their heads up and down and pairs knocking their bills together noisily. When feeding young, it will carry several fish in its bill at once. Although it frequently stands upright, it also rests with its breast on the ground. It is sociable when nesting, but at other times it is seen in ones and twos. Large 'rafts' of Puffins gather on the sea near breeding colonies in late winter.

VOICE
Generally silent, but at the colonies it makes a low growling 'arrrh' often repeated to sound like hoarse laughter.

HABITAT
Breeds on offshore islands and on tall sea-cliffs. Outside the breeding season it lives at sea.

FOOD
Puffins catch small fish. The most common species are sand-eel, Sprat, Herring and Caplin, although many other species are also eaten.

BREEDING
Returns to colony in March and April. Nests in burrow in the turf and sometimes in crevice between rocks.

Will either dig a burrow or use a Rabbit burrow. Nest is usually 70–110 cm from entrance and lined with grass, roots and any dry material to be found. The single egg is laid in mid-May and incubated by both parents for 36–43 days. Newly hatched chick is covered in down, but remains in its burrow for 38–44 days until it flies down to the sea where it has to fend for itself.

MOVEMENTS AND MIGRATIONS
Puffins disperse from their colonies after breeding. Those from east-coast colonies mostly remain in the North Sea with some reaching southern Norway. Some from northern and western colonies also reach Norway, but others cross the Atlantic to the Grand Banks off Newfoundland and yet others move south to the Bay of Biscay, with some reaching the Mediterranean. Oldest known Puffin lived for over 33 years.

POPULATION
About 500,000 Puffins nest in Scotland, or 83% of the British and Irish population. Some colonies have increased while others have decreased, but overall numbers appear largely stable.

winter

juvenile

summer

CONSERVATION
Threats come in many forms: weather conditions, variable food supplies, the introduction of rats by humans onto islands, oil and other pollution at sea and overfishing are all important factors. Many of the most important colonies are in places that have been given special protection either as nature reserves or other sites of national importance.

DISTRIBUTION
Breeds widely around the coast of Scotland on cliffs and islands, including in the Firth of Forth. There are colonies in Ireland, Wales and south-west and north-east England. Also breeds in North America, Greenland, Iceland and Europe, as far south as northern France. In winter Scottish birds mainly disperse into the North Sea and North Atlantic.

WOODPIGEON COLUMBA PALUMBUS

IDENTIFICATION
40–42 cm. Our largest pigeon. It has a small head, broad wings, longish tail and bulging chest. The adult is blue-grey with white crescent on wing, black band on tail and white patch on neck. The neck has a green and purple sheen and breast has a pink flush. The juvenile is similar to adult, but has no white on neck. The annual moult may last for 8–10 months. It begins in April, is suspended while the bird breeds and continues in the autumn. Some individuals suspend moult again during the winter and do not finally complete their feather growth until the following February.
SEE ALSO: Stock Dove p143.

HABITS
When disturbed, it clatters noisily out of trees and bushes. In aerial territorial display it flies up steeply, then claps its wings together above its back with a sharp slap before gliding down steeply. Often repeats this manoeuvre several times. May be seen singly, but often in large flocks when not breeding. Drinks without lifting its head from water.

juvenile

VOICE
Call is a soft, restful 'orr-oo-cooo, orr-oo-oo-coo'.

HABITAT
Breeds on lowland farmland where there are hedges or trees and also in woods, copses and, increasingly, in towns and city centres. In winter, largely dependent on farmland.

FOOD
It eats mainly plant material, especially buds, leaves and seeds. The most commonly eaten plants include clover, cabbage and other brassicas, ash, Ivy and peas. Cereal crops such as Wheat and Barley are also eaten. Animal food includes insects such as beetles.

BREEDING
The Woodpigeon has been observed breeding in every month of the year, but, in Scotland, mostly between July and September. Flimsy nest of twigs is built in a tree or bush. The 2 eggs can sometimes be seen from below. Incubation is by both adults and lasts for 17 days. The young are brooded for the first 7–8 days and then left. The parents feed their young (squabs) on 'crop milk'. Young fly at 33–34 days, but it may be as

early as 16–21 days if the nest is disturbed. Young are fed by their parents for about a week after their first flight. There are two or three broods each year and the same nest may be reused.

MOVEMENTS AND MIGRATIONS
Most Woodpigeons in Scotland are fairly sedentary, and thus spend all their lives here, although one Scottish-ringed bird reached south-west France. Migrants from northern Europe are seen in spring and autumn, the largest numbers occurring in the Northern Isles or sometimes moving through glens in eastern Scotland on their way south. Oldest known bird was 17 years.

POPULATION
Up to 600,000 pairs nest in Scotland each year, with numbers growing to over 1.5 million in winter.

CONSERVATION
Woodpigeons have been expanding their range and numbers for the last 150 years. They suffered a decline in the 1950s and 1960s caused by agricultural chemicals, but their numbers have recovered and they have recently colonised western Ireland and some of the Scottish islands. Considered a pest on arable crops, the spread of intensive arable cultivation, especially of oilseed rape, may explain the rise in population. There have been attempts to control numbers by regular shoots, but these have had little effect on the total population.

STOCK DOVE (PIGEON) *COLUMBA OENAS*

IDENTIFICATION
32–34 cm. Similar in size and shape to the Feral Pigeon and smaller than the Woodpigeon. This pigeon is blue-grey with an iridescent sheen on its neck, a pale rump and no white on its neck or wings. In flight, it has dark edges to the plain grey wings and two small but distinct bars near the body. The underwing is grey. The juvenile is duller and browner and lacks the iridescence on the neck. Moult takes place gradually between July and November with the primary feathers being some of the first to be lost.

SEE ALSO: Woodpigeon p142, Rock Dove p145.

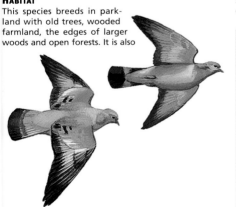

HABITS
The flight is noticeably different from that of the Woodpigeon with birds looking more compact, their flight more direct and with a more flickering wing action. In display it flies with slow deliberate wing-beats and glides in a wide arc with wings held in a shallow 'V'. In the breeding season pairs may nest close to each other or on their own. At other times it will join with flocks of Woodpigeons or sometimes feeds in small flocks with its own species.

VOICE
The song is a soft, deep 'ooo-woo, ooo-woo'.

HABITAT
This species breeds in park-land with old trees, wooded farmland, the edges of larger woods and open forests. It is also found where there are cliffs or quarries or around old buildings. It frequently feeds on arable farmland.

FOOD
It eats mainly plant material. It feeds on seeds of cereal crops such as Wheat and Barley, and plants such as Rape, goosefoot, dock and buttercup.

BREEDING
It nests in a hole in a tree, in nestboxes, in a building, a cliff or, very occasionally, a hole in the ground. Very little nest material is used and the same site may be used year after year. It usually lays 2 eggs which are incubated for 16–18 days by both sexes. Both male and female care for the young (squabs), which are fed on special milk that forms in their parents' crop. Incubation may start with the first egg and results in the young being different ages. The age of the first flight is variable, between 20–30 days, and the young birds become independent soon afterwards. There may be further broods, and up to five in a year have been reported from other parts of its range.

MOVEMENTS AND MIGRATIONS
Most Scottish birds are resident, seldom moving far. European populations are migratory, and small numbers – presumably from Europe – are seen in the Northern and Western Isles, especially in spring. Oldest known bird was 12 years.

POPULATION
10,000–15,000 pairs nest in Scotland. The population in the British Isles increased throughout most of the 19th and 20th centuries. Recent trends in Scotland are not clear. Some areas where the species once nested have been abandoned, while colonisation of a few new areas has also been reported.

CONSERVATION
The expansion of its range in the 19th century resulted in the Stock Dove breeding in Scotland for the first time around 1866. Its arrival has been linked to the expansion of arable farming, while a decline in the 1950s and early 1960s coincided with the widespread use of chemical seed dressings. Since a ban was placed on these chemicals the population has recovered in Scotland. This species can be assisted by the erection of suitable nestboxes.

DISTRIBUTION
Breeds mainly in central and eastern Scotland.
Widespread in the rest of Britain and parts of Ireland.
In Europe it breeds from southern Scandinavia to the Mediterranean; it also breeds east to central Asia and south to North Africa.

COLLARED DOVE *STREPTOPELIA DECAOCTO*

IDENTIFICATION

31–33 cm. Smaller than Woodpigeon, with a longish tail. This is a pale pinkish-buff dove with dark flight feathers and, when seen from below, a broad white band at the tip of the tail. The back is plain and unmarked and there is a thin black bar on the side of the neck. Moult begins in spring, after March, and continues into the autumn, with some suspending the moult of their flight feathers during the winter and not completing the growth of all new feathers until the following February – thus moult can last for 10 months. SEE ALSO: Woodpigeon p142.

HABITS

Seen singly or in pairs in the breeding season, but may form flocks at other times. It feeds on the ground and frequently perches in the open. It sings from roofs and overhead wires. In its aerial display flight it rises steeply and then glides down on fanned wings – often calling as it lands. This species can become used to humans.

VOICE

It has a harsh, excited 'kwurr' call. The song is a loud and repetitive 'coo-oo-cuk, coo-oo-cuk'.

HABITAT

The Collared Dove is associated mainly with human activity, such as farms (especially where there is spilt grain for food) and also gardens with a bird table. Many live in towns where there is a varied habitat of gardens, parks and churchyards but it tends to avoid city centres. Although it is widespread, it avoids uplands, especially moorland and mountainous areas.

FOOD

It is mainly vegetarian, feeding on grain and other seeds and fruits. Wheat, Barley and Oats are all eaten when available, as are seeds from knotgrass, bindweed and various grasses. Berries such as Elder are eaten in autumn. It will sometimes feed on aphids and also caterpillars.

BREEDING

In Scotland, Collared Doves nest mostly between February and November. The clutch is generally 2 eggs. The nest is a delicate, thin structure of rather thin twigs and the eggs are sometimes visible from below. Incubation is by both parents and lasts 14–18 days. The young remain in the nest for 15–19 days and are cared for by both parents. They are fed on 'crop milk' for the first 10 days after hatching. They become independent of the adults after about a week out of the nest. It is possible for a pair to raise five broods in a year although three broods are more usual.

MOVEMENTS AND MIGRATIONS

It is mainly a resident species but the young disperse after leaving the nest and many show a tendency to move west. Although some return to their original breeding areas, this habit has led to the rapid expansion westwards since about 1930. Oldest known bird survived for more than 16 years.

POPULATION

Between 8,000 and 12,000 pairs breed in Scotland. The species arrived here in the 1950s, having expanded its range across Europe. The population now appears stable.

CONSERVATION

The expansion of this dove's range has been quite remarkable. Spreading from south-east Europe, it moved west and eventually reached Scotland by 1957. There are no special conservation measures associated with this successful species.

juvenile

DISTRIBUTION

It is found throughout Scotland except for upland areas. The species originated in southern Asia and the Middle East and is now found across central Europe as far south as Greece and north to southern Scandinavia. The Collared Dove continues to expand its range across North America and the Caribbean.

Rock Dove/Feral Pigeon COLUMBA LIVIA

IDENTIFICATION

31–34 cm. Smaller than Woodpigeon. This species includes the familiar town pigeon. In its wild form it is blue-grey with a pale grey back, dark bars on wings and white rump. Head and breast are darker with iridescent green/purple sheen to feathers on side of neck. Feral form varies from pure white to almost black and includes plumages that are various shades of grey and brown. Some of the feral population resemble their Rock Dove ancestors. In flight, it shows white on the underside of the wing and white rump. Adults moult between June and November with the flight feathers being replaced gradually. Feral birds may moult at any time of year. SEE ALSO: Stock Dove p143, Woodpigeon p142.

HABITS

Sociable. Flight fast, and it also glides and wheels. Has been domesticated for centuries and these domesticated forms may have exotic plumages, tumbling flight action, or be used for racing. In the past they have also been a source of food and used for carrying messages. Some previously domesticated birds or their descendants now breed in the habitat used by wild Rock Doves.

VOICE

Call during display is a gentle 'orr-roo-cooo'.

HABITAT

In Scotland its traditional home is rock faces and cliffs, usually with caves and near the sea. In other parts of its range it will use suitable cliffs miles inland. Feral form is usually associated with towns and cities where it lives around buildings that provide nest sites and accessible supplies of food.

FOOD

Feeds on the seeds of cereal crops such as Wheat, Barley and Oats. Also eats peas and seeds of plants, including Wild Radish, Shepherd's Purse, dock and buttercup. Feral birds eat grain, but will take a wide range of other, mainly vegetarian, foods available by scavenging in towns.

BREEDING

Colonies of wild birds nest in semi-darkness in holes in rock faces or on ledges in caves. Urban birds use cavities in buildings. The rather loosely constructed nest is made from grasses, seaweed and other local material.

Eggs may be laid at any time of year, but peak nesting is in spring and autumn. The normal clutch is 2 eggs, and five or more clutches may be laid in a year. Incubation is by both parents and lasts for about 17 days. Young (squabs) are fed on a substance that forms in the birds' crop known as 'crop milk' that the young take by reaching inside the adults' mouths. They fly at 35–37 days, but may be fed by their parents for up to 10 days after fledging.

MOVEMENTS AND MIGRATIONS

Wild Rock Dove is mainly resident, seldom moving far from its nest site. Domesticated birds have remarkable powers of navigation, hence their use in racing (homing) and as message carriers. Rock Doves may live to 20 years or more.

POPULATION

It has been estimated that there may be up to 78,000 pairs of this species breeding in Scotland, but of those only 1,000–5,000 may be pure Rock Doves. These birds are to be found on the Inner and Outer Hebrides and in parts of Orkney and Shetland.

CONSERVATION

The spread of the Feral Pigeon has been so successful that nothing can be done to stop its gradual hybridisation with the wild form.

feral variants

DISTRIBUTION

Scotland still has a small population of apparently pure Rock Doves, with the majority of these in the Hebrides. The other 'pure' populations in the British Isles are thought to be in south and west Ireland. The wild Rock Dove is also found in Europe, North Africa and south-west Asia. The feral descendants are found in all continents except Antarctica.

CUCKOO *CUCULUS CANORUS*

male

IDENTIFICATION
32–34 cm. Size of Collared Dove. Superficially it resembles small bird of prey, with its slim body, long tail, small head and pointed wings. Bill short and slightly curved; legs very short. Upperparts, head and breast plain blue-grey and underparts white with back barring. Tail rounded with white tip. At rest the bird droops its wings well below the level of the long tail. Female is slightly browner than male, especially on its breast. Juvenile grey-brown or reddish brown with black barring and white feathers on the back of its head. There is a rare form of the adult female that is reddish brown like a female kestrel. Adults partly moult during June or July, but have a complete moult in Africa during the winter.
SEE ALSO: Sparrowhawk p77, Kestrel p80.

HABITS
In flight the pointed wings move below the level of the body and wingbeats are rapid. Perches in the open; on wires or at top of trees or on bare branches, often with tail cocked and spread and wings drooped. A male will adopt this pose as he swivels his body during courtship. Generally seen singly outside the breeding season. Those present in Britain or Ireland in late summer and early autumn are invariably juveniles.

VOICE
Call of male is the famous 'cuc-oo'. It also makes a harsh, laughing 'gwork-gwork-gwork'. Female makes a very different bubbling call.

HABITAT
Found in most habitats except built-up areas although it does visit large parks. Especially favours reedbeds, moorland, birch woodland and agricultural land with old hedges. In Africa in winter, found in savannah and forests.

FOOD
Feeds mainly on insects, especially caterpillars – including those that are hairy, such as the Fox Moth and Northern Eggar, or that have warning colours. Other insects include beetles, flies, sawflies and ants. Will also eat eggs and small nestlings of other birds, sometimes from the nests that it parasitises.

BREEDING
Some maintain territories, others gather where there is a high density of 'host' species. Individuals parasitise particular species: Meadow Pipit, Dunnock and Reed Warbler are the most common, although more than a hundred others have been used. Female makes no nest; instead she watches a suitable area. Then, when she is ready to lay, she selects a nest, takes out an egg in her bill and lays her own in its place. She flies off with the host's egg and swallows it. Up to 25 eggs may be laid in a season and their colour usually resembles that of the preferred host. Incubation is by the host and the young Cuckoo hatches after 12 days. The blind and naked chick then instinctively pushes other eggs or young out of nest. Other small birds, such as Wrens, are sometimes attracted to feed the giant baby. Young Cuckoos leave the nest after about 19 days and continue to be fed for a further 3 weeks.

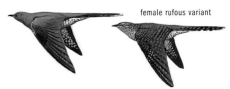

female rufous variant

MOVEMENTS AND MIGRATIONS
Most breeding birds arrive in April and leave again in August. Juveniles follow a month or so later. Oldest bird was 12 years.

POPULATION
There may be up to 4,400 pairs breeding in Scotland. Numbers appear to be stable, but a decline has been noted elsewhere in the UK.

CONSERVATION
The recent decline in the UK has been linked with fewer host species and the lack of invertebrates as a result of agricultural changes. These declines have been less obvious in Scotland. As a migrant, the species may also be affected by changes in its winter quarters in Africa.

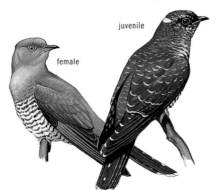

juvenile

female

LITTLE OWL *ATHENE NOCTUA*

IDENTIFICATION
21–23 cm. Size of Starling. Scotland's smallest owl. Small and plump with a rather flat head and short tail. The brown or greyish-brown upperparts and wings are heavily spotted with white and the pale breast is heavily streaked. The black eyes with yellow irises stare from under white 'eye-brows', giving a fierce expression. Juvenile is duller than adult and lacks white spots on its crown. In flight, wings are quite long and rounded at the ends. Moult begins in July and continues to November, with male starting before female.
SEE ALSO: Tawny Owl p148.

HABITS
May be seen in daylight as it perches with an erect attitude in the open on a telegraph pole, branch or rock. Mainly hunts from dusk to midnight and again before dawn. It bobs curiously when alarmed. It frequently hunts on the ground where it hops or runs on its rather long legs. Flight is often deeply undulating, rising with rapid wingbeats and dipping down with closed wings, but can also be direct and 'bat-like'.

VOICE
The most frequent call is a sharp, mewing 'kiew, kiew' that is most common in March and April during courtship, when the male also gives a pure, single hoot 'woop'.

HABITAT
It lives mainly on open lowland farmland where there are hedges and copses, as well as old trees to provide suitable nest sites, mainly in the Borders region of southern Scotland.

FOOD
It feeds on small mammals, birds, insects and invertebrates. Mammals include shrews and voles. Insects include beetles, caterpillars and adult moths, especially common species that hatch in large numbers, and cockchafers. It regularly feeds on earthworms, which it hunts on the ground.

BREEDING
The most usual nest site is a hole in a tree, about 3 m off the ground. It also uses clefts in rock faces, holes in buildings and sometimes holes between tree roots and in rabbit burrows. Eggs are laid during April and May. Most clutches are of 3 or 4 eggs and incubation is by the female. The young hatch after 29–31 days. For the first 2 weeks they are almost constantly brooded by the female, later both parents hunt for food. They can fly after 37 days, but before this they may leave the nest chamber and clamber about around the nest-site.

MOVEMENTS AND MIGRATIONS
The species does not migrate. Young birds disperse from their nest sites in late summer, but seldom travel far. The oldest surviving ringed bird was over 10 years old.

POPULATION
Fewer than 10 pairs regularly breed in Scotland. The species spread into southern Scotland from England and first nested here in the mid-20th century. In recent years it appears to have become more scarce again, with fewer regular breeding sites.

CONSERVATION
The Little Owl was introduced to the British Isles from Europe in the 19th century. Two schemes were successful: one in Kent and the other in Northamptonshire. From these introductions the species gradually colonised southern Britain, breeding in Scotland for the first time in 1958. There are concerns for the European population, which appears to have been in decline for the last 40 years owing to pesticides reducing its insect prey, changes in land use depriving it of nest sites, and road casualties.

DISTRIBUTION
A few nest in southern Scotland. In Britain it is most abundant in central and southern counties. It does not breed in Ireland. The species is a native of central and southern Europe, North Africa, the Middle East and parts of Asia.

TAWNY OWL *STRIX ALUCO*

IDENTIFICATION
37–39 cm. As large as Woodpigeon. Has a tubby body, large round head and rounded wings. Its face is surrounded with a ring of dark feathers and the eyes are dark and create a friendly expression. Upperparts are usually reddish brown with dark and white marks forming a broken line on its wings and on the crown of the head. Underparts are pale buff with dark streaks. A few birds are paler with greyer feathers. Flight is fast, direct and silent, and often higher than other owls. Feathers are moulted gradually between June and December.
SEE ALSO: Long-eared Owl p149, Short-eared Owl p150.

HABITS
Nocturnal. Generally seen during the day only if it is disturbed. Roosts in hollow trees, up against a tree trunk or amongst ivy, and is remarkably difficult to see. If it does emerge during the day it often attracts small birds that mob it. May hunt from a perch or hover in flight. Defends its nest aggressively, even attacking human intruders. The Tawny Owl relies on knowing its hunting territory very well and checks every part of it.

VOICE
Song is the familiar hoot 'hooo-hoo-hooo' of the male that proclaims his territory and is used during courtship. Female also has a hoarse version of the hoot. Another commonly heard call is a sharp 'kee-wick', made by both male and female. Occasionally calls during daylight.

HABITAT
Deciduous and coniferous woodland. An adaptable species that also lives in farmland and gardens where there are suitable nest sites. It has colonised town and city centres where there are parks, squares and churchyards with large trees. In some places, especially outside Britain, it inhabits more open countryside and will nest among cliffs.

FOOD
The most common food is small mammals, especially voles, mice and shrews. Also eats insects such as beetles, birds such as Starlings, finches, thrushes and sparrows and also frogs and earthworms. Surprisingly, it is also known occasionally to eat fish that it presumably snatches from the water surface.

BREEDING
The nest is in a natural or man-made hole, including specially designed nestboxes, and only rarely on the ground. Nesting may begin in late February or March.

The female incubates the clutch of 2 or 3 eggs for 28–30 days. At first the young are brooded by the female while the male hunts. After about 15 days both parents hunt for food. Owlets often leave their nest after 25–30 days and hide among nearby branches. They fly at 32–37 days, but are dependent on their parents for a further 3 months.

MOVEMENTS AND MIGRATIONS
Mainly resident with established pairs probably never leaving their territories. Young birds disperse in any direction in autumn. Juveniles seldom travel further than a few kilometres, but those breeding in northern Europe often travel much farther. Oldest ringed bird survived more than 23 years.

POPULATION
There may be 6,000 pairs nesting in Scotland, and although the species is still widespread a small decline in the population may have occurred in recent years.

CONSERVATION
This owl, like other birds of prey, has been persecuted in game-rearing areas. It is also a frequent victim of traffic on busy roads. Agricultural changes may also reduce vole numbers, a key food.

grey type   rufous type

DISTRIBUTION
Widespread in Scotland, England and Wales, but not found in Ireland. Breeds from central Scandinavia to north-west Africa and the Middle East, and east to western Siberia and the Himalayas.

LONG-EARED OWL   *ASIO OTUS*

IDENTIFICATION
35–37 cm. Smaller than Woodpigeon. Often looks rather long and thin with head feathers known as 'ear-tufts' (which are not ears) that may be raised and lowered. The cat-like face changes from round to narrow when the bird is stretched up and roosting. Plumage is rich buff-brown with darker brown streaks, and underparts are streaked boldly to below belly. In flight, long wings are more uniform than Short-eared's and do not have a pale buff edge. Base of the flight feathers is orange-brown. Short tail is finely barred. Eyes are deep orange. 'Ear-tufts' are held flat in flight. Adults moult gradually between June and December with male starting first. Flight feathers are moulted gradually over 3 months.
SEE ALSO: Short-eared Owl p150, Tawny Owl p148.

HABITS
Nocturnal; only occasionally hunts during the day. Roosts in bushes and trees during the day and is reluctant to fly unless an observer approaches too close. It is not a colonial breeding species, but groups may migrate together and small communal roosts are not uncommon in winter. Its flight is slow and wavering.

VOICE
Variety of sounds is large. Song is a quiet but penetrating low 'hoo-hoo-hoo-hoo'. The small young have jingling calls, but later they make a drawn-out squeak that has been likened to an un-oiled gate.

HABITAT
In Scotland it nests mainly in conifer woods, although some nest in broadleaf woodland and a few in open or rocky areas in Sutherland and Shetland.

FOOD
The main method to study its diet is to examine pellets that are ejected by the owl at its roost. Food is small mammals, especially voles and mice, and also birds that are caught at their roosts.

BREEDING
Nest is usually in a tree, in a sturdy old nest of another bird such as a Magpie or crow, or in a squirrel's drey. Occasionally, in areas with few trees, these owls nest on the ground. Nesting begins in late March or April. Female incubates clutch of 3 or 4 eggs for 25–30 days. Male feeds female and provides most of the food for young. At about 21 days young leave the nest and live among the branches. They can probably fly at 30 days and remain dependent on their parents until they are 60 days old.

MOVEMENTS AND MIGRATIONS
Northern populations are migratory, whereas southern birds are resident or move only relatively short distances to find food. In Scotland some birds leave and fly south, while others remain. In addition, small numbers of birds from Scandinavia and Russia arrive in autumn. Some of these will overwinter here, while others fly on southwards. Oldest ringed bird was 17 years.

POPULATION
This is a very difficult species to census. There may be between 600 and 2,200 pairs in Scotland. Its population has cycles, reflecting the abundance of prey, and Long-eared Owls reportedly abandon areas if Tawny Owls move in. There may now be a contraction of the range of this species in Scotland.

CONSERVATION
Its range over the whole of the British Isles appears to have contracted in recent years and numbers are lower, but populations fluctuate as these owls achieve better breeding results in years when rodents, especially voles, are numerous – and such years tend to be cyclical. Some pairs can be encouraged to nest in man-made sites such as willow baskets.

DISTRIBUTION

Widespread in Scotland and thinly distributed in the rest of the British Isles, with fewest birds in the south and west of England and Wales. Inhabits a band around the northern hemisphere, including North America, Europe and Asia, with some isolated populations in North Africa.

SHORT-EARED OWL *ASIO FLAMMEUS*

IDENTIFICATION

37–39 cm. Medium-sized owl that is mottled brown with staring yellow eyes surrounded with black patches within a pale face. 'Ears' are hard to see. Has long wings, which are very pale below with a black tip and a black curved bar at the base of the flight feathers. Upperwings are mottled brown and buff and have a white trailing edge. Tail shows four strong bars. Breast is heavily marked with dark streaks, but rest of underparts are paler than a Long-eared's. In flight, often keeps low. It has deep wingbeats followed by a glide, with wings in a shallow 'V'. Adults start to moult in June or July. Moult begins with flight feathers and by November all feathers have regrown.

SEE ALSO: Long-eared Owl p149, Tawny Owl p148.

HABITS

This owl quite commonly hunts in daylight, but especially at dawn and dusk. In spring, it has an aerial display as it flies high above its territory and claps its wings below its body. Often solitary, but does sometimes gather in groups to roost, occasionally mixing with Long-eared Owls. Regularly perches on the ground, on a post or in bushes or trees. On the ground it is less upright than other owls. Winters on coastal grasslands and inland marshes.

VOICE

Usually silent, but has a low, hollow 'boo-boo-boo-boo' and also a hoarse bark.

HABITAT

Open country: moorland, coastal marshes, rough grassland and dunes. Has also benefited from grasslands enclosed when young conifers are planted.

FOOD

Main food is small mammals, especially Field Voles, rats and mice. Birds up to the size of thrushes are eaten, and insects and amphibians are occasionally caught.

BREEDING

The first eggs may be laid during March in a nest that is a shallow scrape made on ground by female and lined with local vegetation. Site is usually in grass, rushes or heather.

Female incubates clutch of 4–7 eggs for 24–29 days. Incubation starts with first egg and young hatch over a period of a week or more. Both adults feed the young. At about 15 days the owlets leave their nest and hide in the surrounding vegetation until they fly at 24–27 days.

MOVEMENTS AND MIGRATIONS

Northerly populations are migratory, and some birds from northern Europe reach Scotland each autumn, where they may be seen on the east coast. Most Scottish breeding birds leave their nesting sites soon after the young can fly and move to coastal marshes and other lowland areas. Many migrate south, with immatures often travelling further than adults and reaching as far as Spain. Some from Europe travel further, crossing the Sahara Desert to winter in central Africa. Some populations are nomadic and breed or winter where food is plentiful. Oldest known bird lived 20 years.

POPULATION

The Field Vole population rises and falls in a cycle, and Short-eared Owl breeding densities have a corresponding fluctuation, with between 125 and 1,250 pairs breeding in Scotland. With such wide variations trends are hard to monitor, but there appears to be an overall decline.

CONSERVATION

The species initially benefited from the establishment of new conifer plantations in the 20th century, but replanted areas seem to be less attractive, perhaps owing to the presence of fewer voles. Persecution on sporting estates is still a problem in a few areas. The loss of rough hill ground and moorland to improved agriculture pasture has reduced food availability.

DISTRIBUTION

Breeds mainly in south and east Scotland, with some on the Hebrides and Orkney. Also breeds in northern and eastern England and in parts of Wales, but is scarce in Ireland. Elsewhere it breeds in Iceland, in Europe from the Arctic as far south as northern France, in Asia, and in parts of North and South America. Some reach Africa in winter.

Barn Owl *TYTO ALBA*

IDENTIFICATION
33–35 cm. Smaller than Tawny Owl. It has a heart-shaped face that can change shape, long and rather narrow wings and long legs. The honey-coloured upperparts are flecked with darker marks with some grey on the back. The underparts, including under the wings, are snowy white with only light spotting. The female has a little more spotting on breast and more streaking and spotting on back. The race found in central Europe has buff underparts. Body feathers are moulted gradually throughout the year. Flight feathers are moulted between July and December.
SEE ALSO: Short-eared Owl p150.

HABITS
Its buoyant flight is typically slow, low over the ground and wavering, and it frequently hovers when hunting. Generally a nocturnal hunter, but may be seen during the day. Territories are occupied for the whole year and birds hunt singly. When perched has an upright position.

VOICE
A piercing shriek, especially during courtship. Call for food is a loud 'snore' made mainly by the young, but also by adults during courtship.

HABITAT
Open country, usually below 300 m, especially farmland, but also coastal marshes and forest edge. Nests and roosts in buildings, hollow trees or cliffs. Hunts over areas of rank grassland, along field edges, ditches, riverbanks, railway embankments and roadside verges.

FOOD
Feeds mainly on small mammals such as mice, voles and shrews, and it also eats larger mammals including small rats. Birds such as finches and thrushes are sometimes taken at their roosts and some individuals also catch and eat bats.

BREEDING
The nest is in an enclosed space in a barn, ruined building, hollow tree, cliff-face or a specially made nestbox. Some nests are among hay or straw bales in modern barns. During courtship the male feeds the female. No nest is made and the clutch of 4–6 eggs is laid onto a pile of old pellets. Incubation by female takes about 30 days and starts with the first egg, so the young hatch at intervals of 2 or 3 days and therefore the oldest may be 2 weeks older than the youngest. Young fly after about 55 days and are dependent on their parents for a further 3–5 weeks. Often two broods.

MOVEMENTS AND MIGRATIONS
Most adults are resident and seldom move far. Juveniles randomly disperse once they are fully independent and they may travel up to 50 km, with a few going further. After good breeding seasons in some European countries, birds may disperse, with a few reaching eastern Scotland. Oldest wild bird survived over 17 years.

POPULATION
500–1,000 pairs of this owl nest in Scotland. Population fluctuations are due to changes in food availability, but following a serious decline in the mid-20th century numbers have been increasing again in recent years.

CONSERVATION
Specially protected. Once it was widespread both here and in Europe, but along with other birds of prey it suffered declines during the 20th century owing to agricultural intensification and the use of pesticides. In Britain, the use of second generation rodenticides has been a cause of some mortality. Re-establishing hay meadows, conserving areas of rough grassland rich in voles wherever possible, especially alongside watercourses, field edges and woods will help to ensure this species continues to have sufficient feeding areas. The provision of new nest sites in areas where natural holes are in short supply is also helpful.

DISTRIBUTION
It is widespread in mainland Scotland on land below 300 m, but is only a vagrant on the Northern Isles and the Outer Hebrides. It is one of the world's most widespread species, with as many as 28 different races breeding in all continents except Antarctica.

NIGHTJAR CAPRIMULGUS EUROPAEUS

IDENTIFICATION
26–28 cm. Smaller than Kestrel. Long, pointed wings, a long tail and a rather large, flat head. Eyes are large and dark, bill is short and mouth very wide for catching flying insects. Plumage is grey-brown with beautiful camouflage markings. Adult male has white marks near the tips of its wings and on the outer tips of its tail. Females and juveniles lack the white marks. Adults begin to moult in July and some inner flight feathers may be moulted before migration, but rest of moult takes place in Africa.
SEE ALSO: Kestrel p80, Cuckoo p146, Grasshopper Warbler (song) p185.

HABITS
Males are territorial and it is unusual to see more than one or two birds at a time, although small groups may gather at rich feeding sites. In flight, twists and turns, and flies as silently as an owl – sometimes almost seems to float on the air. During display flight it will clap its wings together above the back making a 'slapping' sound. Most active around dusk and dawn when it feeds. At rest, during the day, perches along a branch instead of across it, like most other birds, to gain maximum camouflage, or on the ground.

VOICE
Flight call is a loud, liquid-sounding 'coo-lik'. Song is a long, drawn-out churring that rises and falls as the bird turns its head.

HABITAT
In Scotland it usually nests in open woodland, often amongst Bracken. Clearings in forestry plantations below 200 m are often used, but birds need to move on as new trees grow. In winter in Africa it also lives in clearings in forests as well as in open steppe country.

FOOD
Feeds on insects. Catches prey in flight and takes a wide variety of moths, beetles and flies.

BREEDING
Nest is a shallow scrape on bare ground, usually among dead branches and broken sticks; either in a clearing in a wood or in a more open location. Usually lays 2 eggs, incubated mostly by female, with male taking over at dawn and dusk. Eggs hatch after 17–18 days. Young fly after 18–19 days and become independent about 16 days later.

MOVEMENTS AND MIGRATIONS
This is a difficult species to study and its migrations are poorly understood. All are long-distance migrants. Juveniles from first broods are thought to leave Europe in late July with adults and other juveniles following later. They reach their African wintering grounds between October and November. Scottish birds return in early May, with the males returning a few days before the females. The oldest wild bird survived 11 years.

male

POPULATION
This species declined during the latter part of the 20th century. There have been only 20–30 males holding territory in Scotland in recent years, mainly in the south-west.

CONSERVATION
It is unclear why the Scottish Nightjar population is decreasing while the population in England, especially in the south and east, is increasing. The influence of a changing, wetter climate seems the most likely explanation, as many sites apparently favourable to Nightjars remain in Scotland. The maintenance of a mosaic of woodland habitat, retaining open areas within forests, is important for the future of this species and the large flying insects upon which they depend. Work by the RSPB and the Forestry Commission is now targeting this species.

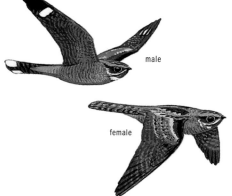

male

female

DISTRIBUTION
Relatively small numbers breed in southern Scotland. Occasional passage birds are seen on the Northern Isles. The largest concentrations in the British Isles are to be found in southern and eastern England. Breeds from southern Scandinavia to North Africa and east into central Asia. It winters in central and southern Africa, as far south as South Africa.

KINGFISHER _ALCEDO ATTHIS_

IDENTIFICATION
16–17 cm. Size of sparrow with large head and long dagger-like bill. Tail is short and wings broad and rounded. Underparts and cheeks are orange and upperparts electric blue or oily green depending on the light. Has a white throat and neck-patches. Male has an all-black bill and female has a red base to lower part of bill. Juvenile is duller and greener. Feathers are moulted gradually between July and November with the main flight feathers taking between 90–100 days to moult and re-grow. Some that moult late may suspend their moult during cold winter weather.

HABITS
Flight fast and straight, and often low over the water although it will fly higher when taking 'short-cuts' across land. Perches motionless when fishing or sometimes hovers before plunging into the water after a fish. Once prey has been caught it is taken to a perch and the bird may hit the fish until it is stunned before turning it in its bill and swallowing head first. Courtship involves high-speed chases. Despite its bright colours, its small size and rapid flight makes it hard to observe. The distinctive call is usually the best clue to its presence.

male

female

VOICE
Call is a shrill 'chree' or a double note 'chee-kee'.

HABITAT
Breeds in lowland areas where there are large, slow-flowing rivers and their tributaries, especially those that have suitable banks for nesting and shallow edges for fishing. Also visits other smaller waters, including ornamental ponds and, sometimes, garden ponds. In winter, may visit estuaries and coasts.

FOOD
Feeds on fish and some aquatic insects. The most common fish are Bullheads, loaches, Minnows, sticklebacks and small Chub. Insects include mayflies, stoneflies, dragonfly nymphs and water beetles.

BREEDING
Birds pair in February or March. Breeding territory usually between 1–1.5 km long. Nest is in a chamber at the end of a tunnel that is dug by both birds. Tunnel is dug into a vertical bank, usually, but not always, close to water. First clutches are laid in early April and there are normally 5–7 eggs. Eggs are incubated for 19–21 days by both sexes. Both sexes feed young until they leave nest at 23–27 days. Young become independent a few days after leaving nest and many pairs attempt to raise a second or even a third brood.

MOVEMENTS AND MIGRATIONS
Scottish Kingfishers do not usually move very far unless forced out of their territories by hard weather. Juveniles disperse after becoming independent, but seldom travel more than 12 km from their original nest site. Northern and eastern European populations are migratory and many winter around the Mediterranean. Oldest ringed bird was 15 years old.

POPULATION
There may be between 330 and 450 pairs breeding in Scotland. In the past, numbers have fallen after harsh winters or as a consequence of polluted waterways, but in recent years, helped by mild winters, the Scottish population appears stable.

CONSERVATION
Specially protected. It has declined in Europe and this is attributed to river pollution. To conserve this species the culverting of streams and rivers should stop and government agencies should continue to control polluters, including pollution from animal waste slurries and from silage clamps which frequently finds its way into watercourses.

DISTRIBUTION
Found mainly in southern and eastern Scotland, south of the Forth–Clyde line. It is more numerous south of the border in central and southern England, in Wales and in Ireland. This race of Kingfisher is found across Europe, east to the Caspian Sea and to Spain. Other races are found in south-east Europe, North Africa and parts of Asia.

GREEN WOODPECKER *PICUS VIRIDIS*

male

IDENTIFICATION
31–33 cm. Size of a town pigeon. The largest of the British woodpeckers with a heavy-looking body, short tail and a strong, rather long bill. Green-grey upperparts, duller greyish underparts, vivid yellow-green rump and red crown. It has black around the eye. The 'moustache' mark of male is dull red while that of female is black. Juvenile is heavily spotted and barred. Flight deeply undulating as the bird closes its wings after 3–4 flaps. Moult takes place between June and November with the first flight feathers being lost around the time the young fledge. Juveniles moult quickly after fledging and gain their adult plumage between August and November.

FOOD
Insects are extracted from the nest chambers with the woodpecker's extremely long and sticky tongue. Diet consists chiefly of ants; as eggs, larvae, pupae and adults. Also eats beetles, flies and caterpillars.

BREEDING
Nests in mature trees, especially oak, Ash and birch. Nest is at the bottom of a specially excavated chamber in a tree trunk or large limb, generally about 4 m from the ground. Diameter of hole is 6 cm and the nest chamber averages 28 cm deep. The 4–6 eggs are laid between March and mid-June. Incubation is by both adults and young hatch after about 19 days. Both parents feed the young, which fly after about 21 days and become independent after a further 3–7 weeks.

MOVEMENTS AND MIGRATIONS
Resident, with individuals seldom moving far from their original nest site. Young birds may disperse in autumn and winter and exploit feeding areas away from woods and trees. Oldest known bird survived 15 years.

female
male
juvenile

POPULATION
First recorded nesting in Scotland in 1951. This was followed by a rapid colonisation northwards to beyond the Great Glen. Since then it has retreated to the south and east, but it is still widespread, especially in Fife, Perthshire and Lothian and Borders. There are now 600–900 pairs breeding.

CONSERVATION
The recent success of the species in Scotland has not been repeated in mainland Europe, where it has declined in some places. Loss of habitat for feeding, especially areas of short turf with concentrations of ants, is a problem in some places, and the effects of climate change may further restrict distribution in future.

HABITS
Spends a lot of time feeding on the ground where it moves in a series of hops. On the ground it often looks hunched-back as it feeds, but adopts an upright posture when alert. On a tree trunk it will climb in a series of jerks with its stiff tail feathers pressed against the trunk for support. Often hides from an observer by moving behind the trunk or limb. Outside the breeding season it is generally solitary, although several individuals have been observed roosting together. Call is given from a regular song-post near the nest.

VOICE
Call is a ringing, laughing 'peeu, peeu, peeu' and it also makes a feeble drumming.

HABITAT
Mainly a lowland species that breeds in open deciduous woods, parkland, orchards, farmland, heaths and, less often, conifer woods. Often feeds away from trees in open grassy areas such as pasture and occasionally garden lawns where there are ants' nests.

DISTRIBUTION
Found in southern, central and eastern Scotland south of the Great Glen, but common nowhere. Widespread in England and Wales, but absent from Ireland. Breeds in Europe from Scandinavia south to the Mediterranean and east throughout Europe and into south-west Asia.

GREAT SPOTTED WOODPECKER — *DENDROCOPOS MAJOR*

IDENTIFICATION
22–23 cm. Similar in size to Blackbird. A medium-sized black and white woodpecker with dirty-white underparts and crimson feathers under its short stiff tail. On its shoulders it has two large white patches with small white spots on the folded wings. The shoulder marks show as oval patches in flight. Male has a crimson patch on the back of head. Juvenile has duller white plumage and a red centre to its crown. Flight is bounding with wings closing after several flaps. Adults undergo a complete moult between June and November.
SEE ALSO: Green Woodpecker p155.

HABITS
Less likely to be seen on the ground than Green Woodpecker. Generally solitary outside the breeding season. When danger threatens, it will spiral up a tree trunk or branch and often 'freeze' on the side facing away from the danger. When attacking food with tough shells it will wedge it in a crevice in a tree trunk or branch and hammer it open with its powerful bill. During courtship pairs engage in noisy chases among the trees.

VOICE
Sharp and loud 'kick kick' may be heard throughout the year and is often the best indication of the presence of the bird. 'Song' is an instrumental sound made by drumming with its bill on a branch. The short bursts of drumming last around 5 seconds and accelerate before fading away at the end. Most drumming takes place in late winter and early spring.

HABITAT
Likely to be found almost anywhere there are trees, both in coniferous and deciduous woods – provided the trees are large enough to support the nest holes. Some live in parks and large mature gardens in urban locations.

FOOD
Feeds mainly on insects in summer and seeds and nuts in winter. A great variety of insects are eaten, including adults and larvae of wood-boring beetles, which the woodpecker reaches by chipping away at dead wood and using its long tongue to reach into the insects' chambers. Will also create a hole in a nestbox to reach the young birds inside, which it then eats or feeds to its own young. May visit bird tables and will frequently cling to hanging feeders.

BREEDING
Nesting begins in April. Both sexes excavate a nest chamber in a tree trunk or large branch. A variety of trees are used, but birches or oaks are most often selected. Hole is 5–6 cm in diameter and the average nest

male

chamber is 28 cm deep. The 4–6 eggs are incubated by both parents for about 15 days. The young are fed by both adults and fly at about 20 days. After fledging, the adults continue to feed their young for a week or more.

MOVEMENTS AND MIGRATIONS
Young birds may travel a few kilometres from their nest sites, but generally the species is resident. Young of northern populations may 'erupt' in years when food is in short supply, and a few of these reach the Northern Isles and the east coast of Scotland in winter. Oldest ringed bird survived for over 12 years.

POPULATION
Up to 10,000 pairs breed in Scotland. In recent years the population has been growing, following earlier declines during the two World Wars, when the demand for timber removed much suitable nesting habitat from the countryside.

CONSERVATION
The distribution of this woodpecker has changed over the last 200 years, from being widespread it retreated south. However, Scotland was re-colonised after 1887 and now it is widespread again. More recently it benefited from the dead wood resulting from Dutch elm disease.

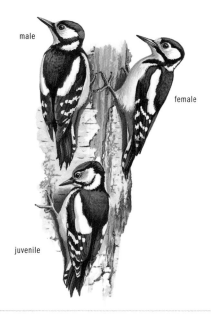

male

female

juvenile

SKYLARK *ALAUDA ARVENSIS*

fresh, autumn

IDENTIFICATION
18–19 cm. Larger than sparrow, but smaller than Star-ling. Has a short crest that may be raised or lowered. Back is brown with darker streaks, breast streaked, underparts are off-white and tail has white outer feath-ers. In flight, broad wings have obvious pale trailing edge. Crest and tail are both longer than those of Wood-lark but pale stripe over eye is less prominent. Juvenile looks more scaly. Skylarks undergo a complete moult between July and September with the flight feathers being lost and regrown over a period of about 58 days. SEE ALSO: Meadow Pipit p163.

HABITS
Spends most of its time on the ground and crouches when nervous. Will also land on posts and other low perches. On taking off, its flight is fluttering. Its direct flight is slightly floppy and undulating, with rapid flaps followed by a glide. Song flight begins as it rises steeply and hangs in the air over its territory, gradually getting higher until it is sometimes lost to human view. Para-chutes down with an extra rapid descent for the last few metres. Generally flocks outside the breeding season and in winter these may attract hundreds of birds.

VOICE
Chief call is a loud 'chirrup' often given in flight or when it is alarmed. Song is a long pleasant liquid warbling, usually given in flight, but sometimes from a perch or from the ground.

HABITAT
Breeds in open country, especially on ungrazed grass-lands, arable crops, dunes and grassy moorland. Out-side the breeding season it moves to lowland areas, and flocks gather on unploughed stubbles and coastal marshes.

FOOD
Feeds on both plant and animal material. Invertebrates include springtails, flies, bugs, beetles, moths, spiders, slugs and snails. Plant food includes grain, and also seeds and leaves of a wide variety of plants, including nettles and docks.

BREEDING
Nesting begins in late March or April. Site is usually amongst short vegetation and nest is in a shallow depression lined with grass. The 3–5 eggs are incubated by the female for 10–12 days. Both parents feed young. They leave the nest after about 8 days and fly after

16–20 days, but are cared for by their parents for up to 10 days after fledging. Up to three broods may be raised in a season.

MOVEMENTS AND MIGRATIONS
After nesting, Skylarks move from upland breeding territories to lower feeding areas and many migrate south of the border. More appear on the coast and in the Northern Isles in autumn; these are migrants from the Continent, especially from Scandinavia. Some of these birds will stay in lowland Scotland while others may fly on to winter in Ireland. Oldest ringed bird sur-vived over 9 years.

POPULATION
There are thought to be between 290,000 and 557,000 pairs nesting in Scotland. For the most part the popu-lation remains stable here, but there has been a con-siderable decline elsewhere in Britain, particularly on lowland farmland.

CONSERVATION
Skylark mortality increases in cold winters, especially after periods of prolonged frost and snow. The recent and rapid decline of the Skylark in England has been attributed to the change from spring to autumn sow-ing of cereals, which results in taller, denser vegetation at the time the birds are nesting. This has not been a major problem in Scotland, but the introduction of 'Skylark plots' of bare soil within cereal fields has been proved to maintain populations.

juvenile

DISTRIBUTION
Widespread. Found breeding in many parts of Scotland, apart from the highest hills. Also present on many of the islands. In winter it is found on coasts and lowland farmland. It is widespread in the rest of the British Isles. In Europe it breeds from northern Scandinavia to the Mediterranean and east into central Russia. There are other races in southern Europe, North Africa and Asia.

Shore Lark or Horned Lark
EREMOPHILA ALPESTRIS

Identification
14–17 cm. Smaller and slimmer than Skylark. Has a pinkish-brown streaked back, pale almost unstreaked underparts, boldly patterned yellow and black face and black throat. Adult male has black band on forehead ending with two small 'horns' on top of rear crown. Face markings of female have less contrast and both sexes are poorly marked in autumn and early winter. Juvenile moults before arriving in Britain but is more spotted on its back, more streaked on its underparts and with a less distinct face pattern. Complete moult takes place between June and September. After moult the face pattern becomes obscured as new feathers have yellow fringes. These fringes abrade (break off) during the winter revealing the bold black and yellow spring breeding plumage.
SEE ALSO: Skylark p156, Lapland Bunting p237.

male

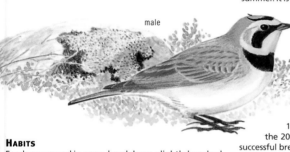

Habits
Feeds on ground in open, head down, slightly hunched or crouched and either shuffles along or makes small hops. Feeding flocks are constantly on the move. Although it will often allow a close approach, it can be difficult to observe, owing to its excellent camouflage. In winter, usually seen in small flocks, sometimes with Snow or Lapland Buntings. In flight, has a more bounding flight than a Skylark.

Voice
Voice in its winter flocks is a shrill 'tsee-tsi'. On breeding grounds has a warbling Skylark-like song usually given in flight.

Habitat
In Scotland in autumn and winter, it is found mostly near the east coast, often feeding along the strand line or on coastal grazing marshes, dune systems, stubble fields and rough pastures. Breeds in stony mountain areas or on Arctic tundra. Other races live on prairies, deserts and ploughed fields, in habitats similar to those used by Skylark.

Food
In summer, feeds on insects and some seeds. In winter, feeds mainly on seeds. Insect food includes springtails, flies and beetles. Plant food includes seeds from sedges, grasses, docks and grain.

Breeding
Nest is on the ground, often in the open amongst short vegetation, in a depression built by the female. Female incubates 2–4 eggs for 10–11 days. Young are cared for and fed by both adults. They leave the nest at 9–12 days but do not fly until 16–18 days. There can be one or two broods.

Movements and migrations
Northern races are migratory, while those living further south are largely resident. In Scotland, the Shore Lark is seen mainly on passage in April and May, and again between September and November. A small number remains in Scotland for the winter, and occasionally a pair has been observed in suitable breeding habitat in summer. It is probable that wintering birds are from the Scandinavian breeding population.

Population
The largest numbers are seen in autumn. The wintering population in Scotland comprises generally fewer than 50 birds, with the most reliable area to see them being East Lothian. Up to three pairs may attempt to breed in upland areas in some years. First recorded wintering in Scotland in 1859, the species increased gradually during the 20th century, but it remains a rare bird with successful breeding proven on only one occasion.

Conservation
A specially protected species. Secrecy to prevent nest robbery or disturbance is the key conservation measure if breeding is suspected again.

female
(fresh, autumn)

DISTRIBUTION

Wintering and passage birds in Scotland are seen mainly in the east and on the Northern Isles, and are rare inland. Occasionally, breeding may be attempted in the Highlands. In Europe, it nests in the mountains of Scandinavia and on the Arctic tundra. Other races are found in south-east Europe, Asia and North America.

SWIFT   *APUS APUS*

IDENTIFICATION
16–17 cm. Shorter body and longer wings than Swallow. Body, wings and tail are plain sooty brown and chin is noticeably pale. In bright sunlight plumage may appear lighter brown, but more often it appears black against the sky. Wings are long and scythe-like and tail is short and forked. Juvenile resembles adult, but with a more obvious pale throat and pale fringes to its wing feathers that creates a scaly appearance. Moult begins in August and at least some begin to moult their flight feathers before migrating. Moult continues in Africa and may not be completed until February or March.
SEE ALSO: Swallow p160, House Martin p161.

juvenile

HABITS
Flight is rapid and flickering, followed by long glides on sickle-shaped wings. Often parties will chase rapidly around their nest sites, screaming noisily. Spends more time in flight than any other species and regularly sleeps on the wing at night when not nesting. Also feeds, drinks, gathers nest material and sometimes mates in flight. Grounded Swifts find it difficult, and sometimes impossible, to take off again.

VOICE
Usual call is a harsh scream 'screee'.

HABITAT
An aerial species that ranges widely in its search for food and to avoid storms. It may be seen over most habitats, even mountains. Most breed in buildings in towns and villages, especially in older buildings or where there is access to the roof space. Some nest in traditional cliff sites, and a few in holes in trees or in specially erected nestboxes in forest areas.

FOOD
Feeds almost exclusively on flying insects, with some birds catching up to 10,000 a day when feeding young. Prey includes beetles, aphids, flies, hoverflies, craneflies, moths, butterflies, thrips, leafhoppers, ants and lacewings. Also catches airborne spiders.

BREEDING
The Swift starts breeding in May. Both sexes build the nest, which is a shallow cup of straw and other material gathered on the wing and cemented together with saliva. The site may be under eaves of a house, in a church tower or any other building that provides a suitable cavity. In Abernethy it regularly uses holes in trees and sometimes nestboxes. Clutch of 2 or 3 eggs is incubated by both sexes for 19 days, but incubation may be longer if the weather is cold. Young are brooded continuously for the first week. They remain in the nest for 37–56 days depending on the weather and are independent as soon as they leave the nest. Young Swifts do not breed until their fourth year.

MOVEMENTS AND MIGRATIONS
Summer migrant. Arrives in late April or early May and leaves again in August with only a few birds seen in Scotland in September. Its migratory journeys are rapid with autumn migrants arriving in Africa by mid-August. In Africa birds respond to changes in the weather and food availability by moving large distances. The oldest known Swift survived 21 years.

POPULATION
Difficult to census, but there are thought to be 6,000–8,000 pairs in Scotland. The population appears to have fallen in recent years, perhaps by as much as 50%.

CONSERVATION
There are problems for the species in that modern buildings lack suitable nest sites and some older buildings have cavities wired against pigeons that also prevent Swifts from nesting. It is possible to make Swift nestboxes, and this is recommended to owners of modern houses and also to managers of northern forests.

DISTRIBUTION

Mainly seen in central, southern and eastern Scotland, although it also visits offshore islands. It breeds throughout the British Isles, with the largest numbers in the south and east. Elsewhere it breeds from the Arctic Circle south to North Africa and east into Asia. Winters in southern Africa. Passage birds seen in the Northern Isles.

Sand Martin *RIPARIA RIPARIA*

Identification

12 cm. Smaller than Swallow and slimmer than House Martin. Tail is only slightly forked. Upperparts uniform brown and underparts white with distinct brown band across breast. Wings are pointed and often appear narrower than those of House Martin. Juvenile has pale edges to back feathers, giving a less uniform appearance and the breast band is less distinct. Adults start to moult between July and September, as they finish nesting, continuing during the early stages of migration, but moult may be suspended until the bird reaches Africa.
SEE ALSO: Swallow p160, House Martin p161.

Habits

Breeds in small or large colonies and many feed together at suitable sites. Often migrates in flocks and gathers in large evening roosts. Flight is fast and agile, but looks weaker and less graceful than a Swallow and glides less often. Feeds by catching insects in the air. Often perches on wires.

Voice

Song is a harsh rattling or twittering, given frequently in flight and also when perched. The song is usually associated with courtship, but is also heard at other times.

Habitat

Depends on vertical sandy banks for nesting. These sites are usually close to rivers and sand or gravel quarries. Feeds over open country and especially over water, and tends to avoid built-up areas, woods and mountains. On migration flocks roost in reedbeds.

Food

Feeds on insects that it catches in flight, especially midges, flies and aphids, but a wide variety of other insects are eaten. When feeding nestlings, many insects are caught in a single foraging flight and the mass is brought back and fed to the young.

Breeding

Older birds return to colonies first. The nest is in a hole in a bank and occasionally in an artificial site such as a drain pipe. Both adults excavate a 35–119 cm tunnel with a chamber at the end that contains a nest of grass and feathers. Both birds incubate the 4 or 5 eggs for 14–15 days. The young are cared for by both adults and leave the nest at about 22 days. In years with good weather, a second brood is reared. If the survival of the first brood is poor the female may leave the young for the male to feed. She may pair with a new mate and start a second family. Males, too, may change mates after the young become independent.

Movements and migrations

One of the earliest migrants to return to Scotland in spring, arriving in March and April. Young from first broods leave their colonies after fledging in June and generally spend several weeks exploring a wide area, often visiting other colonies and gathering at communal roosts. In August adults and juveniles head southeast to make the shortest sea-crossing across the Channel and then fly on to Africa, crossing the Sahara Desert. In winter they may be nomadic, moving east before returning north in February and March. Oldest bird survived 10 years.

Population

There are between 20,000 and 60,000 pairs in Scotland. There was a crash in the population in 1968–9, which reduced numbers significantly throughout the British Isles, including Scotland. Since then numbers have somewhat recovered, but they still vary from year to year.

Conservation

The population crashes in the 20th century have been linked to drought conditions in its wintering areas in Africa, which may be caused by overgrazing and by climate change. In Europe the protection of breeding colonies and management of river systems to provide nest sites will help this species.

DISTRIBUTION

Widely distributed in Scotland, particularly along major rivers, but not in the uplands or remoter offshore islands. Relatively common throughout the rest of the British Isles where there are suitable banks for nesting. Breeds in most of Europe, Asia and North America. European birds winter in Africa.

SWALLOW   *HIRUNDO RUSTICA*

IDENTIFICATION
17–19 cm. Smaller than Swift. Has a small broad bill, long pointed wings, (usually) long tail-streamers and white spots on underside of deeply forked tail. Upperparts are iridescent blue-black, underparts are off-white, face is reddish-brown and it has a blue-black chest-band. In spring tail-streamers of male are noticeably longer than those of female. Juvenile has much shorter tail-streamers and browner, less-shiny feathers. Flight is strong and agile with frequent swoops and glides when feeding. Moult is slow so as not to interfere with ability to hunt. Moult starts in September and most birds moult while in Africa.
SEE ALSO: House Martin p161, Sand Martin p159, Swift p158.

HABITS
Although much time is spent on the wing, frequently perches on wires and other prominent perches. Also lands on the ground, especially when gathering nest material. Flight usually low as it catches its prey on the wing or snatches food from the surface of the water. Does not breed in colonies, but flocks form outside the breeding season.

VOICE
The alarm call is a loud 'tswit', which is often given in flight. The song is a hurried dry twittering trill.

MOVEMENTS AND MIGRATIONS
A migrant that arrives mainly in April. First juveniles disperse in various directions during July. In September they move south with most having left Scotland by early October. Migrates by day, feeding as it flies, and roosts at traditional sites. Autumn migration takes about 6 weeks and is on a broad front, including crossing the Sahara Desert. The return takes about 4 weeks. Oldest known Swallow was 11 years.

POPULATION
There are 80,000–120,000 pairs nesting in Scotland. Numbers fluctuate, and although there are some local declines the total population is largely stable.

juvenile

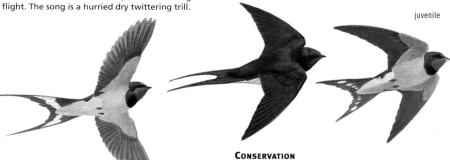

HABITAT
Breeds in open country where there are safe nest sites and abundant food, often in areas with water close by. In Scotland it is seen mostly in lowlands where there are farms with livestock, sometimes in villages but seldom in towns. It feeds around water, cattle, manure heaps and along hedges or woodland edges. In winter in Africa it is nomadic as it searches out food supplies.

FOOD
Feeds almost exclusively on flying insects. The large range includes bluebottles, house flies, bees, hoverflies, mayflies, aphids and flying ants. Even moth caterpillars hanging from trees are snapped up. A brood of Swallows needs 6,000 flies a day to survive.

BREEDING
Nesting begins in April or May. Older birds return first; males before females. Nests in barns and other buildings (not under eaves like House Martin). Nest cup is built by both sexes from mud and lined with feathers and grass. Previous year's nests are frequently re-used. For about 18 days the female incubates 4 or 5 eggs. Young fly after 18–23 days and are fed for a further week. Two broods.

CONSERVATION
Population fluctuations appear to be related to changes in Africa. In Scotland the loss of traditional nest sites, such as old barns, and food availability owing to changing farming practices cause concern for the future. Climate change and drought in parts of Africa may limit the number returning to breed each year. The loss of extensive livestock farming and flying insects may have an impact on Scottish breeding birds.

DISTRIBUTION
Found throughout Scotland, but scarce in the far north-west and in upland areas. Breeds across the British Isles and Europe; also in Asia, North Africa and North America. European populations winter in southern Africa, and North American birds winter in South America.

HOUSE MARTIN *DELICHON URBICA*

IDENTIFICATION

12.5 cm. Smaller than Swallow. Small, plump, aerial feeder with broad, rather pointed wings and a forked tail. It is blue-black above, pure white below with an obvious white rump. It lacks both the breast-band of Sand Martin and the tail-streamers of Swallow. Its tiny legs and feet are covered with white feathers. Juvenile is browner than the adult. Flight is less agile than a Swallow's; it is fast, direct but with fewer twists and turns and is rather more fluttery. The prolonged adult moult takes places mostly in Africa, all the feathers being replaced between late October and March. SEE ALSO: Swallow p160, Sand Martin p159.

HABITS

Most of the time is spent in the air and it often feeds at higher levels than the Swallow. It seldom lands on the ground except to gather nest material but frequently perches on wires, roofs and other prominent objects. It is a sociable species, inclined to nest in loose colonies and feed and migrate in small flocks. Large numbers will sometimes gather at migration times. Outside the breeding season it roosts in trees and is also suspected of sleeping on the wing at high altitudes.

VOICE

The main call is a hard 'prrit' and the song is a soft twittering that is heard during the summer.

HABITAT

Found in towns and villages throughout Scotland and in some places it nests on cliffs – especially sea cliffs. Tends to avoid city centres and is most abundant in lowland agricultural areas.

broad front, but the whereabouts of the main wintering grounds in Africa are uncertain. The oldest ringed bird survived over 14 years.

POPULATION

Between 38,000 and 74,000 pairs nest in Scotland, with the highest numbers in the south and central lowlands. While there are frequently marked changes in local populations, overall numbers appear to be increasing slowly.

CONSERVATION

As most House Martins have adapted to nesting on houses their nest sites depend on the co-operation of the property owner. Although nests and eggs are protected, ignorance and prejudice results in some nests being knocked down. Birds that have to rebuild are less likely to rear three broods in a summer, and therefore produce fewer young. Climate change and intensification of agricultural management could affect this species in future.

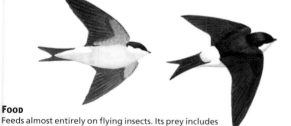

juvenile

FOOD

Feeds almost entirely on flying insects. Its prey includes aphids, gnats, flies, beetles and ants.

BREEDING

Nesting begins in late April or May. Both adults build the cup-shaped mud nest on the outer walls of buildings, especially under the eaves of houses. A few use traditional cliffs, either inland or by the sea. Old nests are re-used or, if necessary, repaired. Nesting tends to be in colonies and sometimes several nests are built side by side. Both adults incubate the 4 or 5 eggs for 14–16 days and both care for the young. From about 15 days the parents and other House Martins attempt to lure the young from the nest. The young will continue to roost in the nest and are fed by their parents after their initial flight. Two or sometimes three broods in a season, with late broods still in the nest in October.

MOVEMENTS AND MIGRATIONS

A summer migrant that returns in April and May and leaves between August and October. It migrates on a

DISTRIBUTION

Found in most parts of Scotland, but scarcer in the north-west and in he uplands. The species is widespread in the rest of the British Isles and also in Europe, Asia and North Africa. European birds winter in Africa, where they are most often seen in central highland areas, but they are probably also distributed across central and southern Africa.

TREE PIPIT *ANTHUS TRIVIALIS*

song flight

IDENTIFICATION

15 cm. Smaller than Skylark. Similar to the usually more common Meadow Pipit, but a little larger and sleeker with a heavier bill, much finer and thinner streaks on the flanks, more prominent head marks, sometimes a more obvious pale stripe over its eye and a different flight call. Has dark olive-brown streaked upperparts, a yellowish breast that is lightly marked with large streaks, fine streaking on the flanks and a white belly. Legs are flesh-coloured. Both Tree and Meadow Pipits have white outer tail-feathers. In late summer in worn plumage it becomes drabber. Adults have a complete moult between June and September and a partial moult in winter quarters, before return migration.
SEE ALSO: Meadow Pipit p163, Skylark p156.

HABITS

Unlike Meadow Pipit it frequently perches on trees and bushes. Song flight starts with a bird taking off from a prominent branch or other perch, singing as it rises at about 60 degrees and then parachuting down with legs dangling to land on the same or a nearby perch. Regularly feeds on the ground, where it moves with greater determination, rather than the jerky movements of Meadow Pipit. If disturbed it takes off steeply and circles before landing on the ground or on a tree or bush. Not a particularly sociable species, but small groups may form on migration.

VOICE

The call is a sharp 'teeze', often given in flight. Song may be given from a perch or during an obvious song flight. Generally the bird sings as it rises. Song is a series of

feed the young. Young fly at 12–14 days, but generally leave the nest before they can fly.

MOVEMENTS AND MIGRATIONS

Arrives in Scotland in April and May and leaves in late summer, flying directly to the Iberian Peninsula and from there to Africa. In spring and autumn birds from Scandinavia may visit Scottish coasts and islands. Oldest bird was 8 years.

POPULATION

There may be 43,000 pairs nesting in Scotland. The population here appears stable, although it is falling rapidly in other parts of the British Isles.

CONSERVATION

Maturing forests and loss of rough grassland and scrub may reduce Tree Pipit numbers, but more significant may be the effect of climate change on its wintering grounds and hunting at its stop-over points on migration.

summer   juvenile

summer (fresh, spring)

single notes and trills 'zit, zit, zit, wich, wich' and ending with 'swee-u, swee-u' as the bird lands.

HABITAT

Breeds in open countryside with scattered trees, rough grassland and shrubs, and also in open birch woods, young conifer plantations, clearings in forests, woodland edges and rough ground at the edge of farmland. It requires some trees or taller shrubs from which to launch its song flight. In winter in Africa it occupies similar habitats, including savannah.

FOOD

Mainly feeds on invertebrates especially weevils, beetles, caterpillars, ants, spiders and a variety of insects. Some plant material such as seeds and berries also eaten.

BREEDING

Nests on the ground among low cover in a nest in a depression that is made by female. The normal clutch of 4 or 5 eggs is incubated by female, although both adults

DISTRIBUTION

Locally common in many parts of Scotland where the habitat is suitable, including Mull, Argyll, Dumfries & Galloway and the central Highlands. Also breeds in England and Wales, from northern Scandinavia to northern Spain and Greece, and in Asia, where there are other races. Most European birds winter in tropical Africa, but some winter on Greek islands.

MEADOW PIPIT *ANTHUS PRATENSIS*

IDENTIFICATION

14.5 cm. Smaller than Skylark and also slightly smaller than Tree Pipit, with finer bill and distinctive call. Upperparts are olive-brown with darker streaks. Face is relatively plain with, sometimes, a small pale stripe over the eye. The bold streaks and spots on the greyish or yellowish breast continue at the same thickness along the flanks. Belly and outer tail feathers are white. Juvenile is more pinkish buff than adults in late summer and lacks the dark streaks on flanks. Adults moult between July and September, with flight feathers being lost and regrown over about 50 days. Partial moult before breeding.
SEE ALSO: Skylark p156, Tree Pipit p162, Dunnock p171.

summer

HABITS

Song flight generally starts from the ground and continues as the bird rises and parachutes down on half-spread wings. In suitable habitats the population may be high, but it is not colonial. Outside the breeding season it is commonly in loose flocks, sometimes feeding alongside Skylarks. Feeds on the ground, and on migration and in winter it seldom perches on vegetation, but on its breeding territories it is more likely to perch on prominent plants. On the ground it may sometimes appear quite upright, and it moves with jerky movements.

VOICE

In flight it usually strings three calls together – 'sweet-sweet-sweet'. Song is given during the aerial display and is a series of plaintive and accelerating 'seep, seep' followed by repeated 'tseut, tseut' and ending with a trill.

HABITAT

Breeds in open country, especially upland moors where it is usually the most abundant species, also on lowland heaths, salt marshes, rough grasslands and dune systems. In winter it feeds on agricultural land, including ploughed fields, coastal marshes and along the edges of lochs and rivers.

FOOD

Eats mainly invertebrates (with some seeds) including flies, especially craneflies (daddy long-legs) and mayflies, and also beetles, moths and spiders.

song flight

BREEDING

Nesting begins in late March in lowland areas and is later in the uplands. Female builds the nest on the ground amongst vegetation. Usually 4 or 5 eggs that are incubated for 13 days, mostly by female. Both parents feed the young, which fly between 10–14 days. The young usually leave the nest before they are able to fly. Two broods are usually raised.

MOVEMENTS AND MIGRATIONS

The species is a resident, summer visitor and migrant, and is found in all seasons. In late June and early July birds start to move off the hills into lower country and around the coast for the winter. Many leave Scotland and may reach the Continent and even North Africa. Birds breeding in the uplands return in late March or April. Other passage migrants from Scandinavia and Iceland move through Scotland in spring and return in autumn, sometimes in very large numbers. Oldest bird was 7 years.

POPULATION

Up to 1.6 million pairs may nest in Scotland, or over half the British population, and up to 50,000 remain for the winter. Numbers are largely stable, although there has been a slight decline in recent years.

CONSERVATION

South of the border declines have been caused by habitat degradation, especially on agricultural land. This has been less of a problem in Scotland, but the optimum habitat of heather, bog and rough grassland needs conserving to ensure populations survive.

juvenile

winter
(fresh, autumn)

DISTRIBUTION

A widespread breeding species in Scotland, and also common in much of England, Wales and Ireland. It breeds in northern Europe, as far south as northern France and east into Russia, Siberia and western Asia. It also nests in Iceland and eastern Greenland.

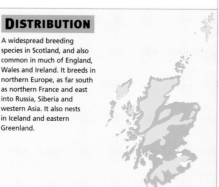

ROCK PIPIT *ANTHUS PETROSUS*

IDENTIFICATION
16.5–17 cm. Larger and darker than
a Meadow Pipit and smaller than a
Starling. A large, stocky pipit that has dusky
olive-brown upperparts with darker streaks that are
not as well defined as on the smaller pipits. The underparts are dirty white with dark streaking. Its legs and
bill are dark and the outer tail-feathers dirty grey. It has
a broken pale stripe over its eye. In winter it becomes
duskier and with less contrast in its plumage. The young
are more streaked than the adults. The northern race
(*littoralis*) is cleaner-looking with a more prominent
stripe over the eye and plainer underparts. Adults moult
between June and September and the flight feathers
are moulted and re-grow within 42 days.
SEE ALSO: Meadow Pipit p163, Skylark p156.

HABITS
It hops, walks and runs as it forages for food among
rocks and boulders, and it frequently perches on prominent rocks. It has a song flight that is similar to other pipits that involves a steep aerial climb and a parachuting flight down on half-closed wings. It is fairly tame
and can be approached more easily than most other
pipits. Many birds retain their territories throughout
the year, but some form small
groups during the winter.

VOICE
The call is 'pseep', which is more
metallic and less squeaky than
a Meadow Pipit's and often given
singly. The song is similar to that of
Meadow Pipit, but is stronger and
with a more obvious trill. The song is
mainly heard between March and July.

HABITAT
It breeds along the rocky shorelines and on small islands
around the coasts of Scotland where there are cliffs
and rock-strewn beaches, and it avoids sandy beaches.
It is rare inland.

FOOD
It feeds mainly on invertebrates that it finds on the
ground along the strand line and amongst seaweed.
Prey includes flies and midges and their larvae, beetles,
fish, small shellfish and seeds.

BREEDING
Nesting begins in April. The female builds the nest in
a hole or a hollow in a cliff. The nest includes some seaweed in the lining. The usual clutch is 4 or 5 eggs and
most of the incubation is by the female with the males

helping only occasionally. The eggs hatch after 14–15
days and the young are fed by both parents. They
leave the nest after 12 days. There may be two
broods in a summer.

MOVEMENTS AND MIGRATIONS
Most of the Rock Pipits around Scottish coasts are
resident, although juveniles are more likely to
make local movements away from their nesting
area, often visiting agricultural land near the
coast. Northern populations are more mobile,
and some birds move southwards after the
breeding season.

POPULATION
There are thought to be around 20,000 pairs
of Rock Pipits breeding in Scotland. There
may have been a recent decline, especially in
Shetland and along parts of the east coast.

CONSERVATION
The reason for a decline in the breeding population is
unknown. In some places south of the border disturbance by holidaymakers may be one cause, but this
is unlikely in many of the Scottish sites. Climate
change, pollution and a reduced food supply are
more probable causes here.

summer *littoralis*

DISTRIBUTION
Found almost all round the
Scottish coast, aside from
extensive areas of mud flats.
It is also found on rocky
coasts of England, Wales and
Ireland, and in other parts of
western Europe, from
northern Norway to northern
France. The northern race is
seen occasionally on the
Scottish east coast.

PIED WAGTAIL *MOTACILLA ALBA*

IDENTIFICATION

18 cm. Larger than sparrow. Black and white bird with a long black and white tail that constantly bobs. In Britain and Ireland male has black upperparts, rump, chest and throat and white face. Wings black and white, and underparts white. Female has dark grey, slightly blotchy back and less black on crown and throat. Juvenile brownish-grey above, creamy below and has dark breast-band. Race that breeds in Europe, known as White Wagtail, has pale grey (not black) back, rump and crown. Some immature Pied Wagtails have pale backs, but their rumps and crowns are almost black. Moult takes place between July and September and there is a partial moult into fresh breeding plumage between January and March.

SEE ALSO: Grey Wagtail p167, Pied Flycatcher p197.

female summer

male summer

HABITS

When feeding has jerky walk and frequently runs. Flight is bounding and occasionally in spring it makes a song flight, similar to that of Yellow Wagtail. Mostly feeds singly and males defend a winter feeding territory, into which it sometimes allows a female or juvenile when food is plentiful. It roosts communally outside the breeding season with dozens, and occasionally hundreds, of birds coming together for the night. Pre-roost flocks form before dusk, sometimes gathering in urban areas such as car parks and on flat roofs.

VOICE

Usual call is a sharp 'twissi-vit' or 'chizzwit' that is often given in flight. Song is quiet twittering interspersed with occasional call notes.

HABITAT

Found in a variety of places, often, but not always, near water. Breeds in open country such as moorland edge and farmland, and sometimes in towns and parks. More abundant in areas of mixed farming. In winter it is even more widely distributed and a frequent visitor to urban areas and sometimes suburban gardens. Also a common winter visitor to sewage farms, and groups regularly feed on arable fields, sometimes with other species such as Meadow Pipits.

FOOD

Chief food is insects, especially flies and midges and also caterpillars. Most food is taken from the ground, but also from shallow water or by catching flying insects in the air.

BREEDING

Nesting begins in April. Most nests are in holes, clefts or on ledges and sited in banks, ditches and buildings. Old nests of other birds such as Blackbirds are also used. Both sexes build the nest, with the female taking the largest share and completing the lining of hair, wool and feathers. Incubation of the 5 or 6 eggs is by both adults and lasts for about 13 days. Young are also fed by both adults and fly at about 14 days. They continue to be fed for a further 4–7 days.

MOVEMENTS AND MIGRATIONS

Present throughout the year, but many move south in autumn while others leave upland and island territories to winter in lowland areas. Juveniles are likely to travel further south than adults, with records from France, Spain and Portugal. Groups of passage migrants of the white, continental race are regularly seen in spring and autumn, and are mainly birds from Iceland. Oldest bird was 11 years.

1st-winter

POPULATION

There are probably over 100,000 pairs breeding in Scotland. Just one or two 'White Wagtails' breed in the Northern Isles; others hybridise with the pied form. The population is stable or possibly expanding.

CONSERVATION

There are no special conservation measures for this species. Research has shown the survival of young birds has improved in recent years.

DISTRIBUTION

Found throughout Scotland, except for the highest mountains. It is common in the rest of the British Isles, with the largest numbers being in the south in winter. Various races are found across Europe and Asia, and some from Europe reach North Africa in winter.

'white' wagtail

YELLOW WAGTAIL *MOTACILLA FLAVA*

male summer

female summer

IDENTIFICATION
17 cm. Smaller and sleeker than Pied Wagtail, with a shorter tail. Adult males in summer have bright yellow underparts and faces, olive-green upperparts and brownish wings. Head colours, markings and the intensity of the colours vary between geographical races. British race has a mainly yellow head while the nearest other race in Europe is the Blue-headed Wagtail, which is occasionally seen in Britain. Adult female is duller with browner back, pale throat and pale stripe above eye. Juvenile is like female, but with dark necklace and pale streak on cheek, below eye. Annual moult between July and September may not be completed before migration. Has a further partial moult in Africa between January and April.
SEE ALSO: Grey Wagtail p167, Pied Wagtail p165.

HABITS
Frequently follows cattle and other large animals in its search for food. Like other wagtails it runs or walks with its head moving backwards and forwards and its tail pumping up and down. Sometimes flutters into the air to catch insects. Normal flight is in long undulating curves. Regularly perches on vegetation, posts or wires. Territorial when nesting, but flocks form in late summer and loose parties migrate together. Often large numbers gather at roost sites.

VOICE
Call is a loud 'psweep' that is given in flight and from a perch. Sings from May until July. Song is a variation on the call, interspersed with a rather feeble warble.

HABITAT
Traditionally associated with lowland pastures, water meadows and marshes, many pairs today are found in, or close to, arable fields, especially those growing potatoes, peas and beans.

juvenile

FOOD
Feeds on small invertebrates, including flies and beetles in summer. Many of the flies are caught around the feet or dung of farm stock.

BREEDING
Nesting begins in April. Female builds a cup-shaped nest on the ground amongst vegetation. Made from grass and lined with hair, wool or fur. Both adults share the incubation of the 4–6 eggs for about 14 days, and both feed the young. The young leave the nest at about 11 days and fly 5 days later. They stay with their parents after fledging and may begin their migration as a family.

MOVEMENTS AND MIGRATIONS
This species is a scarce summer visitor to Scotland, spending the winter in Africa, south of the Sahara Desert. Birds leave in late summer, and while the route of Scottish birds has not been traced, we know birds from elsewhere in Britain fly to the French coast around the Bay of Biscay or direct to Portugal, and from there on to Morocco and then Nigeria. A few migrant birds from Continental races are seen in spring and autumn, usually on the east coast or Northern Isles. Oldest bird was 8 years old.

POPULATION
Scotland is at the northern edge of the species' range in Europe, and only 25–35 pairs breed annually. Numbers have been declining steadily in recent years.

CONSERVATION
A species such as this on the edge of its range is susceptible to local population expansions and contractions. Drainage and agricultural improvements of pastures that allow higher stocking densities of cattle and sheep may be significant factors. When these are combined with climate change, both here and on its route to Africa, it is no surprise the species appears to be contracting its range.

DISTRIBUTION

Small numbers breed in southern and eastern Scotland. The species is more numerous in southern England, with some in eastern Wales. The race that breeds in the British Isles (flavissima) also breeds in parts of western Europe. Other races breed from northern Scandinavia to North Africa and east across Russia and Asia. European birds winter in central and southern Africa.

GREY WAGTAIL *MOTACILLA CINEREA*

male summer

female summer

IDENTIFICATION
18–19 cm. Similar size to Pied Wagtail. Graceful, long-bodied bird with a very long tail that is constantly moving. Male has a yellow breast and bright egg-yellow under its tail. Upperparts blue-grey with white stripe over eye and black throat. Female has pale throat with only, usually, a few dark feathers. In winter, eye-stripe of male becomes less obvious, throat becomes pale and yellow breast is paler, but it retains yellow undertail. Juvenile resembles a female but with buffer underparts. Flight is bounding, in deep curves. Moults between July and September and has a second, partial moult into its breeding plumage in February and March.
SEE ALSO: Yellow Wagtail p166.

HABITS
Usually seen singly or in pairs. Undulating flight is often low before perching on boulders in water, although it sometimes perches on overhanging trees and bushes. Distinctive song-flight during which male parachutes down from a high perch on open and fluttering wings. Some Grey Wagtails defend a winter territory.

VOICE
Usual call is a loud, hard, sharp 'tswick' that is shorter than the Pied Wagtail's. Song, heard mainly between March and May, is a quiet trilling and quite melodious, given in flight or when perched.

HABITAT
In summer, mainly found in upland areas near fast-flowing water bordered by trees and where there are rocks and open ground such as shingle banks. In winter, it leaves the highest ground and visits a wider variety of habitats, including water treatment works, farmyards, ornamental ponds, canals, lowland rivers and streams, coastal areas and even city centres close to water.

FOOD
Feeds mainly on insects and other invertebrates that it picks up from the ground, from shallow water or snatches in the air. Insects include midges, stoneflies, mayflies, beetles and ants. Other prey includes spiders, small water snails, freshwater shrimps and tadpoles.

BREEDING
Nesting may begin late March, but mostly in April or May. Nest is built in a hole or crevice in wall, bank or other protected site such as under a bridge or among tree roots. Both sexes build the outer structure of grasses, small twigs and roots and the female lines it with moss and hair. Incubation of the 4–6 eggs is by both sexes and lasts for 11–14 days. Young fly after 13–15 days and are dependent on their parents for a further 2 weeks, and they may return to their nest to roost. It may have a second or even a third brood.

MOVEMENTS AND MIGRATIONS
In autumn, many Grey Wagtails leave upland areas and move to lowlands, and there is also a movement to the south and west and towards coasts. Most local breeding birds remain in Scotland, and some stay on their territories throughout the winter, while others travel to southern England and Ireland. Those in northern Europe travel furthest, and may reach southern Europe and North Africa in autumn. Passage birds from Scandinavia may pass along Scotland's east coast in spring and autumn. Oldest bird was 8 years.

POPULATION
Up to 17,500 pairs breed in Scotland. There has been a modest expansion in range in recent years.

CONSERVATION
Populations are affected by hard weather, and a recent run of mild winters has helped numbers to increase. Climate change and poor water quality in the species' feeding areas may influence its expansion in future.

juvenile

DISTRIBUTION

Widespread in Scotland, especially near streams and stony rivers in summer, and in lowland and coastal areas in winter. South of the border it is most numerous in upland areas of England, Ireland and Wales, where it usually moves to lower streams and rivers for the winter. Breeds from southern Scandinavia to North Africa and east into central Asia. Other races are found on small islands off the West African coast and in eastern Asia.

WAXWING BOMBYCILLA GARRULUS

IDENTIFICATION
18 cm. Smaller than Starling. Stocky bird with prominent crest and soft-looking plumage. Reddish-brown with grey rump, black bib, small black mask, yellow and white pattern in the wings, and yellow-tipped tail. Tips of its secondary flight feathers have a series of spikes which look like pieces of bright red wax. The undertail feathers are a rich chestnut. In flight, wings are 'triangular', rather like those of a Starling. First-winter birds usually have a single pale yellow stripe in the folded wing, adults have yellow and white borders to the wing-tips. The adults moult between August and November, but may suspend their moult and continue after migration. SEE ALSO: Starling p218.

HABITS
Generally gregarious. Numbers vary from small groups to large gatherings outside of the breeding season. Usually perches in the tops of trees, but comes lower to find food, often sitting immobile among the branches. Relatively tame and can often be approached to within a few metres. It is acrobatic when feeding; almost tit-like as it adopts a variety of feeding positions. Flight is strong with gentle undulations as birds periodically close their wings – a flight action recalling a Starling. They also catch flying insects rather like a large flycatcher.

VOICE
Call is a high-pitched, trilling 'sirrrrr', like a bell.

HABITAT
In winter in Scotland its arrival is sporadic and it visits any habitat that provides food. It can be a surprising find in parks and gardens, even in busy public places where there has been amenity planting of berry-bearing trees and bushes. First sightings in winter are often along the east coast, but groups rapidly travel inland in their search for food. It breeds in dense northern forests where there are old lichen-covered pines.

FOOD
Chief winter food is berries (it eats two or three times its own body weight in a day!). Favourites are Rowan, Whitebeam and Hawthorn, but in Britain it also eats cotoneaster, rose and many other winter fruits and seeds. Insects, especially mosquitoes and midges, and other invertebrates form a large part of its diet on its breeding grounds.

BREEDING
Does not breed in Britain or Ireland. On its northern breeding grounds it does not start breeding until mid-June. Cup-shaped nest of twigs, grass and moss is built by both sexes. Female incubates the clutch of 5 or 6 eggs for 14–15 days. Both parents care for the young, that eventually fly after 14–17 days.

MOVEMENTS AND MIGRATIONS
Partial migrant and some birds will overwinter in their northern breeding areas. Some regularly migrate south, but the species also 'erupts' when the population becomes too large for the food available. These eruptions have become more frequent in the last 20 years. Waxwings first arrive in October/November and normally stay until April. Oldest bird survived for 8 years.

POPULATION
Because of the species' irruptive behaviour, numbers vary from year to year. There may be as few as 50 or as many as 15,000.

CONSERVATION
There are no specific conservation measures for this species, but the planting of berry-bearing shrubs and trees in public places and in gardens can help their survival in winter.

1st-winter

DISTRIBUTION

In autumn, the first arrivals are usually seen along the east coast. As they move inland they may occur almost anywhere where there are suitable berry-bearing trees, including in towns, along roadsides and in parks. Waxwings breed in northern Scandinavia and Siberia, and another race breeds in North America. In winter, northern European and Siberian birds move south-west in search of food.

DIPPER   *CINCLUS CINCLUS*

IDENTIFICATION
18 cm. Smaller than Starling. Plump bird with short tail that is frequently cocked, and a habitual bobbing action. It is dark sooty brown and black with broad white breast and throat, and chestnut band on its belly. When blinking, the white eye-lid is obvious. Wings are short and rounded, and it frequently flies fast and straight above the water. Juvenile is dark grey with brown feather margins, creating a scaly effect on upperparts and wavy grey scalloping on underparts. Moults between July and October. Dippers in moult are reluctant to fly, and they may be flightless for a time.

HABITS
Frequently stands bobbing on rocks in the water. Will enter water and walk below surface in its search for food, or sometimes will swim and dive. Holds a territory throughout the year and is usually solitary when feeding. Pairs tend to roost together under bridges, even after breeding. Some roosts attract other Dippers, and up to nine have been observed roosting together.

VOICE
Call, frequently given in flight, is a sharp 'zit, zit' that carries above the sound of the river. Song is a sweet rippling warble, heard from October to July and again in late summer.

HABITAT
Swift-flowing upland burns and rivers and also the shallow edges of upland lochs. Sometimes follows rivers down into built-up areas in winter. Found on some lowland rivers where there are weirs and bridges.

FOOD
Principal food is small invertebrates picked from the bottom of burns or rivers up to 50 cm deep. It takes both adults and larvae of species such as caddisflies, stoneflies and mayflies and a few freshwater crustaceans such as freshwater shrimps.

BREEDING
Nesting begins in February and continues until June. Nests are usually within 1 m of running water and sites include riverbanks, ledges on rock faces, riverside walls, tree roots, and especially holes and ledges under bridges. The domed nest of moss, grass and leaves is built by both adults and lined by female. Mainly the female incubates 4 or 5 eggs for about 16 days. If disturbed, young leave the nest from 13 days, but usual fledging is 20–24 days, with young sometimes returning to nest to roost. Some males take a second mate, although these second families often produce fewer young. There may be a second brood.

MOVEMENTS AND MIGRATIONS
Few adult British Dippers move more than 2.5 km from their breeding sites, whereas juveniles disperse 5–8 km or more, with females travelling farther than males. Some northern European populations are partial migrants and travel considerable distances, a few occasionally reaching Scotland. Oldest bird survived over 10 years.

POPULATION
10,000–15,000 pairs nest in Scotland. Numbers may be temporarily affected by severe winter weather or flooding, but overall the population appears stable.

CONSERVATION
Dipper's habitats have been affected by sewage and toxic chemicals running into rivers, and by conifer forests trapping acidifying air pollutants, causing the water to become more acid and less productive for invertebrates. Not planting conifer trees along streams in the uplands will help reduce pollution.

juvenile

DISTRIBUTION
There are 13 subspecies of Dipper, three of which may be seen in Scotland: one occurs across most of Scotland, England and Wales; another is present in Ireland, the Outer Hebrides, and a third is a black-bellied form found in Europe, which is a scarce winter visitor to the British Isles, including Scotland. Dippers breed throughout much of Scotland, and also in uplands south of the border.

WREN *TROGLODYTES TROGLODYTES*

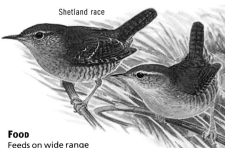

Shetland race

IDENTIFICATION
9–10 cm. One of our smallest birds. Tiny, dumpy and energetic bird that is always on the move. Has long thin bill and large feet. Small tail is often cocked above its back, and short neck gives the appearance of a small brown ball. Has reddish-brown upperparts and buff underparts, both with delicate dark bars. Has long pale stripe above eye. Flight is fast, straight and generally close to the ground. Wings are broad and rounded. Moults between July and October, the primary feathers taking 60 days to be lost and re-grown.
SEE ALSO: Treecreeper p208, Dunnock p171, Goldcrest p198.

HABITS
Constantly searching for food, but inconspicuous as it hunts among bushes, vegetation and in crevices in tree trunks, roots and rocks. Usually keeps low, but will sometime go higher and may sing from an elevated perch. Most Wrens defend territories throughout the year, but will sometimes form communal roosts in cold weather; there are records of 43 birds using a House Martin nest at Dunkeld.

FOOD
Feeds on wide range of insects and other invertebrates. Prey includes beetles, spiders, flies and their larvae, moth caterpillars and ants. Sometimes paddles to reach insects, small fish and tadpoles.

BREEDING
Nesting begins in the second half of April. The male builds 5–8 nests in hollows, crevices or holes in banks, walls or trees. The nest is made from moss, leaves and grass. It is a domed structure with a hole in the side. Female chooses one and lines it with feathers and other material. She lays 5 or 6 eggs that she incubates for about 16 days. Both adults feed the young, which fledge after 15–19 days and are tended by their parents for a further 9–18 days. There are often two broods and some males in woodland have two mates.

MOVEMENTS AND MIGRATIONS
Many Wrens defend a winter territory, but some breeding areas support fewer birds in winter, and there are some movements, usually southwards. On the Continent this movement is even more marked, with northern Wrens travelling considerable distances. Oldest ringed bird was 6 years old.

POPULATION
This is one of our most numerous species, with about 1.5 million pairs breeding in Scotland. Following a run of relatively mild winters, the population has grown in recent years.

CONSERVATION
Up to 80% mortality in cold winters, but is capable of recovery in just a few years. This is one of several species breeding earlier owing, it is assumed, to climate change.

VOICE
Call is a loud 'tic-tic-tic' that has a rattling quality. Song is powerful for such a diminutive bird, and it trembles as it sings a cascade of notes, generally ending with a loud and distinctive trill.

HABITAT
Occupies wide variety of habitats. Chief breeding habitat is deciduous and mixed woods, especially alongside streams. Also occurs on farmland, moorland, cliff tops and offshore islands. Visits and breeds in mature gardens and, in winter, many move into reedbeds, a marginal habitat that tends to be used by less successful birds.

DISTRIBUTION

There are 43 subspecies of Wren, many found on isolated islands. Five are present in Scotland. The most numerous by far is sometimes called the British Wren and is found throughout Scotland, England, Wales and Ireland. Other distinct races occur in the Outer Hebrides, St Kilda, Shetland and Fair Isle. The most distinctive of these races is found on the remote St Kilda group. The species also breeds throughout Eurasia, North Africa and North America.

DUNNOCK PRUNELLA MODULARIS

IDENTIFICATION
14.5 cm. Size of House Sparrow but with thin, pointed bill and pinkish legs. Rich brown upperparts with streaky back and wings and streaks on the flanks. Apart from a brown crown, the head and breast are blue-grey. Moves with shuffling walk, with body close to ground. Juvenile is less grey and more boldly striped than the adult. Moult begins as soon as they finish breeding, between July and October, with Dunnocks in the north starting before those in the south.
SEE ALSO: Wren p170, House Sparrow p219, Warblers pp185–195.

adult displaying

HABITS
For most of the year tends to be solitary although up to six may come together where food is plentiful. Creeps mouse-like on the ground, often giving a nervous flick of its wings. In courtship individuals flick open their wings and wave them above their backs while calling shrilly. Courtship includes a wing-shivering display by the female, after which the dominant male pecks her cloaca until she ejects a package of sperm. Mating then follows. Often two males mate with one female and the less dominant male helps feed the young. Dunnocks are frequent hosts for Cuckoos.

VOICE
Call is a shrill, piping 'tseep' that is also heard while the birds are displaying. The short, fast warble is often given from a prominent perch in low trees and bushes. Males sing in the winter, but most song is heard between January and July. Males copy parts of neighbouring Dunnock's songs and incorporate them into their own.

HABITAT
Breeds in a wide variety of habitats, especially gardens. Other habitats include low thick scrub, Bramble patches, farmland where there are hedges, Bracken on moorland, conifer plantations and deciduous woodland.

FOOD
Most food is found on the ground. Takes invertebrates, including beetles, snails, spiders, flies, worms and springtails. It also eats berries, seeds and grain. It visits gardens for bird food, but is an unusual visitor to a raised bird table, and more likely to feed underneath.

BREEDING
The pairing arrangements are unusual. Some pairs are male and female, some males have two females, some females have two or more males and there are complex arrangements with several males sharing several females. Nesting begins in March with the female building a cup-shaped nest of roots, leaves and grasses, and lined with softer material. The female incubates the normal clutch of 4 or 5 eggs for 14–15 days. The young are cared for by both sexes and by any additional males. Young fledge at 12–15 days and are fed for a further 14–17 days. There are up to three broods.

MOVEMENTS AND MIGRATIONS
It is very sedentary – seldom moving more than 1 km. Scandinavian populations are migratory and some Dunnocks from the north arrive in eastern Scotland in autumn. Oldest ringed bird survived 11 years.

POPULATION
There may be as many as 400,000 pairs nesting in Scotland. In Britain as a whole, Dunnock declined in the 1970s and 1980s, and this was reflected in parts of Scotland. Since then numbers appear to have recovered significantly.

CONSERVATION
The decline mentioned above caused concern about the species' long-term future. Climate change has affected the time of its breeding, and changing agricultural and forestry practices can have an impact on both its food supplies and breeding sites.

DISTRIBUTION
There are two subspecies of Dunnock in Scotland. Most belong to the British subspecies, which is also found south of the border. The other is the Hebridean subspecies, found in the Hebrides and along the west coast. The species also breeds in central and northern Europe and east into Russia. Some, from northern Europe, winter around the northern shores of the Mediterranean.

ROBIN *ERITHACUS RUBECULA*

IDENTIFICATION
14 cm. Size of House Sparrow. Familiar bird that has a body shape that varies from rotund to sleek. Upperparts are olive-brown: face, neck and breast are orange-red. A band of grey-blue separates the red from brown, with white feathers under the tail. Eye is large and prominent, bill short and thin, and legs long and black. Juvenile lacks the red breast and is heavily speckled until its first moult, and has a light brown wing-bar. Adults moult between June and September. Juveniles have a partial moult from their speckled juvenile plumage when 6–7 weeks old.
SEE ALSO: Bullfinch p234, Chaffinch p221, Redstart p175, Dunnock p171.

HABITS
On the ground moves in a series of hops, sometimes with wings drooped. May be rather tame, especially in towns and gardens. Defends a territory all year round; males and females hold separate territories in winter – the female usually travelling the furthest. There are a few records (mostly from eastern Scotland) of birds forming communal winter roosts. Robins have elaborate courtship displays, when the red breast of the male is used as a visual signal to attract females and deter rivals.

fresh, autumn

VOICE
Makes an urgent 'tic, tic' and a high-pitched 'tsweee'. The song may be heard almost throughout the year. It is varied and melodious and takes two distinct forms. After moulting in autumn it is rather sad and wistful, whereas from around Christmas it becomes stronger, faster and more vigorous.

HABITAT
Breeds in woods and copses with plenty of undergrowth. Also found in dense hedges, gardens, parks and other shrubby places and, sometimes, in more open country.

juvenile

FOOD

Hunts from a perch, watching for movements, or when hopping on the ground. Mostly eats invertebrates in summer and some fruits and seeds in winter. Invertebrates include spiders, beetles, sawflies, other flies and worms. Fruits include berries from Elder, Bramble and Rowan. Seeds include grain.

BREEDING
Starts to nest in late March with the first eggs in April. Nests are built by female and consist of leaves, moss and grass. Nest site is usually quite low in a hollow in a bank, a tree stump, among tree roots or a man-made site – such as a gap in a wall or a shelf in a garden shed. The 4 or 5 eggs are incubated by female for about 15 days. Both parents feed the young, but male continues alone if female starts another brood. Young fly after about 13 days and become independent 16–24 days later. There are two, sometimes three, broods.

MOVEMENTS AND MIGRATIONS
Robins are seen in Scotland year-round, and some remain on territory all winter. However, many move away from their nesting areas to feeding sites close by, and an unknown proportion move further south and cross the border to winter in England or Ireland. Large numbers from the Continent arrive in Scotland in autumn and return again in spring; what proportion of these birds remain and how many move on south for the winter is unknown. Oldest bird was 11 years.

POPULATION
Up to 1.25 million Robins breed in Scotland and as many as a million more arrive from the Continent. Populations fall in cold winters, but a recent run of milder winters has allowed the Scottish population to expand.

CONSERVATION
There are no special conservation measures in place to help it in Britain, but there have been concerns about the level of hunting of migrant Robins around the Mediterranean in winter.

DISTRIBUTION
Found across Scotland, except for the treeless uplands and exposed islands. It breeds from the Arctic Circle south to the Mediterranean and North Africa, and east into Russia and Asia. Some of the northern European population winters around the Mediterranean basin.

BLUETHROAT *LUSCINIA SVECICA*

IDENTIFICATION
14 cm. Robin-like but more upright, longer tailed and longer legged. Dark brown with buff underparts, a prominent white stripe over eye and bright chestnut sides to base of tail. In spring, male has bright blue throat bordered with narrow bands of black, white and chestnut. Throat pattern varies from race to race, with those from northern Europe having a red spot and in the south a white spot. Males in autumn show varying amounts of blue and chestnut. Females have a pale throat with a black breast-band and, sometimes, a hint of blue. Juvenile is spotted like juvenile Robin, but with rusty-red at the base of the tail. Moult begins in July after breeding and is completed in 40–45 days, before the birds migrate.
SEE ALSO: Robin p172, Redstart p175.

HABITS
Often a skulking species that feeds on the ground, usually amongst thick vegetation. Even on migration searches out crops and other vegetated areas and if disturbed will often fly only a short distance before dropping back into cover. On the ground tends to flit from feeding area to feeding area. Hops like Robin and often cocks tail and droops its long wings.

male summer
white-spotted race

VOICE
Call is short, hard 'tacc, tacc' or a plaintive warbler-like 'hweet'. Song may be given from a perch or in a short song-flight and is a clear, repeated 'zruu, zruu, zruu' accelerating and ranging up and down the scale. Mimics other species and other sounds.

HABITAT
Usually seen as a passage migrant on the coast, seeking out scrub, gardens and other grassy areas. In Scotland birds are occasionally seen in potential breeding habitat, which is scrub with dense vegetation and woodland, often close to rivers or marshes. Elsewhere in Europe the species may breed around salt-water marshes, fens, and in scrub close to rivers or in uplands.

FOOD
It mainly eats beetles, spiders, moth caterpillars and a variety of other invertebrates. It also eats berries in autumn.

BREEDING
A very rare breeding species in Scotland. Nest is on the ground amongst dense vegetation. It is a cup of grass, leaves, moss and roots and is built mostly by female. Normal clutch is 5–7 eggs that are incubated mainly by female, but with some help from male. Incubation lasts for 13–14 days and both parents feed the young, which fly

male summer
red-spotted race

female summer

after about 14 days. White-spotted birds are sometimes double-brooded.

MOVEMENTS AND MIGRATIONS
It is mainly Red-spotted Bluethroats that are seen occasionally as passage migrants in spring and autumn. Most visit the Northern Isles or sites along the east coast such as Fife Ness and St Abbs Head. Those that breed in Scandinavia either migrate to Africa or head south-east to Pakistan and northern India. Those that arrive in Scotland in spring usually come on southeasterly winds and have presumably overshot their Scandinavian habitats. Oldest known bird was 11 years.

POPULATION
First nested (unsuccessfully) in 1968, and since then breeding has been proved or suspected on a number of occasions. Up to 40 may be seen on spring passage in some years, and very rarely individuals of the White-spotted race are also seen.

CONSERVATION
The few that nest, or attempt to nest, in Scotland need safeguarding from egg thieves, therefore breeding sites are generally kept secret.

female 1st-winter

DISTRIBUTION
Regular passage migrant. Most are seen in Scotland, in the east and on the Northern Isles during September. Also regular along the English east coast. The species breeds from northern Scandinavia south to central Spain and east across Siberia. There are several distinct subspecies, which are separated geographically. In western Europe the Red-spotted breeds in the north and the White-spotted in the south.

Black Redstart PHOENICURUS OCHRUROS

male **female**

IDENTIFICATION
14.5 cm. Similar in size to Robin but slimmer. Has many of the characteristics of Redstart, but the plumage is darker and those in western Europe have no trace of red on their breasts. Males are slate-grey above, sooty black around the face and breast with white flashes on the folded wings and orange-red sides to the tail. Males are greyer in autumn. Female is a uniform dusky grey-brown with a red tail. Juvenile is similar to female but with slight flecking and barring. Adults moult between July and October, before migration. The new feathers of male have pale fringes that give a hoary appearance. These fringes wear away as the breeding season approaches, revealing the striking black plumage.
SEE ALSO: Redstart p175.

HABITS
Its bright tail is constantly quivering. Commonly seen on the ground where it runs rather than hops and it also regularly perches on buildings or rocks. Will often fly up from a perch, sometimes hovering for a moment, as it catches insects.

juvenile

VOICE
Most common call is an urgent 'tucc, tucc'. Song is a short warble with some metallic jangles at the end. It is heard from March to July and sometimes in late summer.

HABITAT
In Scotland most are passage migrants most likely to be seen near the east coast, on rocky beaches or around old buildings. Elsewhere, it nests in holes in rock faces or buildings – frequently in town centres or industrial sites such as power stations.

FOOD
Feeds on insects such as midges, small flies, aphids, moths, ants and beetles. Also eats spiders, worms, berries and seeds.

BREEDING
Nests from late April to July. Nest site is a ledge, crevice or other hole in a rock or wall. Female builds a nest of grass and leaves, lined with hair, wool and feathers. The 4–6 eggs are incubated by the female for 12–16 days. Both parents feed the young, which leave the nest after 12–19 days. After fledging, young are cared for by their parents for a further 11 days. Two, sometimes three, broods.

MOVEMENTS AND MIGRATIONS
The Black Redstart is a common breeding species in much of central and southern Europe, and it migrates south in autumn to winter around the Mediterranean and as far as the Sahara Desert. A few spend the winter in southern England and, very rarely, in Scotland. Those that arrive on the Northern Isles and along the east coast of Scotland are presumed to be on passage to or from southern Scandinavia. Oldest ringed bird was 10 years old.

POPULATION
First nested successfully in Scotland in 1994, and there have been a few other successful attempts since then. The number of passage birds varies between 25 and 100 in both spring and autumn. A few overwinter.

CONSERVATION
The Black Redstart's arrival in Scotland as a breeding species followed its gradual colonisation of southern Britain, where it famously started nesting in the bombsites of London after the Second World War. In the British Isles it is at the edge of its range and no special protection measures are required other than keeping any nesting birds free from the impact of building works or nest robbery.

DISTRIBUTION
Mainly visits the east of Scotland and the Northern Isles. South of the border, it breeds mainly in southern England. Elsewhere, it is found in central and southern Europe and in parts of North Africa. There are other distinctive races in Turkey and the Middle East. It winters in southern and western Europe, including Britain and Ireland, North Africa and the Middle East.

REDSTART   *PHOENICURUS PHOENICURUS*

juvenile

IDENTIFICATION

14 cm. Similar size to Robin but slimmer with longer wings and a longer tail that constantly quivers up and down. Tail and rump are bright orange-red. Male in spring is striking, with blue-grey upperparts, black face and throat, white forehead and orange breast and flanks. Female has grey-brown upperparts and orange-buff underparts; warmer coloured than female Black Redstart. Juvenile is mottled like a juvenile Robin, but with reddish tail. Adults moult between June and September, before autumn migration. After moult the bright colours are obscured by buff tips to the feathers that wear off in late winter, revealing the bright, fresh breeding plumage.
SEE ALSO: Black Redstart p174, Robin p172.

HABITS

Song is given from a prominent perch. At other times it is constantly on the move and often fluttering or hovering to catch insects in the air. Some of its actions are reminiscent of a Robin, but it is much more likely to be seen in trees than on the ground. Among the leaves it can be hard to see, but the long tail and slim rear body give it a distinctive profile.
Flight is gently undulating.

VOICE

Call a rather sweet, warbler-like 'hooweet'. Song is a loud warble ending with distinctive mechanical jangle.

HABITAT

In Scotland it is found in broadleaf or mixed woodland in hill country, or where there are scattered copses of old trees, hedges and rough pastures. It also occurs in old Caledonian pine forests. It requires trees with holes for nesting, and the number of these that are available will determine breeding numbers.

FOOD

Insects, especially flies, beetles, moths and ants, but also a wide variety of other invertebrates, including spiders and worms. Fruits from a variety of plants are also eaten.

BREEDING

Nesting begins in April. Nest is in a hole in a tree or some other crevice and nestboxes are often used. Nest built by female and consists of grass, moss and other local materials. Incubation of the 5–7 eggs is by female only and lasts for 13–14 days. Both parents feed the young, although the female appears to provide most food. Young fly after 16–17 days and are independent 2–3 weeks later. There are frequently two broods in a season.

MOVEMENTS AND MIGRATIONS

Summer migrant, returning in April and May and leaving in late August. Most European birds move southwest although some from northern Scandinavia take an eastern route around the Mediterranean. The greatest numbers are on the move through Europe in September, when varying numbers of passage migrants visit the Northern Isles and, particularly, the east coast, where large falls of over 100 birds are occasionally recorded. From southern Europe most over-fly the Mediterranean and the Sahara Desert in a single flight. Oldest bird 10 years.

POPULATION

20,000–30,000 pairs breed in Scotland. A decline in the 1960s has been followed by a partial recovery, but in Scotland it is suspected that the species' range may be contracting, particularly in the north.

CONSERVATION

There has been a recent decline in the Redstart population in much of Europe. Drought in Africa was a probable cause in the 1960s and early 1970s from which the species partly recovered. More recent problems are loss of mature woodlands and their associated nest-holes; the impact of grazing animals, especially sheep and deer, which have an effect on the invertebrate populations; and climate change, which affects the species' winter quarters.

female

male

DISTRIBUTION

In Scotland, it is found mainly in the south, west and central Highlands. Elsewhere in Britain it is found mainly in the south and west of England and in Wales, but it is rare in Ireland. It is widespread across Europe, North Africa, the Middle East and Russia. All birds return to central Africa for the winter.

WHINCHAT *SAXICOLA RUBETRA*

IDENTIFICATION
12.5 cm. Slightly smaller and shorter-tailed than Robin. Slimmer than Stonechat with flatter head, longer wings, heavier bill, white sides to base of tail and black spotting above tail. Male has streaky brown upperparts, orange-brown breast, prominent white stripe above eye and a smaller one below its dark cheeks. Female is duller, with buff eye-stripe and buff breast. Juvenile resembles female with less distinct eye-stripe and slightly spotted breast. Flight usually low and white base of tail is conspicuous. Adults have a complete moult between July and September, before autumn migration.
SEE ALSO: Stonechat p177, Wheatear p178.

male summer   male summer

HABITS
Rather upright when perched and frequently bobs and flicks its tail and wings. Perches on tops of bushes, small trees and wires. Flies low to a new perch with a rather jerky flight. Usually seen singly or in pairs, but family groups may be obvious in late summer.

VOICE
Call is a sharp 'tic, tic', similar to, but not as hard as, a Stonechat's.

HABITAT
Breeds on moorland edges, amongst Bracken, in young forestry plantations with areas of grass and where there is a mosaic of short grazed grassland, prominent perches to hunt from and thicker vegetation to nest in. Also found in other rough grassland areas, including water meadows, upland farms – especially transitional zones between farmland and scrub-covered slopes.

FOOD
Eats invertebrates and some seeds. Mayflies, caddisflies, other flies, moths and their caterpillars, beetles, spiders, snails and worms are eaten. Plant food includes blackberries.

BREEDING
Nesting takes place mainly in May and June. Female builds the nest with male occasionally helping to select some material. The nest is often in an open site among long grass or Bracken or sometimes off the ground, low

down in a bush. The nest is a cup-shaped structure of grass, leaves and moss. There are usually 5 or 6 eggs which are incubated by the female for 12–13 days. Young are fed by both parents and leave the nest after 12–13 days. They start to fly at 17–19 days and remain dependent on their parents until 28–30 days. Pairs sometimes rear a second brood.

MOVEMENTS AND MIGRATIONS
Summer migrant to Europe, arriving in April and May. They leave their nest sites between July and mid-September and peak passage through western Europe is in September. Migrants concentrate in traditional areas in western France and northern Spain, or in Portugal and southern Spain. After breaking their migration to feed they appear to make a single crossing of both the Mediterranean and the Sahara Desert. On their return, however, many stop in North Africa before flying into Europe.

POPULATION
Up to 20,000 pairs breed in Scotland. There are fluctuations in numbers from year to year, but overall the population here appears to be stable.

female summer

CONSERVATION
Once more common in the lowlands, but has retreated to areas of rough grazing, woodland edge and hill slopes. A general tidying-up of the countryside, more productive farmland and overgrazing at nest sites have all combined to reduce the number of pairs. Also many tracts of young forests that were planted 30–40 years ago and provided home for many Whinchats have matured and are now unsuitable as nest sites. Agricultural grants could be targeted to restore mosaics of moorland edge habitats for this bird.

juvenile

DISTRIBUTION

In Scotland, the largest concentrations tend to be in the south and west, but the species can be seen in upland areas in suitable habitat. It also breeds in England, Wales and Ireland. It is found from northern Scandinavia south to northern Spain and east into Russia, and in parts of the Middle East. It winters in central and southern Africa.

STONECHAT *SAXICOLA TORQUATA*

male

male

IDENTIFICATION
12.5 cm. Slightly smaller than Robin. Similar size to Whinchat, but plumper, with shorter wings, rounder head and no eye-stripe. Male in spring has black head with white patch on side of neck, white patch in wings, small white rump, dark brown back and orange-red breast. At other times the colouring of the male is much duller. Female lacks the black head, has a less obvious white neck patch and a browner, streaked back. Juvenile resembles a dull female, but with spotting and barring on its breast and back. Adults moult between July and October. It has only one period of moult, the colour change in late winter into breeding plumage is caused by the duller feather tips being worn away.
SEE ALSO: Whinchat p176.

HABITS
Perches very upright and constantly flicks its wings, spreads its tail and is generally active and restless. In flight, it appears large-headed and short-tailed and has been likened to a large bumble bee. Drops to the ground to feed. Perches on the tops of bushes, especially gorse, and small trees. Usually seen singly or in pairs and in Britain and Ireland pairs remain together outside the breeding season.

MOVEMENTS AND MIGRATIONS
Both a resident and a partial migrant. Many Scottish Stonechats leave their summer territories and winter around the coast. Some travel further and have been recorded in England, France and Spain. Many European birds winter around the Mediterranean and in North Africa. Oldest ringed bird survived 8 years.

POPULATION
As many as 30,000 pairs may breed in Scotland. Numbers can be significantly reduced after cold winters. In recent years the population has increased substantially, perhaps as a response to milder winters.

CONSERVATION
Suffers in severe winter weather. Once it was far more common, but the range contracted between the early 1970s and late 1980s. Since 1994 its abundance has fluctuated and breeding performance has improved. In Europe it also declined, but there appears to have been a recent recovery. It benefits from low-intensity agriculture, with few pesticides, plenty of scrub and lower numbers of grazing animals.

juvenile

male
(fresh, autumn)

VOICE
Call is a hard 'hweet, chac, chac', the last two notes being remarkably similar to two pebbles being knocked together. The variable song is rather like that of a Dunnock and sometimes given during a short song-flight.

HABITAT
Breeds on lowland heaths, coastal sites with plenty of gorse, dune systems and in young conifer plantations with heather. Other sites include golf courses and moorland.

FOOD
Feeds mainly on insects, especially weevils, ichneumon flies, shieldbugs, moths, caterpillars of butterflies and moths, and ants. Spiders, snails and worms are also eaten. Plant food includes seeds and blackberries.

BREEDING
Female builds a nest among grasses, either in the open or, more often, under a gorse bush or another shrub. Sometimes the nest is off the ground in a bush. The nest is a rather untidy cup of grass and leaves and lined with hair, feathers and wool. Incubation of the 5 or 6 eggs is by female and takes 12–15 days. Young are fed by both parents and fly at 12–15 days. Adults continue to feed the young for 4–5 days before the female ceases and concentrates on the next brood while the male continues feeding for a further 5–10 days. Pairs rear two or three broods in a season.

female

DISTRIBUTION
The species is widespread in Scotland, with the highest breeding densities in the north and west. In winter it is mainly found in coastal areas or on low ground with rough vegetation, old heather and scrub. It is also present in central and southern Europe, and there are subspecies in Africa, Russia, Siberia and eastern Asia. Some European birds migrate to Africa for the winter.

WHEATEAR OENANTHE OENANTHE

IDENTIFICATION
14.5–15.5 cm. Larger than Robin. Neat, sleek and rather short-tailed. Has an extensive area of white on rump and upper-tail, with black 'T'-shaped terminal band. Back of male is blue-grey, wings black and underparts white with an orange flush on breast. Cheeks are black with white stripe over eye and across forehead. After moulting it is browner, but retains darker cheeks and pale stripe over eye. Female is sandy brown with less well-marked face and browner wings. Juvenile is spotted or mottled on upperparts and breast. Moult takes place before migration, between late June and early September. The brighter spring plumage is revealed as the pale feather fringes are lost in spring.
SEE ALSO: Whinchat p176.

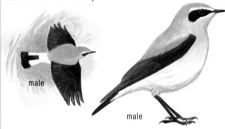

male

male

HABITS
This is an upright species. Most obvious feature in flight is white rump and black 'T' shape on end of tail. Feeds on the ground; active and restless and frequently bobs. Moves in a series of swift, short runs and perches on rocks and posts. Sometimes it flutters up to catch a flying insect. Mainly solitary or in pairs, but groups may form on migration, especially at coastal sites.

VOICE
Call is a hard 'chack, chack'. It also has pleasant warbling song that is given on the ground or during a short song-flight.

HABITAT
Breeds in rocky and stony places, upland pastures with drystone walls and on moorland. Found on short, grazed, unimproved grassy areas in the lowlands, particularly on coastal sites. On migration it is widespread, stopping in open places, often near the coast.

FOOD
Mainly insects and other invertebrates. Individual items include beetles, springtails, moths and their caterpillars, flies, small snails, worms and berries from Blackberry, Rowan and Elder.

BREEDING
Nests between April and July. Nest site is a hole in a wall or rock-face or a hole in the ground, such as a Rabbit burrow. Female builds a rough cup of Bracken, grass or leaves and lined with finer grass stems, moss and lichen. Incubation of the 5 or 6 eggs is by female and takes around 14 days. Both adults feed the young and those in holes in the ground may leave the nest during the day at about 10 days old. They can fly from about day 15 and become independent from 28–32 days.

MOVEMENTS AND MIGRATIONS
Summer migrant that arrives between March and May. Most start to leave in August and migrations take place mainly at night. Movement is south-west through Europe on a broad front and many land on the North African coast before setting off again for their wintering grounds. The slightly larger Greenland race has a remarkable migration that takes it from Africa to its Arctic breeding grounds. For many the return journey necessitates a 30-hour, 2,400 km non-stop flight from Greenland to western Europe. Oldest bird lived more than 9 years.

POPULATION
Between 35,000 and 95,000 pairs nest in Scotland. Although the population is thought to be stable, the species has disappeared from some lowland areas in recent years. Wheatears of the Greenland subspecies also pass through Scotland in varying numbers in spring and autumn.

CONSERVATION
The main threat to the Wheatear is habitat loss. The species disappeared from much of lowland Britain in the last century, but this has been more marked in England and Wales than in Scotland, although even here improvement of pastures and afforestation still poses threats. Hunting along migration routes and unknown threats from climate change are also problems for this species, which is a long-distance migrant.

male Greenland race (autumn)

female

female (fresh, autumn)

REDWING _TURDUS ILIACUS_

IDENTIFICATION
21 cm. A little smaller and thinner than Song Thrush with rusty-red flanks and underwings, creamy white stripe over its eye and pale stripe below the cheek. Upperparts are dark brown and the yellow-buff breast is heavily spotted and streaked. Lower belly and under the tail is white. Icelandic race is darker and more heavily spotted. Juvenile has buff spots on its back and first-year birds retain pale tips to some of the wing feathers. In flight, the slightly pointed wings and flight silhouette are sometimes reminiscent of a Starling. Adults moult between June and September, which means that some start to replace their flight feathers while still feeding young.
SEE ALSO: Song Thrush p182.

HABITS
Generally rather shy. The red on the flanks may often be hidden under the folded wings, but the boldly patterned face is the best identification feature. Much of its behaviour is similar to a Song Thrush, but it is a sociable species outside the breeding season, with flocks migrating and feeding together, and large communal roosts developing in suitable habitats. Will feed and roost with other thrushes, especially Fieldfares.

VOICE
Soft thin 'seeip' call, usually given in flight, is frequently heard after dark during migration. Song is variable and seldom heard in Britain or Ireland; it consists of jumbled, but repeated notes.

HABITAT
Breeds in open broadleaf or mixed woodland and scrub. In autumn, frequents hedges and orchards. Later in winter, feeds in open areas of short grass. Visits farmland, parks and large gardens. Roosts in thick hedges and scrub. In Europe breeds in forest bog, birch and willow scrub and in parks and gardens.

FOOD
Newly arrived autumn migrants feed on fruit such as windfall apples and a wide variety of berries, especially Hawthorn. As supplies of fruits are exhausted it switches to feed on earthworms. In summer it feeds on worms, snails, slugs and insects.

BREEDING
The nest may be in a tree, a low bush or on the ground. Female builds a cup-shaped nest of grasses, twigs and moss. Female incubates the 4 or 5 eggs for 12–13 days. The young are fed by both parents and leave the nest at 10–15 days. They continue to be fed by their parents for another 14 days, and the male will continue feeding while the female starts another brood. There are usually two broods in a season.

MOVEMENTS AND MIGRATIONS
Migrating Redwings start arriving in Scotland from early September, with the main movements later in September and October. Northern populations move on a broad front between September and November. Icelandic birds tend to winter in Scotland and Ireland, while those from Scandinavia winter in southern Britain and farther south in Europe. Wintering flocks roam widely. Migrants may winter in quite different areas in different years. Oldest ringed bird lived for over 17 years.

POPULATION
Between 40 and 80 pairs nest in Scotland in the north and west. The highest numbers were recorded in the 1980s, since when the population appears to have declined here.

1st-year (fresh, autumn)

CONSERVATION
The Redwing first nested in Scotland (Inverness) in 1932 and the population has grown gradually since that time, although secrecy and varying observer effort from year to year make it difficult to assess the long-term trend. No special conservation programme is needed to help this species aside from preventing disturbance to nesting birds.

DISTRIBUTION
A few Redwings breed in northern Scotland, mostly north of the Great Glen. Scotland is also visited by large numbers of Icelandic and Continental Redwings in winter. The species breeds in Iceland, Scandinavia, north-east Europe and northern Russia. It winters in south-west Europe, including the British Isles, and also reaches the Mediterranean and North Africa.

RING OUZEL   *TURDUS TORQUATUS*

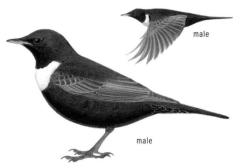

male

male

IDENTIFICATION
23–24 cm. Similar size to Blackbird, but slimmer and longer winged. Male is sooty black with whitish crescent on breast and silver-grey edges to many wing feathers that create a pale wing panel. There are faint 'scaly' marks on the flanks and under the tail. In late summer has pale tips to many of the body feathers giving a scaly look, especially to the underparts. Female is brown with a duller crescent on breast and scaly marks on underparts. After moult the crescent may be obscured. Juvenile lacks pale crescent and is spotted like juvenile Blackbird, but less rufous, with scaling on underparts and paler wings. First-year bird may also lack pale crescent, but scaling and pale wings are distinctive. In flight, wings appear paler than body. Adults moult between July and September, before migration. Newly grown body feathers have brown edges that obscure the breast marks and create a scaly appearance.
SEE ALSO: Blackbird p181.

female 1st-year
(fresh, autumn)

HABITS
Less approachable than Blackbird, often taking flight a good way from an observer, but fiercely protects its nest. On the ground it is more upright than Blackbird. May be loosely colonial when nesting, and seen singly or in groups when migrating. On territory it sings from a prominent perch and sometimes rival males will sing against each other.

VOICE
Call is a rattling or chattering 'tac, tac, tac'. Song is strong and flutey as it sings out a phrase of a few notes, pauses and sings another phrase. Quality is similar to Mistle Thrush.

HABITAT
Breeds in gullies on moorland and in mountains, and also around hill farms, fringes of forestry plantations and old quarries. It requires open hillsides, where deep heather, grassy knolls and small patches of scrub are found. Nest site frequently near water. On migration it regularly stops over on open areas of short grass near the coast and on steep grassy hillsides.

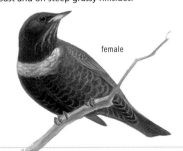

female

FOOD
In summer, feeds on beetles and their larvae, flies and other insects. Also eats worms and spiders and other invertebrates. Feeds on berries from Elder, Hawthorn, White-bryony, Blackberry and blaeberry.

BREEDING
Nest site is in a crag, gully or rocky outcrop, or it may be on the ground or even in a low bush; occasionally a nest may be below ground level, in an old mine. The 3–5 eggs are laid in late April or early May. Incubation is mostly, but not exclusively, by female and takes 13–14 days. Both parents care for the young, which fly after 12–16 days. Most pairs rear a second brood.

MOVEMENTS AND MIGRATIONS
Scottish breeding birds arrive back in late March and April. Other Ring Ouzels, en route to Scandinavia to breed, appear on the coast in late April and May. After nesting they fly to southern France and northern or central Spain, and from there many fly on to Morocco, where they spend the winter in the Atlas Mountains. Oldest bird survived for 9 years.

POPULATION
4,300–5,500 pairs breed in Scotland. The species declined in the 20th century and recent surveys indicate that this decline is continuing.

CONSERVATION
This species has retreated to the remotest uplands. Upland forestry has destroyed some previously suitable sites and grazing pressure may have removed sources of late-summer food. Recent research suggests that climate change is affecting the survival of birds in winter.

DISTRIBUTION
Widespread on open hillsides in upland areas of Scotland. Occurs in other places on migration, especially the coast. It also breeds in the Pennines, Wales and Ireland. Elsewhere, it breeds in Scandinavia. It winters mainly in Spain and Morocco. There are other races in the mountains of southern and eastern Europe.

BLACKBIRD *TURDUS MERULA*

male

male

male 1st-year

IDENTIFICATION
24–25 cm. Larger than Starling. Plump with round head and medium-length tail. Male is matt black with yellow bill and yellow ring round eye. First-year male is dull black with paler, browner flight feathers and horn-coloured bill. Female is dark brown with darker wings and tail; variable markings on breast that are usually obscure, but can be quite spotted on some individuals. Juvenile is similar to female but more rufous and with streaks on both upperparts and underparts. Adults begin moulting after breeding, between May and October. Juvenile moults its body feathers between July and October, but the main flight feathers are retained until the following year.
SEE ALSO: Ring Ouzel p180.

HABITS
Flight direct and lands with a characteristic raising of the tail and wings slightly drooping. Blackbirds that migrate are relatively gregarious; others may be territorial throughout the year. Tends to feed under or close to cover and turns over leaves to search for food. On sunny days, mainly in summer, it may be seen sunbathing, with wings spread, feathers ruffled, bill open and eyes closed. Sings from a prominent perch, often a rooftop in an urban area.

VOICE
Noisy species that has a beautiful, mellow song that is a slow, clear warble which 'tails-off' at the end. If disturbed it makes a loud 'tchook-tchook-tchook'. At dusk many birds will give nervous 'chink, chink, chink' calls. Song is mainly heard between March and July.

HABITAT
An adaptable species. Primarily a woodland bird that also lives in gardens, parks and hedgerows, as well as more open areas in cultivated and uncultivated places.

FOOD
Eats insects, worms and berries. Earthworms are eaten all year round – as long as the soil is damp. Other invertebrates include insect larvae, caterpillars, beetles and snails. Plant food includes berries from Hawthorn, Elder, ripe fruit such as fallen apples and pears and also kitchen scraps.

BREEDING
Nesting may begin in February in mild weather. Female mainly constructs the nest. It is a cup-shaped structure of grass, straw and small twigs, plastered on the inside with mud and lined with fine grasses. It is built in a bush or small tree. Female incubates the clutch of 3–5 eggs for about 14 days. Young are fed by both adults and fly after 14 days. On leaving the nest the brood is split between the two adults, with the male generally caring for his group longer than the female, which may leave them to begin another brood. There may be two or three broods in a season.

MOVEMENTS AND MIGRATIONS
Although many Scottish Blackbirds are resident, there is a movement away from the hills after breeding, with birds congregating in the coastal and Central Lowlands and in urban areas in winter. In northern and eastern Europe this species is a summer migrant, and in October and November an influx of these migrant Blackbirds from the Continent arrives along the Scottish coast from the north and east. Oldest known bird was 21 years.

POPULATION
The population of Blackbirds in Scotland is estimated at between 600,000 and 1 million pairs. While there are local fluctuations, the population is considered stable and may have increased as planted forests have matured.

CONSERVATION
The Blackbird evolved as a woodland species, and its move into man-made habitats such as agricultural areas, towns and gardens took place during the 19th and 20th centuries. There are no special conservation measures required for this successful species, although any agricultural changes potentially affect its future.

juvenile

female

DISTRIBUTION

Widespread in Scotland, although densities are low on moorland and upland areas and it is absent from mountains. Breeds throughout Europe and parts of Russia. Other races occur in southern Europe, North Africa and Asia.

SONG THRUSH *TURDUS PHILOMELOS*

IDENTIFICATION
23 cm. Smaller than Blackbird. Stocky thrush with a relatively short tail, medium brown upperparts and small black spots all over buff breast and flanks. There is a slight buff wing-bar. Differs from Mistle Thrush in smaller size, browner plumage, smaller spots, plain brown tail and orange underwing, which shows in flight. A recently fledged juvenile has pale streaks on its upperparts. Adults moult all feathers slowly between June and October.
SEE ALSO: Mistle Thrush p183, Redwing p179.

HABITS
A rather upright thrush that flicks its wings when excited. Territorial during the breeding season and many birds maintain the same territories during the winter – especially males. Outside breeding season usually seen singly except for loose flocks of migrants. Flight strong and direct without the undulations of Mistle Thrush. Sings from prominent song post, often a small tree or bush, not as high as Mistle Thrush.

VOICE
Far-carrying musical song comprises a series of short phrases, each repeated 3–5 times. Pattern of song is distinctive; individuals may have a repertoire of 100 phrases. Sings during the day and also at dusk, after most other birds finish singing. It sings from March to July and again briefly in autumn and during mild winter weather. Flight call is a thin 'tsic', not as hard as Robin's 'tic' alarm note. It can be heard at night as migrants pass over.

HABITAT
Found in a variety of habitats where there are trees and bushes; gardens, parks, coniferous and deciduous woodlands and hedgerows. Often feeds under trees and bushes and seldom far from cover.

FOOD
In dry weather it specialises in feeding on snails, which it opens by hitting them against a hard object ('anvil'). Generally prefers to eat earthworms, caterpillars and other insects, especially beetles, and fruits, especially berries, in autumn.

BREEDING
Nesting starts in March. Female builds the nest in a tree or shrub, usually close to the trunk. It is made of twigs, grass and moss and lined with a smooth layer of mud. The 3–5 eggs are incubated mainly by the female for 14–15 days. Both adults feed the young and they leave the nest after 13 days. The brood may be split between the two adults, but young are soon independent. Sometimes a second brood is reared, and in the south of its range a third or fourth brood.

MOVEMENTS AND MIGRATIONS
In Scotland the species is both a resident and a migrant. After breeding, it moves away from upland areas to lower ground and coastal areas, and many leave altogether, heading south or south-west to winter in England or Ireland. Breeding birds gradually return to their breeding sites from late February. The pattern is confused by the migration of Continental Song Thrushes, which pass through Scotland in varying, but often large, numbers in spring and autumn. It is not known what proportion of these migrants stay for the winter, but most head on south. Oldest wild bird lived 10 years.

POPULATION
About 250,000 pairs nest in Scotland. There has been a modest recovery in numbers since a population crash in 1970–90.

CONSERVATION
In much of the UK the Song Thrush has declined markedly in lowland areas, particularly in the drier east of the country where drainage leads to a shortage of invertebrate food and poor breeding success. Loss of permanent grazed pastures, hedges and damp areas is a continuing threat.

juvenile

MISTLE THRUSH *TURDUS VISCIVORUS*

IDENTIFICATION
27 cm. Larger than Song Thrush with longer wings and tail. Has grey-brown upperparts, large bold spots on a whitish breast and white tips to the outer tail-feathers. Pale-edged feathers create a pale panel on the closed wing and the cheeks are pale with darker marks. In flight, underwing is white. Juvenile has a pale head and pale spots on its upperparts. Adults moult between May and September, and moult may begin before they have finished nesting.
SEE ALSO: Song Thrush p182, Fieldfare p184.

HABITS
On the ground it is very upright and usually feeds in the open, well away from cover. Sings from the tops of tall trees and other exposed perches, and the song can often be heard during stormy conditions. Flight is strong, but sometimes deeply undulating at low levels: the bird dipping as the wings are closed at regular intervals. Outside the breeding season it is often seen in small groups. A bold and often aggressive thrush. An individual or a pair will sometimes defend a food-source, such as a Holly tree, during winter.

VOICE
Call is a loud rattling and chattering often given when the bird is alarmed, but also when travelling in flocks. Song is powerful, rather like a Blackbird, but louder with song phrases repeated again and again, with pauses between phrases.

HABITAT
Requires open woodland and other places where there are tall trees for nesting and for song posts, and also areas of short grass for feeding. In Scotland, the largest numbers occur on upland edges where pastures, woodland and scattered trees are found. After nesting it travels more widely in search of food, including on moorland.

FOOD
Feeds on insects, especially beetles, earthworms, slugs, snails and other invertebrates. Also takes plant material, especially fruits and seeds. Favourite berries include Yew, Hawthorn, Rowan and Holly.

BREEDING
Nesting may begin in February. Nest site is usually in a fork of a tree or shrub. Female builds a cup-shaped nest of grass, roots and leaves with some earth, and lines it with finer grasses. Incubation of the 3–5 eggs is mostly by female and lasts for 15–16 days. Both adults feed the young, which fly after 14 days, but they continue to be cared for by their parents for a further 14 days. There are often two broods.

MOVEMENTS AND MIGRATIONS
Most Mistle Thrushes in Scotland are resident, and many remain close to their breeding sites, but there is a movement away from the uplands in winter. After breeding, nomadic parties roam the countryside in search of food, some moving onto moorland for the craneflies and berries found here. Other individuals travel further, and there are records of Scottish birds reaching France. On the continent, Mistle Thrushes from the north migrate to southern Europe and around the Mediterranean for the winter, but very few of these stray across the North Sea to Scotland. Maximum age is 21 years.

POPULATION
Up to 50,000 pairs breed in Scotland. While the population in Scotland has been increasing, it appears the population south of the border has been declining.

CONSERVATION
Unlike its relative the Song Thrush, the Mistle Thrush has not been affected to the same extent by changes in agriculture, and populations in Scotland are healthy.

juvenile

DISTRIBUTION

Widespread in Scotland in summer, with the exception of the Outer Hebrides and the Northern Isles. Retreats to lowland and coastal areas in winter, with a higher density in central and southern areas. It also breeds extensively across England, Wales and Ireland, and on the Continent – from Scandinavia to the Mediterranean – and in parts of North Africa and Asia.

FIELDFARE *TURDUS PILARIS*

IDENTIFICATION
25.5 cm. Slightly smaller than Mistle Thrush. Large, plump thrush with rather long tail. Has grey head with dark streaks on crown, long pale grey rump, chestnut back and wings and black tail and flight feathers. Breast is yellow-orange and is heavily spotted. In flight, underwing shows white. Adults moult between June and September, before leaving breeding area.
SEE ALSO: Mistle Thrush p183.

HABITS
On the ground it is rather upright. Its flight appears leisurely with loose wingbeats alternating with short glides. In Britain and Ireland it is generally seen in small noisy flocks, with larger numbers gathering when migrating. In winter, flocks are nomadic as they travel the countryside in their search for food. They will sometimes travel with, and feed alongside, other thrushes and Starlings. At dusk in winter large roosts gather in thick hedges and other dense cover. When breeding it may nest singly or in small colonies. An individual will use well-aimed defecation to deter a predator from approaching a nest.

VOICE
The call is a loud 'chacker, chack, chack' and a nasal 'ee-eep' often given in flight. Song is a rather feeble warble with several hard, harsh notes and not often heard in Scotland.

HABITAT
In winter feeds along hedgerows and in copses. It may be seen in open places such as pastures and other areas of short grass, and on arable fields. Feeding sites are often close to woodland and tall hedges. In Scandinavia breeds in scrub, woodland and also in parks. The few that nest in Scotland use upland birch woods and the fringes of plantations, often in fairly remote locations.

FOOD
Insects and their larvae, worms and other invertebrates. Plant material is chiefly berries, especially from Rowan, Juniper, Elder, Hawthorn and Holly.

BREEDING
Breeding starts in April or May. Nest is cup-shaped and mostly built by female from twigs and roots, lined with mud and with an inner lining of finer material. Incubation is by the female and lasts 11–14 days. Both adults feed the 5 or 6 young, which usually fly at 12–15 days old. The young become independent at about 30 days. In Scandinavia there are often two broods.

MOVEMENTS AND MIGRATIONS
Mainly a winter visitor to Scotland from Scandinavia, with migrants being first seen here in September and the largest numbers arriving between mid-October and mid-November. The majority winter in the Central Lowlands, Dumfries & Galloway and along the east coast. They leave between March and May. Flocks are nomadic in their search for food, especially autumn berries, and they may fly further south if supplies are short or in response to severe weather. Oldest bird survived for 18 years.

POPULATION
The Fieldfare is a rare breeding species in Scotland, with no more than five pairs attempting to breed in most years. The winter population is estimated at 100,000–150,000 birds, but the number on passage may be as high as 1.5 million.

CONSERVATION
Specially protected. In the 1970s it looked as if the Fieldfare was set colonise Scotland. Following an expansion of its range in Europe, it first nested in Orkney in 1967 and possibly in northern England at the same time. It then nested in Shetland and further south in Scotland. However, from a peak of 13 possible nesting attempts in 1991, numbers have now fallen to 0–5 pairs.

DISTRIBUTION
A rare breeding species, but a common winter visitor. Seen throughout Scotland, with the exception of the highest mountains, between October and March. The species breeds from Scandinavia south to France and east to Russia, Asia and China.

GRASSHOPPER WARBLER *LOCUSTELLA NAEVIA*

IDENTIFICATION

12.5 cm. Smaller than House Sparrow. This secretive small warbler is olive-brown with dark, broken streaks on upperparts and a faint pale stripe over eye. Underparts are buff with some dark streaks on breast and under the tail. Feathers under the tail are very long. Tail graduated; wings short and rounded. Sometimes individuals appear yellow-brown. Juvenile often brighter and more yellow below than adults. It appears that some adults begin to moult before migration, but most moult in their winter quarters, although this aspect of the bird's life cycle is poorly understood.
SEE ALSO: Sedge Warbler p186.

yellowish variant

1st-winter

HABITS

Shy; generally lives in deep cover and is difficult to observe. A newly arrived migrant may, for a short time, sing from exposed perches at or near the top of a small bush. If disturbed it will slink down and disappear. During courtship it may flit short distances from bush to bush. It has complex displays that involve raising and waving its wings above its back. Most of the time it slips with ease, mouse-like, through dense vegetation and spends much time foraging on the ground amongst grass or shrubs and is reluctant to fly.

VOICE

Song is a remarkable insect-like trill that can be sustained for several minutes without a break. Trill is uniform in pitch and has been likened to the mechanical sound made by an angler's reel. Volume appears to change as the bird turns its head while singing. Song comprises 26 double notes per second and is heard mainly between April and July, during the day and at night, and especially at dawn and dusk. The ability of humans to hear the song decreases with age!

HABITAT

Breeds in a variety of wet and dry habitats in lowland areas, including thick scrub, thickets, edges of marshes, fens, heaths, farmland and young forestry plantations. Requires a combination of dense cover, suitable perches and an abundance of food.

FOOD

Eats mainly insects that it picks off the ground or from vegetation. Food includes bugs, beetles, moth caterpillars, lacewings, flies and ants. Also known to eat elderberries in late summer.

BREEDING

Nest is a thick cup built by both sexes in dense cover on or near the ground. The 5 or 6 eggs are incubated by both adults and hatch after 12–15 days. Both parents feed the young for 12–13 days. It is not known how long it takes for them to become independent. In the north only one brood is reared, while in the south of the range two broods are normal.

MOVEMENTS AND MIGRATIONS

A summer migrant to Scotland, arriving in mid-April and May and leaving after nesting in July and August. Its migrations are poorly understood, but it seems likely it flies to southern France or Portugal before heading on to West Africa for the winter, possibly stopping in Morocco en route. It appears to make long, non-stop flights, with much migration taking place at night.

POPULATION

Between 900 and 3,700 pairs nest in Scotland. There are large fluctuations from year to year, and in Britain as a whole numbers have declined, but the picture in Scotland suggests that where good habitat persists there may have been local increases.

CONSERVATION

Difficult to census, but it appears that the population fluctuates from year to year. Loss of suitable breeding habitat and drought in its winter quarters, or on migration, means it is vulnerable to drainage, agricultural improvements and the effects of climate change.

DISTRIBUTION

Widespread but thinly populating much of lowland Scotland; particular hotspots are Dumfries & Galloway and parts of Argyll. It is also found in suitable areas throughout the rest of Britain and Ireland. Elsewhere it breeds from southern Scandinavia to northern Spain and east into Russia. Its wintering area is not precisely known, but is likely to be West Africa.

Sedge Warbler
ACROCEPHALUS SCHOENOBAENUS

Identification
13 cm. Brown warbler with rather flat head. Has blackish streaks on back, dark streaky crown and prominent white stripe above its eye. Has a dark streak from eye to base of bill. The reddish-brown, unstreaked rump is especially noticeable in flight. Underparts are creamy white. It is duller as its plumage becomes worn in summer. Juvenile is fresh-looking and yellower than adult with boldly marked upperparts, pale crown stripe and some fine streaking on the breast. Adults begin to moult while still on their breeding grounds, then suspend moult while migrating and continue again during winter. Moult is completed by March.
SEE ALSO: Reed Warbler p187.

Habits
Clambers amongst plant stems and frequently feeds on the ground within tangled vegetation. For much of the time it can be hard to observe, but when singing it perches on the outside of a bush and may make a short, jerky song-flight. If newly fledged young are disturbed they will adopt a Bittern-like posture with bill pointing to the sky.

Voice
Song is loud, strong and repetitive; a mixture of varied fast chattering phrases, sweeter-sounding notes and some mimicry that often includes sparrow-like chirrups. Call is a scolding 'tuk', or grating 'chrirr'. Sings during the day and sometimes at night.

migration. Also feeds on plant material, especially berries in autumn.

Breeding
Nesting begins in late April with most clutches laid during May. Nest is a deep cup of grasses, moss, plant stems and spiders' webs and lined with soft grass, flower heads, hair and plant down. Generally close to ground amongst thick tangled vegetation and woven around vertical stems of plants, and sometimes suspended over water. Female builds nest and lays 4 or 5 eggs. Incubation is chiefly by female and lasts for 13–15 days. Young remain in the nest for 10–14 days and are fed by both parents.

Movements and Migrations
Summer migrant that arrives in mid-April and leaves its breeding sites in July, with the adults leaving before the juveniles. They move to pre-migration feeding areas where they build up large fat reserves that are sufficient for some to fly 3,900 km from southern Britain to Africa. The oldest known individual lived for 10 years.

Population
About 90,000 pairs nest in Scotland. Despite occasional huge fluctuations, the population remains stable overall.

Conservation
This is a dynamic species that has experienced rapid declines due to climate change on its migratory route to Africa and harsh management of the countryside, especially drainage of habitats such as wet ditches, the loss of rough fen vegetation and unsympathetic management of river banks. Yet there have been local expansions into drier habitats, including scrub adjacent to arable crops. Future threats come from further drainage of agricultural land and the desertification of land the species must cross during its migration.

fresh, spring

juvenile

Habitat
Breeds in thick vegetation in mainly wet places. Present in marshes, reedbeds with some trees and bushes, riverside scrub, damp ditches and nettle-beds. Also breeds in dryer habitats, including Bramble and Hawthorn thickets, young forestry plantations and fields of Rape and other crops.

Food
Finds most of its food low down in dense vegetation. Chiefly eats insects and other invertebrates, including flies, beetles, spiders, worms and small snails. Plum-reed aphids are an important source of food prior to

Distribution
Widespread in lowland Scotland, particularly the south-west and the east coast. Found throughout the British Isles and across much of Europe – from northern Scandinavia to western France and east across central Europe and into Russia. It winters in Africa, south of the Sahara Desert.

REED WARBLER *ACROCEPHALUS SCIRPACEUS*

IDENTIFICATION
13 cm. Plain, unstreaked warbler that has warm brown upperparts, and reddish-brown rump. Underparts are buff, graduating to white on throat. Has rather flat forehead, the suggestion of a peaked crown and rather long bill. Slight pale stripe over eye. By late summer adults are greyer. Juvenile is fresher, warmer rusty-brown with orange-brown flanks. Like all members of its family the feathers below the tail are quite long – reaching beyond the wing-tips. Between July and September adults have a partial moult before migrating. Moult is completed in Africa.
SEE ALSO: Sedge Warbler p186.

HABITS
Spends most of its time amongst dense reed stems where it is well camouflaged and easily overlooked unless singing. Frequently, song is given from within reedbed and not from an obvious perch. Climbs amongst the reeds with ease, often grasping different reeds with legs apart. May leave reeds to feed in neighbouring shrubs. When nesting will defend a small territory within a large or small colony. Solitary outside breeding season.

VOICE
Song is a noisy, unmusical, repetitive chatter and churring with frequent changes in pitch. It is more even, less varied and lower pitched than Sedge Warbler's song and full of 'rrr' and 'zzz's.

juvenile

fresh, spring

HABITAT
Breeds in Common Reed (*Phragmites*) in old fenland, ditches and along the edges of lochs and slow-flowing rivers. It prefers reeds that grow in water, although it occasionally breeds in drier places and other vegetation such as willowherb and arable crops. Migrants turn up almost anywhere, including orchards, gardens and in crops – often some way from water.

FOOD
Feeds mainly on insects, spiders and small snails. Insects include aphids, beetles, flies and small bugs.

BREEDING
Nesting begins in May. The female makes a deep cup of grasses, leaves and reed heads suspended between reed-stems. It takes 4 days to build and 3 days to line with hair, feathers or other soft material. Both sexes incubate the 3–5 eggs for 9–12 days and both adults feed the young. Young birds leave the nest at 10–13 days and become independent 10–14 days later. Sometimes they raise a second brood. Nests are frequently parasitised by Cuckoos.

MOVEMENTS AND MIGRATIONS
A summer visitor to Scotland, arriving from late April to mid-June and leaving in August and September. The journey to its winter quarters in West Africa is made in relatively short stages, with birds first heading for the Atlantic coast of France, then on to Spain and Portugal. From there they cross into Africa via Morocco. Migrant Reed Warblers from Scandinavia reach Scotland in autumn, being seen mainly in the Northern Isles and along the east coast. Oldest bird was 12 years.

POPULATION
There are 50–60 pairs nesting in Scotland. The species is a relatively recent colonist, with nesting first recorded on Shetland in 1973, although most birds are now found on the Tay and at sites like Mersehead on the Solway.

CONSERVATION
Historically, this species suffered from loss of habitat due to the drainage of wetlands and loss of large reedbeds. In the 19th century it spread north through England, but this expansion halted until the last quarter of the 20th century, when first Cumbria and then a few parts of Scotland were colonised. The conservation of reedbeds within nature reserves has helped this spread, as has the establishment of new reedbeds.

DISTRIBUTION
A scarce breeding species in Scotland. The largest concentrations in the British Isles are in East Anglia and along the south coast of England. It also breeds from southern Scandinavia to North Africa and in parts of the Middle East and Russia. It winters in central Africa.

BLACKCAP *SYLVIA ATRICAPILLA*

male

female

IDENTIFICATION
13 cm. Slightly smaller than House Sparrow. One of the larger warblers. Male has grey-brown upperparts, ash-grey underparts and a jet-black crown and forehead extending to eye level. Back of neck and face is grey. Female is browner above and brown-grey below and has a reddish-brown cap. First-winter birds are like a dull version of female, but during winter some black feathers start to appear. Adults moult between July and September, with late starters completing their moult quicker than the early ones. Moult is usually completed before migration.
SEE ALSO: Garden Warbler (song) p189, Marsh Tit p206, Willow Tit p205.

HABITS
An active and lively warbler. Generally it keeps within cover, but often it is a little easier to observe than a Garden Warbler. It is frequently aggressive towards other small birds – especially in winter when feeding at a bird table.

VOICE
The sweet and melodic song is one of the most lovely sounds of summer. Similar to that of Garden Warbler, but Blackcap has more obvious phrases, rich clear notes, varying tempo and generally ends with a flourish. Call is a hard 'tack' and a grating 'churr'. Sometimes individuals will mimic songs and calls of other birds.

HABITAT
In summer, it lives in deciduous or mixed woodlands, copses, thickets and other bushy places, including mature gardens and parks. It generally needs a mixture of trees and bushes, unlike Garden Warbler that prefers thickets. Those that are seen in winter are usually in areas with shrubs and bushes and frequently visit urban and rural gardens.

FOOD
Summer food is chiefly insects such as caterpillars, flies and beetles. In autumn and winter, feeds on berries such as Honeysuckle, Holly, Mistletoe and Sea Buckthorn. An opportunist feeder in winter. Will feed on windfallen apples and visit bird tables and other feeders where it takes bread, fat and other scraps. Also feeds on nectar.

BREEDING
Nests in a tangle of Brambles and other dense vegetation. Nesting begins in April or in May. Male builds several rudimentary nests from which the female chooses one to fashion into a neat, rather delicate cup-shaped nest. Both adults incubate the 4 or 5 eggs for 13–14 days and they both feed the young for 10–12 days before leaving the nest.

MOVEMENTS AND MIGRATIONS
The breeding population arrives in Scotland in April and May and leaves in August and September. These birds appear to move first through England, and then fly to their winter areas around the Mediterranean, both in Iberia and North Africa. Migrants from the Continent arrive in autumn; most of these move on, but some overwinter here. In the last 30 years, part of the European population has changed its migratory direction to west-south-west, and a small population from Germany and north-east Europe now arrives in winter in the British Isles, with increasing numbers in Scotland. Oldest bird was 11 years.

POPULATION
56,000 pairs of Blackcaps breed in Scotland. The population appears to have increased through the 1980s. Wintering birds were first observed in the 1970s, and there may now be 200 or more, mainly in the lowlands of the south and east.

CONSERVATION
There are no special conservation measures for this successful species. The recent increase in numbers has been linked to climate change, especially global warming.

DISTRIBUTION

Widespread in Scotland in lowland areas, mainly south of the Great Glen in summer. Also a common breeding species in much of England, Wales and Ireland. It breeds from northern Scandinavia to North Africa and east into Russia. Blackcaps mainly winter around the Mediterranean, with some travelling to West Africa, and a small population also winters in the British Isles.

Garden Warbler *SYLVIA BORIN*

IDENTIFICATION

14 cm. Similar size to Great Tit. Rather plump and large plain brown warbler with no obvious features. Has brown upperparts and buff underparts. Bill is rather short and thick, and the blue-grey legs are quite stout. Adults become greyer as breeding season progresses. Suggestion of grey on side of neck, but otherwise this is a rather nondescript species. Sexes look the same. Juvenile resembles adult except it may appear more olive in fresh plumage in late summer when compared with the greyer adult. A few adult birds moult while they are in Britain, others start and suspend their moult, but most appear to delay and undergo a complete moult in their winter quarters.

SEE ALSO: Blackcap (song) p188, Chiffchaff p194, Reed Warbler p187.

HABITS

An active bird but spends most of its time amongst cover and can be very difficult to see even when in song. When seen it does not usually appear as nervous as many other warblers, with no wing-flicking or tail-fanning.

VOICE

Song may be heard between April and July, an attractive stream of sweet, musical phrases that is confusingly similar to that of Blackcap. Tends to be more even, subdued and hurried in its delivery and carries on in the same way for a long time – often singing non-stop for a minute or more. Calls are a hard 'tacc, tacc' and grating 'churr'.

fresh, spring

HABITAT

Breeds in deciduous or mixed woodland and scrub with dense ground cover. Often frequents dense scrub and overgrown hedges at the edge of farmland. Not really a garden bird, except in large, mature gardens with suitable habitat.

FOOD

When nesting eats mainly invertebrates, especially caterpillars, larvae and adult beetles, larvae and adult flies, aphids, worms and spiders. At other times it eats berries and other fruit, including figs while migrating through the Mediterranean region.

BREEDING

Cup-shaped nest of grass, leaves and small twigs is built low in a shrub, small tree or among other plant stems. Usually the male builds a number of unfinished 'cock nests' from which the female chooses one to complete. Eggs are laid in May. A clutch usually comprises 4 or 5 eggs. Incubation is by both sexes and lasts for 11–13 days. Both adults feed the young, which leave the nest after 9–10 days, often before they can fly properly. They continue to be looked after by the adults for a further 10–14 days.

MOVEMENTS AND MIGRATIONS

A long-distance migrant that arrives in Scotland in late April and May and departs July–September. Migrating birds pause to feed along the south coast of England before flying to Spain or Morocco and then on to their winter quarters in West Africa, especially Ghana. The number of stops they make is unclear, but they are capable of long, sustained flights. Other migrants from northern Europe pass through Scotland, especially in autumn. Oldest bird was 14 years.

POPULATION

Between 10,000 and 18,000 pairs nest in Scotland. The species appears to be expanding its range in the north, while in parts of the south numbers are falling.

CONSERVATION

The recent changes in the distribution in Scotland may be due to competition from Blackcaps, which occupy the best territories as they undertake a shorter migration and therefore arrive back earlier in spring than Garden Warblers. Climate change could also affect this species in the same way as it has affected other trans-Saharan migrants in recent years.

DISTRIBUTION

Breeds in the lowlands of southern and central Scotland and in the southern Highlands. There are small populations north of the Great Glen. Widespread south of the border, especially in central and southern England, Wales and parts of Ireland. A summer visitor to most of Europe, from northern Scandinavia to Spain and east to Russia. Winters in central and southern Africa.

LESSER WHITETHROAT *SYLVIA CURRUCA*

male

IDENTIFICATION
12.5–13.5 cm. Smaller than Great Tit. Compact and generally rather grey warbler that is a little smaller than Whitethroat with more uniform grey wings and slightly shorter grey tail. Has a grey-brown back and grey head with contrasting dark grey cheeks. Underparts are usually off-white, but may be tinged pink in early spring. Has white outer tail-feathers. Legs are dark grey. First-winter birds are very white below, still with obvious dark cheeks; some have slight pale stripe from bill over eye. Adults moult between July and September, before they migrate for the winter. Moult is rapid with flight feathers being lost and regrown in about 40 days.
SEE ALSO: Whitethroat p191.

HABITS
Skulking. It is the call or song that is most likely to attract an observer's attention. This species is most obvious when the young are out of the nest. It maintains a territory in spring, but is sociable outside the breeding season, with reports of flocks of 20 migrating together and in Africa in winter it forms mixed feeding groups with other warblers.

BREEDING
Nests in bushes or small trees. Male builds several incomplete 'cock-nests' and pairs work together to complete one of them. Nest is a loose, deep cup of grass and roots. Usually 4 or 5 eggs in a clutch. Incubation is by both birds and lasts for 10–16 days. Both adults feed the young and juveniles leave the nest at between 10–13 days, when they are only able to flutter.

MOVEMENTS AND MIGRATIONS
Returns to Scotland in April and May, having flown from its African wintering grounds, around the eastern end of the Mediterranean, and from there probably non-stop to Britain. From mid-July return migration begins as birds move south. Once they leave Britain it appears they fly direct to a small area in northern Italy where many rest and feed before flying on south-east, across the Mediterranean and Egypt to their wintering area. The oldest ringed bird survived for over 7 years.

POPULATION
There are about 400 pairs nesting in Scotland. The species has expanded its range here in recent years, whereas in the rest of the UK numbers have been falling.

CONSERVATION
The small Scottish population appears stable, but the rest of the British population has been falling since the 1980s. Loss of habitat – especially thick hedges and 'scrubby corners' in an increasingly 'tidy' countryside – has been an issue. Even more serious is its reliance on specific stop-over points on its migration. Any deterioration either here or on its African wintering grounds could have a damaging long-term effect.

fresh, autumn
or early spring

juvenile

VOICE
Song usually delivered from within dense cover such as a bush or hedge. Call is a hard 'tac, tac' rather like a Blackcap but shorter. Its song is heard from late April to late June and is a dry rattle on the same note, very similar to the start of a Yellowhammer's song. At close quarters a more musical warble can be heard before the rattle, and often a quiet 'stic, stic'.

HABITAT
Generally found around Hawthorn or Blackthorn scrub, hedgerows, shrubberies, overgrown railway embankments, disused and overgrown industrial sites, and sometimes venturing into gardens – especially in late summer.

FOOD
Chiefly feeds on invertebrates such as beetles, ants, flies, midges and caterpillars, and also some fruit, especially Elderberries and Blackberries.

DISTRIBUTION
A local breeding species, mainly in southern Scotland, with half in Lothian and the Borders. A few isolated pairs are found on the east coast between Fife and Aberdeen. Also breeds in England, especially the south-east, and in Wales, but rarely in Ireland. Elsewhere, it breeds in northern and central Europe, east into Russia and China, and also in the Middle East.

WHITETHROAT *SYLVIA COMMUNIS*

male summer

female summer

IDENTIFICATION

14 cm. Similar size to Great Tit and slightly larger than Lesser Whitethroat. Tail rather long, and crown peaked, especially when male is alarmed or displaying. Male also has a grey head, white throat and brown back with reddish-brown edges to wing feathers giving a rufous look to the closed wing. Underparts are buff or slightly pinkish and the outer tail-feathers are white. As plumage becomes worn during the breeding season, the colours of male become more drab. Female has a browner head and is generally duller than male. The first-winter is similar to female, but is a warmer brown with orange-brown feathers in the wing and off-white underparts. Most adults moult between July and September. It has a further partial moult in March and April when it acquires its bright spring plumage.
SEE ALSO: Lesser Whitethroat p190.

HABITS

Jerky song-flight in spring, but also sings from a perch. At other times skulks in bushes and hedges, and flits between areas of cover. Maintains a territory during the breeding season and some males may have a second female. Some newly independent young flock together in late summer, often with other species such as Blackcap, Willow Warbler and Blue Tit.

VOICE

Common calls are hard 'tacc, tacc' and scolding 'tchur-rrr'. Song is a jumble of unmusical phrases. Also has a more musical song that is sometimes heard early in the breeding season.

HABITAT

Breeds in thick hedges, scrub, young plantations, along woodland edges, in glades with thick bushes, Brambles, nettles or gorse and other places where there is tangled vegetation. It will sometimes venture into parks and gardens if there is dense vegetation. In Africa in winter many birds live in woodland areas – especially prior to their return migration.

FOOD

During the breeding season, feeds on beetles, aphids, caterpillars and flies. At other times it will eat fruit, especially berries in late summer and also in its winter quarters in Africa prior to migrating northwards.

BREEDING

Male builds several 'cock nests' and female selects one and completes the structure. It is cup-shaped and built low down in a bush. Egg laying begins in April and peaks in May. Both sexes incubate the 4 or 5 eggs (the female generally at night) for 12–13 days. Both adults feed the young. Young leave the nest after 12–14 days and

juvenile

remain with their parents for 15–20 days. Sometimes the brood is split between the two parents. There may be two broods.

MOVEMENTS AND MIGRATIONS

Summer migrant arrives between mid-April and mid-May, with the male returning before the female. It makes long migratory flights; when leaving Britain and Ireland in autumn it flies south-east to France then changes direction to south-west to Spain and Portugal. From Iberia flies to Africa. Appears to adopt a different strategy on return in spring, and flies directly north into France. The oldest survived 6 years.

POPULATION

Between 70,000 and 133,000 pairs nest in Scotland. The population fluctuates; following a huge crash in 1969 the species has gradually recovered, but it is probably still not back to its original numbers.

CONSERVATION

The sudden dramatic decline in the late 1960s was due to droughts in the Whitethroat's wintering quarters in the Sahel area of North Africa. While in Scotland habitat quality needs to be maintained, the global issue of climate change affecting Africa is the most obvious threat.

DISTRIBUTION

Breeds mainly in lowland areas of southern and eastern Scotland, but avoids mountainous or urban areas. It is widespread elsewhere in the British Isles. In Europe it breeds from the Arctic Circle to North Africa and east into Russia. Migrants are seen on the east coast and Northern Isles.

YELLOW-BROWED WARBLER
PHYLLOSCOPUS INORNATUS

IDENTIFICATION

10 cm. Smaller than a Chiffchaff and paler, with whiter underparts. It has a conspicuous long pale stripe over the eye to the nape and below this a narrow dark line through its eye. Its cheeks are mottled. The back is grey-green and the wings show two creamy wing-bars – the lower one thicker than the upper one. The inner flight feathers are conspicuously edged creamy white creating white stripes on the closed wing. It has a fine, tiny dark bill. It is slightly larger and longer than a Pallas's Warbler with a green, not yellow rump, and it is not so bright green or stripy. Some birds have the suggestion of a stripe on the crown and dark lines bordering the pale stripe above the eye, but this is never so clear as the marks on a Pallas's. The legs are usually yellowish, not grey like Pallas's.
SEE ALSO: Pallas's Warbler p249.

incubates, but both adults help to feed the young. They leave the nest at 11–15 days and stay with their parents for about another 13 days.

MOVEMENTS AND MIGRATIONS

This is a remarkable small migrant. It breeds in Asia from the Ural Mountains east to Korea. It normally leaves its breeding habitat in August and September to winter in South-east Asia. Each year many juveniles 'reverse' migrate, and their journey brings them to western Europe, where they arrive during September and October. They are regularly seen in the Northern Isles or along the east coast of Scotland, but are rarely seen inland, although a few do reach the Outer Hebrides.

fresh, autumn

HABITS

It can often be difficult to observe among the leaves of trees and bushes and it is the call that usually attracts attention. It is constantly on the move as it feeds from ground level to the canopy of tall trees, but often it moves actively right through the canopy.

VOICE

The call is similar to that of a Coal Tit and is a loud single rising note 'suu-eet'. Individuals often call repeatedly, especially if others are calling in the locality.

HABITAT

On migration it will feed in whatever cover is available – migrants on offshore islands will often visit gardens. Usually it feeds in willow trees and taller sycamores. It breeds in deciduous or mixed forests, including birch forests in the foothills of the Himalayas.

FOOD

It feeds mainly on insects, including beetles and flies, and also some other small invertebrates. It will sometimes hover to take prey from the underside of leaves or fly up to snatch an insect in flight.

BREEDING

It does not breed in Britain or Ireland. The nest is domed with an entrance at the side. The female

POPULATION

Between 50 and 300 arrive in autumn. It is a very rare vagrant in spring.

CONSERVATION

There are no special conservation measures in place for this species.

DISTRIBUTION

In Scotland it is most likely to be seen near the coast, especially the Northern Isles and migration 'hot spots' on the east coast. It breeds in parts of eastern Russia, China and other parts of Asia. Most winter in India and South-east Asia.

WOOD WARBLER *PHYLLOSCOPUS SIBILATRIX*

IDENTIFICATION
12 cm. Larger than Willow Warbler with 'broad shoulders', relatively short tail and rather long wings. Appears bright and clean, with yellow-green upperparts, pale yellow stripe above eye, bright yellow throat and breast and pure white underparts. Flight feathers have yellowish edges that give a yellow cast to the closed wing. Plumage becomes a little greyer during summer. Legs are yellowish brown. First-winter birds are similar to adults but duller and browner above. It has a partial moult between June and August and a full moult in its winter quarters in Africa.
SEE ALSO: Willow Warbler p195, Chiffchaff p194.

HABITS
An active species that sometimes hovers to pick insects from the underside of leaves and also captures them in flight. When perched it frequently droops its wings and does not flick its tail like some other warblers. It moves with great agility along branches. When displaying it has a beautiful 'butterfly-like' flight among the trees. Outside breeding season generally seen singly and seeks out dense cover at the tops of trees.

VOICE
Call is a loud, sweet sounding, rather plaintive 'pew-pew'. Song a remarkable series of 'tsic, tsic' notes that accelerates into a shivering trill, with the bird trembling as it sings. Song is not usually given for a second time from the same perch and sometimes it will sing during its display flight. Also has a second song that is made up of the 'pew' notes.

HABITAT
Prefers mature upland oakwoods or mature birch stands with a high canopy and limited ground vegetation. Also breeds in Beech woods, and elsewhere in Europe it uses woods of pine, Alder, birch or mixed deciduous woods. Winters in forests in equatorial Africa.

FOOD
Feeds mainly on insects such as moth caterpillars, craneflies and other flies and beetles. Also eats spiders. Takes very little plant material.

BREEDING
Males defend individual territories, but these territories are sometimes in 'clusters' within suitable woodlands, and males will often try to attract a second mate. Nests on the ground where there is ample cover, or under a fallen tree trunk or branch. Female builds the nest. There are 5–7 eggs, incubated by the female for 12–14 days. Both adults feed the young until they leave the nest at 11–13 days. They continue to feed them for a further 2–3 days and sometimes the family is split between the two parents, or the family may stay together for up to 4 weeks.

MOVEMENTS AND MIGRATIONS
A summer migrant that returns to Scotland in late April and early May and leaves again in July and August. Wood Warblers seem to arrive directly on their breeding sites, and small numbers are seen in the Northern Isles and along the east coast in August. It appears British Wood Warblers make unbroken flights to southern Europe, often Italy, and then on to the southern fringe of the Sahara Desert. In spring they break their journey on the North African coast. Oldest bird was 10 years.

POPULATION
About 3,000 pairs nest in Scotland. The UK population has fallen by as much as a half in recent years; the Scottish population has also fallen, with the species now absent from many previous breeding sites.

CONSERVATION
Like a number of woodland species, Wood Warbler populations have declined in recent years and the reason is far from clear. The cause may be changes in woodland management, but is more likely to be changes in their winter habitats, possibly linked to climate change.

fresh, spring

1st-winter

DISTRIBUTION
In Scotland, most nest in the central and western broadleaf woodlands. In the rest of Britain it also has a westerly distribution, with the highest density in Wales and a few also in Ireland. It breeds from Scandinavia to Italy and east into Russia.

CHIFFCHAFF PHYLLOSCOPUS COLLYBITA

IDENTIFICATION
10–11 cm. About the size of Blue Tit. Slightly smaller, more compact and with more rounded head than Willow Warbler. In spring and summer, upperparts are dull green or olive-brown and the rump slightly paler. Underparts are dull yellowish. The rather short wings are marked with yellowish lines, which are the edges to the flight feathers. There is a dark line through the eye and a pale stripe above the eye. Plumage becomes duller during the summer. Legs are dark brown or black. First-winter birds look fresh and browner than the adults, with slightly yellower underparts. Adults moult any time between June and early October. Moult is completed before they migrate for the winter.
SEE ALSO: Willow Warbler p195, Wood Warbler p193.

HABITS
Active and restless; frequently flicks its wings and twitches or wags its tail. Often difficult to see within shrubs and trees, but will also frequently sing from an exposed branch. Flight looks a little jerky as it moves from tree to tree. Will flutter out to catch insects in the air and sometimes hover to pick an insect from under a leaf. Usually solitary outside the breeding season, but large roosts of a hundred or more sometimes occur where it is common in winter.

fresh, autumn

VOICE
Call is loud, rising 'huitt' and the song a distinctive repeated 'zip-zap, zip-zap, zip-zap'. Between song phrases it sometimes makes a much quieter 'terric, terric' call.

HABITAT
Breeds in woods, copses and other shrubby places where there is thick undergrowth and trees, but not usually in coniferous woodland. In autumn and winter, it may visit parks and gardens.

FOOD
Feeds mainly on insects including midges, other flies, aphids and caterpillars of moths. It sometimes takes plant material such as seeds and berries, but this is not a common food.

BREEDING
The first eggs are laid in late April or early May. The site is generally among leaves, low down in bushes, especially Bramble, or amongst grass. The female builds a domed nest with a side entrance. The female incubates the 4–6 eggs for 13–15 days. The young are mostly fed by the female and they leave the nest after 12–15 days. The young are sometimes split between the parents until they become independent 10–19 days later.

MOVEMENTS AND MIGRATIONS
Migrant Chiffchaffs arrive in Scotland in late March and April and generally leave again in the last 20 days of September. Most head south-east into France and then to the Mediterranean region, and some fly on to West Africa. In October and November migrant Chiffchaffs from the Continent arrive and a few of these remain for the winter. Maximum known age is 7 years.

POPULATION
Around 50,000 pairs breed in Scotland, with more Scandinavian birds passing through on passage in autumn, and up to 75 overwintering. Its range in Scotland has expanded northwards in recent years and increasing numbers are being seen in winter.

CONSERVATION
Like other trans-Saharan migrants, the numbers returning each year can be variable, but since the 1970s the population in Scotland has been stable or on the increase. However, any alteration to the Chiffchaff's favoured habitat in Africa and any changes to the climate that result in increased desertification may adversely affect this species.

juvenile

DISTRIBUTION
Found in low-lying woodlands throughout Scotland, including the Inner Hebrides. Also widely distributed in England, Wales and Ireland. The species is found from Sweden to northern Spain and east through Italy, Greece, Turkey and Bulgaria. There are other species and subspecies of Chiffchaffs. The northern subspecies, known as the Scandinavian Chiffchaff, visits Scotland in large numbers in autumn.

fresh, autumn
or spring

IDENTIFICATION
10.5–11.5 cm. The size of a Blue Tit. A small, slim, warbler with greenish-brown upperparts and yellowish-white underparts. It becomes less yellow as the summer advances. It has pale legs, a dark line through the eye, a pale yellowish stripe over eye and no suggestion of a wing-bar. Differs from Chiffchaff by having longer wings and slightly longer body, cleaner yellow underparts and clearer stripe above eye. The best difference is, however, the voice. Juvenile is variable, but many have very yellow underparts. Unique among Scottish warblers in having two complete moults a year; one between June and early September, before migration, and another in Africa between December and April. SEE ALSO: Chiffchaff p194, Wood Warbler p193.

HABITS
Often difficult to see this species as it feeds in trees and bushes, but frequently sings from a prominent perch. It occasionally flicks its wings and twitches its tail, but generally it is less restless than Chiffchaff.

VOICE
The song is a pretty, liquid series of descending notes that starts softly and ends with a flourish. The common 'hoo-ee' call is almost two notes run together.

HABITAT
Nests in young woods and plantations, scrub, along woodland edges and rides and in forest clearings. Also breeds in birch woods, on the edge of moorland and on former industrial land and gravel workings where there is a growth of bushes.

juvenile

FOOD
It feeds mainly on insects such as flies, caterpillars, beetles and midges. It also eats spiders and will feed on berries in late summer and autumn.

BREEDING
Some males are polygamous, having more than one mate at any one time, and while most are single-brooded, some males have a second family with a different female. Nesting begins in late April and May. It usually nests on the ground in a well-concealed domed nest with an entrance at the side. The nest is made from leaves, mosses, lichens and is built by the female. The female incubates the 4–8 eggs for 12–14 days. Both adults feed the young, which fly when they are 13–16 days old.

MOVEMENTS AND MIGRATIONS
Summer migrant that arrives between March and June, with most arriving in April. By July young birds disperse in random directions, but by August they are starting to head south. At first migration is generally short flights in a southerly direction, but after refuelling in Iberia they make longer flights to their winter quarters in West Africa. Willow Warblers breeding in east Siberia also migrate to Africa – a journey of 11,250 km. The oldest ringed bird lived for more than 10 years.

POPULATION
Over half a million pairs nest in Scotland, with another 10,000–20,000 migrants passing through en route to and from Scandinavia. The long-term population trend in Scotland indicates a modest increase.

1st-winter
(fresh, autumn)

CONSERVATION
While populations are declining in much of southern Britain, those in Scotland appear to be faring better, perhaps in response to the planting of mixed broadleaf woodland. There are, however, worrying signs for the future: survival rates have been falling and more broods are failing while in the nest, and females, which migrate later, are returning in fewer numbers, perhaps as a result of changing weather conditions on the species' wintering grounds.

DISTRIBUTION

Abundant and widespread on the mainland, except for the highest hills, but thinly distributed in the north and on islands, and rare on Shetland. It is a common summer migrant in other parts of the British Isles. On the Continent it is the most numerous summer migrant, breeding across northern Europe and into Russia and Asia. It winters in central and southern Africa.

SPOTTED FLYCATCHER   *MUSCICAPA STRIATA*

IDENTIFICATION
14.5 cm. Size of House Sparrow. The dark bill is long and wide, the head quite rounded and the wings and tail rather long. Has grey-brown upperparts, off-white underparts, streaks on breast and fine streaking on crown. There are pale edges to wing feathers. Very upright when perched. Sexes are similar. Juvenile has a more scaly or spotted appearance, rather like a juvenile Robin. Adults are unusual in that sequence of moulting flight feathers is often irregular. Adults split their moult, having a partial moult between July and September before migration and a complete moult between November and March in Africa. Some may not complete moult before spring migration and will complete it on their breeding grounds.
SEE ALSO: Dunnock p171, Tree Pipit p162.

1st-winter

juvenile

FOOD
Mainly feeds on flying insects, especially larger flies and it also catches butterflies. In cooler weather when large insects are not flying it resorts to searching amongst foliage for insects such as aphids and smaller flies. Prior to egg-laying, females may feed on calcium-rich food such as small snails and woodlice. Cool wet weather in spring can significantly reduce the food available and results in the loss of young.

BREEDING
Nest site is a natural or artificial ledge or niche where the nest is usually sheltered. Sites may be among Ivy and other creepers on a tree trunk or a wall, in the old nest of another species or in a specially made open-fronted nestbox. The rather loose cup-shaped nest of twigs, grasses and roots is built by both sexes. The female incubates the 4 or 5 eggs for 13–15 days. Both adults feed the young until they leave the nest at about 13–16 days. The young remain dependent on their parents for a further 12–32 days.

MOVEMENTS AND MIGRATIONS
It is a summer migrant, with most returning in late May – one of the last migrants to return. Its arrival depends on weather conditions in southern Europe. It is a long-distance migrant with most wintering south of the equator. Our breeding birds start to leave in July and August. Birds from further east arrive as passage migrants in September. They are nocturnal migrants. The oldest known bird lived for 11 years.

POPULATION
Between 10,000 and 20,000 pairs nest in Scotland. There has been a serious long-term decline across the whole of the British Isles, which has been most noticeable in the south-east of England.

CONSERVATION
The population decline appears to have started in the 1960s. Breeding productivity in Scotland is good, yet the survival rate of young birds is poor. The reasons for this are believed to relate to problems on the species' migration route or in its winter quarters in Africa. The issue may be deteriorating habitats due to drought, or the actions of man, or both.

HABITS
Regularly hunts from a bare branch or other prominent position. Flies out, often chasing its prey erratically, and seizes a flying insect, before returning to the same perch or another close by. It can be tolerant of humans.

VOICE
Call is a thin repeated 'tzee' that has been likened to a squeaking wheelbarrow! The alarm is a sharper clicking 'eez-tchick'. Song is a rather quiet series of high-pitched notes and low scratchy warbles.

HABITAT
A bird of woodland glades and woodland edge, large mature gardens and parks with a mixture of mature trees and younger trees or bushes. It occurs in mature pine forests and at the edges of plantations near scrub and isolated stands of trees.

DISTRIBUTION

A widespread summer visitor to most of Scotland, apart from the Northern Isles and Outer Hebrides. It also breeds in England, Wales and most of Ireland. It is found from Scandinavia to North Africa and east into Asia. It winters in southern Africa, and some northern European birds even reach South Africa.

PIED FLYCATCHER *FICEDULA HYPOLEUCA*

IDENTIFICATION
13 cm. Slightly smaller than House Sparrow. Smaller and plumper than Spotted Flycatcher, with a proportionally shorter tail with white edges. Adult male in spring is black and white. Upperparts are mostly dull black with a bold white patch on the folded wing and a white spot above the bill. Underparts are white. After breeding it moults into brown or grey plumage with blackish rump and tail and buff underparts, but it retains the white in the wing and tail. Female resembles the non-breeding male but has browner rump and tail. Juvenile resembles female in colour, but has spotting on upperparts and some speckling on underparts. Moult sometimes begins while the adults are feeding young in June and is mostly completed before the birds migrate. There is a partial moult into breeding plumage in January and February while it is still in winter quarters.
SEE ALSO: Pied Wagtail p165, Spotted Flycatcher p196.

male summer

male winter

HABITS
Often cocks its tail and flicks its wings nervously. Darts out from a perch to catch a fly, but (unlike the Spotted Flycatcher) it usually returns to a different perch. Sometimes clings to branches like a tit and occasionally feeds on the ground. Can be quite obvious when nesting but after the young leave the nest they and their parents disappear quickly from the neighbourhood, feeding high in trees or in dense shrubs as they prepare for migration.

VOICE
Call is a sharp 'whit' and also a 'tic'. Song is a simple series of rather sweet notes 'suee-suee-sweet-sweet'.

HABITAT
Breeds in mature deciduous woodland, especially oak woods and sometimes birch woods on hillsides. Where numerous, it uses gardens and parks, often near streams and rivers. In other parts of range nests in mixed woodland or sometimes in pine woods with suitable nest sites.

FOOD
Feeds mainly on invertebrates and some fruits and seeds. Insect food includes caterpillars, flies, beetles, bugs and ants. Spiders and millipedes are also taken.

BREEDING
Female builds the nest in a hole in a tree – often an old woodpecker's hole. Nestboxes are also used. Nest is a loose structure of leaves, grass, roots and moss. The 6 or 7 eggs are incubated by female for 13–15 days. Young are fed by both adults and

juvenile

female

leave after 16–17 days. Some males have a second or third mate. Such males feed the first brood, but are less supportive to others.

MOVEMENTS AND MIGRATIONS
Summer migrant from late April through to early June, with males returning ahead of females. In August and September it makes a non-stop flight to northern Spain and Portugal where it mixes with other Pied Flycatchers from elsewhere in Europe; all refuelling ready for the next leg of their journey to Africa. They return from Africa by a more easterly route. Falls of Scandinavian migrants arrive in the Northern Isles and on the east coast, particularly in September and early October. The oldest ringed bird survived 10 years.

POPULATION
300–400 breeding pairs are present in Scotland. Following the species' colonisation of Scotland in the 19th century and its expansion in the 20th century, numbers have largely been on the decline except in the south and west, where they are stable or increasing.

CONSERVATION
The species has been helped at some sites, such as Wood of Cree and Inversnaid, by nestbox programmes. Such schemes are especially valuable where there is shortage of natural holes or where the best potential holes are taken up by other species before these late migrants return in spring.

DISTRIBUTION
Breeds in central and southern Scotland, especially the south-west. Also breeds in western England and Wales, and from Scandinavia across northern Europe, with further populations in France and Spain. All Pied Flycatchers winter in Africa.

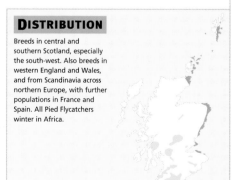

GOLDCREST *REGULUS REGULUS*

IDENTIFICATION
9 cm. Britain and Ireland's smallest bird. Tiny, rather round-looking species with small rounded wings and large eyes. Upperparts are dull green, underparts off-white and it has a yellow or orange patch on the crown of its head that is bordered with black. Crown patch is more yellow on females and, when raised in display, shows deep orange on males. There are two whitish wing-bars. Juvenile is similar to adult, but lacks the yellow/orange crest. Adults have a complete moult between June and October. Sometimes it begins its moult after rearing the first brood, but it suspends its moult if it begins a second brood.
SEE ALSO: Pallas's Warbler p249, Yellow-browed Warbler p192.

HABITS
A very small, hyperactive species that always seems to be on the move. Tit-like, it will feed among branches and sometimes hover to snatch food from the undersides of leaves. It sometimes ignores an approaching observer. Outside the breeding season it often joins flocks of other small birds such as tits and warblers as they forage for food in woods and hedgerows. In parts of Europe small groups of Gold-crests defend winter territories.

VOICE
Call is a high-pitched, thin 'tsee' that is useful for locating this species. Song is sometimes heard in winter and regularly from February. It is a high-pitched, wheeling 'tee-lee-de, tee-lee-de'.

HABITAT
Stronghold is in coniferous woodland and also in conifer plantations, but it will nest in churchyard Yews, in parks and in large gardens. Outside the breeding season it appears in a variety of habitats where there are at least some trees or thick bushes. Some migrants that arrive on treeless islands or headlands can be seen flitting around boulders and cliff edges.

FOOD
It feeds almost exclusively on insects and spiders and sometimes it eats small seeds. Insect food includes flies, beetles and small caterpillars.

BREEDING
Nesting begins in late April. Nest is a deep, rounded cup of moss, lichen and spiders' webs, and is suspended in a fork of twigs at end of a conifer branch. Male may build nest, but usually both birds work on it. Female incubates the 6–8 eggs for 16–19, days which hatch over 1–4 days. Young are fed by both adults. They leave the nest after about 18 days and become independent 2 weeks later. A second nest may be built and eggs laid before young of first brood leave the first nest. At these times the responsibility of feeding the first brood falls to the male.

MOVEMENTS AND MIGRATIONS
Scottish Goldcrests are mainly resident, but those farther north in Scandinavia and east in Poland and Russia are migrants, making night-long flights, stopping to feed and then moving on. Migration from Scandinavia peaks when there is high pressure over the Baltic Sea. Some of these migrants reach Scotland, especially in October, and they will remain until March. Occasionally, in autumn, exceptional numbers arrive along the east coast. The oldest known Goldcrest lived for 7 years.

POPULATION
300,000–750,000 pairs nest in Scotland, and in winter the population may rise to 3 million. Numbers are stable or increasing.

male displaying

female

juvenile

CONSERVATION
Vast forestry plantations in Scotland have allowed this species to spread to new areas, and population growth is probably higher here than in the rest of Britain. The species suffers adversely in severe winters, although generally numbers recover after a few years.

DISTRIBUTION
Widespread in Scotland wherever mixed or plantation forests and woodland occur. Common in the rest of the British Isles, except treeless areas such as the East Anglian fens. Breeds from northern Scandinavia to northern Spain and east into Asia. The most northerly territories in Europe and Russia are abandoned in winter.

BEARDED TIT *PANURUS BIARMICUS*

IDENTIFICATION

16.5 cm. Larger than Long-tailed Tit. Small, dumpy, ginger-brown bird with a long tail. Male has a lavender-grey head, black 'moustache' and black under the tail. Has white outer-tail feathers and strongly marked white, black and orange-brown wings. Female is duller and lacks the 'moustache' and the black under the tail. Juvenile similar to female, with a shorter tail, a dark centre to the back and dark edges to the tail. Wings are short and rounded. Flight is weak-looking with whirring wings. Adults moult between June and early October. Young moult at the same time; those fledged early in the season take about 55 days to moult and re-grow their primary flight feathers while those fledged later complete their primary moult in just 40 days.

male

female

juvenile

HABITS

Clambers about on reed stems or hops about on ground, usually close to cover. Flight is often loose and jerky with characteristic fanning and twisting of tail as it flies low over the tops of the reeds, but it goes higher at times of irruption. Can be hard to see in a dense reedbed and it is often the distinctive call that attracts attention. Sociable, and flocks travel together for much of the year.

VOICE

Call is a metallic ringing 'ping, ping' that may be given from cover, but also frequently by groups in flight. Song is a rather quiet twittering.

HABITAT

Found almost exclusively in dense reedbeds or vegetation around the edge of a reedbed. At times of irruptions and migrations it may sometimes visit another habitat such as rank grass.

FOOD

Feeds mainly on invertebrates and seeds. In summer, the invertebrates include beetles, caterpillars, flies, especially midges, spiders and snails. In winter, feeds on the seed of the Common Reed.

BREEDING

Breeding begins in April. Nest is built among reeds where the plants grow thickly. The nest is a deep cup made from reed leaves and other marsh vegetation, and lined with fluffy reed heads. Both sexes help to build the nest and more material may be added during egg-laying and incubation. The 4–8 eggs are incubated by both sexes for about 10–14 days. Young leave nest after 12–13 days. They are able to feed themselves after a week and become independent after another week. There may be two or possibly three broods in a season.

MOVEMENTS AND MIGRATIONS

The species is largely sedentary, although groups will form and roam the local reedbeds in winter. In autumn there is occasionally a large dispersal from a particular breeding site, triggered by cold or food shortage, and this may lead to the colonisation of new reedbeds. The species' arrival in Scotland in 1972 may have been the result of eruptions from either Leighton Moss RSPB reserve or from Denmark, or both. Oldest bird was 6 years.

POPULATION

Over 250 pairs breed in Scotland, or about 30% of the UK total. First observed in 1972, with the first breeding record in 1991. This species has since made a rapid colonisation and is now established on the Tay.

CONSERVATION

This species has been affected by the historic loss of many large reedbeds, which has resulted in a very fragmented habitat. Its population also falls if there are periods of prolonged ice and snow in winter. Better protection and improved management of the remaining reedbeds, along with recent schemes by the RSPB and other bodies to create new ones, will help this species. Also, a new technique for helping them involves making artificial nest sites within reedbeds.

DISTRIBUTION

Breeds in a few sites in east Scotland. The main stronghold in the British Isles is East Anglia and southern England, with a few notable sites elsewhere. It is locally distributed in western and southern Europe and east to China.

LONG-TAILED TIT *AEGITHALOS CAUDATUS*

IDENTIFICATION
14 cm, of which 9 cm is tail. Tiny round bird with a long narrow tail, rather short rounded wings and a stubby bill. Pinkish-brown above, pinkish-white below, with dark marks on sides of head and a white crown. Wings are blackish with pale lines caused by pale edges to the major flight feathers. Tail has white outer feathers. Eastern birds have all-white heads. Flight appears weak and undulating, with the long tail the most obvious feature. Juvenile is similar to an adult but with a smoky grey head. Adults moult between late May and early October.
SEE ALSO: Pied Wagtail p165.

flock in flight

HABITS
Highly sociable species producing large broods of young and travelling through woods and along hedges in family flocks for much of the year. They roost in groups and during cold weather huddle together to conserve body heat. Restless and acrobatic as they feed actively among branches of trees and bushes, often hanging upside down to reach food. In spring, it has a butterfly-like display flight.

VOICE
Common call is a thin, high-pitched 'see, see, see' often interspersed with a short, rolling 'thrup'. Song rarely heard – an elaborate version of the calls.

HABITAT
Breeds along deciduous woodland fringes, in scrub, hedgerows, parks and in other bushy places. Outside breeding season travels more widely and sometimes visits gardens, where there are bushes and trees.

FOOD
Feeds on invertebrates, including flies, beetles and spiders, also on eggs, larvae, pupae and adults of moths and butterflies. Also eats seeds, and has adapted to feeding at bird tables and on hanging food. This behaviour has become more widespread in recent years.

BREEDING
Nesting begins in late March and early April. Male and female build the nest in Bramble, gorse or other thick shrubs. It is a delicate round or oval structure made from moss, bound with cobwebs and lined with lots of feathers. The outside is covered in lichens. The result is a rather elastic nest that expands with the growing young inside. The entrance hole is at the side. Female incubates 6–8 eggs that hatch after about 15 days. Young fly after 15–16 days and are fed by both parents, and for a further 2 weeks or so after fledging. Some adults, especially males that fail to rear their young, frequently help to feed a neighbouring family.

MOVEMENTS AND MIGRATIONS
Most are sedentary but some make local movements after nesting. Wintering birds have a feeding territory and move around this area in flocks that are made up of families from the previous breeding season plus additional helpers. Sometimes family flocks will join together and frequently attract other small birds such as tits and warblers to travel with them. There are occasional eruptive movements, which account for small numbers arriving on Shetland and other unexpected places. The oldest known bird survived over 10 years.

POPULATION
30,000–45,000 pairs nest in Scotland. The population is stable or growing, spreading to the Inner Hebrides in recent years and some birds reaching the Outer Hebrides.

CONSERVATION
Greatest influence on this species is the winter weather, when severe frost can in a few days reduce the population. Like other small birds, Long-tailed Tit populations recover quickly from such disasters. Habitat changes have not adversely affected this species, and there is evidence it is breeding more successfully, and possibly benefiting from recent climate change.

juvenile

DISTRIBUTION
Widespread in Scotland, although scarcer in the north-west and in the uplands. Breeds throughout England, Wales and Ireland. Elsewhere, it breeds from northern Scandinavia to the Mediterranean and across into parts of the Middle East and Asia.

BLUE TIT   *PARUS CAERULEUS*

juvenile

IDENTIFICATION

11.5 cm. Smaller than Great Tit, with blue cap, wings and tail. Has a green back, yellow underparts, white cheeks and a black line through the eye. Has a small pale patch on the back of the head and small single white wing-bar. Blue cap is sometimes raised to form small crest. Males tend to be brighter than females. Juvenile is also duller than male, with greenish cap and yellowish cheeks. Adults moult between late May and September. Their moult usually begins a few days before the young leave the nest. Adults in the north start later and moult quicker than those in the south. Juveniles have partial moult between July and October.
SEE ALSO: Great Tit p202.

HABITS

Much of its food is on outer twigs and branches where it frequently hangs upside down to feed. Outside the breeding season groups of Blue Tits will join foraging parties of other small birds such as Long-tailed Tits. Some will not move far from their territories, but others are more nomadic in their search for food.

VOICE

Call is a thin 'see, see, see' and it has a churring alarm call that rises at the end. Song can be heard at any time of year, but particularly from late winter into summer. It is a 'see, see, see-chu -chu -chu' and ending with a short trill.

HABITAT

Lives in a variety of habitats, but most are in deciduous woodland, especially oak woods. Populations in conifer woods tend to be at lower densities. Also breeds in parks and gardens, and even in the centres of towns. It regularly feeds in hedgerows and other places with trees and bushes.

FOOD

Feeds mainly on insects and spiders in summer, especially caterpillars. In autumn, feeds on insects but also eats berries and nuts. Regularly visits bird tables to feed on peanuts, sunflower seeds, other bird food and household scraps.

BREEDING

Nesting generally begins in late April and early May. Male courtship feeds female. Nests in a natural hole or other crevice, usually in a tree, but may be in a building. Nestboxes are frequently used. Female builds a nest of moss, twigs and grass. The 8–10 eggs (pairs in gardens tend to have smaller clutches) are incubated by female for 13–16 days. Both adults feed the young, which leave nest after 18–21 days.

MOVEMENTS AND MIGRATIONS

Largely resident in Scotland and only a small proportion ever move more than 10 km, but it will make regular trips to feeding sites. On the Continent it often travels further and large movements may be triggered by food shortages; some of these birds arrive in Scotland in autumn. Oldest known Blue Tit survived 9 years.

POPULATION

Up to 750,000 pairs nest in Scotland. There is no evidence of any marked population change and there may even be a modest expansion of the species' breeding range and numbers.

CONSERVATION

Provision of nestboxes helps this species, both in gardens and in young woodlands where there is a shortage of suitable nest sites. Cold winter weather can significantly reduce the population as can unseasonal weather when young are being fed, especially if this coincides with the spring emergence of woodland caterpillars.

DISTRIBUTION

Widespread where there are deciduous woods in Scotland, including some of the larger islands in the Inner Hebrides and in small numbers on the Outer Hebrides. Common across the British Isles. Also found in Europe, from Scandinavia to the Mediterranean. Breeds as far east as the Moscow region of Russia.

GREAT TIT *PARUS MAJOR*

male

IDENTIFICATION
14 cm. Size of House Sparrow. Largest member of the tit family. Has a black cap, collar and throat, and a black line running down the yellow breast and belly. Cheeks are white, back is greenish and wings are blue-grey with a single white wing-bar. Blue-grey tail has white outer feathers. Male is brighter with a wider black breast-stripe that becomes wider between the legs. Juvenile is duller than both parents with yellowish cheeks. Adults moult between late May and October and may begin before the young leave the nest.
SEE ALSO: Blue Tit p201, Coal Tit p204.

HABITS
Although it sometimes occurs in small flocks and mixes with other species, it is less social than some other members of the tit family. It often feeds low down and on the ground, but it will also feed in trees and bushes although a little less acrobatic than other, smaller tits. It is often a skulking species, although in gardens it may become quite tame.

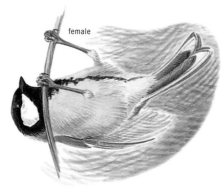

female

VOICE
Has a very wide variety of different songs and calls, and vocabulary is complex. Most familiar call is a sharp 'chink', rather like a Chaffinch, and a scolding 'cha-cha-cha' when alarmed. In flocks, makes a softer 'tsee'. Song is variations on 'teacher-teacher' which has been likened to a squeaky bicycle pump and is heard between January and June, and sometimes in autumn.

HABITAT
Breeds in deciduous broad-leaved woodland, parks, farmland, trees in hedgerows, conifer plantations where there are some suitable nest sites and also in some gardens. In winter, it may spread to other neighbouring habitats in search of food.

FOOD
Mainly insects, especially caterpillars, in summer and fruits, seeds and nuts in autumn and winter. It is capable of opening Hazel nuts, and Beech mast provides a popular food supply in years when abundant. In gardens it feeds on peanuts, sunflower seeds and kitchen scraps.

BREEDING
Nests in a hole or cavity in a tree or building and frequently uses nestboxes. Nest is of moss and is lined with hair, fur or feathers. Female incubates clutch of 7–9 eggs for 13–15 days. Young are fed by both parents. They leave the nest after about 18 days and the young continue to be cared for out of the nest for 4–6 days for first broods and longer for second broods.

MOVEMENTS AND MIGRATIONS
In Scotland mostly a resident that seldom travels far, although some nesting in upland areas move to lower areas in winter, especially in northern Scotland. In central and northern Europe it moves (or erupts) at times when the population is high and a few of these continental Great Tits, which are slightly smaller, visit the Northern Isles and east coast of Scotland. Oldest was 15 years.

POPULATION
There are 300,000–450,000 pairs nesting in Scotland. The population has been increasing since the 1960s.

CONSERVATION
In the last 100 years has gradually expanded its range northwards, perhaps aided by milder winters. A successful species that may have benefited from the food people put out in gardens in winter. Providing suitable nestboxes in areas where there is a shortage of natural nest-holes and where food is plentiful can further assist Great Tits.

juvenile

DISTRIBUTION
Widespread in the lowlands of mainland Scotland and the Inner Hebrides. Found throughout the rest of the British Isles, where it is particularly abundant in central and southern England. Breeds across Europe and Asia, and into the Far East.

CRESTED TIT *PARUS CRISTATUS*

IDENTIFICATION
11.5 cm. Size of Blue Tit. Has a brown back and pale buff underparts, rather like a Marsh or Willow Tit, but its face is off-white with a black bib, speckled forehead and crown and a long pointed crest. Has a blackish mark through the eye and curving round its cheeks. Also has a thin black collar. Juvenile has slightly less distinct head marks and slightly shorter crest, but is otherwise similar to adult. Adults have a complete moult between July and September.
SEE ALSO: Blue Tit p201.

HABITS
An active and restless feeder, constantly moving as it searches for food by hanging on tree trunks or upside down as it searches the underside of branches. After nesting it forms small social groups that will also join with other species such as Coal Tits and Goldcrests. They travel together, but seldom go beyond the boundaries of their winter feeding territory. Social flocks start to break down in February and March.

VOICE
Call is a thin high-pitched trill often repeated rhythmically. It is similar in quality to the call of Long-tailed Tit, but sharper. It also makes a high-pitched 'see, see, see' call. Song is combination of the various calls run together.

HABITAT
In Scotland usually associated with Scots Pine although it may sometimes be seen in other conifers and even in Rowan, Alder and birch in winter. When breeding, it prefers old native Scots Pine forest, especially where there are stands of older trees, often with heather nearby. Elsewhere in its range it is also associated with pine forests, but also some mixed woodland and even Beech forests are inhabited in the Pyrenees.

FOOD
Spends most of its feeding time foraging in pines, often in the larger trees in summer, and sometimes in smaller trees in winter. May feed in the crown of the trees and on the ground. Feeds mainly on insects such as moths, caterpillars, aphids and beetles and other invertebrates, especially spiders. Also feeds on seeds, particularly in winter, and sometimes, where it is common, it visits bird tables in gardens. In Norway it is known to store food, including the larvae of insects.

BREEDING
In Scotland, selects rotten tree stumps or dead trees in which the female excavates a nest chamber and lines it with moss and other soft material. Female incubates the clutch of 4–6 eggs for 13–16 days. The young are fed by both parents and they leave their nest after 18–22 days. They are usually dependent on their parents for about 23 days before becoming independent and forming pairs for the winter.

MOVEMENTS AND MIGRATIONS
Highly resident and very few have been seen away from the normal breeding areas. In the east of its range it may exceptionally wander farther in winter. Oldest known bird lived for 11 years.

POPULATION
There are 1,000–2,000 pairs in Scotland. When Scotland was more forested the species would have been more common, but currently the population is stable.

CONSERVATION
Specially protected. Protecting the remaining native Scots Pine forest, the retention of dead and decaying timber and the planting of new Scots Pine woods (rather than non-native species) will help, as will the provision of nestboxes – especially if filled with wood shavings and sawdust. These boxes give birds a chance to excavate their own nest.

juvenile

DISTRIBUTION
In Britain restricted mainly to the remnants of the old native Scots Pine forest and some mature plantation pine forests in the Highlands between the Spey valley and the Moray Firth. Often seen at Loch Garten near the RSPB's osprey centre. Breeds from central Scandinavia south to the Mediterranean and east into western Russia as far as the Balkans.

COAL TIT *PARUS ATER*

IDENTIFICATION

11.5 cm. Smaller than Great Tit. Small tit with a short tail and rather large head. Head is black with white cheeks, like Great Tit, but it also has white stripe on the back of its head. Back, wings and tail are a dull blue-grey. Underparts are plain and buff with no black central stripe and it has two small white bars on its closed wings. Those on the Continent tend to have greyer backs. Juvenile looks like a duller version of the adults with yellow (not white) wing-bars. Adults moult between late May and early September. Juveniles mostly moult before the winter, but the yellow wing-bars may be retained until the following spring.
SEE ALSO: Great Tit p202, Crested Tit p203.

HABITS

An active and very agile bird that often feeds high in the canopy of trees and also searches the trunks of trees for food, rather like a Treecreeper. Hangs upside down and also hovers to reach food on the underside of branches and leaves. Outside breeding season it frequently accompanies roving flocks of other small birds such as Long-tailed Tits and Goldcrests as they move through the woods and along hedgerows.

juvenile

VOICE

Many calls sound like a high-pitched Great Tit. Makes a thin 'see. see, see' call and has a loud song that is a repetitive double note 'pea-chew, pea-chew', but there is variety in these songs.

HABITAT

Chief habitat is conifer woods and plantations, but also common in Sessile Oak woods, and birch woods of north-west Scotland. Often visits parks and gardens outside the breeding season. Elsewhere in Europe more closely associated with conifer woods in the north and breeds in more varied woodland in the south.

FOOD

Main food is adults and larvae of insects, including caterpillars. Also feeds on other invertebrates, especially spiders, and many seeds are eaten in autumn and winter. Much of the food is found among the leaves and needles of its favourite trees, but it will feed on the ground at sites where there is a supply of food such as Beech-mast. When food is plentiful the Coal Tit will hide some of it and retrieve it later. It will also visit bird tables in gardens in winter where it will feed on peanuts and other bird food.

BREEDING

Nests in a hole in a tree or some other crevice and sometimes in the ground. Female makes a cup-shaped nest of roots, moss and other soft material. Female incubates the clutch of about 9 or 10 eggs for 14–16 days. Young are fed by both adults and leave their nest after 16 days. There is sometimes a second brood – especially by pairs nesting in conifer woods.

MOVEMENTS AND MIGRATIONS

In Scotland, it is mostly sedentary, with most birds moving no further than 10 km from their nesting sites. After the breeding season there is a tendency for young birds to roam wider and perhaps leave their native woods and forests. A few make longer movements of around 100 km. In Europe many northern and eastern populations travel further and may irrupt at times of food shortage; some of these birds may be seen on Scotland's Northern Isles and east coast. Oldest wild bird lived 8 years.

POPULATION

200,000–400,000 pairs nest in Scotland. The population increased over the last 50 years and is now regarded as stable.

CONSERVATION

For a species that is mostly resident, the abundance of food and the weather are the biggest influences on the size of the population. The Coal Tit has, therefore, benefited from the planting of commercial conifer forests and from recent mild winters.

DISTRIBUTION

Widespread on the mainland, but not breeding in the Northern Isles or most of the Outer Hebrides. Also abundant in Wales and Ireland, and in parts of England. Elsewhere it breeds from Scandinavia south to the Mediterranean and parts of North Africa, and its range extends east to eastern Asia.

WILLOW TIT *PARUS MONTANUS*

IDENTIFICATION

11.5 cm. Size of Blue Tit. Plain brown with a rather large head and thick neck, a black cap and pale cheeks. Differs from the Marsh Tit by having a different call, a dull-black crown that extends farther down the back of the head, less extensive white cheeks, a pale patch that is often apparent on the closed wing and brown (rather than grey) flanks. The black bib below the bill tends to be larger and fades into the breast (rather than having clearly defined edges) and the plumage often appears 'looser' than the rather sleek Marsh Tit. Juvenile is similar to an adult but with fresher plumage in late summer and is almost inseparable from the juvenile Marsh Tit. The race breeding in parts of northern and eastern Europe has whiter cheeks, paler underparts and a more grey-brown back than other races. Adults moult between mid-May and September.
SEE ALSO: Marsh Tit p206, Blackcap p188.

HABITS

Outside the breeding season it will often join with flocks of other small birds as they move through its territory, but will not normally follow the flock beyond the boundaries of its own winter territory.

VOICE

Call is a nasal 'eez, eez, eez' which is very different from the call of the Marsh Tit. Makes a series of nasal-sounding 'tchair' calls, but that sound is similar to one of the calls of the Marsh Tit. It also makes a harsh 'tchay' call that is unique. The sweet warbling song is not often heard. The young tend to be more noisy than young Marsh Tits when begging food from their parents.

HABITAT

Breeds in birch woods, willow scrub and other deciduous woodlands. Prefers damp woods, woods close to rivers and streams, Alder carr and other places where trees and bushes grow close to water.

FOOD

Its bill is not quite as strong as that of the Marsh Tit and the food is slightly different. Like the Marsh Tit it eats invertebrates in summer and mostly plant material in autumn and winter, but the seeds (e.g. Alder and birch) are smaller or softer. It frequently hoards food if it has the opportunity.

BREEDING

Nesting begins in mid-April. It excavates a new nest hole every year. Nests are in rotten wood and usually quite close to the ground. Female excavates the nest, carries away the wood chippings and lines the hollow with wood chips and a little plant material. The 6–8 eggs are incubated by the female alone for 13–15 days. The young are fed by both adults and fly after about 17 days.

MOVEMENTS AND MIGRATIONS

Scottish Willow Tits are highly sedentary. In Europe they may wander considerable distances and may even irrupt into new areas if food becomes scarce. The oldest ringed bird survived over 10 years.

POPULATION

There may be 300–1,100 pairs nesting in Scotland. There has been a marked reduction in numbers in recent years and this decline continues.

CONSERVATION

This species has been declining since about 1970. The lack of dead wood, the drying out of some woodland, the loss of the shrub layer caused by changing woodland management and competition for nest sites with the more numerous Blue Tits and Great Tits are all possible causes for the decline, but the complete picture is poorly understood.

juvenile

DISTRIBUTION

Apart from a small population in the Clyde area, the bird is restricted to the south-west of Scotland; a favoured area is the RSPB's Ken-Dee Marshes reserve. The species is locally distributed in parts of England and Wales. It breeds from northern Scandinavia to central Europe and east through Russia and the Far East, including Japan.

MARSH TIT *PARUS PALUSTRIS*

IDENTIFICATION
11.5 cm. Size of Blue Tit. Plain brown bird with a rather sleek black cap and pale cheeks. Best way of separating this species from the similar-looking Willow Tit is by its call. Also has a more glossy black cap that does not extend as far down the back of its neck, pale cheeks that extend farther back on the head, rather plain wings, pale grey flanks and a smaller and a well-defined black 'bib' under the bill. Juvenile has a duller cap than adult and is, therefore, even more like a Willow Tit. Adults moult between mid-May and mid-September.
SEE ALSO: Willow Tit p205, Blackcap p188.

HABITS
Usually feeds in shrubs and low vegetation and is less likely to be seen in the canopy of the trees. A restless feeder, always on the move. Can be difficult to observe in dense vegetation, but not usually shy of humans. Outside the nesting season it can sometimes be seen with flocks of other small birds. When it discovers a ready supply of food, such as sunflower seeds at a bird feeder, it will methodically secrete large numbers in nooks and crevices as a store for the future.

juvenile

VOICE
Call is a loud and clear 'pit-chu', quite unlike call of Willow Tit. Also makes a series of nasal 'tchair' calls, but that sound is similar to call of Willow Tit. Song is a series of 'chip' notes that run into each other to become a trill. Also has a more rarely heard song that is a rich 'yu-yu-yu'.

HABITAT
Breeds in open deciduous woodland, parks and farmland with woods and copses. Will visit large mature gardens, especially in winter. Often found around the shores of lochs and other water bodies.

FOOD
Feeds on insects, especially scale insects, and other invertebrates in summer. Eats seeds in autumn and winter. Often extracts the seeds from small berries, such as Honeysuckle. Has a strong bill and can tackle quite hard seeds and small nuts.

BREEDING
Nesting begins in April. Nests in natural holes and does not often use nestboxes. It may enlarge an existing hole or cavity but does not excavate its own hole, unlike the Willow Tit. Nest is usually low down. The female lines the nest with a cup of moss, hair and other soft materials. The female incubates the 7–9 eggs for 14–16 days. Young leave the nest after 17–20 days and are fed by their parents for a further week. Families stay together as a group for about 2 weeks after nesting and then the young join mixed flocks of tits and other species as they travel around local woods and hedges in search of food.

MOVEMENTS AND MIGRATIONS
This is a resident species that roams a territory of about 5–6 ha. It appears that once settled neither male nor female will leave the territory again. They may join groups of itinerant small birds passing through their territories, but they leave the flock as it reaches the territory boundary. Maximum recorded age 11 years.

POPULATION
40–50 pairs breed in Scotland. The Scottish population has never been large and is probably now stable, but in Britain as a whole there has been a large decline since the 1960s.

CONSERVATION
The recent decline may be a result of lower survival rates caused by poorer management of woodland, leading to less understorey and greater fragmentation of its habitat.

DISTRIBUTION
Scotland is at the edge of its range in Britain, with small numbers in the Borders. The species is widespread elsewhere in England and Wales, but not in Ireland. Elsewhere it is generally found from southern Scandinavia, through France and northern Spain, eastwards to Poland and the Balkans. Other races are to be found in south-east Europe and parts of Asia. Sedentary.

NUTHATCH *SITTA EUROPAEA*

IDENTIFICATION
14 cm. Size of Great Tit. Resembles a small woodpecker. Plump with long black pointed bill, rather large head, short neck, short stiff tail and short strong legs. Has blue-grey upperparts, buff underparts, chestnut on flanks and broad black stripe running through its eye to back of head. Juvenile similar to adult, but with less chestnut on the flanks. Wings are rounded at the ends. Adult has a complete moult between late May and mid-September.
SEE ALSO: Blue Tit p201, Great Tit p202.

HABITS
Rather elusive. At times can be very vocal. Its action on trees is distinctive as it moves up and down branches and tree trunks with jerky movements, often on the underside of branches. No other Scottish species descends a tree trunk head first. Also feeds on the ground and on thin branches. In winter, a resident pair defends a territory, and although they may accompany roving flocks of other small birds, they will not usually go far beyond their territories.

open with its powerful bill. It will sometimes visit bird tables to feed on peanuts and other bird food. Sometimes it hides seeds – when they are abundant – by wedging them into cracks in bark, or into crevices and covering them with moss or bark.

BREEDING
Nests in natural holes in trees and sometimes uses a hole in a wall or a nestbox. To prevent larger birds entering the nest the female reduces the size of the entrance hole with mud. The nest cavity is filled with dead leaves or pieces of bark. The 6–8 eggs are laid in April or May and incubated by the female for 16–17 days. The young are fed in the nest by both adults for 23–24 days.

MOVEMENTS AND MIGRATIONS
In general, adults seldom travel far from the woods where they nest, but juveniles may disperse a little further afield. In Scotland, juveniles dispersing further are responsible for the colonisation of new woodland. In Europe, there are irruptions and invasions of Nuthatches in some years of high population. Oldest bird lived for 12 years.

POPULATION
There are about 260 pairs in Scotland. The species first nested in Scotland in 1989 and continues to extend its range northwards, and sightings are now more frequent in the central belt.

CONSERVATION
Scotland has benefited from a growing population in England, especially in Northumberland and Cumbria. From about 1970 the species expanded its range northwards. Good forestry practices that retain deciduous trees of mixed ages help Nuthatches. Sometimes, when there is a shortage of natural holes, the birds will breed in nestboxes.

VOICE
Call is a loud 'tuit, tuit, tuit-tuit' that becomes more strident when alarmed. This call is territorial and may be heard at any time of year. Also has a loud rattling 'pee, pee, pee' trill that is most frequently heard in spring. Song is very varied and loud with whistling notes up and down the scale.

HABITAT
Found in deciduous woodland, mature woods, established parkland with old trees and mature gardens. Rarely nests in conifer woods.

FOOD
Feeds mainly on insects, such as small beetles, and also spiders in summer. In autumn and winter, eats nuts and seeds such as Hazel nuts, acorns, Yew seeds and pine cones. It gets its name from its habit of wedging the nut or seed in a crevice in the bark and hammering it

DISTRIBUTION

The species' stronghold in Britain is central England and Wales, with a small but expanding population in southern Scotland. It nests in woods such as the Hirsel in the Borders and the RSPB's Ken-Dee Marshes reserve in Dumfries & Galloway. It breeds from southern Scandinavia to the Mediterranean and North Africa, and east to Japan and South-east Asia.

TREECREEPER CERTHIA FAMILIARIS

IDENTIFICATION
12.5 cm. Smaller than Great Tit. Mouse-like with long down-curved bill and long, stiff, pointed tail feathers. Upperparts are mottled and barred brown with pale streaks. Underparts are white and the rump is a richer brown. Has a ragged pale stripe over eye and a buff wing-bar. In flight, wings are long and rounded with the wing-bar sometimes obvious. Juvenile is almost identical to an adult, but newly hatched birds still have some downy feathers on the body until early autumn.
SEE ALSO: Wren p170.

HABITS
Never still. Moves up (never down) a tree trunk or branch, often spiralling. Jerky movements are characteristic as it presses its tail against the wood for support and rapidly probes the bark for insects. Once at the top, or perhaps 16 m up a tall tree, it flies down and repeats its search on a neighbouring tree. It will often join roving flocks of tits and other small birds that move through its winter territory. Generally solitary, pairs sometimes stay together outside the breeding season. At night they roost in crevices in tree trunks and sometimes communal roosts form in winter. A favourite roost is on the trunks of a redwood tree (*Wellingtonia*) where they excavate oval hollows in the soft bark.

VOICE
Call is a thin, high-pitched 'tsee, tsee' call. Song is heard from February to April and again in autumn, a high-pitched trill followed by a warble that can be hard for humans to hear.

HABITAT
Most birds are found in woodland below 300 m. Breeds in deciduous and coniferous woods, particularly Scots Pine forests, and is scarce in spruce plantations. Also breeds in small copses, parks and gardens with mature trees and often follows roving tit flocks into thick hedges in autumn and winter.

FOOD
Diet of insects includes stoneflies, crickets, earwigs, lacewings and various caterpillars. Some small seeds are eaten in winter, especially pine or spruce.

BREEDING
Male selects potential nest sites. Female builds a nest behind loose bark or in some other cavity such as behind Ivy stems or on a building. Cavity is partly filled with local material such as small twigs and pine needles. A delicate nest cup is built of moss, spiders' webs, fine grasses, hair, feathers and other soft material. Female incubates 5 or 6 eggs for about 14 days and young are fed by both adults. Young fly after 15 days and are independent a week later. It may raise two broods a year – especially in conifer woods.

MOVEMENTS AND MIGRATIONS
Resident. It may leave its breeding territories in autumn, but most range no further than 20 km. Some northern and eastern European Treecreepers are partial migrants and occasionally reach the Northern Isles. Oldest lived for more than 8 years.

POPULATION
Between 40,000 and 70,000 pairs breed in Scotland. There was an expansion of the species' range in the 20th century, and since then the population is thought to have remained stable.

CONSERVATION
Expanded northwards in the 19th and 20th centuries, and has been assisted by new forestry plantations. For the past 30 years population has been more or less stable with the only falls being attributed to severe winter weather. The provision of specially designed nestboxes can help Treecreepers, especially in young plantations.

DISTRIBUTION
Found in much of mainland Scotland and on offshore islands such as Skye, Mull and Islay. Also found in central and northern Europe, Russia and parts of Asia. Scarce in the Low Countries, France and Spain, but there are isolated populations in coniferous forests in the mountains of southern Europe. There are other races in Asia.

RED-BACKED SHRIKE *LANIUS COLLURIO*

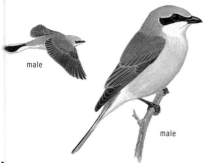

male

male

IDENTIFICATION

17 cm. Slightly smaller than Starling. Rather like small bird of prey with black hooked bill, pointed wings and rather long tail. Male has powder-blue crown and rump, reddish-brown back, pink breast, black 'mask' through its eye, and white throat. Tail is black with white sides, especially towards base. Female is duller; a rich brown, less obvious face markings and crescent-shaped marks on its pale breast and flanks. Juvenile is brown or grey-brown with barred upperparts and crescent-shaped barring on underparts.
SEE ALSO: Great Grey Shrike p248.

HABITS

Frequently perches in open: on a branch of a bush, on a fence or on some other prominent perch. When perched its tail is often fanned, flicked up and down or moved from side to side. Flight over a long distance is undulating, with a final swoop up to a perch. Flight between perches is often low to the ground. Also hovers, or makes a sudden dash after its prey. Like other shrikes it will sometimes store surplus prey in 'larders' by impaling victims on thorns or barbed wire.

VOICE

Call, a harsh 'chack, chack'. Song, a scratchy warbling, now hardly ever heard in Britain.

HABITAT

Found in open countryside with old hedges and thorn thickets, and in other open places with widely spaced bushes, including railway embankments and scrub-covered hillsides. Also inhabits birch–pine plantations, peat bogs and lowland heath. Migrants generally seen in coastal areas where there are bushes or other cover.

FOOD

Eats mainly insects, especially beetles. Also captures small birds, small mammals, and reptiles such as lizards. Sometimes pursues and catches insects in flight.

BREEDING

Nest is usually built low down in dense cover, but some are in more open positions. Male and female make the main structure from local materials such as plant stems, leaves and roots, and often incorporate paper, string and other man-made materials. Nest has a lining of softer materials. Female incubates the clutch of 4–6 eggs for 12–16 days. Both adults feed the young, which fly after 14–15 days.

MOVEMENTS AND MIGRATIONS

A passage migrant that is seen mainly in May and June and again in September and October. The spring birds are migrants heading north from Africa to their breeding grounds in Scandinavia and northern Europe. Many of the autumn birds are juveniles migrating south. The oldest known wild bird survived for over 7 years.

POPULATION

There are up to 250 sightings in spring and 100 in autumn, but these numbers are highly variable. Occasionally a pair remains for the summer to breed in Scotland. The species has declined to a point where it no longer breeds regularly anywhere in Britain.

CONSERVATION

The reason for the species being so rare is uncertain. It ceased to breed regularly in England in 1988, but after a pair nested in Caithness in 1977 there was hope of colonisation of Scotland by birds from Scandinavia. Unfortunately, the northern European population declined, and now the Red-backed Shrike breeds here only very rarely. Egg-stealing was a problem for the last few pairs, but habitat changes due to agricultural intensification and effects of a changing climate, both in Britain and on the species' migratory route, are probably important factors in its disappearance.

1st-winter

female

female

DISTRIBUTION

The species is a rare breeding bird in north-east Scotland, with more being seen in spring and autumn, mainly in the Northern Isles but also on the east coast. It is a passage migrant to the east coast of England. In Europe, it breeds from Scandinavia to northern Spain and east to Greece. Two other races occur in Siberia and Asia Minor. It winters in southern Africa.

JAY *GARRULUS GLANDARIUS*

IDENTIFICATION
34–35 cm. Smaller than Woodpigeon. Small colourful crow. Has a pinkish-fawn body, rounded head with a small pale streaked crest that can be raised in display or when the bird is excited, and a small black 'moustache'. There is a bright blue patch and also a white patch on the wing, which is delicately barred with black. The longish tail is black and the rump is white. Bill is short and powerful. In flight, wings appear broad and rounded. From behind, the white rump and black tail are distinctive. Adult has a complete moult that begins in June or July and is finished by October.

HABITS
For most of the year a secretive woodland bird that is more likely to be heard than seen. Individual birds or, sometimes, small groups will travel away from woods, especially in late summer and autumn, as they search out new supplies of food, especially acorns. On the ground it moves with a series of hops. Flight can appear laboured and 'floppy', but it is manoeuvrable in woodland. Territorial when breeding, but in spring gatherings of 3–30 Jays may take place.

VOICE
Call is a harsh screech that travels considerable distance through the woods. It also has other, less obvious calls, including a mewing sound.

HABITAT
Essentially a woodland species that lives in both coniferous and deciduous woods, especially where there are oak trees. Birds are often seen in the autumn, moving between woodland blocks as they disperse in search of food.

FOOD
Acorns are eaten all year round, and sometimes fed to the young. This is possible through the Jay's habit of hiding food and recovering it later. Food may be hidden in crevices in trees, but is most often buried and covered. Also eats insects, especially caterpillars, cockchafers and other beetles, fruits, nuts, eggs, nestlings of other birds and small mammals.

BREEDING
Nesting begins in mid-April. Nest of twigs lined with fine roots and hair is built by both adults on a branch or in a fork of a tree. Female incubates 4 or 5 eggs for about 18 days. Young are fed by both adults and leave their nest after about 21–22 days, but continue to be fed by their parents until they are 6–8 weeks old.

MOVEMENTS AND MIGRATIONS
Mainly sedentary, with British birds seldom moving more than 50 km. It is more eruptive on the Continent, and in years when there is a high population and shortage of acorns or other food large numbers of Jays may move considerable distances, generally in a westerly direction. Oldest known wild bird survived over 16 years.

POPULATION
6,000–10,000 pairs breed in Scotland. Following historical declines the population is now growing and gradually expanding northwards.

CONSERVATION
The Jay's habit of stealing eggs and young birds made it unpopular on sporting estates, and past declines were largely a result of systematic killing by gamekeepers. During the 20th century the species increased again owing to a reduction in keeping and the expansion of new forests.

DISTRIBUTION

Widespread in mainland Scotland, mainly south of the Great Glen. It is commonest in mature woodland in Perthshire, the Borders and the south-west. Breeds across much of England and Wales, and also in Ireland, where there is a separate subspecies. Beyond the British Isles there are more subspecies breeding from northern Scandinavia to North Africa and east across Asia.

MAGPIE *PICA PICA*

IDENTIFICATION

44–46 cm. Longer than Woodpigeon. Medium-sized crow that appears black and white with a very long, wedge-shaped tail. Crown of head is rather flat and bill medium-sized and powerful. Body is black with an iridescent blue-green sheen to the black wings and tail. Belly and the outer half of the wings are white. Wings are short, broad and rounded. Flight action is direct, but not fast. Male is slightly larger than female. Juvenile is duller, shorter tailed, less iridescent, and the white feathers appear dirty. Moult begins in June or July and ends in September or October.

HABITS

May be seen singly, perched on top of a bush or tree, but frequently travels in pairs or larger groups – some numbering 100 or more. Territorial when nesting, but territories may be visited by a flock of non-breeding, mainly young birds. Stores food when it is plentiful by hiding it in a scattering of locations within the territory. On the ground it walks or hops, usually with its tail lifted above the level of its back.

VOICE

Frequently noisy with a 'chacker, chacker, chacker' call that is both fast and scolding. It also has a commonly heard 'cha-ka' call and a rarely heard quiet bubbling, repetitive song.

HABITAT

Found on lowland farmland, upland moors and in towns – often close to city centres – wherever there are suitable trees for nesting – and sometimes on pylons and other man-made structures.

FOOD

Eats almost anything, from fruit and berries to carrion, and from beetles to dog faeces. Will catch and kill live prey such as small mammals and young birds and will also raid nests of other species. In general the summer food is insects and other invertebrates and the winter diet is vegetable material, but there are many exceptions to this.

BREEDING

Nest building may begin in mid-winter. Both birds build a substantial structure of twigs, small branches and mud with a softer lining. The nest is usually high in a tree or tall shrub, often in a hedgerow and sometimes in an isolated tree. Generally the nest is domed with an entrance at the side. The 5 or 6 eggs are laid from late March and are incubated by the female for about 20 days. Young leave their nest after 26 days and stay with their parents for a further 6 weeks.

MOVEMENTS AND MIGRATIONS

In the northern European populations some birds disperse after nesting and in some autumns there appears to be a local southerly movement, although it is not thought any of these birds reach Scotland. Maximum age reached is over 21 years.

POPULATION

There are 14,000–17,000 pairs in Scotland. There has been a growth in the population since the 1980s and some extension of the range northwards, but the species is still scarce or absent in the west and on the islands.

CONSERVATION

Because of their reputation for taking eggs, Magpies have long been persecuted by gamekeepers. During the 20th century fortunes reversed and Magpies increased, helped by new forests and a reduction in gamekeeping, and they colonised towns. The Magpie has retained its reputation as a destroyer of nests and eggs, but the case for it causing the decline of small-bird populations is unproven despite thorough research.

DISTRIBUTION

Patchily distributed in Scotland, mainly south of the Great Glen; commonest in the Central Belt; often in urban situations. A common resident in the rest of the British Isles except for treeless uplands. Breeds throughout most of Europe and Asia, and is also found in North Africa and North America.

CHOUGH PYRRHOCORAX PYRRHOCORAX

juvenile

IDENTIFICATION
39–40 cm. Larger than Jackdaw, but with smaller head and long, slim, red down-curved bill and red legs. Plumage is black, but appears blue and purple at close range. In flight, wings are broader than those of Jackdaw and have more obviously 'fingered' ends. Juvenile is browner with less gloss on its feathers and a shorter less-curved yellowish-pink bill that gradually becomes red. Adults completely moult their feathers between June and October. Primary flight feathers are lost and regrown over a period of 92 days.
SEE ALSO: Jackdaw p213, Rook p214.

HABITS
A master of flight as it dives and swoops with agility and ease in the up-draughts around rock-faces. Noisy. Pairs and larger groups often fly and feed together, with the largest flocks often forming in September and October. Individuals or groups will frequently feed amongst the short grass on the tops of sea cliffs.

VOICE
Usual calls have some of the qualities of a Jackdaw, but are less abrupt, higher pitched and slightly more musical, a drawn-out 'kyaa' and 'kyeow' being the most common.

HABITAT
In Scotland, it is found mostly on rocky coastal cliffs, grazed dunes and cliff-top pastures in the Inner Hebrides. It feeds on areas of short grass such as pasture, and sometimes in harvested arable fields, sand-dunes and along the tide-line of sandy beaches – scavenging the strand line. In other parts of Europe it is most numerous in inland mountains and other areas of highland where there are crags and rocky valleys.

FOOD
Insects and other invertebrates and their larvae that live in the soil, especially beetles, caterpillars, craneflies, ants, spiders and flies. It also eats worms, berries, grain, small mammals and birds. When feeding, it habitually probes, digs and turns over stones, seaweed, cow pats and other objects.

BREEDING
Nests in sea caves, other crevices in rock faces and sometimes in old buildings. The nest of sticks and plant stems is often mixed with some mud and lined with hair or wool. Female incubates the 3–5 eggs for 17–18 days. Both adults feed the young, which leave the nest at about 38 days. Other Choughs may visit the nest and help feed the young; these birds may be immatures reared by the same pair in previous years.

MOVEMENTS AND MIGRATIONS
Seldom moves far from its original nest sites, although there is a tendency for young females to move farther than young males. The main movements in Scotland are to and from feeding sites. Oldest wild bird lived for more than 16 years.

POPULATION
There were 83 pairs in 2002. There has been a historic decline in the species' range and numbers, but since 1982 the population has fluctuated, perhaps due to poor weather in the breeding season.

CONSERVATION
The population in parts of Europe has also declined and its range contracted. Loss of habitat, persecution, predation and bad weather have all contributed. Choughs require short, open vegetation with abundant soil invertebrates. This habitat is mostly associated with low-intensity grazing, but is less common due to changing farming practices.

DISTRIBUTION
Found in south-west Scotland, particularly on Islay and Colonsay, with occasional birds seen on Mull and the coast of Dumfries & Galloway. Breeds in Ireland, Isle of Man and in Wales (both on the coast and inland in Snowdonia), and has recently returned to traditional haunts around Land's End in south-west England. Also breeds in Brittany in France, parts of southern Europe including the Pyrenees and Alps, some Mediterranean islands, the Canaries, Morocco and Algeria. Other subspecies are found in Africa and Asia.

JACKDAW *CORVUS MONEDULA*

IDENTIFICATION
33–34 cm. Smaller than Carrion Crow. Neat, stocky, small crow that is mainly black, but with a slight purple sheen on its back and head, and a grey 'hood'. Eye is watery grey and the short bill and legs are black. Male is similar to female, but the grey of the male's 'hood' tends to be paler. Juvenile is more of a sooty brown with a less contrasting grey 'hood' and a darker eye. Annual moult starts between May and July and immature birds in their second year generally start before the full adults. Moult is completed sometime between August and October.
SEE ALSO: Chough p212, Carrion Crow p215, Rook p214.

HABITS
Usually seen in pairs or in flocks. Even in flocks pairs remain together and will often join flocks of Rooks or Starlings. Flight is light, agile, but can sometimes appear jerky. Also very aerobatic and individuals will often tumble and free-fall, especially around cliff-faces. Like other members of the family it frequently hides food. On the ground it has a rapid walk and sometimes runs or hops. Forms communal roosts that may be used throughout the year.

juvenile

VOICE
Call is a familiar hard 'tchack' from which it gets its name. Also makes a loud 'ky-ow'. When mobbing a predator its cawing 'kaarr' calls sound rather like Rooks and Carrion Crows.

HABITAT
Lives in a variety of habitats, from open woodland, farmland, parkland, towns, villages, mountain sides and rocky sea cliffs. May be seen feeding on grassland or pasture, alongside sheep and cattle or scavenging on the sea shore.

FOOD
Finds its food mainly on the ground, but also feeds in trees. Eats insects and other invertebrates, grain, seeds, fruits and berries, eggs and young birds. Will scavenge at rubbish tips and take a wide range of human scraps, and also visits garden bird tables.

BREEDING
Nests in loose colonies – either close together or often spaced out – depending on the nest sites available. Sites selected are holes in trees, crevices in cliffs or in buildings, including chimneys. Will also use large nestboxes. The nest of sticks is lined with wool, hair or other soft materials and is built by both adults. Female incubates the 4–6 eggs for 18–20 days. Both adults feed the young, which remain in the nest for 30–33 days. It may be a further week before the young are flying strongly.

MOVEMENTS AND MIGRATIONS
Scottish Jackdaws seldom move far from their breeding colonies – most stay within a radius of 100 km. In Europe the species is more mobile and birds undertake migrations, but it is unclear if any of these ever arrive in Scotland. Oldest known Jackdaw lived 19 years.

POPULATION
80,000–120,000 pairs nest in Scotland. The population appears to be stable, or very slightly increasing.

CONSERVATION
The Jackdaw is still regarded legally as a 'pest' species, and as a result it may be killed by landowners or people working for them. On the whole it is a successful species that has plenty of nesting places and an improved survival rate among its young.

DISTRIBUTION
Common in Scotland except for the north-west Highlands and Shetland, but scarce in the treeless uplands. Breeds throughout England, Wales and Ireland. Outside the region it breeds from southern Scandinavia to the Mediterranean, with a few in North Africa, and east across Europe and into Russia.

ROOK CORVUS FRUGILEGUS

juvenile

IDENTIFICATION
44–46 cm. Only slightly smaller than Carrion Crow with purplish-black plumage and bare greyish skin at base of bill, flattened forehead and rather peaked crown. Long, dark bill has a pale base and is more slender and pointed than a Carrion Crow's. Also wingbeats are deeper, tips of the wings narrower and more 'fingered', base of the wings is narrower where they join the body and the tail more wedge-shaped. Feathers appear 'looser', especially at the top of the legs, giving it a 'baggy trouser' look. Juvenile has feathers at base of bill and resembles a Carrion Crow, but has the different bill shape and more peaked crown. Moults between May and October, starting with first-year birds, then older females. Onset of moult is closely connected to the end of breeding.
SEE ALSO: Carrion Crow p215.

HABITS
Feathers on crown are raised when the bird is excited. Gregarious, with large autumn roosts – sometimes numbering over 10,000 individuals – forming at traditional sites. Rookeries may either be occupied throughout the year or reoccupied on sunny or mild winter days. While flight is usually direct and purposeful, individuals in flocks sometimes tumble and free-fall, especially in autumn.

VOICE
Most common call is a raucous 'kaah'. Song begins after moult has been completed and consists of not very tuneful caws, croaks and squeaks.

HABITAT
The main requirement is tall trees. In Scotland most Rooks nest in pines, but some birds uses broadleaved trees such as oak, Beech and Ash. Most rookeries are on lowland farmland, but some are in towns and villages and others on the edge of moorland. Away from the nest the Rook feeds on farmland, the verges of busy roads and rubbish tips.

FOOD
Earthworms and grain are important foods, but takes a variety of other food, including nuts, beetles, caterpillars, flies, craneflies and their larvae, small mammals, birds, especially eggs and nestlings, and carrion. Food is carried to nestlings in an extendable pouch in the base of the bird's mouth.

BREEDING
Nests are in colonies at the tops of tall trees. Rookeries vary in size from only one or two, to 2,000 nests or more.

Male selects nest site and begins the process of building before female joins in. Nest comprises large and small sticks and is solidified with earth and tufts of grass with a lining of moss, leaves and other softer material. Female incubates the 3 or 4 eggs for 16–18 days. Young are fed by both parents and fly at 32–34 days old. They continue to be fed for about 6 weeks.

MOVEMENTS AND MIGRATIONS
Most Rooks are resident within Scotland and many do not move far from their colonies. In autumn, smaller rookeries are often abandoned and the occupants join with other local Rooks to form large evening gatherings. These aggregations usually roost in woodland, sometime choosing a wood where there is already a large rookery. Rooks on the Continent are more migratory; influxes of these birds sometimes reach the Northern Isles and eastern Scotland, where they probably overwinter with locally bred birds. Oldest bird was 22 years.

POPULATION
There are between 300,000 and 500,000 nests in Scotland. The population has declined modestly over the last 50 years.

CONSERVATION
Traditionally, Rooks were shot as agricultural pests although any damage may be more than offset by their consumption of invertebrates, and much of their food is of little commercial value. A recent partial recovery in population may be due to the species being an omnivorous and opportunist feeder.

DISTRIBUTION

Breeds in lowland agricultural areas throughout Scotland but is absent from the central Highlands and much of the north-west. Widespread in England, Wales and Ireland. Breeds in central and eastern Europe, and across Russia and Asia. Winters as far south as the Mediterranean.

CARRION CROW *CORVUS CORONE*

IDENTIFICATION
45–47 cm. Slightly larger than Rook and smaller than Raven. All black with a very slightly bluish sheen. The deep bill, legs and feet are black. Sometimes inter-breeds with Hooded Crows and produces young with some of the characteristics of a 'Hoodie'. In flight, closed tail is squarer than Rook's, but more evenly rounded when spread and the wings are proportionally shorter, broader and less obviously 'fingered' at the ends. Juvenile is duller and browner than adult. Moult begins between May and July, with the second-year birds beginning to moult first. All birds complete their moult between August and October.
SEE ALSO: Hooded Crow p216, Rook p214, Raven p217.

HABITS
Not usually as gregarious as the Rook, but immatures and non-breeding adults may form small, and occa-sionally large, flocks, especially in winter. Feeds on the ground where it moves with a walk or hop. Flight is quite slow and deliberate and less aerobatic than the Rook's although it is surprisingly successful at robbing other birds, such as gulls, of their food while in flight.

VOICE
Has a variety of calls including the deep and resonant 'kaarr' and a hard 'konk, konk'.

HABITAT
It occurs in a wide variety of habitats: the centre of cities, arable farmland, pasture, upland hills, moors, woodland and sea cliffs. Will frequently visit the sea shore and estuaries to feed and is a regular visitor to rubbish tips.

FOOD
Food is very varied, including carrion, injured and young birds, mammals, eggs, insects and other inver-tebrates, especially worms and beetles, and also veg-etable matter such as grain, fruit and seeds. Adapt-able and has found a variety of sources of food.

BREEDING
The nest is usually in a tree, but sometimes on a cliff ledge, a building or a pylon. Both sexes build the nest of sticks and other tough vegetation and line it with smaller plant material. The 3 or 4 eggs are incubated by female for 18–20 days. Young are fed by both adults and leave their nest at about 30 days. They become independent after 3–5 weeks.

MOVEMENTS AND MIGRATIONS
This species is largely sedentary in Scotland. There is some dispersal after breeding but it is unusual for a

bird to travel more than 100 km. Nevertheless, this northern population is more mobile than Carrion Crows south of the border. Many birds also make local flights to join communal roosts in winter. An increas-ing number of Carrion Crows are visiting the Northern Isles and offshore installations, especially in spring. Ornithologists believe these are Scottish birds that have moved south for the winter, but have then over-shot on their return journey.

POPULATION
There are 100,000–200,000 pairs breeding in Scotland. The species increased its range and numbers during the 20th century, and that process may still be contin-uing.

CONSERVATION
The Carrion Crow is considered a pest and may be legally controlled, although the damage it does may be exaggerated. It does take eggs and chicks of other species, particularly ground-nesting birds, and this can be a problem for gamebirds such as Grey Partridge and other threatened species.

juvenile

DISTRIBUTION

Breeds in the south and east of Scotland. There is a hybridisation zone with the Hooded Crow in Argyll, Perthshire and along the north-east coast from Moray to Wick. It breeds in western Europe, from Germany to southern Spain and east to northern Italy. There is another subspecies in Asia.

HOODED CROW   *CORVUS CORNIX*

IDENTIFICATION
45–47cm. Larger than a Jackdaw. Black head, wings and tail and a pinkish-grey body with a black 'bib'. Juvenile has similar markings to the adult but is browner with a mottled back. Those nesting close to Carrion Crows will sometimes hybridise with them and produce young that have the charactistics of both species. In flight, the tail appears square when closed, but rounded when fanned, and the wings are shorter, broader and less obviously 'fingered' at the ends than a Rooks. Moult begins between May and July, with the second-year birds moulting first. All birds complete their moult between August and October.
SEE ALSO: Jackdaw p213.

HABITS
Not as gregarious as the Jackdaw, but immatures and non-breeding adults may form flocks. Mostly feeds on the ground where it hops or walks. Flight is quite slow and deliberate although it is surprisingly successful at robbing gulls and other birds in flight. It will also frequently mob large birds of prey such as Ospreys and eagles.

VOICE
Has a variety of calls including the deep and resonant 'kaarr' and a hard 'konk, konk', which may be harder and more rolling than that of Carrion Crow – although this is difficult to detect as there is considerable variation between individual birds.

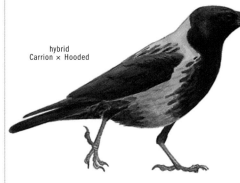

hybrid
Carrion × Hooded

HABITAT
It occurs in a wide variety of habitats: arable farmland, pasture, upland hills, moors, woodland, sea cliffs and sometimes in towns and cities. Will frequently visit the seashore and estuaries to feed and is also a regular visitor to rubbish tips.

FOOD
It has a varied diet, including carrion, injured and young birds, mammals, eggs, insects and other invertebrates, especially worms and beetles, and also vegetable matter such as grain, fruit and seeds. Adaptable and has been observed dropping shellfish, such as mussels, onto rocks in order to open them.

BREEDING
It usually tree-nests, but will use a cliff ledge in the absence of a suitable tree. Both sexes build the nest of sticks and other tough vegetation and line it with smaller plant material. The 3–6 eggs are incubated by female for 18–19 days. Young are fed by both adults and leave their nest at about 28 days. They become independent after 3–5 weeks.

MOVEMENTS AND MIGRATION
It remains in Scotland for the whole year. There are local movements to and from its communal roosts, which may sometimes involve 100 birds or more. There are also some other movements that are not properly understood, these resulting in small numbers of birds arriving on the west coast or even on the remote island of St Kilda. Traditionally, some birds were seen on the east coast in autumn and winter, and it was thought these were migrants from Scandinavia. However, these have become much scarcer in recent years, though a few are still seen in most winters.

POPULATION
25,000–45,000 pairs breed in Scotland. Numbers have been falling and the range contracting north and west for some decades.

CONSERVATION
The 'Hoodie' is legally regarded as a pest, and its numbers are still controlled on sporting estates and by shepherds. However, the main threat to the species appears to be the expansion of the range of the Carrion Crow, which has been spreading northwards while that of the Hooded Crow has been declining. Until recently, Hooded and Carrion Crows were considered to be two races of a single species, but they have now been officially recognised as two distinctly different species.

DISTRIBUTION
The Hooded Crow breeds in the west and north of Scotland. It also breeds in Ireland but is an unusual winter visitor to England. In Europe it is found in Scandinavia, Italy, Greece and Russia, and it also occurs in parts of the Middle East. Northern European birds migrate to southern Europe for the winter.

RAVEN CORVUS CORAX

IDENTIFICATION
64 cm. The largest crow, which is bigger than Buzzard. Massive all-black bird with very large and powerful bill, rather flat head, shaggy throat feathers, long wings with fingered ends. When soaring it has rather long thick neck, wedge-shaped tail and, over all, an almost cruciform shape. At close quarters the black feathers have a purplish or reddish sheen. Juveniles are similar, but a little duller with paler eyes. Adults have a complete moult that starts between April and June and ends in October.
SEE ALSO: Carrion Crow p215.

HABITS
Flight powerful, majestic and slower than that of other crows. Frequently glides and soars, but will also flip over on its back and tumble and dive, especially around cliffs and rock faces. On the ground it moves with a walk or an occasional hop. Usually seen in pairs throughout the year, but groups may gather at feeding sites and sometimes roost together. Breeding territories are usually defended all year round, even during severe winter weather.

VOICE
Voice is suitably powerful for such a large bird. Usual flight call is hollow-sounding 'kronk, kronk' or a echoing 'toc, toc, toc'.

HABITAT
In Britain and Ireland mainly a bird of western mountains and coastal cliffs, but also breeds on moorland.

been in use for very many years – and a pair tends to alternate between two traditional sites. Nest is made from large sticks, lumps of grass and moss with an inner lining of softer material. Female incubates the 4–6 eggs for 21–22 days. Both adults feed and tend the young, which leave the nest after 35–49 days. Young remain with their parents until 4–6 months after fledging.

MOVEMENTS AND MIGRATIONS
The Scottish population is sedentary, with most adults remaining around their territories for the whole year. Juveniles in their first autumn may disperse further, but only rarely more than about 50 km. Ravens in northern Europe and Asia are likely to make longer journeys. Oldest wild Raven lived for 21 years.

POPULATION
2,600–6,000 pairs nest in Scotland. The population is currently increasing, particularly on the coast, and in the south west.

CONSERVATION
Historically, the Raven was familiar as a scavenger throughout much of Scotland and, indeed, most of the rest of Britain. However, it was persecuted in Scotland by gamekeepers and by many shepherds, who saw its habits as a threat to their employment. During the latter part of the 20th century, numbers were affected by habitat change, afforestation of the uplands and agricultural intensification. More recently, the population has recovered again, benefiting from increased sheep farming and larger numbers of deer on the hills.

FOOD
Feeds chiefly on the ground where it takes carrion, mammals, birds and eggs, insects and other invertebrates. Sometimes at a carcass it feeds on the blowfly maggots rather than rotting meat. Like other crows, known to habitually store food when it is plentiful.

BREEDING
Nesting starts early in the year, with most eggs laid between mid-February and mid-April. Nest is usually on a cliff ledge, but sometimes in a tree or on a man-made structure. Nest sites are often reused – some have

DISTRIBUTION
Widespread in the north and west. More local along the east coast and in upland areas managed as grouse moors. Elsewhere it breeds from the Arctic south to Portugal and east into the Caucasus, and also in Asia. Other races are found in Iceland, in the Faeroes, around the Mediterranean, in the Sahara, in Asia and in North America.

STARLING STURNUS VULGARIS

1st-winter

fresh, autumn

juvenile

male

IDENTIFICATION
21.5 cm. Smaller than Blackbird. Stocky bird with pointed bill that is dark in winter, but turns yellow in breeding season. Feet and legs also change from brown to pink in spring. Feathers are blackish and strongly tinged with a green-blue sheen. In autumn, plumage is speckled with white. In spring, male is slightly less spotted and more glossy than female and its yellow bill has a blue base. In flight, wings are almost triangular and the short tail is square-ended. Moults between late May and early October, with those in the north starting later than those in the south. Fresh autumn plumage is spotted, but the spots wear away during the winter.
SEE ALSO: Blackbird p181.

HABITS
On the ground it has a jerky walk. Flight is straight and direct. Feeds in groups during the day and forms large roosts in the evening (some roosts attract thousands of birds) which frequently performs breathtaking aerial manoeuvres. Bathes in water at any time and sometimes sunbathes during the summer months.

VOICE
Has a 'tcheerr' call. Both sexes sing throughout year, but especially before egg-laying. Song consists of harsh and rattling notes, including wheezy warbling and musical whistles, and often incorporates calls of other birds such as chickens, curlews, ducks. Mimics noises such as telephones and car alarms. Song is often accompanied by a visual signal, when the throat feathers are ruffled and the wings waved energetically.

HABITAT
Feeds on open grassland that, in Scotland, may be garden lawns, farm fields, playing fields and parks. It is adaptable and exploits rubbish tips, the strand line or town centres. Nests in suburban estates, trees in open countryside, farms and towns.

FOOD
Probes for cranefly larvae (leatherjackets), but also eats spiders, caterpillars and other invertebrates. It sometimes catches insects in the air, such as 'flying ants'. In autumn and winter it eats soft fruit and seeds.

BREEDING
Nests in holes in trees, rocks, and buildings. Male starts building an untidy nest of leaves and grasses that is completed by female before egg-laying. Both adults incubate the 4 or 5 eggs, but female takes longer shifts. Incubation lasts 12–15 days. Young are fed by both parents and remain in the nest for about 21 days. They are fed by their parents for a few days before joining other young birds and forming summer flocks. Mating system is flexible and pairs may change mates between broods. Male sometimes has several females, and it is not uncommon for females to dump their eggs in another Starling's nest. It may have two broods.

MOVEMENTS AND MIGRATIONS
Resident and sedentary in Scotland, with some movements away from uplands in autumn. Young disperse after becoming independent and roam the countryside – sometimes in large flocks. Those in northern and central Europe are migrants; they leave their breeding sites to winter farther south or west. Some migrants reach Scotland in autumn and leave again in spring. Oldest bird survived 22 years.

POPULATION
170,000–300,000 pairs nest in Scotland, with the population in winter possibly rising to 3 million birds. There are 10,000–20,000 pairs nesting on Shetland, these belonging to a distinct subspecies known, appropriately, as the Shetland Starling. In Britain as a whole, the Starling has been declining sharply for some years. This trend has affected Scotland less, but numbers have declined since the early 1970s.

CONSERVATION
The surprising decline of the Starling in Britain is attributed partly to agricultural change and the loss of permanent pasture. So far it appears Scottish birds have not been affected to the same degree. Improved building maintenance has resulted in the loss of some nest sites in buildings, especially for urban birds. These birds can be helped by the provision of nestboxes.

DISTRIBUTION

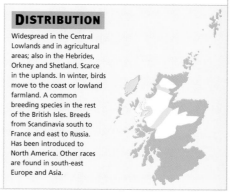

Widespread in the Central Lowlands and in agricultural areas; also in the Hebrides, Orkney and Shetland. Scarce in the uplands. In winter, birds move to the coast or lowland farmland. A common breeding species in the rest of the British Isles. Breeds from Scandinavia south to France and east to Russia. Has been introduced to North America. Other races are found in south-east Europe and Asia.

HOUSE SPARROW   *PASSER DOMESTICUS*

males

female

IDENTIFICATION

14–15 cm. Familiar small plump bird with thick bill, which becomes black when breeding, and rather short legs. Male has a chestnut-brown back with blackish marks, brown head with a grey crown, pale grey underparts, grey cheeks and a black bib. Has a small white wing-bar. Female and juvenile have streaked backs, pale underparts and cheeks, pale brown, not grey, crown and often a distinct straw-coloured line above and behind the eye. Flight is rapid with whirring wings. Moults between July and October with males beginning before females. Fresh plumage has pale fringes to many of the feathers that obscure the brighter colours until the breeding season.
SEE ALSO: Tree Sparrow p220.

HABITS

Historically it has been associated with human activity and uses buildings as nest sites. Can be both tame and wary. Feeds mainly on ground, but has adapted to take food from hanging bird feeders, and will some-times chase flying insects. A social species, often nesting in colonies and feeding in flocks throughout the year. In winter, flocks may be large and it often forms evening roosts. Sometimes engages in aerial chases of other species, especially pigeons.

VOICE

Makes several simple calls, and insistent chirping and churring notes. Song is monotonous repetition of a single chirp.

HABITAT

Usually lives on cultivated land near houses and other buildings, also in towns, parks, gardens, farmyards and industrial areas with open ground.

FOOD

Forages around domesticated animals. Also eats seeds from plants such as docks and rushes. Takes household scraps, eats peanuts from bird feeders, scavenges litter and visits rubbish tips. Nestlings are fed on inverte-brates such as aphids, weevils and caterpillars.

BREEDING

Pairs often stay together for life, but infidelity accounts for 10–20% of young. Both adults build the loose round nest of grass and straw with a side entrance. Usually it is in a hole or crevice and sometimes in a House Martin's nest. Some nests are in a tree or bush, under the eaves of a house, or on some other structure. Incubation of the 4 or 5 eggs is by both adults and lasts for 11–14 days, with the female taking the largest share. Both parents feed the young. The young leave the nest at 14–16 days and are fed for a further 11–19 days. There are two or three broods, and nests have been observed in nearly every month of the year.

MOVEMENTS AND MIGRATIONS

Most House Sparrows are sedentary. Young disperse from their nest sites, but generally nest close by. Adults may commute to rich feeding areas. Juveniles from northern and eastern Europe make migrations. Oldest ringed bird was over 19 years old.

POPULATION

600,000–900,000 pairs nest in Scotland. The wide-spread decline noted in southern England has not occurred in Scotland, but numbers are now lower than in the 1970s. Declines have been most noticeable in urban areas, especially Edinburgh, and on upland hill farms that no longer grow crops.

CONSERVATION

The extent of the decline of the House Sparrow is sur-prising. Across Britain the fall was 62% between 1974 and 1999, and this has continued, albeit more slowly. The species has disappeared from strongholds like town centres and suburban gardens, as well as from the wider countryside. The farmland decline has been attributed to agricultural changes – such as autumn sowing, result-ing in fewer stubble fields; more efficient harvesting; and the loss of weed seeds. The species' disappearance from gardens and towns is more of a mystery. What is clear is that survival of young in some localities is not sustainable owing to food shortages.

DISTRIBUTION

Widespread in Scotland, missing only from the highest mountains. One of the most widespread species in the world, having been introduced into every continent except Antarctica. In Europe it breeds from north of the Arctic Circle to the Mediterranean.

TREE SPARROW *PASSER MONTANUS*

IDENTIFICATION
14 cm. Slightly smaller, sleeker and neater with more rounded head than House Sparrow. Plumage similar to House Sparrow but has pale collar around back of neck, chocolate-brown cap with no grey on crown, small isolated dark patch on cheeks and smaller black bib. Also has double white wing-bar that can be difficult to see in the field. Male and female look alike. Juvenile is duller than the adult. Adults moult between June and September, but there is little change in the overall appearance at this time.
SEE ALSO: House Sparrow p219.

HABITS
Rather shyer than House Sparrow, but in flight it is a little more agile. Less associated with humans in Europe, although in parts of Asia it fills a similar niche to the House Sparrow and is common around houses. A social species that nests in loose colonies. In winter, will join flocks of House Sparrows, finches and buntings.

VOICE
Basic call is a distinct 'chip' that is higher pitched than call of House Sparrow. Rudimentary song is a variation on call 'chip, chip, chippi, chip'.

juvenile

HABITAT
Nests in places where there are suitable nest holes. These include open woodland, farmland with hedges and hedgerow trees, parks, orchards and quarries. In winter, feeds on agricultural land, especially any stubble or other unploughed fields.

FOOD
It eats seeds from grasses, cultivated cereals such as Wheat and Barley and also seeds from small wild herbs. It takes small invertebrates such as aphids, caterpillars, weevils and beetles. Food is found in trees, on the ground and also, to a lesser extent, by catching insects in flight.

BREEDING
It nests in holes and crevices in trees, buildings, cliff faces and in banks, including Sand Martins' nest holes, and can be encouraged to use nestboxes. It uses the same one or two sites year after year. Sometimes it usurps a site that is already being used by another species and builds a nest on top of an existing nest, even if that first nest contains eggs or young. Both adults help build the nest and incubate the 5 or 6 eggs for 11–14 days and both adults feed the young, which fly after 15–18 days. Once out of the nest, parents continue to look after young for a further 10–14 days. There are two or three broods a year.

MOVEMENTS AND MIGRATIONS
It is mainly sedentary. Young disperse from their breeding areas, but seldom travel far. Some breeding in northern Europe and Russia make short migrations. However, when the population is large there are occasional eruptions of birds away from their breeding areas in autumn and some will then cross the North Sea. The oldest wild bird survived over 13 years.

POPULATION
4,600–8,100 pairs nest in Scotland. Like populations elsewhere in Britain, the species has declined sharply here in recent years, but nestbox schemes and the retention of set-aside have helped it in some localities.

CONSERVATION
The decline appears to be similar to the falling populations of other farmland birds. Intensification of agriculture, especially autumn-sowing reducing the number of stubble fields, the use of herbicides and insecticides, and the loss of insect-rich wetlands have all combined to make winter survival more difficult.

DISTRIBUTION

Fairly widely distributed in Scotland on agricultural land, mainly in the south, the Central Belt and the lowlands near the east coast. South of the border and in eastern Ireland, it has a similar localised distribution. Also found across Europe and Asia, including Scandinavia, the Mediterranean region and North Africa.

CHAFFINCH FRINGILLA COELEBS

male

male

IDENTIFICATION

14.5 cm. Size of House Sparrow. Plump finch with medium-sized bill, slightly peaked crown, rather long wings, white shoulder-patch and a white stripe in its wing. Tail is quite long with white outer feathers. Rump is greenish. Male has blue-grey head, pinkish-brown breast and cheeks, and chestnut back. The white in the wing forms a distinctive pattern on the closed wing and is also an obvious feature in flight. Female is paler yellowish brown and has the same pattern in the wing. Juvenile is similar to female but lacks greenish rump. Adults moult between June and September. After moult birds are less colourful, but pale tips of the new feathers abrade during the winter and gradually reveal the contrasting breeding plumage.
SEE ALSO: Brambling p222, Bullfinch p234.

HABITS

Flight is undulating and the white wing marks are prominent. Forms flocks outside of the breeding season, sometimes joining with other finches, buntings and sparrows. In winter, single-sex flocks of all males or all females are frequently seen. Perches in trees and bushes, but generally feeds on the ground.

VOICE

Sings mainly between February and June. Song is short, fast and rather dry. It is a descending series of trills that accelerates and ends with a flourish. Call, which may be heard throughout the year, is a loud 'pink, pink'.

HABITAT

Widespread, nesting wherever there are trees or bushes: in coniferous and deciduous woodland, scrub, hedges with trees, parks and large gardens. Feeds in open areas: on lawns, on the woodland floor, but mainly on farmland outside the breeding season.

FOOD

Eats seeds from a very wide variety of plants, such as goosefoot, chickweed and grasses, but in summer it feeds on insects, especially caterpil-

male
(fresh, autumn)

lars and other invertebrates that it finds in trees and bushes. Eats Beech mast when it is plentiful.

BREEDING

Pairs form in late winter. Female builds a beautifully neat cup-shaped nest into the fork of a tree or tall bush. It consists of an outer layer of lichen and spiders' webs and inner layers of moss and grass with a lining of tiny rootlets and feathers. The 4 or 5 eggs are laid between late April and June. Female alone incubates the eggs, which hatch at about 12 days. Both parents feed the young. Most young leave their nest after 13 days and their parents continue to feed them for a further 3 weeks.

MOVEMENTS AND MIGRATIONS

It is both sedentary and migratory. Most Scottish Chaffinches do not move more than 10 km from their nests – a few travel further, but a movement of more than 100 km would be highly unusual. Some birds nesting in upland forests move downhill, away from snow and ice, but most will return to their territory year after year. Other populations are migratory – some birds from Scandinavia are seen on the Northern Isles and along the east coast in autumn. Oldest known bird survived 14 years.

POPULATION

There are 1–1.5 million pairs breeding in Scotland, making this species one of the commonest passerines here. Given the variations of other bird populations, the Chaffinch is remarkably successful and its numbers remain stable.

CONSERVATION

Has benefited from the planting of new forests in upland areas. Numbers appeared to fall in the 1950s and it was assumed this was as a result of agro-chemicals used on agricultural land, but have since recovered.

female

DISTRIBUTION

One of the most widespread and abundant birds in Scotland. Breeds wherever there are trees and bushes and is therefore scarce on some of the northern islands. Also breeds from northern Scandinavia to the Mediterranean and into western Asia. There are other races in north-west Africa.

BRAMBLING *FRINGILLA MONTIFRINGILLA*

male

male

IDENTIFICATION
14 cm. Similar in size to Chaffinch with marginally shorter and more deeply forked tail, and stubbier bill. Chief differences are the long white rump, which shows best in flight, white belly, no white outer tail-feathers and an orange breast and shoulder patches. Male in spring is striking with a black head and back. In autumn and winter the black areas become mottled brown and the orange less bright. Female is orange-brown with a mottled back and a mottled brown head with grey on the sides and back of neck, and duller orange breast. Juvenile resembles female but is paler. Has a complete moult between July and September after which the bright plumage is obscured by the pale fringes to the newly grown feathers. These fringes wear away to reveal the bright plumage in late winter.
SEE ALSO: Chaffinch p221.

HABITS

female

This is the 'northern Chaffinch' and it resembles that species in many ways. Gregarious outside breeding season and large flocks sometimes form in winter. There are occasional reports of more than 1,000 birds flocking in Scotland. Food supplies are irregular and the presence or absence of Brambling flocks in a locality changes from year to year, depending on the food supply.

VOICE
Call, heard both in flight and when perched, is a rising 'tchway'. Song, which is rarely heard in Britain or Ireland, is a slow, wheezing 'dzwee'.

HABITAT
As most Bramblings are seen in winter they are mostly concentrated around supplies of food – especially Beech trees that produce crops of Beech mast. They feed on the ground and may be seen on farmland, woodland glades, country parks and sometimes in gardens.

FOOD
In winter, chiefly a seed-eater that finds its food on the ground, taking a wide variety of seeds, especially Beech mast. Regularly visits feeding stations at reserves and country parks. In summer, feeds mainly on insects such

male (fresh, autumn)

as beetles and the caterpillars of moths that it finds in trees and bushes. Also catches insects in the air.

BREEDING
A very rare breeding species in Scotland. Female builds the nest in a fork of a tree or bush. Nest is larger and more untidy than that of Chaffinch. It is made from grass, small roots, lichen and pieces of bark, and lined with hair and feathers. Female incubates the 5–7 eggs for 11–12 days. Both adults feed the young, which leave the nest after 13–14 days.

MOVEMENTS AND MIGRATIONS
Mainly a winter visitor to Scotland. Birds from northern Europe migrate south-west on a broad front to winter mostly in central and southern Europe. Flocks congregate where food is plentiful; these locations can change from year to year depending on the quantity of mast found on Beech trees. Many birds from Norway and other parts of Scandinavia arrive in Scotland in late September and October. Some continue their migration southwards, while others form the Scottish wintering population. Most leave Scotland in April and May, but some males linger and may be heard singing, and very rarely breeding takes place. Oldest bird was 14 years.

POPULATION
One or two pairs breed in some years. The winter population is highly variable, numbering between 1,000 and 100,000 birds.

male 1st-year
(fresh, autumn)

CONSERVATION
A rare breeding species that is specially protected. The first successful breeding in Scotland was in 1981, and in 1982 up to nine pairs were seen in potential breeding habitat. This apparent colonisation did not continue, and now only one or two pairs are found in some years.

DISTRIBUTION

Mainly a passage migrant and winter visitor to Scotland; found mostly in the Central Lowlands and eastern areas. Winters commonly in England, Wales and Ireland. Breeds from Scandinavia east to Siberia, and winters in southern and western Europe.

GREENFINCH CARDUELIS CHLORIS

male

male

IDENTIFICATION

15 cm. Similar in size to House Sparrow. Chunky-looking finch with large head, rather short, slightly forked tail and heavy-looking conical bill. Male is olive-green with brighter back and rump and bright yellow patches in wings and tail. Female is duller than male with less yellow and slightly streaky upperparts. Juvenile similar to female but browner. Adults have a complete moult between July and November. Feathers are duller after moult and brighten towards the breeding season owing to feather wear.

SEE ALSO: Siskin p225, Goldfinch p224, Common Crossbill p231.

HABITS

Undulating flight. Usually seen feeding in small groups or, in winter, in larger flocks. Will often join flocks of other finches, buntings and sparrows and sometimes gathers in large communal roosts. Feeds on the ground and in trees, and will feed like tits on hanging bird feeders in gardens. A dominant species at a feeder and will often drive away other species. Sings from high perches and has a song-flight in which it makes deep, slow, exaggerated wingbeats with its body rolling as it weaves among the trees.

VOICE

Song is heard mainly between March and July. Makes a variety of wheezy notes and trills, repetitive 'too-eee', and loud twittering trill that is often followed by a drawn-out wheezing 'dzeee'. In flight gives a repeated 'chichichichi' and a dry 'jup, jup, jup'.

female

HABITAT

Widespread in lowlands in woods, plantations, gardens with trees and bushes, churchyards and farmland with tall hedges. In winter, even more widespread and feeds on farmland, woods, gardens and the sea shore.

FOOD

Eats a variety of seeds, including chickweed, groundsel and dandelion. Will also take grain from cereal crops and it will visit garden bird feeders where it feeds on peanuts, sunflower seeds and other bird food. Its bill can open larger seeds and it favours Dog's Mercury in summer, Yew and Hornbeam in autumn, and rose and Bramble in winter.

juvenile

BREEDING

Female builds a nest in a tall shrub or small tree. It is a bulky structure of twigs, moss, grass and lichen and lined with rootlets, hair and other soft material. It lays 4 or 5 eggs, incubated by the female for 12–14 days. Both adults feed the young, which leave the nest after 13–16 days. The parents feed the young out of the nest, and the male may continue alone if the female starts another brood. There are two and sometimes three broods in a season.

MOVEMENTS AND MIGRATIONS

Mostly sedentary in Scotland – while birds will frequently move to new feeding areas and roosts, the majority seldom travel more than 10 km. A few make longer movements, perhaps undertaking short migrations within Scotland. It seems likely that some of the birds that breed in Scandinavia and Russia may join the Scottish wintering population. Oldest bird lived for 12 years.

POPULATION

The Scottish breeding population comprises 120,000–250,000 pairs. Numbers have increased in recent years.

CONSERVATION

This is a successful species that has maintained its population at a time when other birds that depend on agricultural land have declined. Feeders in gardens are believed to have helped it. The increase in Oilseed Rape as a common farm crop may also be important in maintaining numbers. Oldest bird lived 12 years.

DISTRIBUTION

Widespread in Scotland, with the largest numbers on lowland arable farms and along the east coast in winter. It is a common resident throughout the rest of the British Isles, and from Scandinavia south to North Africa and east into Russia.

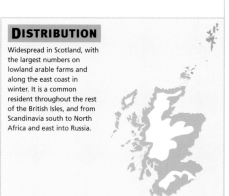

GOLDFINCH *CARDUELIS CARDUELIS*

IDENTIFICATION
12 cm. Smaller and slimmer than Chaffinch. Delicate, small finch that has sandy brown body with white belly, black wings with broad yellow bar, black tail with white marks, red face, black crown and white cheeks. Bill is quite long and thin, and is pale with a dark tip. Female is similar, but slightly duller with less red on the face. Juvenile has similar wing and tail marking to adults, greyer and streaky body and no red on the face. Flight is particularly 'bouncy' but the black and yellow wings are not always easy to see on a flying bird. Adults moult after the breeding season with some individuals beginning in July and others not completing their moult until October. After moult birds appear less colourful, until the tips of the newly grown feathers wear away.
SEE ALSO: Greenfinch p223, Siskin p225.

HABITS
Usually seen in small groups outside the breeding season. These groups are often family parties but larger flocks sometimes form around popular feeding areas in autumn and winter. Frequently seen feeding with other finches.

VOICE
Most common call that is often given in flight, is a pleasant tinkling 'whit-a-whit, whit', heard all year round and is often the best clue to the bird's presence. Song is a liquid tinkling with trills and more nasal notes.

HABITAT
Breeds where there are scattered bushes and small trees. Uses gardens, parks, orchards, cultivated land and also the edges of woods. Feeds on open land, such as industrial wasteland and roadside verges where there are low-growing plants.

FOOD
Feeds mainly on or near the ground. Its relatively long bill and its light weight allows it to extract seeds from thistles, teasels, dandelions, burdocks, groundsels and ragworts. Also takes the seeds from garden plants such as forget-me-not, aster and pansy. Recently it has started to take food from hanging bird feeders. Insects and other invertebrates are also eaten, especially in summer.

BREEDING
Nest often seems precarious; built towards the end of a branch of a small tree or tall bush. It is a neat cup made by the female from moss, small roots, grasses, lichen and lined with plant down, hair and feathers. The 4–6 eggs are incubated for 13–15 days. Young hatch after 14–17 days. After leaving the nest they are fed by their parents for a week. Usually two, sometimes three broods.

MOVEMENTS AND MIGRATIONS
A partial migrant. Fewer are present in winter, as many move south. Some remain in Scotland, but others winter in England and a few reach Belgium, France and Spain. More females leave than males, and some individuals migrate in some winters and not others. There is passage of birds in the Northern Isles and along the east coast in spring and autumn, and it is assumed that many of these are migrants from northern Europe. Oldest bird was 11 years.

POPULATION
40,000–60,000 pairs breed in Scotland. The population has been increasing steadily in range and numbers.

CONSERVATION
The Goldfinch was once captured in large numbers and kept as a cage bird, but as this tradition largely died out, so numbers of wild birds increased. The

juvenile

population grew during much of the 20th century, with birds spreading northwards; this continues today with the recent colonisation of Strathspey and most of the Inner Hebrides. The species has also taken advantage of gardens and bird-feeders. Agricultural changes have reduced some 'weedy' areas in the countryside, but fields of Oilseed Rape have provided an alternative food supply, as has the introduction of wild-bird cover crops for game species.

DISTRIBUTION

In Scotland, the Goldfinch breeds in the lowlands and in upland valleys, to an altitude of about 300 m, and is absent from much of the north and west. It is widespread in most of England, Wales and Ireland. Elsewhere it breeds from southern Scandinavia to North Africa and across into western Asia. In winter, some migrants reach the Middle East. It has been introduced to Australia, New Zealand and Argentina.

SISKIN *CARDUELIS SPINUS*

male

IDENTIFICATION

12 cm. Smaller than Greenfinch. Small, lively finch with distinctly forked tail and rather long narrow bill. Male has streaky yellow-green body with pale belly and blackish crown and bib that varies in intensity from bird to bird. Rump is greenish yellow and it has yellow wing-bars and yellow sides to its tail. Female is paler, greyer and more streaky than male. Juvenile is duller and browner than female and more heavily streaked. Adult has a complete moult between June and October. After moulting, the black cap and bib of the male is obscured by pale feather-tips until the tips wear by spring.
SEE ALSO: Greenfinch p223, Common Crossbill p231.

HABITS

Mostly feeds near the tops of trees and is less common on the ground than most other finches. Resembles a member of the tit family as it often hangs upside down on a branch or twig to reach food, and is attracted to bird feeders in gardens. Flight is light and bouncy. Sociable outside the breeding season and sometimes forms large flocks in winter. Has a song flight in which it circles with tail spread and with slow exaggerated wingbeats.

female

VOICE

Call, frequently given in flight, is a clear, loud 'tsuu' or a ringing 'tszing'. Song is a sweet twittering that includes a drawn-out wheeze.

HABITAT

It nests mainly in coniferous forests, but will also use birch woods. It has been able to adapt to feed on the seeds of Sitka Spruce and European Larch, and is thus found in many of the new plantation forests.

FOOD

Feeds on seed, especially from spruce and pine trees. Also eats seeds from Alders and Silver Birches. Feeds on the seeds of plants such as dandelion, dock, thistle and Meadowsweet. Eats insects and other invertebrates in summer and sometimes feeds on peanuts in gardens.

BREEDING

Nesting season depends on the food supply. It nests in late winter or early spring when there has been a good crop of spruce seeds, but if the crop fails breeding may be delayed until May or June. The small neat cup-shaped nest is built by female from conifer twigs, grass, heather, moss and spiders' webs, and lined with hair and other soft material. Female incubates the 3–5 eggs. Both adults feed the young, which fly at 13–15 days.

juvenile

MOVEMENTS AND MIGRATIONS

Birds that feed on conifer seeds need to be mobile, as the supplies of their food vary from year to year and from place to place. Some move to new forests, while others supplement their food by visiting lowland woods or garden feeders. In autumn, many Scottish birds move south of the border and some travel further into Europe. Other Siskins from northern Europe arrive in the Northern Isles and along the east coast in September and October, but it is uncertain how many will stay in Scotland for the winter and how many will continue southwards to England and beyond. Oldest bird was 13 years.

POPULATION

This is a very difficult species to census, but there are likely to be between 500,000 and 3.5 million pairs breeding in Scotland. There has been a rapid population growth in recent years in response to the planting of European Larch, Sitka Spruce and pine forests.

CONSERVATION

Extended its range during the 20th century due to the planting of commercial conifer forests. The population depends on spruce seeds being available. Siskins move on if the cone crop fails, which happens periodically. Winter feeding in gardens can help when other food is in short supply.

male   female

DISTRIBUTION

An abundant species over much of Scotland that spreads its range even wider in winter. It also nests in England, Wales and Ireland where there is suitable habitat. Its breeding range extends from close to the Arctic Circle south to the Pyrenees and east into Russia and Asia Minor.

ROSEFINCH
CARPODACUS ERYTHRINUS

male 1st-year

female

male

IDENTIFICATION
14.5–15 cm. Size of House Sparrow, with short bulbous bill, round head, beady eye set in plain face, and distinctive call. Wings brown with two pale wing-bars. The longish brown tail is deeply notched. Older males have reddish-pink head, breast and rump; younger males lack the red colouring and have mainly plain brownish upperparts and off-white lightly streaked underparts. Has dumpy, short-necked appearance. Female resembles a young male and is rather nondescript olive-brown. Juveniles are like female but more heavily streaked. Adults moult in their winter quarters, between September and November. After moulting the red of male is subdued, and becomes brighter during the winter due to the wear of the feathers.
SEE ALSO: Crossbill p231, Lesser Redpoll p229, Linnet p227.

HABITS
Males breed in their first year, before they have the bright red plumage. In Scotland generally seen singly at migration times. May mix in with flocks of House Sparrow, Linnets or Greenfinches. Feeds mainly on the ground, flying to a fence, wires or bushes if disturbed. Forms groups and larger flocks on its Asian wintering grounds.

VOICE
Most usual call is a loud 'chew-ee, chew-ee' like the contact calls of young Willow Warblers but louder and the first syllable harsher. Song is a simple, but very variable 'swit-too-swit-too'.

HABITAT
In Scotland generally a passage migrant that arrives in coastal areas and may be seen in low scrub or small trees. Those few that establish territories select open country with clumps of trees for song posts and scrub or thick hedges for nest sites. Where it is most numerous it often selects swampy areas and wet woodland.

FOOD
Seeds and buds from trees such as Rowan and Alder. Also berries from honeysuckle, Elder and Juniper. Diet includes weed seeds, grain and some insects such as aphids.

BREEDING
Female builds a loose-structured nest of plant stems and grass, lined with roots and hair. Nest is usually in a low bush or other dense cover. Female incubates 4–6 eggs for 11–12 days and young stay in the nest for 10–13 days while both adults feed them. Young often leave the nest before they can fly and both parents continue to care for them for about 2 further weeks.

MOVEMENTS AND MIGRATIONS
Summer migrant to Europe that arrives in May and leaves again by August or September. Regularly appears in Scotland in spring and autumn. Most are seen near the coast and the largest numbers are recorded in the Northern Isles. Occasionally, a pair will stay and attempt to breed. In Asia some migrate for the winter, others that live in mountains migrate downhill to a more hospitable climate. Oldest ringed bird was over 9 years.

POPULATION
There have been five breeding records in Scotland, the first in 1982. Numbers seen on passage vary widely from year to year, with 10–96 in spring and up to about 100 in autumn. The largest numbers of passage migrants are reported from the Northern Isles, with smaller numbers along the east coast in weedy fields.

CONSERVATION
Following its expansion across northern Europe, the arrival of the Rosefinch had been expected. It is specially protected at all times, but there is no other conservation action that will help it except, regrettably, secrecy to ensure breeding pairs are not disturbed and their nests robbed by egg collectors.

DISTRIBUTION

Mainly seen in the Northern Isles and along the east coast in spring and autumn. Also visits the east and south coasts of England. Elsewhere its stronghold is in Russia, but it is also found over much of northern Asia and eastern Europe. In recent years it has gradually been spreading westwards. It winters in southern Asia.

LINNET CARDUELIS CANNABINA

IDENTIFICATION
13.5 cm. Smaller than House Sparrow. Small slim finch, with longish, forked tail and short bill. Has white edges to the flight feathers, which form a short white panel that shows on both the closed and open wing. Has white edges to brown tail. Male has an unmarked chestnut back, crimson patches on either side of breast, crimson forehead and grey head. Female is more streaky and lacks any crimson marks. Juvenile is similar to female but slightly paler and more boldly striped. Moults between July and October. After moulting males are browner and more streaky without red foreheads and breasts. The bolder, distinctive spring plumage emerges as the dull tips of the autumn feathers wear away.
SEE ALSO: Redpolls pp229–230, Twite p228.

BREEDING
Usually breeds in colonies. Eggs are laid from mid-April. Female builds the nest – made from grasses, small roots, small twigs and lined with hair or wool – in a low bush or tussock. Early nests often in evergreen shrubs such as gorse or in bramble. Female incubates the 4 or 5 eggs for 13–14 days. Both adults feed the young for 13–14 days. Together with the Twite is unique among British and Irish finches in feeding its young entirely on seeds. The parents continue to feed them for a further 14 days or so and there may be two or three broods.

MOVEMENTS AND MIGRATIONS
Linnets may be seen in all seasons, but they become more nomadic outside the breeding season, with flocks gathering where food is abundant. In autumn birds withdraw from uplands and move towards the coast. A few may cross the border and leave Scotland, while others from the Continent – probably Scandinavia – arrive in the Northern Isles. Oldest bird survived 9 years.

POPULATION
70,000–90,000 pairs breed in Scotland. The Linnet population fell between 1970 and 2000, but since then there has been a partial recovery.

male

male

female

juvenile

HABITS
Nervous species that is difficult to approach. More often seen on the ground or in low bushes than in trees. Outside the breeding season it is seen in flocks and sometimes forms large roosts in the evenings. Some flocks comprise only Linnets but others associate with other finches and buntings. Flight is light and wavering.

VOICE
Song of male, which may be heard at any time of year, but especially in spring, is a rather fast and pleasant warbling that has a slightly wheezy quality. Flight call is a rapid twittering 'chi, chi, chi, chit'.

HABITAT
Lives in open country, lowland farms, rough ground with some scrub (especially gorse) and in coastal areas. It sometimes breeds on the edges of towns in places such as cemeteries or disused industrial sites with Hawthorns and birch scrub. Outside the breeding season flocks feed on farmland, in weedy stubble, on wasteland and on coastal marshes.

FOOD
Eats seeds, especially common weeds such as Fat-hen and chickweed. Also eats seeds of charlock, dandelion and buttercup. Increasingly, Oilseed Rape seeds are an important food source. Some insects are eaten in summer, but they are not a large proportion of the diet.

CONSERVATION
Once commonly sold as a cage bird, the Linnet is now more familiar as an inhabitant of lowland agricultural land, and like many other farmland species it suffered a decline in the last quarter of the 20th century. This decline was less evident in Scotland owing to the prevalence of spring-sown cereal crops and winter stubble fields. The spread of Oilseed Rape has provided a new supply of food, and countryside stewardship schemes, which have encouraged wild-bird 'crops', have helped restore numbers.

DISTRIBUTION

Widespread and abundant away from the uplands. Moves to lowlands and coastal districts in winter. Found mainly in the south and east, with modest numbers on Arran, Islay and other islands of the Inner Hebrides. Breeds from northern Scandinavia to North Africa and east into Russia and the Middle East. In winter it reaches Egypt and Iraq.

TWITE *CARDUELIS FLAVIROSTRIS*

IDENTIFICATION
14 cm. Linnet-sized, but more slender, with darker upperparts, buff wing-bar, orange-buff throat, longer more- forked tail and well streaked on the back and the underparts. Generally it resembles a redpoll more than a Linnet, but is longer tailed than either. Rump of male is pink in the breeding season; female has a streaked rump. There is a buff wing-bar. Flight feathers are edged white and show as a white panel in the wing both in flight and when perched, but this feature is not as obvious as on a Linnet. Bill is yellow in winter (Linnet's is grey). Young resemble female, but are darker and more streaked. Moults between July and October, but the fresh plumage is not significantly different from breeding plumage.
SEE ALSO: Linnet, p227, Lesser Redpoll p229.

female

male

HABITS
Feeds mainly on the ground, but perches on posts, fences and in trees. Habits are similar to a Linnet and it is gregarious outside the breeding season, with, sometimes, quite large flocks forming in winter.

VOICE
Call usually incorporates a harsh 'twaaay', similar to a Linnet's, but more 'nasal'. Also makes a more drawn-out 'tchway' and 'tchway-de-wee'. Song is a variety of these individual notes, and not as well-formed as that of Linnet.

HABITAT
Lives on the edge of moorland and on associated farms and crofts, particularly where arable crops are still found and where seeds are available. Beyond Scotland it breeds on Arctic and alpine tundra, cold steppes and stony mountains. In Europe it winters mainly on or near the coast, or on stubble fields and other cultivated land.

FOOD
A seed-eater that prefers sorrels, dandelions, grass seeds, thistles and hardheads. In winter, on the coast takes the seeds of Sea-aster, Marsh Samphire, Sea-rocket and Thrift. Inland feeds on mayweeds, milfoil and cultivated species such as Golden Rod. Young are fed only on seeds. Adults eat some invertebrates.

BREEDING
Arrives on breeding grounds in March and it breeds between April and August. Nests in heather, Bracken or other tall vegetation. Female builds a bulky nest of grasses and other plants, and incubates 4–6 eggs for 12–13 days. Both adults feed young, but female sometimes does most work. Young leave at 14–15 days and continue to be fed for about 2 weeks. Where seed crop is good there will be a second brood.

MOVEMENTS AND MIGRATIONS
Most Scottish birds move from their breeding areas in late summer to winter near the coast, with many populations visiting traditional areas. Most stay within Scotland, but Twite from the west Highlands winter in Northern Ireland and those from the Inner Hebrides winter in north-west England. Some Continental birds may reach Scotland, but for the main part Scandinavian birds move south-east to winter around the Baltic. Many of the Twite on Scottish islands remain for the winter. Oldest bird survived 6 years.

POPULATION
Up to 13,800 pairs nest in Scotland, or 94% of the population of the British Isles. The population is experiencing a long-term decline.

CONSERVATION
In Britain it has been retreating northwards. The causes are the loss of flower- and herb-rich hay meadows, the abandonment of fodder crops that also contained weeds, and more intensive grazing may affect nests. Encouraging agricultural change through Stewardship and other incentives may help this species. Given this decline across Britain, safeguarding the Scottish population becomes even more important.

juvenile

male

male

DISTRIBUTION
A common breeding species on the north coast and hills of the west and north of Scotland, the Hebrides and the Northern Isles, with smaller numbers in the south. Also breeds in the English Pennines, north Wales and western Ireland. The species is also found in Norway, and another population spreads from Turkey to Tibet and western China. Many European Twites winter around the Baltic and North Sea, including on salt marshes along the east coast of England and Scotland.

LESSER REDPOLL *CARDUELIS CABARET*

IDENTIFICATION
11.5 cm. Slightly smaller than Linnet with stripey brown body, red forehead, tiny black bib, pale double wing-bar and dark-streaked rump. Triangular bill is small and quite fine and tail is forked. Males have a red flush on their breasts in the breeding season, but this and the intensity of the red forehead varies between individuals. Forehead of female also varies from dull red to yellow or brown. Often impossible to separate males from females. Moults between July and October. After moult it is browner, with red appearing during the winter owing to the abrasion of the feathers.
SEE ALSO: Linnet p227, Twite p228, Common Redpoll p230.

HABITS
Small and active, with behaviour rather like a tit as it hangs upside-down to reach food. Sometimes nests in loose colonies. Gregarious outside the breeding season. Small flocks feed together and larger numbers occur at roosts and during times of migration or irruption. Frequently mixes with Siskins. Song flight takes place before territories have been established: flying in an undulating course, it loops and circles on shallow wing-beats with occasional glides.

BREEDING
Nest is built in a tree or tall bush. It is an untidy structure of grasses, moss, old flower heads and small roots, and lined with feathers, hair and other soft material. The 4 or 5 eggs are laid between late April and late May and are incubated by female for 10–11 days. Young leave the nest after 12 days. They may leave the nest before being able to fly and they are independent after about 26 days. Often two broods in a season.

MOVEMENTS AND MIGRATIONS
Lesser Redpolls retreat from upland areas after breeding, many of them moving south for the winter, often across the border. Others will remain where food is plentiful, and the numbers and localities usually vary from year to year depending on the abundance of the food supply. There are occasional emigrations, when large numbers leave an area and breed in a new locality; these movements are usually triggered by food availability. Oldest known ringed bird lived for 6 years.

POPULATION
Between 7,500 and 15,000 pairs nest in Scotland. The population reached a peak in the 1970s and 1980s, and then declined markedly. This decline now appears to have halted.

male

juvenile

female

VOICE
Flight call is a purring trill. Its song incorporates the trill and a twittering 'chi, chi, chi, chi' that is usually given in its song flight.

HABITAT
Breeds in broadleaf or coniferous woodland, particularly birch woods, alder thickets and young conifer plantations. Also found in woodland margins, parkland and large gardens on the edges of towns. At other times it visits agricultural land where there are tall hedges, more open countryside and wasteland.

FOOD
Main food is birch seeds. In spring, takes flowers and seeds of sallow, and insects that are attracted to the opening buds of trees such as larch. At other times, feeds on grass seeds and other small seeds from low-growing plants, especially willowherb, dandelion, chickweed, sorrel and Tansey. A special favourite in winter is the seed of Alders.

CONSERVATION
The rise and fall in the Lesser Redpoll population has been linked with the introduction of conifer forests in Scotland. The species makes good use of young plantations, particularly where birch and Alder occur, but birds move out as trees mature. Availability of food is also crucial; changed agricultural practices have reduced the food available in the wider countryside.

DISTRIBUTION
Widely distributed across mainland Scotland and on many Inner Hebridean islands, especially in summer. In winter, flocks occur wherever food resources are found. Also found in parts of western Europe and in the Alps. There are other closely related redpolls in northern Scandinavia and Siberia, Asia and North America and it has been successfully introduced into New Zealand.

COMMON REDPOLL   *CARDUELIS FLAMMEA*

IDENTIFICATION

12.5 cm. Slightly larger than a Lesser Redpoll. It is a variable species but is more robust and generally paler and greyer than the Lesser Redpoll. In late winter it has clean whitish flanks with lines of contrasting brownish streaks, a rather clean 'frosty' appearance and an almost white rump. In the breeding season the forehead and breast become rose-pink and it has a small black 'bib'. However, these features vary between individuals. The female lacks the pink breast and sometimes has a larger black 'bib'. The breast is buff with darker streaks that join with the marks on the flanks. Immature males resemble females but sometimes have a trace of pink on their face and rump. It moults between July and October. The fresh autumn plumage is darker and browner and for a time obscures the paler breeding plumage. The rump can change from being strongly streaked to virtually plain white. Feathers abrade during the winter to reveal the paler plumage, red forehead and breast.
SEE ALSO: Lesser Redpoll p229, Linnet p227.

HABITS

Its behaviour sometimes recalls a tit as it hangs from a slender branch in its search for food. Like the Lesser Redpoll it is gregarious and flocks form outside the breeding season. In Scandinavian forests its nests are often in the vicinity of nesting Fieldfares, which help to guard it against predators.

VOICE

The call is a trilling 'tji-tji-tji'.

HABITAT

A winter visitor to the Northern Isles and, in small numbers, along the east coast. It frequently visits areas with birch, Alder and spruce trees. In Scandinavia it breeds in inland spruce forests.

FOOD

It feeds on very small seeds from birch, Alder and spruce. It also eats insects and other invertebrates, both adults or as larvae.

BREEDING

A very scarce breeding species in the Outer and Northern Isles. In years when the spruce has a good crop of seeds Common Redpolls may start nesting in March while there is still snow on the ground and the temperature as low as –20 °C. The female builds a cup-shaped nest in a tree and incubates the 4–6 eggs, which hatch after 10–12 days. The young are fed by both parents and leave the nest at 9–14 days. It is single- or double-brooded. In years when spruce seeds are unusually plentiful the Common Redpoll breeds for longer and populations increase accordingly.

MOVEMENTS AND MIGRATIONS

It is predominately a passage migrant and a scarce winter visitor to Scotland. Most Common Redpolls move south-east in autumn, and some from Scandinavia cross the North Sea to reach the Northern Isles and the east coast of Scotland between September and November. Birds from Greenland are seen in most years on Shetland and the Outer Hebrides. In some years there is an eruption, with more birds travelling in larger numbers. These movements are linked to food shortages.

male

female

POPULATION

Numbers vary from year to year, with most in late autumn and winter. Between 50 and 2,000 birds present.

CONSERVATION

The Common Redpoll has been recognised as a full species only in recent years. Until then it was considered by most ornithologists to belong to the same species as the Lesser Redpoll. However, there is no evidence that they interbreed as they would do if they belonged to the same species. Common Redpoll populations have natural fluctuations and there are no specific conservation actions that will help.

DISTRIBUTION

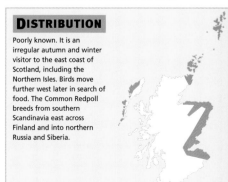

Poorly known. It is an irregular autumn and winter visitor to the east coast of Scotland, including the Northern Isles. Birds move further west later in search of food. The Common Redpoll breeds from southern Scandinavia east across Finland and into northern Russia and Siberia.

COMMON CROSSBILL *LOXIA CURVIROSTRA*

male

IDENTIFICATION

16.5 cm. Larger than Greenfinch. Large finch with heavy-looking body and large head and bill. Tips of bill are crossed. Tail is forked. Male is brick-red and slightly brighter on its rump. Some males are orange or yellow, or sometimes a mixture of both with streaked backs. Young males may be any of these colours, but most likely to be grey-green with paler yellow rumps. Wings are dark without any markings, although a few individuals may show thin, pale wing-bars. Female is greenish grey and slightly streaked. Juvenile is paler brown and more heavily streaked above and below. Most moult between July and November, but those that breed later or earlier in the year may moult at other times. Early moulting males tend to be yellow, later ones are more likely to be red.
SEE ALSO: Parrot Crossbill p233, Scottish Crossbill p232.

HABITS

Versatile and acrobatic feeder. Climbs with its feet and bill and flutters from branch to branch rather like a small parrot. Can be rather tame. Frequently comes to the edges of ponds, streams and puddles to drink. Gregarious for most of year, even when nesting. Family groups roam the woods after nesting and some join together to make larger flocks. Flight is fast and undulating, and often at tree-top height.

juvenile

VOICE

Call in a sharp 'chip, chip, chip' and sometimes a loud 'teu'. At dusk it makes a Blackbird-like 'chink-chink'. Song is an unremarkable soft twittering.

HABITAT

Spends most of its life associated with coniferous trees, especially Sitka, Norway Spruce, Scots Pine and larch. Norway Spruce produces larger seeds than Sitka Spruce and in larger quantities – it is therefore sought by crossbills, Siskins and Red Squirrels. It may be in commercial plantations, larger forests and mixed woodlands and sometimes parkland.

FOOD

Chief food is conifer seeds. Cones are wrenched off and held under the feet while the seeds are extracted. Can extract seeds from cones of any age, but prefers older ones. Also eats buds, shoots and seeds from trees and from low-growing plants. Some insects and other invertebrates are also eaten.

BREEDING

Across its range has been found breeding in every month of the year. Nesting commonly begins in February and continues into spring, but may begin in August and continue through the winter – if the trees provide enough cones. Typical nest is high in a tree and is built by female on a base of twigs. It consists of grass, moss, lichen and bark and lined with moss, hair and feathers. Female incubates 3 or 4 eggs for 14–15 days. Both adults feed the young which leave the nest after 20–25 days. The parents feed them for 3–6 weeks after fledging.

MOVEMENTS AND MIGRATIONS

Good cone crops are sporadic and occur in different areas in different years. Crossbills regularly leave forests where crops are poor and search out new feeding areas. If the crop is substantial the birds will stay and breed and moult before moving on. There is, therefore, only one movement most years rather than two-way migration. Occasionally there are huge irruptions caused either by food shortage or over-population. At these times Crossbills arrive in new woods and may be seen on the east coast. Oldest known bird survived over 6 years.

POPULATION

The breeding population varies from year to year; for the most part it numbers 5,000–50,000 nesting pairs, but in years following invasions it may be higher. The species' range in Scotland has extended owing to the planting of new conifer forests.

CONSERVATION

Because of its nomadic nature there is little practical help that can be given to the Crossbill. Has been helped by establishment of conifer plantations during the 20th century.

female

SCOTTISH CROSSBILL *LOXIA SCOTICA*

male

IDENTIFICATION
16.5 cm. Larger than Greenfinch. Similar to Crossbill, although it is a slightly larger bird with a heavier, stronger bill and a larger head. Colours are similar, with brick-red, orange or yellow males and green and slightly streaked females. Young are also yellow-green and more heavily streaked than females. Positive identification is very difficult and proximity to known breeding areas is one of the safest criteria, but even this is not indisputable as Crossbills will sometimes visit the favoured habitat of the Scottish Crossbill at times of invasions. Adults have their annual moult between July and November.
SEE ALSO: Common Crossbill p231, Parrot Crossbill p233.

HABITS
Its habits are similar to those of the Crossbill. It spends most of its time around the tops of trees, but it will also regularly visit pools and running water to drink. Flight is strong and undulating. It commonly forms flocks when not breeding and feeding flocks tend to be quite noisy.

VOICE
The call is a hard, sharp 'chup, chup'; difficult to separate from Parrot Crossbill.

HABITAT
Restricted to areas in the north-east Scottish Highlands. It may nest in commercial plantations or traditional Caledonian pine forest. The nest may be in dense woodland or in isolated clumps of pines. Generally it selects sunny parts of the wood in preference to the dark forest interiors. Favoured sites generally have access to water for drinking. It is usually seen in small flocks outside the breeding season.

FOOD
The chief food is seeds from Scots Pines. It extracts the seeds either with the cones attached to the branch or by removing the cone and flying to a perch where it holds it down with its foot as it removes the scales. It also eats some invertebrates in summer.

BREEDING
It normally nests between February and June. The female builds the nest. The usual site is in an old Scots Pine, but sometimes in other conifers. The nest is a bulky structure made from twigs, heather, moss and grass, and lined with softer material such as fur, hair and feathers. The female incubates the 3 or 4 eggs for 12–14 days. Both parents feed the young and they fledge after about 21 days. They remain with their parents and are fed by them for about the next 8 weeks. There are two broods if there is sufficient food.

MOVEMENTS AND MIGRATIONS
It is a resident, but within its range it shows the typical Crossbill tendency to disperse after breeding and to follow the best food supplies. Like the Crossbill in Europe, when large populations start to build up after several successful breeding seasons, there is general movement to find new areas where there is plentiful food and some birds may stay to breed there in the autumn.

POPULATION
The latest estimage is that some 6,800 pairs nest in Scotland. This is the only known population of this species and it does not occur in other parts of the British Isles. It is a difficult species to monitor, but probably extended its range following the planting of new forests. Scottish Crossbills overlap with Common Crossbills, and sometimes Parrot Crossbills, but in late winter and early spring birds within the range and in Scots Pine woods are likely to be 'Scottish'.

CONSERVATION
Evolution is thought to have taken place after the last ice age (7000 BC) in Scots Pine forests. However, birds are now known to use non-native pines and spruces on occasions. This habitat had declined from 600,000 ha to 12,500 ha by 1987. Careful management of this fragile habitat and its gradual enlargement where possible will help not only Scottish Crossbills but assist other native species of the Scottish Highlands.

female

PARROT CROSSBILL *LOXIA PYTYOPSITTACUS*

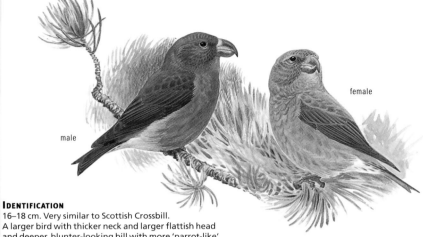

male

female

IDENTIFICATION
16–18 cm. Very similar to Scottish Crossbill.
A larger bird with thicker neck and larger flattish head and deeper, blunter-looking bill with more 'parrot-like' bulge on lower mandible than other crossbills. Heavier looking and rather short-tailed. Plumage colour similar to other crossbills, but male tends to be slightly duller with more grey on nape. Greenish female tends to also be greyer with less black on wings. Heavy and 'front-loaded' appearance in flight. Juvenile's bills less pronounced and hardly separable from other juvenile crossbills. Moults between June and November.
SEE ALSO: Common Crossbill p231, Scottish Crossbill p232.

HABITS
Behaviour similar to other crossbills. Secretive although may allow observer to approach when feeding. Usually feeds high in trees, but frequently comes down to puddles and other water to drink. May travel in family groups or small flocks and will join flocks of other crossbills. It has a butterfly-like song-flight prior to nesting.

VOICE
Similar to Common Crossbill although some observers have described a deeper emphatic 'quop, quop' call. Song tends to be lower, slower and slightly better enunciated than Common Crossbill's.

HABITAT
Found in pine and spruce forests, and in the remains of the ancient Caledonian forest of the Scottish Highlands.

FOOD
Specialist feeder on seeds of conifer trees, especially Scots Pine, and also spruce and larch. Seeds and buds from other plants including Alder and Rowan are also taken. Some invertebrates are also eaten when nesting.

BREEDING
In Scotland the species breeds mainly in ancient Scots Pine forests and also in some mature Scots Pine plantations. Nests are built by the female 6–20 m off the ground and composed of twigs, lichens, moss, bark and pine needles. Clutches of 3–5 eggs are laid between February and May and are incubated for 14–16 days. The young fledge at about 22 days but they will continue to be fed by their parents for 6 weeks or more.

MOVEMENTS AND MIGRATIONS
Like other members of this family, invasions take place periodically, usually triggered by food shortage or high population. Breeding birds from northern Europe and Russia head south-west – and some cross the North Sea. The eruptive movements are often in the same years as Common Crossbills, but usually later. At such times Parrot Crossbills may colonise new locations as they apparently did in Scotland in the late 20th century.

POPULATION
The first record of this species breeding in Scotland was in Abernethy Forest in 1991, where all 3 crossbill species occur in some years. It is estimated that there may now be 100 breeding pairs of this species. Others occur as scarce passage migrants in the Northern Isles and a few other places.

CONSERVATION
This is a difficult species to locate. Its main breeding areas appear to be in native Scots Pine forests, which is a habitat that is specially protected by the RSPB and other conservation bodies. The future of this species is uncertain given its eruptive nature and it is not known how long the curent popualtion of Scottish birds has been established.

DISTRIBUTION
A small number breed in Scottish pine forests and very occasionally further south in Britain. The species is found across Scandinavia, Northern Europe and into Russia and, following eruptions, it will move south-west to Denmark and sometimes to the Netherlands and to Scotland.

BULLFINCH   *PYRRHULA PYRRHULA*

IDENTIFICATION
14.5 cm. Similar in size to House Sparrow. A plump finch with large head, thick neck and short black, bulbous bill. Plumage appears soft and cap, wings, tail and bib are all glossy black. Has white wing-bar and gleaming white rump. Lower face and breast of male is rose-pink and the back is grey. Lower face and breast of female is pinkish grey. Juvenile is browner than the female, and with no black on its head. It moults between July and October, but males do not have the duller autumn plumage that is typical of some other finches.
SEE ALSO: Chaffinch p221.

HABITS
Rather secretive; seldom seen far from cover and usually feeds directly from plants rather than on the ground. Often seen in pairs or in small family groups after the breeding season. Larger groups sometimes form in rich feeding areas in winter.

VOICE
Usual call soft but distinctive 'peu, peu' and also quieter piping as birds keep contact in dense cover. Song is a quiet, creaking or piping warble and is seldom heard.

HABITAT
Nests in woodland undergrowth, thickets, young conifer plantations, shrubby areas and thick hedges. Never far from scrub and mature hedgerows. Many of these habitats occur on lowland farmland. Also visits gardens and orchards.

male

male

female

juvenile

FOOD
Main food is native tree buds. Oak, sallow and Hawthorn are commonly eaten and also the buds of fruit trees, especially those in orchards. Other food includes tree-flowers, berries and other soft fruits and seeds. Seeds include Ash, dandelion, buttercup, dock, nettles and Bramble. Young are fed on both plant material and on invertebrates. In the breeding season adults develop pouches in the floor of their mouths to help them carry food.

BREEDING
Nests between May and July, but in some years breeding continues into September. Female Bullfinches build their nest in thick bushes, 1–2 m off the ground. Nest is a remarkably flimsy-looking, rather loose structure made from fine twigs, moss and lichen, with a neat inner cup of roots and hair. Female incubates the 4 or 5 eggs for 14–16 days and young remain in the nest for 15–17 days.

Young are fed by both parents, which continue to feed them for 15–20 days after fledging. Some pairs manage two or more broods in a year.

MOVEMENTS AND MIGRATIONS
Small numbers from Scandinavia and further east are seen on the Northern Isles and along the east coast in spring and autumn. These are larger, brighter birds than ours. Most of our breeding birds are resident but some move up to 28 km during the breeding season. This movement is thought to take place between broods, in order for the family to take advantage of new food sources. Elsewhere it is an altitudinal migrant, moving downhill for the winter, and a true migrant moving south in autumn. Oldest known bird was over 17 years old.

POPULATION
50,000–90,000 pairs breed in Scotland. Sometimes as many as 1,000 larger Continental birds arrive in the Northern Isles in April and October. In Britain as a whole the Bullfinch has been declining in recent years, but in Scotland the species has fared better and has been modestly extending its range.

CONSERVATION
The damage inflicted on commercial fruit crops resulted, for many years, in this bird acquiring the status of an agricultural pest in fruit-growing areas, due to the Bullfinch's liking for the buds found on fruit trees. The loss of hedgerows with standard trees and agricultural intensification is thought to be behind its recent decline in England.

DISTRIBUTION
Absent from treeless uplands and the Northern Isles as a breeding species. Widespread in lowland and coastal Scotland. Breeds in England, Wales and Ireland. Extends from Ireland in the west across Europe and Asia to Japan. In Europe breeds north to the Arctic Circle and south to the Mediterranean.

HAWFINCH COCCOTHRAUSTES COCCOTHRAUSTES

IDENTIFICATION
18 cm. Larger than Greenfinch. Large and heavy-looking finch with massive, conical bill, large head, rather short legs, short square-ended tail and a 'bull-neck'. Has white patch in its wing and broad white tip to the tail. Back is rich brown, head orange-brown, breast pinkish brown and neck grey. Wings are blackish and the bluish-black secondary flight feathers are splayed out at the tips and twisted to present a series of spikes. It has black around eye and below bill. Bill is blue-grey in the breeding season and horn-coloured in winter. Female is only slightly less colourful than male. Juvenile has a more orange head without any black marks, a greenish-yellow breast and dark spotting on its belly. Adult moults between July and September.
SEE ALSO: Waxwing p168.

HABITS
Usually shy and secretive, spending much time in the tree-tops. It looks 'heavy-fronted' in flight, with the large white patches on the wings appearing transparent from below. Flight is rapid, powerful and bounding. Male has a song flight where it switchbacks over its territory before suddenly plummeting downwards. Out of the breeding season it is sociable, often feeding in groups.

VOICE
Most common call is a short 'tic, tic', slightly harder than Robin's alarm call. The rarely heard song is a slow 'deek, waree, ree, ree'.

HABITAT
Inhabits mature deciduous woods and mixed woodland, some large gardens, cemeteries, arboreta and parks as well as orchards and shrubby places with scattered trees. In winter it may be seen in more open habitats. Woodland that has Hornbeam is particularly popular.

FOOD
The main food is large seeds from woodland trees, especially Wych Elm, Hornbeam, Beech and maple. It also visits hedges to search for hips and haws and other autumn fruits. In spring it feeds on buds from oak, and in summer it eats some insects, including large beetles, some of which it catches in flight. It is fond of the fruit of Wild Cherry and is able to crack open the hard seed with its powerful bill.

BREEDING
Nests in trees, usually more than 3 m from the ground. Nest is an untidy and flimsy saucer-shaped structure of twigs, small roots, grasses and lichen. The 4 or 5 eggs are laid between May and July and incubated by the female for 11–13 days. Young are fed by both parents and leave the nest after 12–14 days. Usually only one brood a year.

MOVEMENTS AND MIGRATIONS
Relatively little known about its seasonal movements in Britain and it may be mostly sedentary. On the Continent northern populations are migratory, with juveniles most likely to make the longest journeys and females more likely to migrate than males. A few Hawfinches from northern Europe and Russia arrive in Scotland in spring and autumn, with most occurring on the Northern Isles. Oldest bird lived 12 years.

POPULATION
40–75 pairs breed in Scotland. While the species is declining in Britain, in Scotland there are increases in

female

juvenile male

male

male

some localities and declines in others, and the number seen on passage has increased.

CONSERVATION
Monitoring this scarce and elusive species is difficult. Grey Squirrels may be a possible threat to its future, and responsible woodland management is necessary to safeguard its habitat.

DISTRIBUTION
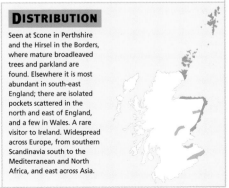
Seen at Scone in Perthshire and the Hirsel in the Borders, where mature broadleaved trees and parkland are found. Elsewhere it is most abundant in south-east England; there are isolated pockets scattered in the north and east of England, and a few in Wales. A rare visitor to Ireland. Widespread across Europe, from southern Scandinavia south to the Mediterranean and North Africa, and east across Asia.

YELLOWHAMMER *EMBERIZA CITRINELLA*

male

male (fresh, autumn)

IDENTIFICATION
16–16.5 cm. A little larger than a Chaffinch. Rather long-bodied bunting with a long and forked tail. In spring, male has a yellow head and breast, rich brown, streaky back and plain reddish-brown rump. There is the suggestion of a reddish-brown band across the yellow breast. In autumn and winter, the yellow is mostly obscured by greenish-brown streaks. Female is much duller than male with pale yellow below the bill and in front of the eyes, lines of brown streaks along the breast and flanks and with two dull wing-bars. In flight, shows white towards the ends of the outer tail-feathers. Juveniles and immature females are darker and only faintly yellow. Adults moult between July and October. After moult the brown feather-tips on the male hide the bright colours until they wear away during winter revealing brighter breeding plumage.
SEE ALSO: Yellow Wagtail p166.

juvenile

HABITS
Flight is in long undulations and looks a little jerky. Frequently perches on the tops of bushes, hedges and overhead wires. Feeds mainly on the ground and outside the breeding season is often seen in small flocks, often mixing with other buntings, finches and sparrows.

VOICE
Call is a sharp, clipped 'zit' or soft 'trillp'. The famous 'little-bit-of-bread-and-no-cheese' description of the song helps to describe the pace and form, which is variable, but tends to be a rapid succession of repeated notes with the last phrase drawn out into a long wheeze. Song is repeated monotonously during breeding season.

female

HABITAT
Breeds in areas of grassland and arable fields with hedges and banks, railway embankments, young plantations and felled areas. Outside breeding season visits larger fields, especially stubble fields, fields with winter fodder crops and other places where grain-eating birds gather, although it is an unusual visitor to gardens.

FOOD
Mainly a seed-eater, but also feeds on insects and other invertebrates, especially in summer. Seeds include grasses, nettle, dock and chickweed, and grain from agricultural crops. Insects eaten include grasshoppers, sawfly larvae, beetles and caterpillars.

BREEDING
Eggs are laid between April and September, but mostly in May and June. The nest is usually on the ground amongst taller vegetation and is made from grass, plant stems and moss, and lined with fine grass and other soft material. The 3–5 eggs are generally incubated by female alone, and hatch after 12–14 days. Young are fed by both parents and leave the nest at 11–13 days. They are not usually able to fly when they leave but become independent of their parents 12–14 days later. There are two or three broods a year.

MOVEMENTS AND MIGRATIONS
Scottish birds are largely sedentary. They form itinerant flocks and join other buntings in their search for food outside the breeding season, but seldom travel far. Continental birds are more likely to be migratory, and small numbers are often seen on passage in the Northern Isles in spring and autumn. Oldest bird survived 13 years.

POPULATION
140,000–220,000 pairs nest in Scotland. This species has declined since the 1970s and disappeared from parts of northern and western Scotland, especially where arable cropping has ceased.

CONSERVATION
The recent decline mirrors that of other mainly farmland species. Possible reasons include poor winter survival because of lack of seed-rich stubble fields due to autumn sowing, the loss of weed seeds owing to herbicides and the lack of invertebrates. Loss of wide field margins, rich in large insects like grasshoppers, have impacted on breeding success.

DISTRIBUTION

Widespread in agricultural areas and upland fringes in the south and east of Scotland. In winter, slightly more widespread, but the general distribution is similar to the summer. It is found from northern Scandinavia to the Mediterranean and east into Russia.

LAPLAND BUNTING *CALCARIUS LAPPONICUS*

female

female 1st-winter

male (fresh, autumn)

male

female 1st-winter

IDENTIFICATION
15–16 cm. Larger than Reed Bunting, but smaller than Snow Bunting. Heavy-looking bunting with short, thick straw-coloured bill, a large head, long wings and relatively short, forked tail. Male in spring has a black face and throat that is separated from the black crown by a 'V'-shaped white band. Back of neck is chestnut. Female in summer lacks the black head. In autumn and winter, adults resemble Reed Bunting but have plainer reddish-buff faces and thin black line around the cheeks. On the wing there is a rich brown panel between two fine white bars. Flanks are sparsely streaked, unlike Reed Bunting's well-streaked underparts. Rump is grey-brown and streaked and there is a slight pale stripe through the crown. Males retain some of the chestnut on the back of the head in winter. Birds often show black mottling in a gorget across the breast. Moults between July and September. Moult takes only about 50 days, necessarily rapid for a bird that breeds in the Arctic. After moulting, the distinctive spring plumage is obscured by the fringes of the newly grown feathers, which wear away by the spring.
SEE ALSO: Snow Bunting p238, Reed Bunting p239.

HABITS
Bounding flight recalls larks and pipits. Spends most of the time on the ground and is often in small flocks, although individual birds and small groups will sometimes join flocks of other buntings, larks and pipits on the British east coast in winter. Larger flocks sometimes form on migration.

VOICE
Flight call is a distinctive dry, rattling 'terrek'. Sometimes it will make a Snow Bunting-like, descending 'teu' call. Song is quite musical and given during a song flight.

HABITAT
Adapted to the Arctic tundra where it breeds among dwarf willows, often in wet areas, or Arctic heath with low-growing shrubs. In autumn, found on coastal heaths. In winter, visits stubble fields and areas of rough grass, usually near the coast, as well as salt marshes.

FOOD
In summer eats invertebrates, but at other times feeds on the seeds of grasses and herbs. Animal food includes flies, craneflies, beetles and spiders. Plant material includes knotgrass, dock and Shepherd's Purse.

BREEDING
It nests on the ground. Female builds a cup-shaped structure of grass, small roots, leaves and lichen, and she incubates the 5 or 6 eggs. Incubation lasts for 11–13 days. Both adults feed the young and they leave the nest after 9–10 days. It is 2–3 days later before the young are able to fly and they become independent of their parents about a week after that.

MOVEMENTS AND MIGRATIONS
After breeding, it departs its near-Arctic breeding sites and moves south. Varying numbers arrive in Scotland from Greenland and Scandinavia. This arrival starts in mid-September and some birds remain for the whole winter. Most have departed again by late May.

POPULATION
Up to 300 individuals may be seen on passage, with smaller numbers remaining for the winter. There has been an increase in passage birds in recent years, and in 1977–80 up to 16 pairs nested in the Highlands.

CONSERVATION
Specially protected. It was found summering in 1968 and in 1977 there were up to 16 pairs at five sites, but colonisation was short-lived and now usually only single birds appear in the breeding season. Secrecy to protect nests from disturbance and the attention of egg thieves is the only conservation action required.

DISTRIBUTION

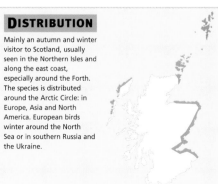

Mainly an autumn and winter visitor to Scotland, usually seen in the Northern Isles and along the east coast, especially around the Forth. The species is distributed around the Arctic Circle: in Europe, Asia and North America. European birds winter around the North Sea or in southern Russia and the Ukraine.

SNOW BUNTING *PLECTROPHENAX NIVALIS*

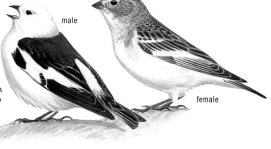

male

female

IDENTIFICATION
16–17 cm. Stocky bunting, slightly larger than Lapland and Reed Buntings. Has a thick pale bill, a rather flat crown, long pointed wings and a short forked tail. Breeding male has a dark bill, snowy white body, a black back, black central tail-feathers and white wings with prominent black triangular tips. In autumn and winter, the head and breast are sandy-coloured and the back is rusty brown with darker marks. In flight, wings always show white in varying amounts, and wing-tips are always dark. Females and immatures resemble winter male, but with less white in the wing. Annual moult is rapid, starting in mid-July and finishing by end of August. In late winter the change in the male from his sandy winter plumage to his white breeding plumage is largely due to the sandy tips wearing away, but it also has a partial moult of its head feathers. SEE ALSO: Lapland Bunting p237.

HABITS
Usually sociable outside the breeding season with flocks of several hundred sometimes forming, and occasionally these flocks mix with other finches. Flocks of juveniles sometimes migrate together. Birds spend a lot of time on the ground, shuffling along with body close to the earth so the short legs can hardly be seen. Often Snow Buntings seem unconcerned about humans nearby.

female
(fresh, autumn)

male

VOICE
Call, usually heard in flight, is a rippling twittering 'tir-rirrirrip'. There are calls that sound like 'seu' and 'sichew'. Song is loud and musical and given from a perch or in flight.

HABITAT
In winter, seen on the seashore, often feeding along the strand-line, or on rough grassland near the coast. Some winter on high hills and mountains. In Scotland breeds on mountain-tops close to the summer snow fields and often among boulders, although there are occasional attempts to breed at ground level in the Northern Isles. In the Arctic it breeds in treeless areas and on rocky coasts.

FOOD
Feeds on seeds, with insects eaten during the breeding season. Seeds are mainly from plants of the bistort family, grasses, herbs and other low-growing plants. Insects include springtails, mites, flies and their larvae, caterpillars and spiders.

BREEDING
Builds a cup-shaped nest of grass, moss and lichen that is lined with hair, wool and feathers. Nest is usually in a crevice amongst rocks and boulders. Female incubates the 4–6 eggs for 12–13 days. Both adults feed the young. Young leave the nest at 12–14 days, a few days before they can fly, and their parents feed them for a further 8–12 days. It has two broods.

MOVEMENTS AND MIGRATIONS
Although most northerly Snow Buntings are migrants, some overwinter close to where they breed. Most migrants arrive in Scotland from late September through to November and leave in April and May. It appears that males are better able to survive in winter and are more likely to remain close to their breeding sites than females. Oldest bird lived 9 years.

POPULATION
50–60 pairs nest in Scotland. In winter between 1,250 and 12,500 individuals are present. Most of these belong to the subspecies that breeds in Iceland, but others come from Greenland and Scandinavia.

CONSERVATION
Specially protected, and large, remote mountain tracts are important. Climate change may influence future breeding status in Scotland.

male (fresh, autumn)

DISTRIBUTION
Breeds in the Highlands on the highest mountains near permanent snowbeds, in a ew other locations in the north-west of Scotland and, occasionally, in the Northern Isles. In winter, it is seen on moorland in the hills, sometimes around feeding cattle; others are found along the east coast and in the Northern Isles. Breeds all round the Arctic Circle, from Scandinavia and Spitsbergen across Siberia to Alaska, Arctic Canada, Greenland and Iceland.

REED BUNTING *EMBERIZA SCHOENICLUS*

IDENTIFICATION

15 cm. About the size of House Sparrow. Little smaller than Yellowhammer with relatively large head and white outer tail feathers. Male has a sparrow-like body, a black head and throat and a broad white collar and a small white downward stripe from the bill. In autumn and winter, the black head marks are largely obscured. There are dull wing-bars. Female has a dull brown head with a pale stripe below the cheeks and a thinner, tri-angular-shaped dark stripe bordering it. Also has a pale stripe above eye that narrows towards back of head and diffuse streaking on breast. In autumn and winter, head markings become bolder. Juvenile is similar to female with yellower plumage and darker streaks. Moults between July and November and also moults its head feathers again between March and May.

Most of the black head feathers of the male are revealed through the fringes of the feathers abrad-ing during the winter.
SEE ALSO: Yellowhammer p236, Lapland Bunting p237.

female

HABITS

Frequently clings to reeds and often sings from near the top of a reed stem or the top of a low bush. Often flicks its wings nervously when calling. After breeding season, forms flocks and joins other buntings, finches and sparrows, or sometimes wagtails and pipits.

VOICE

Usual call is shrill 'tsew' that is given in flight, and also a metallic 'ching'. Song is very simple and repetitive; is a collection of a few metallic notes ending in an unremarkable flourish 'tweek, tweek, tweek, titty-tweek'.

HABITAT

Traditionally this was a bird of wet places such as reedbeds, river margins, fens, marshes and coastal grazing marshes. More recently it colonised drier habitats such as ditches, young forestry plantations and some farm crops, especially Oilseed Rape. On farmland relies on grassland for feeding and seeks out old ditch systems. In winter, it feeds on agricultural land and other open areas, often away from water.

FOOD

Eats mainly seeds from grasses, Saltwort, Shepherd's Purse, plants from the goosefoot family, mare's tails and many other wildflower seeds. In summer it also feeds on invertebrates, including springtails, caterpillars and spiders. Nestlings are also fed on invertebrates.

BREEDING

Nesting begins in April. Nest is often near water. It is built by the female on the ground among a clump of grass or rushes or off the ground in a bush. Made from grass and moss and lined with finer material. Female incubates 4 or 5 eggs for 12–14 days. Both adults feed the young, which leave the nest after 10–12 days, a few days before they fly properly. There may be two broods in a year.

MOVEMENTS AND MIGRATIONS

Fairly sedentary in Scotland, with a mainly southerly dispersal away from breeding areas to feeding and roosting sites in autumn. Females may be more mobile and travel further than males. While most birds remain within Scotland, a few travel further – there are records of Scottish individuals in winter in other parts of the British Isles and on the Continent. Migrant Reed Buntings are seen in the Northern Isles and along the east coast. Oldest bird lived 11 years.

POPULATION

15,000–30,000 pairs breed in Scotland. The population in the UK and in Scotland has declined during the last 30 years, but in Scotland there has been a modest increase in numbers more recently.

CONSERVATION

The Reed Bunting has suffered from increased land drainage, the loss of small wetlands and agricultural intensification, which have removed insect food in summer and seeds and grain in winter. Some have successfully diversified into Oilseed Rape.

male

male
(fresh,
autumn)

DISTRIBUTION

Widespread in lowland Scotland, less common in agricultural glens, and absent from the highest ground and on some offshore islands. Breeds in central and northern Europe, and in Asia, where there are other races. Some European birds reach North Africa in winter.

CORN BUNTING *MILIARIA CALANDRA*

IDENTIFICATION
18 cm. Size of Skylark. Our largest bunting. Plump with heavy straw-coloured bill. Plumage is dull streaked brown with paler, boldly streaked underparts, but without distinguishing features except that some have streaks on their breast clustered in an irregular diamond-shape, looking almost like a wet patch. Sexes are alike. Juveniles similar to adults. Adults moult between July and October. Juveniles replace their feathers in their first autumn after hatching – a feature they have in common with larks and only a few other songbirds. SEE ALSO: Skylark p156, Yellowhammer p236.

HABITS
Rather inconspicuous. Feeds on the ground, often with other species. In winter, forms flocks often comprising 10 birds or less. On winter evenings, where common, larger numbers may form communal roosts in scrub and reedbeds. When singing, sits upright on its perch, opening its bill wide with head thrown back. In flight, over short distances often dangles its legs and flight appears fluttering.

VOICE
Males with several mates sing more than males with only one. Song may start when males visit their territories in January or February and soon sing incessantly throughout the day. Song is an accelerating series of jangling notes that has been likened to jangling of keys. Call is a rather abrupt 'quit'.

HABITAT
Found on open lowland agricultural or croft land, especially in areas of mixed or arable farming. Outside the breeding season it feeds on winter stubble and unimproved grassland, often where there is bare soil and supplies of weed seeds.

FOOD
Most of the year it mainly feeds on plant material. It eats the grain from cereal crops and the tiny seeds from grasses and a variety of 'weeds'. In summer, it eats invertebrates such as beetles and caterpillars. The young are fed on sawflies, aphids, beetles, plant bugs and a vast list of other invertebrates as well as ripening grain.

BREEDING
Most males have one mate, but some have two or more females nesting in their territory, and one individual attracted 18 females, six of which nested. Flocks break down and territories are re-occupied between February and April. Female makes a nest that is a loose cup of grass on the ground or in a low bush, often near the edge of a field. Female incubates 4 or 5 eggs for 12–14 days and it is mostly the female that feeds the young. Chicks leave at 9–13 days, often a few days before they can fly. There may be two broods reared in a year.

MOVEMENTS AND MIGRATIONS
Highly sedentary: seldom moves far, although after nesting flocks will search out favourable feeding and roosting sites. Continental birds are more mobile, and occasionally these birds occur on Shetland. These migrants may sometimes reach other parts of Scotland, but as they are indistinguishable from native birds the size and frequency of their immigration is poorly understood. Oldest bird was 11 years.

POPULATION
About 800 pairs nest in Scotland. Like many other species nesting on farmland, the Corn Bunting has suffered large population declines in the last 30 years, and its range has seriously contracted. Declines continued into the 21st century, although these are not uniform, with birds disappearing from some areas yet remaining relatively stable in others.

CONSERVATION
Numbers declined in the early part of the 20th century, recovered during the 1950s and 1960s before falling again. The loss of stubble fields and earlier harvesting, which has prevented second broods from fledging successfully, are two likely causes. Encouragement for farmers to provide wide, late-harvested field margins will help. Concerted conservation action is required.

DISTRIBUTION

In Scotland, now mainly found from Inverness east around the coastal arable lands and south to Fife. A small separate population is found on the machairs of the Uists. Elsewhere in the British Isles it is mostly restricted to southern and eastern England. In Europe, it breeds from Denmark south to the Mediterranean and east across into Russia. There are other populations in North Africa.

juvenile

RARITIES

These species may sometimes be seen in Scotland and a few nest in very small numbers.

GREEN-WINGED TEAL
ANAS CAROLINENSIS

male

34–38 cm. Smaller than Mallard and similar to Teal, but the drake has a conspicuous neat, vertical white stripe on either side of the breast and lacks the lateral white stripes along sides of its body. Females and eclipse males are generally inseparable from the female Teal, although the crown and eye-stripe tend to be darker.

A rare visitor from North America, with up to 20 birds being seen in recent years. It is mainly a winter vagrant – a few birds arrive with other migrating wildfowl from October onwards. It may occur on any suitable water in Scotland, often with Teal. Most reports are from the Hebrides and Shetland.

female

AMERICAN WIGEON
ANAS AMERICANA

46–53 cm. Smaller than Mallard. The drake in breeding plumage is pinkish brown on the breast and flanks, with a brownish back and a black and white stern. It has a dark green band on the sides of its head, with a distinctive pale, off-white forehead and crown. Ducks (females) and eclipse males lack the distinctive head and tail markings and are more similar to the Wigeon.

A rare vagrant from North America, with 5–20 being seen in recent years. It visits various water bodies, including lochs, with other wildfowl, and has been seen in most parts of Scotland.

male

female

KING EIDER SOMATERIA SPECTABILIS

47–63 cm. The male has a black body, a white oval patch near the tail, a large, round, mostly blue head, a salmon-pink breast and green cheeks. It has a prominent red bulge on the bill, and two back feathers form small 'sails'. The female is similar to a female Eider but has rufous coloration, with a more rounded head, a smaller, darker bill, and crescent marks on the flanks. Its upsweeping gape gives it a 'happy' look, and feathers on the bill stop short of the nostrils. The juvenile is like a dull, uniform female. Immature males take 3 years to gain adult plumage. Individuals may join Common Eiders.

A high Arctic species, with up to 10 reaching the Scottish coast in some years, especially the Northern Isles and east coast. Mainly seen from October to March.

female

male

SURF SCOTER *MELANITTA PERSPICILLATA*

45–56 cm. Smaller than Mallard. A dark sea duck with a large, Eider-like head and long, triangular bill. It has more obvious head markings than other scoters. The drake is black with a multicoloured bill and white patches on the forehead and nape. The blackish-brown female has paler underparts and two pale patches on the side of the head – in front of and behind the eye. Juveniles resemble females but with paler underparts; young males have a large nape patch but lack the mark on the forehead. Individual Surf Scoters may join flocks of Common Scoters. No white in wings in flight.

Breeds in the north of North America; 5–20 have been wintering in Scotland in recent years, mainly on the east coast, with the greatest numbers seen between October and May. Regular in St Andrew's Bay and the Firth of Forth.

male

female

SMEW *MERGELLUS ALBELLUS*

38–44 cm. Only a little larger than a Teal. A small, compact diving duck with a steep forehead and delicate bill. The male is white with a black mask, black back, fine lines on the sides of the breast and faintly barred grey flanks. Feathers on the crown form a crest that may be raised during display. The female is smaller and mottled grey, with a striking reddish-brown head and sharply contrasting white cheeks and throat. Both birds show black-and-white wings in flight.

Breeds from northern Sweden and eastwards across Russia to Siberia. Moves south for the winter, and 10–60 reach Scotland in most years. Mainly seen from November to April in central and south-east Scotland.

adult male moulting

male

female

YELLOW-BILLED DIVER *GAVIA ADAMSII*

76–91 cm. Slightly larger and thicker-necked than Great Northern. Its distinctive long, pale bill is slightly angled and often pointed upwards, and can only be confused with that of Great Northern. The black and white breeding plumage is very distinctive. Other plumages are also similar to those of Great Northern, with the pale bill being the obvious feature, but it has a paler head and neck with more blending between the dark and light areas, and immatures have an overall browner body with a well-marked scaly pattern.

Up to 20 have visited Scotland annually in recent years. Breeds in the far north of Siberia and Arctic Canada. Mostly occurs in the Northern Isles and Hebrides, where a few birds gather in spring, and also along the east coast, as far south as the Forth.

summer

winter

SNOW GOOSE
ANSER CAERULESCENS

65–84 cm. Smaller than Greylag Goose. The white morph is white with black primaries and a pink bill and legs. The so-called 'blue phase', or dark morph, is smoky blue-grey, except for white under the tail and wings and a mainly white head. It also has pink bill and legs. The juvenile white morph has greyish-brown upperparts, neck and crown, while the juvenile dark morph is mostly sooty brown. Juveniles of both morphs have dusky bills and legs.

Breeds in Siberia, Alaska and Arctic Canada. Up to 12 a year join flocks of other migrant geese and winter in Scotland. There is also a small feral population living on Coll. Wild birds mainly arrive in October and November and are seen mostly on the mainland and on Orkney.

white morph

dark morph

LITTLE EGRET *EGRETTA GARZETTA*

55–65 cm. Much smaller than Grey Heron. An elegant white heron with a long, slender neck, a fine black bill, black legs and greenish-yellow feet. In spring it has fine plumes on its breast and back, and two very long plumes on its hind-neck. Immatures lack the plumes and yellow feet, and have a dull grey bill. Often very active when feeding, dashing after prey; sometimes waves its wings to keep its balance.

A very successful species that has expanded its range from southern Europe and first nested in southern England in 1996. Up to 30 a year are now observed in Scotland and breeding may soon follow. Most Scottish birds are seen south of the Great Glen, but there are recent records from Shetland and the Outer Hebrides. Most are seen between April and June.

summer

juvenile

Night Heron *NYCTICORAX NYCTICORAX*

58–65 cm. Tends to be active at dawn and dusk, and often roosts in thick cover during the day. Much smaller than Grey Heron, with a short, thick neck, a large head and a stout bill. Head and body often appear to merge when resting. The adult has a black back and crown, grey wings and body, and three long white head plumes. The juvenile is brown, with large white spots on its back and wings, and pale grey underparts with large brown streaks. Plumage becomes more uniform as birds become older.

juvenile

A rare visitor to Scotland, with occasional vagrants being seen in spring on the Northern Isles and Outer Hebrides. Sometimes seen elsewhere, but sightings are confused by the presence of a small number of free-flying individuals from a population of the North American subspecies that nests in Edinburgh Zoo but wanders quite widely in central Scotland.

Bittern *BOTAURUS STELLARIS*

70–80 cm. Smaller than Grey Heron. Secretive and well camouflaged when standing among reeds. This is a small but stocky heron with a dagger-like bill and longish legs. The golden-brown feathers are mottled with black, and it has a black crown and moustache. The neck is long, but may be withdrawn into the body when resting. Its wings are broad and rounded, and it flies with its neck drawn back into the body.

Historically rather common in Scotland. It declined as marshes were drained and as a result of hunting, both as a game species and as a trophy, and perhaps because of colder winters. Since the middle of the 20th century it has been returning as a winter visitor, with individuals arriving from the Continent during October and November. Most are seen in the south and east, and numbers fluctuate between 2 and 10 each year.

Spoonbill
PLATALEA LEUCORODIA

80–90 cm. Smaller than Grey Heron, but larger than Little Egret. Large white heron-like bird, with long black legs and a black spoon-shaped bill with a yellow tip. In spring and summer the adult has a yellow breast-band and shaggy crest. The juvenile has black tips to its wings and a pale yellow bill. In flight, the neck is extended and the long legs project beyond the tail.

A rare visitor to Scotland, with up to 20 sightings a year in recent years. Most are seen in spring and autumn, mainly at wetlands and coastal areas in the south and east. On a few occasions Spoonbills have been observed displaying and nest-building, and in 2008 a pair nested successfully on the Solway.

juvenile

Hilary Burn

CRANE *GRUS GRUS*

110–120 cm. Much larger than Grey Heron. Graceful bird with long legs, a long neck, a sloping body with obvious 'bustle-like', drooping, curved feathers at the rear, and a pointed bill. Mainly grey with black flight feathers, a black and white head and neck, and a red band at the back of the crown. The juvenile has a paler reddish-brown head and neck. Young take 3 years to acquire adult plumage. Flies with its neck straight and legs protruding well beyond the tail.

Between 10 and 40 Cranes are now being seen in Scotland each year, with most sightings between March and May, and one report of a possible breeding attempt. It has occurred in a wide range of locations, both on the mainland and on islands, with the largest number arriving in the Northern Isles and along the east coast.

HOBBY *FALCO SUBBUTEO*

30–36 cm. The size of Kestrel but more rakish. In flight, the long, pointed wings often appear crescent-shaped, and with the short tail this may prompt thoughts of a large Swift. At rest, the long wing-tips reach to, or beyond, the tip of the tail. Adults have slate-grey upperparts, a conspicuous white half-collar, white cheeks, a black moustache, and pale underparts with lines of black streaking. The undertail and thighs are red. The juvenile has brown upperparts with pale edges to the feathers, and buff underparts with dark streaks. It lacks red 'trousers'.

A scarce passage migrant to Scotland. Up to 20 are seen in most years, between late April and September, in southern and central Scotland and in the Northern Isles. A few remain for the summer, and up to five pairs may breed in some years.

juvenile

Hilary Burn.

GYR FALCON
FALCO RUSTICOLUS

50–60 cm. Our largest and most powerful-looking falcon, with a wingspan equal to that of a Buzzard. Hunts at a lower level than a Peregrine and seldom 'stoops'. The white morph is mostly white, with a variable amount of dark marks on its back and flight feathers. The dark morph is more like a large Peregrine, but with a slate-grey (not bluish) back, coarser, less dense markings on its breast, and a finer and less distinct 'moustache'. Juveniles are browner and lack the distinct 'moustache' of the Peregrine.

Between 5 and 15 of these magnificent falcons arrive in Scotland in most years between September and late April, with the largest numbers occurring in late winter. The species breeds in the far north of Scandinavia, Russia, Iceland, Greenland and Canada. Light-coloured North American and Greenland birds are more migratory and are most likely to reach Scotland, especially the Outer Hebrides and Northern Isles.

AVOCET *RECURVIROSTRA AVOSETTA*

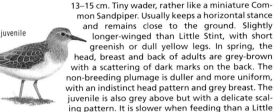

42–45 cm. A distinctive medium-sized wader. Black and white with a long, fine, upturned bill, long blue-grey legs and webbed feet. Has a white body, a black crown and back of neck, and white ovals edged in black on its folded wings. In flight, it shows black wing-tips, a black bar on the wing and two black bars running down the back. Juveniles are browner and have a less distinct pattern. Sweeps its bill from side to side when feeding, and sometimes swims like a duck.

A scarce migrant to Scotland in any month, but most occur between March and May. Numbers vary from 0 to 18, and there have been increasingly frequent sightings – mostly on the eastern side of the country – reflecting the recolonisation of, and growing numbers in, parts of England in the last half of the 20th century.

TEMMINCK'S STINT *CALIDRIS TEMMINCKII*

summer

juvenile

13–15 cm. Tiny wader, rather like a miniature Common Sandpiper. Usually keeps a horizontal stance and remains close to the ground. Slightly longer-winged than Little Stint, with short greenish or dull yellow legs. In spring, the head, breast and back of adults are grey-brown with a scattering of dark marks on the back. The non-breeding plumage is duller and more uniform, with an indistinct head pattern and grey breast. The juvenile is also grey above but with a delicate scaling pattern. It is slower when feeding than a Little Stint, and if disturbed will rise steeply and fly erratically like a Snipe.

Breeds from northern Norway east across Sweden, Finland and Siberia. It winters around the Mediterranean and in Africa. Between 1 and 20 reach Scotland, mostly during spring or autumn migration. Nesting has been confirmed at a number of locations, which may be used for some years and then abandoned.

MEDITERRANEAN GULL *LARUS MELANOCEPHALUS*

36–38 cm. Slightly larger and more robust than Black-headed Gull, with a larger head and slightly drooping bill. Its legs are longer and blood-red. In spring, adults appear white with a black hood from a distance, as the back and wings are pale grey and the wing-tips are all white. In winter, the head looks flatter, as the black is reduced to a smoky-black mask and it has a grey nape. Juveniles have scaly brown backs. First-winter birds have a dark mask and mottled brown wings. In first-summer birds the dark hood is forming. Second-winter birds are pale like the adults but have variable black marks on the primaries.

Following their recent colonisation of parts of southern England, Mediterranean Gulls are being seen more frequently in Scotland, with almost 100 now occurring each year. They are seen at all seasons, especially autumn, and particularly in the south of the country.

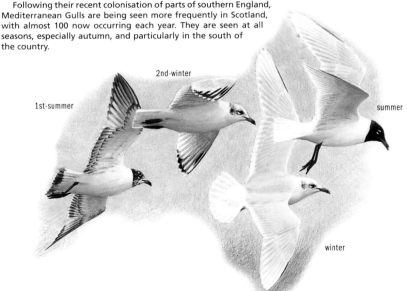

2nd-winter

1st-summer

summer

winter

SABINE'S GULL *LARUS SABINI*

27–32 cm. Smaller than a Black-headed Gull, with long wings, a slightly forked tail and a contrasting wing pattern at all ages. Most likely to be confused with an immature Kittiwake. The adult has a black hood, grey back, black outer flight feathers and a white triangle on each wing. The juvenile is greyish brown on its head and the side of its breast, and has paler buff fringes to the back and wing feathers, giving these a scaly appearance. The wings also show large white triangles. Flight is buoyant and tern-like, and birds are usually found far offshore.

The number of occurrences of this marine species has been increasing in Scotland in recent years, with annual sightings varying between 10 and 90. Most are seen along the west coast when passage birds are blown within view of sea-watchers.

summer

juvenile

winter

ROSEATE TERN *STERNA DOUGALLII*

33–38 cm. Similar size to Common Tern but much whiter looking, with a pale grey back and wings, a jet-black cap, a white body that in spring has a soft pink flush, and long tail streamers. It differs from Common Tern by having faster, shallower wingbeats (almost Kestrel-like), and looks shorter-winged and has a black bill with a little red at the base. By late summer the upperwing has a narrow, dark 'wedge' along the leading edge of the longest flight feathers. The underwing looks very pale. Juvenile has a dark forehead and neat blackish scaly edges to the back feathers, and appears whiter than Common or Arctic terns. Has a distinctive disyllabic 'chewwick' call.

winter

summer

juvenile

A rare breeding species, with as few as 4 pairs nesting in the Forth in recent years. A few more individuals occur on migration, especially along the east coast during May and August.

SNOWY OWL *NYCTEA SCANDIACA*

53–66 cm. Much larger than Barn Owl. This large, bulky owl is unmistakable, with a cat-like face, yellow eyes, broad white wings and a bulky body. The legs and feet are covered in feathers. The fully adult male is almost pure white with a few dark marks on its back and wings. The female is larger, with an all-white face and more dark marks on its back, wings and lower breast. Young in their first winter resemble the female, but young males are less heavily barred. It regularly hunts by day, and in flight its size and shape resemble a large, broad-winged white Buzzard.

A rare visitor from the Arctic, with 1 or 2 being seen in Scotland in most years. From 1967 to 1975 there was a breeding pair in Shetland. Most sightings are during April and May on the Outer Hebrides, the Northern Isles or mainland mountains in the north.

male

female

Hilary Burn

Hoopoe *UPUPA EPOPS*

26–28 cm. Smaller than a Feral Pigeon. This exotic-looking species is slim with a long neck, a long, downcurved bill and a crest that may be raised or lowered. Its body is pinkish buff with bold black and white bars on the wings, tail and back. The crest is pinkish with a black tip. Normally it spends a lot of time feeding on the ground, and the bold pattern helps break up the outline of the bird. Its flight is undulating, with the wings almost closing between each beat.

A scarce passage migrant to Scotland. Mostly seen in late April and May, or in September and October. There is a scattering of sightings across the mainland, but a surprising number overshoot and arrive on Shetland. There are between 5 and 10 sightings in Scotland most years.

Wryneck *JYNX TORQUILLA*

16–17 cm. Slightly larger than a House Sparrow. A slim bird with short legs and bill, a small head and a rather long tail. It is grey-brown with a dark, arrow-shaped mark running from its crown down its back. The plumage is delicately marked, with mottled upperparts and pale underparts that are finely barred. It has a warm buff throat that is barred with fine dark lines. It often feeds quietly on the ground and moves in a series of jerky hops.

Its range has been contracting in north-west Europe for many years and it has disappeared as a breeding species from the British Isles, with just 1 or 2 birds occasionally appearing in its potential breeding habitat of old pines on dry banks in the Highlands. It still arrives as a passage migrant, with 5–40 birds being seen mostly in autumn, along the east coast and on the Northern Isles.

Great Grey Shrike
LANIUS EXCUBITOR

24–25 cm. Similar size to a Blackbird, with striking, clean-cut black, grey and white plumage. Has a long black 'mask' through the eye, a thin white stripe above the eye, a large black hooked bill, black wings with a white patch, a grey body and white, or slightly pink, underparts. The longish, graduated tail is black with a white border. Female has some barring on the breast. It habitually perches on exposed branches or the tops of bushes, from where it swoops down onto its prey.

A scarce passage migrant and winter visitor from southern Scandinavia, arriving mainly in October and with a few remaining for the winter. Annual numbers have recently fallen to about 20 individuals. Sightings tend to be in the east, and from the Northern Isles.

ICTERINE WARBLER
HIPPOLAIS ICTERINA

13.5 cm. Larger and heavier-looking than Willow Warbler. Lacks the bold stripe over the eye and has a faint, pale line in front of the eye. Forehead is rather flat, crown peaks behind the eye and bill appears long. Greenish grey above, with variable amounts of yellow on under-parts. Wing-tips are long, projecting well beyond the other folded wing feathers. Yellow fringes to flight feathers form a yellow panel on the closed wing. Tail is square-ended. Legs are bluey grey. In the adult, yellow plumage fades to greyer tones during summer. A nervous, active bird that may perch upright in the open or fly out to catch a passing insect.

This is a scarce passage migrant, mostly seen in the north and east, and especially on the Northern Isles. Occurs mainly in May, when a few may linger and sing in scrub and scattered deciduous trees, and again in August and September, mainly on the east coast and Northern Isles. Numbers vary from very few to over 100 in some years.

PALLAS'S WARBLER
PHYLLOSCOPUS PROREGULUS

9 cm. A tiny Goldcrest-sized warbler with a large head, compact neck, small, fine bill and short tail. Rather similar to a Yellow-browed Warbler (*see* p192) but with bright olive-green upperparts, off-white underparts and a distinctive pale yellow patch above the rump. It typically has one broad yellowish or white wing-bar, one small wing-bar, a dark stripe through its eye, and a wide yellow stripe over its eye and another along the top of its dark crown. It has a yellow-green edge on its closed wing. Active and restless, it often hovers to pick insects from leaves, its behaviour recalling that of Goldcrest.

A rare but regular migrant to Scotland, mainly seen near North Sea coasts, including the Northern Isles. It breeds in Siberia and Asia, and most winter in China and the Far East, although a few take an opposite route and are seen in Scotland in October and early November. From 5 to 15 usually appear annually, with more in some years.

fresh, autumn

RED-BREASTED FLYCATCHER
FICEDULA PARVA

11.5 cm. The size of a Blue Tit, this small, dumpy flycatcher has a rounded head. The tail juts out from the wing-tips and is black with prominent white patches on either side; it is often cocked. These white patches show as the bird habitually flicks its tail and droops its wings. First-year males and females have drab brown upperparts, buff-white under-parts and the distinctive tail pattern. Older males have a grey face and shoulders and an orange-red chin. The eye is large with a thin, pale eye-ring.

Mainly seen in autumn, especially September and October along the east coast in coastal trees and scrub, and in the Northern Isles. Numbers have increased in recent years, and between 10 and 60 individuals may now be seen annually. It breeds from Sweden across central Europe and into Turkey, parts of the Middle East and Asia.

1st-winter

FIRECREST *REGULUS IGNICAPILLUS*

9 cm. Only marginally larger than a Goldcrest, but more brightly coloured. Has greener upperparts than a Goldcrest, whiter underparts and a strongly striped head, including a dark stripe through the eye and an obvious broad white stripe over the eye with black above it. The male has a startling red and orange stripe on the crown, while the female's crown is more yellow. Both sexes have a distinctive bronze patch on the side of the neck. Juveniles lack the orange or yellow crown but do have the broad white stripe over the eye. Behaves rather like a Goldcrest but often feeds lower down. Has a slightly deeper, more rasping call than a Goldcrest.

Increasing numbers are visiting Scotland as passage migrants, with up to 5 in spring and 20 in autumn. Most are seen along the east coast, with smaller numbers on the Northern Isles and Outer Hebrides.

male

juvenile

ORTOLAN BUNTING *EMBERIZA HORTULANA*

16 cm. Marginally smaller and more compact than a Yellowhammer. It is a relatively long-billed and rather round-headed bunting. The bill and legs are pink. It looks rather blank-faced with no stripes above or through the eye. The male has a greenish-grey head with a yellowish-white eye-ring, a yellowish stripe from the bill along the edge of the cheeks, a yellow throat, orange-brown underparts and a well-marked, stripy brown back. The rump is yellowish brown and streaked. In autumn, the colours of the male are more subdued and it has some streaks on its breast.

A scarce passage migrant to Scotland, with two arrival peaks: May and September. Has become less common in recent years. Most arrive in the east, with by far the largest numbers of sighting coming from the Northern Isles.

male summer

female 1st-winter

GLOSSARY

Auk
A family of seabirds of which the Puffin, Guillemot and Razorbill are the most numerous in our waters.

Brood patch
An area of bare skin on a bird's belly formed when incubating eggs. Feathers are generally lost and veins become more prominent during the breeding season, which results in the best possible contact between the egg and the bird's body.

Courtship feeding
The feeding of one adult member of a pair by the other: generally this is the male feeding the female prior to, or during, the breeding season.

Crop milk
A secretion, similar to mammals' milk, that is produced by adult pigeons and fed to their young.

Dabbling ducks
Ducks that generally feed by sieving or 'dabbling' the surface water to find food.

Diving ducks
Ducks that habitually dive to obtain food from under water.

Dust bathing or dusting
Birds such as partridges and sparrows deliberately engage in behaviour that is similar to water bathing but occurs in places where the soil is dry so that dust runs through the feathers. This behaviour is part of feather care and helps keep plumage in good condition.

Eclipse
Female-like plumage that the males of several species of ducks moult into after breeding. During this period they are flightless, before they acquire their bright breeding plumage again.

Fledge
The gaining of true feathers that allows a young bird to fly for the first time. A young bird recently out of the nest is a fledgling.

Gamebirds
Often used to describe the family that includes pheasants, partridges and grouse. The term also describes species that may be shot for sport, including species from other families such as Snipe and Woodcock.

Incubate
The process of keeping eggs at the right temperature and humidity prior to hatching. In Scotland most species achieve this by 'sitting' on the eggs, but Gannets incubate their eggs under the webs of their feet and some tropical species use alternative forms of heat, such as decaying vegetation.

Juvenile
A young bird that has left the nest but still retains some of its first feathers.

Migrant
The name given to a bird that travels from one area to another and returns again at another season of the year.

Moult
This is the periodic shedding and re-growing of feathers. This includes young birds losing their juvenile plumage and acquiring their first adult plumage. It also includes the replacement of feathers, usually after the breeding season and also the change in many species from dull winter plumage to brighter spring plumage.

Partial migrant
This is used to describe a species part of whose population is resident and another part undertakes an annual migration.

Pellet
A bundle of undigested prey remains that is formed in the stomach and coughed up and ejected through the mouth. Birds of prey pellets may consist of fur and bone and insectivorous birds may form pellets consisting of the hard parts of insects.

Preen
The action of grooming a bird's plumage and is part of essential feather care. This is usually carried out with the bill, but sometimes the foot or head is also used.

Race
A subdivision of a species that generally lives in a defined geographical area and is recognisably different from others of the same species with which it is able to breed.

Resident
A population that does not migrate or undertake other movements away from its breeding areas.

Roost
A period of inactivity when birds are generally sleeping or resting.

Steppe
A geographical term referring to open grassland plains that are treeless and sometimes waterless.

Speculum
The coloured (often iridescent) patch on the secondary feathers of a duck's wing.

Squab
A young pigeon.

Territory
The area defended by a bird or pair of birds for breeding and/or feeding.

BIBLIOGRAPHY

This book is a synthesis of many books and journals as well as the authors' and artists' own observations gathered over very many years. Below we have listed some of the major works, both books and journals, that we used for our research and recommend to readers who would like more information.

In addition to these publications, which cover many different species, there are also a great number of single species' studies and family profiles – especially those published by T & AD Poyser, Christopher Helm and HarperCollins that we thoroughly recommend, but have not been individually listed here.

Beaman and Madge, *The Handbook of Bird Identification*, Christopher Helm
BirdLife International, *BirdLife Conservation Series Number 12*
British Ornithologists' Union, *The British List of British Birds 1977–2000*
British Trust for Ornithology, *Bird Study*
Brown, Urban and Newman, *Birds of Africa*, Academic Press
Campbell and Lack, *A Dictionary of Birds*, T & AD Poyser
Cramp, *Handbook of the Birds of the Western Palearctic*, OUP
Forrester and Andrews, *The Birds of Scotland*, SOC
Gibbons, Reid and Chapman, *The New Atlas of Breeding Birds in Britain and Ireland: 1988–1991*, T & AD Poyser
Ginn and Melville, *Moult in Birds*, BTO
Harris, Tucker and Vinicombe, *Bird Identification*, Macmillan
Harrison, *A Field Guide to the Nests, Eggs and Nestlings of British and European Birds*, Collins
Hollom, *The Popular Handbook of British Birds*, Witherby
Lack, *The Atlas of Wintering Birds in Britain and Ireland*, T & AD Poyser
Mead, *The State of the Nation's Birds*, Whittet
Owen, *Wildfowl of Europe*, Macmillan
Wernham, CV, Toms, MP, Marchant, JH, Clark, JA, Siriwardena, GM, Baillie, SR (eds) 2002 *Migration Atlas: Movements of the Birds of Britain and Ireland*.

INDEX

INDEX

PHOTOGRAPHIC CREDITS
p7 Bluebells, Wood of Cree, Andy Hay (rspb-images.com); p8 Golden Eagle, Mark Hamblin (rspb-images.com); p9 Abernethy, Andy Hay (rspb-images.com); p10 Cairngorms, Niall Benvie (rspb-images.com); p11 Old Man of Hoy, Orkney, Andy Hay (rspb-images.com); p12 top, Osprey centre, Loch Garten, Andy Hay (rspb-images.com); p12 bottom, Crested Tit, Chris Gomersall (rspb-images.com)